The Origins, Prevention and Treatment of Infant Crying and Sleeping Problems

Why do some infants cry a lot, or wake and fuss, while others 'sleep through the night'?

Babies who cry a lot, or are unsettled in the night, are common sources of concern for parents and, consequently, costly problems for health services. In this book, Ian St James-Roberts summarizes new evidence concerning infant crying and sleeping problems to provide an evidence-based approach to these common challenges for parents and health services. The book begins by distinguishing between infant and parental parts of the problems and provides guidelines for assessing each issue.

Topics covered include:

- the pros and cons of 'infant-demand' versus 'limit-setting' forms of parenting
- causes of infant 'colicky' crying and night waking
- effects of night-time separations on infant attachments
- interventions such as swaddling, herbal remedies, and 'controlled crying'.

Since there is now firm evidence that parents' vulnerabilities and cultural backgrounds affect how problems are defined and guidance is acted upon, and that parents who wish to do so can reduce infant crying and unsettled night waking, social factors are considered alongside medical issues.

Translating research evidence into practical tools and guidance, *The Origins, Prevention and Treatment of Infant Crying and Sleeping Problems* will therefore be essential reading for a wide range of professionals including mental health staff, social workers, midwives, health visitors, community physicians and paediatricians.

Ian St James-Roberts is a Professor of Child Psychology in the University of London, UK, with 30 years of experience in carrying out research into infant crying and sleeping behaviour and problems.

The Origins, Prevention and Treatment of Infant Crying and Sleeping Problems

An evidence-based guide for healthcare professionals and the families they support

Ian St James-Roberts

Routledge
Taylor & Francis Group

LONDON AND NEW YORK

First published 2012
by Routledge
27 Church Road, Hove, East Sussex BN3 2FA

Simultaneously published in the USA and Canada
by Routledge
711 Third Avenue, New York NY 10017

Routledge is an imprint of the Taylor & Francis Group, an Informa business

British Library Cataloguing in Publication Data
A catalogue record for this book is available from the British Library

Library of Congress Cataloging-in-Publication Data

ISBN: 978-0-415-60116-0 (hbk)
ISBN: 978-0-415-60117-7 (pbk)
ISBN: 978-0-203-12610-3 (ebk)

Typeset in Times by Garfield Morgan, Swansea, West Glamorgan
Paperback cover design by Andrew Ward

MIX
Paper from
responsible sources
FSC
www.fsc.org   FSC® C004839

Printed and bound in Great Britain by
TJ International Ltd, Padstow, Cornwall

Who else could I dedicate this book to but my children? Claire and Ben are in their 20s now, but I have not forgotten the lessons they taught me. To make the dedication complete I need to include Maggie my wife and my partner in supporting Ben and Claire in their development (and trying to keep one step ahead).

Disclaimer

This book contains information from reputable sources and although reasonable efforts have been made to publish accurate information, the publisher makes no warranties (either express or implied) as to the accuracy or fitness for a particular purpose of the information or advice contained herein. The publisher wishes to make it clear that any views or opinions expressed in this book by individual authors or contributors are their personal views and opinions and do not necessarily reflect the views/opinions of the publisher. Any information or guidance contained in this book is intended for use solely by medical professionals strictly as a supplement to the medical professional's own judgement, knowledge of the patient's medical history, relevant manufacturer's instructions and the appropriate best practice guidelines. Because of the rapid advances in medical science, any information or advice on dosages, procedures, or diagnoses should be independently verified. This book does not indicate whether a particular treatment is appropriate or suitable for a particular individual. Ultimately it is the sole responsibility of the medical professional to make his or her own professional judgements, so as appropriately to advise and treat patients. Save for death or personal injury caused by the publisher's negligence and to the fullest extent otherwise permitted by law, neither the publisher nor any person engaged or employed by the publisher shall be responsible or liable for any loss, injury or damage caused to any person or property arising in any way from the use of this book.

Contents

Figures, tables and boxes

Figures

Tables

Boxes

Acknowledgements

Every 2 or 3 years, an international group of about 50 people involved in infant crying research meet up to discuss the progress they have made. This group is all the more remarkable because it has no formal membership or constitution, no administrative officers, and no membership fee. The success of this arrangement – and enthusiasm of the members – can be judged from the fact that the 11th International Infant Cry Research Workshop took place in the Netherlands in June 2011. This group has been immensely helpful in guiding my thinking and keeping me up to date on developments in this rather specialised area of study. In particular, I am highly indebted to Marissa Alvarez, Ron Barr, Carolina de Weerth, James Green, Gwen Gustaffson, Liisa Lehtonen, Mechthild Papoušek and Dieter Wolke for their many helpful comments and constructive criticisms over the years.

In the 1990s, a collaboration with the aptly named Jennifer Sleep resulted in a study of infant sleeping that first kindled my interest in this topic and the relationship between crying and sleeping. Curiously, these two types of infant behaviour and the problems they give rise to are by and large studied by different groups of researchers. The work with Jennifer led me to think more about the need for practical, evidence-based guidance for parents and professionals. This collaboration also introduced me to Steve Morris and the world of health economics research, resulting in a study to quantify the costs of infant crying and sleeping problems for UK national health services, which Steve led. Since then, publications by, and conversations, with researchers interested in infant and child sleep, most notably Tom Anders, Avi Sadeh and Anat Scher, have improved my understanding of this area and led to new studies and, ultimately, this book. I am most grateful for their inspiration and guidance.

The third group I want to thank is the staff of the Thomas Coram Research Unit, Institute of Education, University of London, where I have worked for the last 20 years. This multidisciplinary unit carried out some of the first systematic studies of infant crying and sleeping back in the 1980s and at one time or other has included anthropologists, educationalists, paediatricians, psychologists, sociologists and statisticians, as well as staff who support computing and the dissemination of research. Psychologists are inclined to focus inside the head, but one of the many salutary insights provided by this diverse group is the need to think about the social context within which infants behave and from which their behaviour acquires its meaning. I am indebted to Peter Aggleton, Julia Brannen, Peter Moss, Charlie Owen, Ian Plewis, Antonia Simon, Marjorie Smith, Barbara Tizard, and to the research officers who have worked with me on projects: Tania Abramsky, Diana Adams, Sue Conroy, Emese Csipke, Jenny Goodwin, Kimberly Hovish, Stephen Hunt, Jane Hurry, Maria Nikolopoulou, Bernice Peter, Marion Roberts and Katie Wilsher. Michelle Cage, Rakhi Kabawala and Serra Pitts have helped to prepare this manuscript.

My day job, so as to speak, has been to teach postgraduate students taking the Masters course in Child Development, or carrying out Doctoral research, at the Institute of Education, University of London. Having to teach something is an effective way of ensuring that a person has his ideas straight and several of the topics discussed in this book – infant attachment relationships, emotional development, behaviour problems, temperament, and the contribution of genetic and environmental factors to children's development – have benefitted from this process of teaching-led refinement. A second group of students, this time of health visitors, mid-wives and other professionals taking primary health care courses, have helped me to develop the materials included in Chapters 9 and 10. Carole Sutton and her colleagues at De Montfort University have supported and influenced this work. There are too many students to thank individually, but I would like to express my appreciation for their kind and formative feedback.

The Wellcome Trust has provided the main financial support for my research into infant crying and sleeping problems and I am grateful to the Trust, Neuroscience Committee and referees for this assistance. The National Health Service Executive, Medical Research Council and charities and commercial organisations have given additional support.

Marissa Alvarez, Kimberly Hovish and Anat Scher have provided helpful comments on sections of this book and I am grateful for their time and care. Any remaining obscurities or inaccuracies are entirely my own.

I am grateful to the following for permission to include material which are their copyright: The National Center on Shaken Baby Syndrome (Figure 1.1); Wellcome Trust Images Custom Medical Stock (Figure 4.1); Wiley & the Journal of Paediatrics & Child Health (Figure 6.1); Elsevier (Table 10.2; Avi Sadeh (Appendix V).

Sleeping like a baby

It is worth acknowledging that two American presidential candidates, Senators Bob Dole and John McCain, have shown considerable insight into infant sleeping. Interviewed on television about their reactions to defeat in presidential elections, they said[1]:

> Well, I've been sleeping like a baby. I sleep two hours, wake up, and cry. Sleep two hours, wake up, and cry.

1 I am grateful to Marc Bornstein for bringing these quotations to my attention. Bob Dole appears to be the original source, but I have cited a report of John McCain's words on the Jay Leno Tonight show November 12th 2008 here. For details see: http://www.timesonline.co.uk/tol/news/world/us_and_americas/article5136102.ece and http://www.mediabistro.com/fishbowlla/mccain-does-bob-doles-material-on-tonight-show_b7536 (Accessed 29/12/2010).

Chapter 1

Overview of infant crying and sleeping problems and this book

The impact of infant crying and sleeping problems on parents and health services

For about 6 months after a baby is born, many parents become pre-occupied with questions about infant crying and sleeping:

> *'Why is she[1] crying so much – is something wrong?'*
> *'Should we always respond to the crying, or will that spoil our baby?'*
> *'Should feeds be given when she cries, or at regular times?'*
> *'Will taking her into our bed lead to bad habits?'*

Then, if all goes well, they forget about these things, at least until the next baby comes along. Occasionally, things do not go so well. In a small minority of cases, the combination of a baby who cries persistently and vulnerable parents can give rise to long-term parent–child relationship problems and child disturbances, or even to 'shaken baby syndrome', sometimes resulting in infant brain damage or death.

More formally, these features of baby care can be translated into a set of facts and figures about the 'costs' of infant crying and sleeping problems for parents, babies and health services. For example, the health economist Steve Morris asked English mothers and health visitors to keep logs of the time spent discussing infant crying and sleeping in the first 3 months after their babies were born (Morris et al., 2001). Translating this time into professional salaries and associated costs, Morris estimated that the average cost was £91 per baby. That does not seem particularly remarkable until you think about the number of babies born each year. Morris calculated that in 1997 the cost to the United Kingdom (UK) National Health Service

---

1 To avoid the awkwardness of 'he or she' and 'him or her' I will refer to individual babies as female. 'She' can be read as standing for both boys and girls. This is to assist brevity and does not reflect any strong preference, except perhaps a desire to even up the historical bias towards the male. There are in any case few sex differences in babies' crying or sleeping behaviour.

(NHS) was over £65 million per year. As he pointed out, with this amount of money it would have been possible to employ 2391 grade E nurses for a year or to treat 1284 patients with HIV for life.

Although other studies have not employed Morris's methods, what might nowadays be called the 'health service burden' of infant crying and sleeping problems is probably comparable in other developed countries. For instance, 23% of North American mothers, and 12–19% of parents in European countries, reported infant crying to be a problem in recent studies (Alvarez & St James-Roberts, 1996; Canivet et al., 1996; Forsyth et al., 1985; Reijneveld et al., 2001). Remarkably, 74% of parents of 4 to 9-month-old infants reported discussing infant night waking and fussing with paediatricians in an American survey of healthcare concerns (Olson et al., 2004). Indeed, with the notable exception of Brazil, problems with infant sleeping seem to be a prominent feature of most contemporary societies – at least 20% of parents in studies in America, Australia, England, China, Finland, Germany, Holland, Italy, Japan, Sweden and Switzerland have reported problems with their infant's sleeping at night. We will return to these findings, including the reason for the low rate of infant sleeping problems reported by Brazilian mothers, later on.

As well as these concerns among parents in general, studies from several countries have documented the consequences in less benign cases. Evidence that persistent crying can trigger parents to shake, smother or hit babies was reported by Dutch researchers in 2004 (Reijneveld et al., 2004) and this was subsequently confirmed by figures collected from California hospitals and by the US National Center on Shaken Baby Syndrome (Barr et al., 2006). As a result, Ron Barr and his colleagues have introduced a campaign in Canada and North America to raise parental awareness about the dangers of 'shaken baby syndrome' and are evaluating its effectiveness.

Figure 1.1 shows the cover of a booklet from this initiative, called the 'Period of PURPLE Crying' program, which is designed to alert parents to common but challenging features of normal infant crying. The word 'PURPLE' is an acronym, with the letter 'P' for instance, referring to the crying 'peak' that occurs in early infancy. This campaign is showing early signs of success (Barr et al., 2009). In the UK, a follow-up study of infants taken to the charity *Cry-sis* because of crying problems (Wolke et al., 2002) found a greatly raised rate of pervasive hyperactivity problems at school age in such cases. Similarly, a group of American, Norwegian and Swedish researchers (Rao et al., 2004) found that prolonged crying after 3 months of age (but not before 3 months), predicted hyperactivity, cognitive deficits, poor fine-motor abilities and behaviour problems when the children reached 5 years of age. Other studies have found a high rate of emotional and behavioural problems where crying or sleeping problems persist (von Kries et al., 2006; Zuckerman et al., 1987). The most extensive clinical research into older (>3 months) infants with crying and sleeping problems

Figure 1.1 Front page from the PURPLE crying booklet (reproduced with permission from the National Center on Shaken Baby Syndrome).

has been carried out by Mechthild Papoušek and colleagues in Munich, Southern Germany (Papoušek & von Hofacker, 1998; Papoušek et al., 2001). Because theirs is a tertiary centre, it is likely that these cases have particularly severe disturbances and Papoušek's findings testify to this. In spite of the consensus that such cases are rare, 1800 families were treated at this centre during its first 10 years.

It is striking that, in contrast to this evidence of the impact of infant crying and sleeping problems on families and services all over the world, there are no standard, tried and tested, health service guidelines for managing infant crying and sleeping in the UK or most other countries. Instead, this area has been dominated by expert opinion, given particularly by writers of popular baby care books, who base their recommendations on personal experience rather than research evidence. Unfortunately, if not surprisingly, they give contradictory advice (see below).

This lack of routine health service procedures for managing infant crying and sleeping is puzzling and food for thought. One reason may be that these problems have traditionally been seen as medical issues, whereas medical expertise has focused primarily on providing treatments for more life-threatening conditions. It is only with the development of health–economic thinking that awareness of the health service costs of common, less serious, complaints has arisen. Another, related reason may be the lack of clear boundaries to delineate which profession infant crying and sleeping problems belong to. Indeed, the question whether infant crying and sleeping problems are principally medical or healthcare issues is a central one for this book. My own interest stems from the fact that these are primarily behavioural phenomena and so legitimately the interest of a developmental psychologist (which I am), but there are few qualified psychologists working professionally with this age group and type of problem. My colleagues in the international research arena include community physicians, gastroenterologists, health visitors, midwives, nurse-practitioners, paediatricians and a variety of care professionals who have become interested in early infancy because of government initiatives designed to prevent child problems at later ages. This diversity provides a rich, multidisciplinary, intellectual environment, but does not make it easy to see who is in charge. It may be no accident that several of these professions have not had a tradition of carrying out systematic research and using it to guide practice.

Whatever the reason for it, the lack of evidence-based guidelines for professionals and parents who support infants in managing their crying and sleeping is striking and at odds with the personal and financial cost of these problems for communities and health services. To some extent, it may be that these are problems whose time, historically speaking, has come. Pressures within society for equality and dual earning have highlighted the difficulties parents face in balancing baby care with employment. Performing effectively in the office after your baby has kept you up at night, night after night, is challenging, to say the least. To a degree, infant crying and sleeping problems are a consequence of modern society – and thinking about them in that way helps to give a more complete understanding.

This book's aim is to develop evidence-based guidance that healthcare professionals can share with parents in order to help babies to manage their crying and sleeping behaviour. So far as possible, it also aims to provide professionals and parents with a 'toolkit' that they can use in carrying out this task. As will become clearer below, the book assumes that parents will want to use tried and tested, evidence-based, forms of baby care. It also assumes that parents generally, and first-time parents in particular, will need expert guidance from a healthcare professional in how to apply the evidence to their own individual baby and circumstances. The book is designed to support this partnership between professionals and parents in anticipating and preventing problems where possible – and guiding interventions if problems arise. Much of the focus will on be on the first year of age, with a good deal of attention being given to the first 6 months, since this is the period when children's crying is most problematic for parents and when most infants stop waking their parents during the night. Consequently, this early period is especially important for *preventing* crying and sleeping problems. The later sections of the book, concerned with treating problems after they have arisen, will span the infant and toddler periods.

The book is divided into ten main chapters. The rest of Chapter 1 examines the distinction between opinion and evidence in more detail and seeks to identify criteria for distinguishing robust evidence, which are then applied in the remainder of the book. Chapter 2 examines the nature of crying and sleeping problems and introduces some distinctions that are helpful in understanding the problems and guiding the provision of services. These include the distinction between crying and sleeping problems, between the problem identified by parents and the infant behaviour underlying the problem, and between the types of cases that present at different ages. In addition, Chapter 2 seeks to clarify the thorny issue of severity, that is, of how to decide when a problem is sufficiently serious to warrant expert help. Chapters 3 and 4 examine the evidence about the nature, and causes, of problematic infant crying behaviour, respectively. Chapters 5 and 6 do the same for infant sleeping problems. Chapter 7 discusses the evidence that parents' cultural backgrounds and beliefs need to be included in an understanding of infant sleeping problems. Chapter 8 focuses on the distinct, and much smaller, group of infants who have multiple, crying, sleeping and other problems after 3 months of age, since infants in this group are much more likely to have poor outcomes. Chapter 9 translates the evidence into guidance and procedures for use in routine healthcare services for preventing infant crying and sleeping problems. Finally, Chapter 10 provides evidence-based guidelines for treatments when problems with infant crying or sleeping are presented.

Expert opinion and the need for evidence-based services

Back in 1979, the eminent paediatrician, Dr Benjamin Spock included a section on 'strictness or permissiveness' in his book on baby and child care (Spock, 1979). For parents, the question whether it is better to impose external limits and boundaries on children's behaviour, or to respond to their wishes and demands, remains a central one, not just during infancy but throughout childhood and adolescence. In relation to baby care, it is a matter for concern, however, how little progress has been made in resolving this issue since Spock's seminal writing. Instead, the pendulum seems to have swung from strictness to permissiveness, and back again, with each succeeding generation of expert writers.

In contemporary society the 'strictness' side of this debate is represented by the terms 'scheduled', 'structured', 'routine-based' and 'limit-setting' care, and perhaps best epitomised by Gina Ford's *The New Contented Little Baby Book* (Ford, 2002). Ford argues that imposition of routines-based care by parents from the early days of infancy is the secret to producing not just satisfied parents but a contented baby as well. This advice has not gone unchallenged and, indeed, has raised strong criticisms from a number of sources. Newspaper reports have highlighted concerns that a routines-based approach encourages parents to neglect babies' needs and can lead to 'convenience' parenting, which ignores babies' well-being in favour of parents' self-interest (Meltz, 2004). A fierce debate has surrounded the associated idea that parents should practice 'controlled crying', that is, deliberately leave babies to cry (Australian Association for Infant Mental Health [AAIMHI], 2002).

On the other, permissive, side books such as Jean Liedloff's (1975/1986) *The Continuum Concept* emphasize innate biological needs and instincts that parents and babies inherit as a legacy of evolution. Liedloff proposes that parents can avoid crying and sleeping problems by following natural instincts to respond quickly, feed in response to babies' cries, and to hold and sleep with them, rather than consciously adopting care that is convenient in an industrial society. Other terms, including 'attachment parenting' (Sears & Sears, 1999), 'infant-led', 'infant-demand' and 'natural' parenting have different origins, but likewise refer to forms of care that aim to be responsive to an infant's expressed, or inferred, need.

Both of these books are based on the deep personal conviction of the author that her approach is effective. Given, too, the experience these writers bring to bear, it is unlikely that either of the approaches they advocate is entirely wrong. On the other hand, it is difficult to see how two such contradictory sets of advice can both be right. Nor are such disagreements unusual. A recent analysis of parenting advice books concluded that about half recommend leaving children to cry by themselves as a way of settling them at night, while half the books recommend bed-sharing (Ramos & Young Clarke, 2006). Amusingly for the general public – if not for parents caught up in these controversies – popular books in this area tend to spawn counter offensives. In response to books with titles like *How to Get Your Baby to Sleep Through the Night* an American journalist Sandi Kahn Shelton has written one called *Sleeping Through the Night . . . and Other Lies* (Shelton, 1999).

Given this inconsistent information, the question, then, is how parents and the health professionals who guide them should make choices. The answer to be offered here, in common with most contemporary scientific and clinical thinking, is that choices need to be based on evidence rather than expert opinions, however wise or deeply held.

What counts as evidence?

In spite of scientific progress, it is sometimes just as difficult to distinguish robust evidence from specious claims nowadays as it used to be in the past. To some extent, this can be attributed to the power of science as a marketing tool in contemporary society. We are familiar with the claim that 'products', including baby care products, are 'clinically' or 'scientifically' tested.

We know, too, that reading the fine print will often identify a great many provisos to the claims made by the manufacturer in its more prominent publicity material. In all fairness, however, it is not just marketing that has sometimes given science a bad name. Career and other pressures can motivate researchers to suspend their critical faculties and make claims for their own findings that go far beyond what the research has actually shown, while even the best-intentioned researchers can be less critical about the limitations of their own studies than they would be about other people's.

It also needs to be admitted that robust evidence is not always easy to identify. Questions can arise about the adequacy of methods used in the original studies – and the applicability of the evidence to the case in hand – which make interpretation difficult. As noted earlier, it is partly for this reason that this book is aimed at healthcare professionals in partnership with parents. Expertise will often be needed in order to apply evidence to particular circumstances and it is not reasonable to expect parents to hold this expertise. Instead, it is assumed that healthcare experts will guide parents by making them aware of evidence (and the areas where there is no adequate evidence) and helping them to make choices. This book is meant to help to support this professional expertise.

Fortunately, the scientific and clinical communities have become aware of this issue of scientific credibility and have taken steps towards resolving it. For instance, the American Psychological Association has published the 'Chambless criteria' (named after the chairperson of the task force who devised them [Chambless et al., 1996]) for identifying 'well-established' treatments for psychological and behavioural problems. Using these criteria, 'well-established' treatments are those proven by at least two between-group experimental studies showing the effectiveness of the treatment above a control condition, or where efficacy has been confirmed by a large series of single-case experimental trials (at least ten), compared with control treatments. Other requirements are that the characteristics of study participants are made explicit, the procedures involved in the interventions are documented in written manuals, and that their effectiveness has been demonstrated by at least two independent research groups.

The Chambless criteria are not the only ones available. In the UK, the Cochrane Library was among the first organizations to publish independent reviews of biomedical research evidence and remains a highly respected source. More recently, the UK National Institute for Health and Clinical Excellence (NICE) has conducted reviews of evidence and made recommendations to government, medical and general communities about a variety of health topics. As David Olds and his colleagues have pointed out (Olds et al., 2007), it is also important that preventive and treatment programmes for children should be acceptable for parents, and that parents should feel motivated to adopt them, since otherwise they may be of little practical use. Collection of evidence to show that parents use, and are satisfied with, services has become a key part of evaluating whether they work (Olds et al., 2007).

The Chambless criteria were designed as benchmarks for identifying effective treatments, whereas the focus here is on prevention as well as treatment, while it may take some time before NICE examines the evidence in this area. Nevertheless, it is possible to extract some principles for identifying robust evidence that are shared by NICE and other bodies and are applicable to research concerned with infant crying and sleeping.

1   The research evidence needs to have been published in scientific journals that employ peer review. The peer-review processes provide the first line of quality control for evidence, since publication in such a journal means that the research underlying it has withstood critical review by other, independent research scientists working in the same area. In practice, scientific journals vary in the rigour with which they carry out peer review. The best ones set very high standards and, as a consequence, turn down all but the best studies submitted to them for publication. The journals publish their acceptance rates, together with other metrics such as their citation index (the number of times articles they publish are cited by other researchers), the make-up of their editorial board and their circulation rate. As a consequence, it is not difficult to identify high-ranking journals and, although publication in them is not a guarantee, it does mean that research they publish has been vetted. This, then, is the first requirement in establishing the quality of a piece of research.

2   The published evidence needs to have been obtained by at least two independent studies by separate research groups. This principle, of replication, has long been one of the cornerstones of scientific evidence, as well as being a key requirement of the Chambless and similar criteria. It goes a long way towards guarding against the likelihood that a set of findings could have occurred by chance or because of some unknown feature of a single study particular to it.

3   The research needs to have been methodologically sound. This is a more complex property to evaluate and, to a large degree, is already taken care of by the two safeguards listed above. It is mentioned here because of the importance assigned to randomized controlled trials in biomedical sciences generally. In line with the Chambless criteria, randomized controlled trials are true experiments, because participants (in our case infants and parents) are assigned at random to the target intervention or to a comparison, control condition group. 'Blinded' randomized controlled trials are those where neither participants nor researchers know which group received the treatment or control provision. Providing group sizes are large enough, research designs of this sort guard against the likelihood that the measured group differences could have been due

to anything other than the experimental condition that distinguished them. Consequently, they provide the final proof of causation and are highly regarded for this purpose. The reification of randomized controlled trails has, however, come in for some criticism (Harrington et al., 2002; Wolke, 2001) and they are not always applicable and certainly not the universal solution for all methodological ills. For example, it is hard to see how mothers could be assigned at random to participate in a study that restricts their diet in order to measure effects of cow's milk protein in their breast-milk on infant crying. Nor could such mothers be 'blinded' to their diet type, so that those who believe infant crying is caused by cow's milk allergy might be biased in their behaviour or in reporting results. Another concern about randomized controlled trials is that they provide evidence under artificial conditions, so that the findings may not apply in the messy circumstances that exist in real life settings. To allow for this, a distinction is drawn between 'efficacy' trials (which measure cause–effect relationships in controlled conditions), and 'effectiveness' studies (which examine whether the causality still applies in pragmatic settings, such as in routine health services). Ideally, both types of information are needed to guide choices. Some of these issues will be re-visited where they are relevant later in this book. For the moment, it is sufficient to recognize the importance given to randomized controlled trials in biomedical research as tests of causation, and to take account of them in evaluating the evidence from studies of infant crying and sleeping.

4   A number of additional safeguards have been introduced to guard against bias in the last few years, including the use of 'meta-analysis' and 'systematic review' to scrutinize evidence across studies, and the requirement that researchers should declare any personal interests they have in the work they publish. Declarations of personal interest allow research that might be biased (for instance, because the researcher has a financial involvement with the company supporting the research) to be identified. Following on from the principle of replication mentioned above, the aim in meta-analysis is to impose standard metrics across separate studies, so that they can be compared directly and the results and sizes of effects can be averaged. This approach helps to show up robust findings and identify doubtful ones. The idea underlying systematic review is that the writer should make explicit the criteria used to select the studies included in the review. For example, the bibliographic reference sources consulted, the dates searched and the keywords used to identify research studies can be specified, making it possible to see what has been overlooked and to consider whether a review might be unrepresentative. Where possible, a systematic review might be confined solely to studies that meet particular methodological standards, such as randomized controlled trials.

Although the value of these attempts to enhance scientific rigour is recognized, it is not possible to adhere to them completely for the purposes of this book. The challenge is that research into infant crying and sleeping problems is not yet sufficiently developed for agreement to exist about measurement methods and criteria. As a result, there are few meta-analyses and systematic reviews available, and adopting these strategies to select and review research into infant crying and sleeping would be unhelpfully restrictive and overlook the majority of the evidence. It is, though, possible to recognize the value of these safe-guards and to go as far as possible towards meeting them. First, as noted above, evidence which has received replication in independent published studies will be given most emphasis. Second, the criteria and procedures involved in searching the research literature will be made explicit, so that these can be duplicated by others and any important oversights can be identified. Similarly, the sources of evidence under-lying the conclusions reached will be specified, so that any omissions can be recognized. For this reason, citation of the original references will be used throughout the book. Appendix I sets out the search criteria used to identify research studies and the reference list documents the studies included. Appendix I also includes a declaration of the author's personal interests.

5   Lastly, one other important consideration in evaluating research evidence is that the findings need to be supported by a plausible theory. This may seem an odd requirement in view of the critical stance towards opinions adopted above, but a set of data is simply an account of past events. To apply the findings to new groups of babies and parents and to generalize them to circumstances beyond those involved in their collection, we need a broader understanding of what the data imply. My criticism is not so much of opinion, although the area of infant crying and sleeping does seem to give rise to more than its fair share of unsubstantiated theories. Rather, the point is that the chief value of opinion is to give rise to research, to provide evidence in support of the theory, or require it to be changed. Opinions and theories need to be supported by evidence.

The principles listed above will be used to distinguish robust from promising evidence, and both of these from speculation and opinion, throughout this book. It needs to be said that this approach does not allow certainty. The only certainty is that improvements in knowledge are likely to occur in the future and require the information contained in this book to be revised. However, this applies to any area of scientific knowledge. With this proviso, the goal here is to summarize current, evidence-based, scientific knowledge about infant crying and sleeping problems, to identify its implications for healthcare professionals and parents, and to be as clear as possible about what we still need to know.

Suggestions for different ways to read this book

Chapters 4 and 6, particularly, are long and detailed and not all readers will want to plough through all this material. These chapters need to be detailed because they provide the analysis of the scientific evidence on which the guidelines for practice in Chapters 9 and 10 are based. My hope is that the first eight chapters can also provide core reading for initial and post-qualification training courses for healthcare professionals, as well as being a continuing source of reference material for practitioners and researchers. Where the reader finds the information too detailed or extensive, the summary section at the end of chapters may prove sufficient, while the guidelines in Chapters 9 and 10 are designed to provide a set of stand-alone tools for evidence-based services. It is possible to start at the back of the book and then come forward, to identify the evidence underlying particular recommendations. As well as the cross-referencing throughout the text, the Index at the back of the book should help the reader to locate particular topics and to navigate around.

Chapter 2

The nature and identification of infant crying and sleeping problems

If we could turn the clock back and start afresh in this area, one of the most useful steps would be to replace some of the existing terms, which are confusing and misleading. For example, the word 'colic' is widely used to refer to the prolonged crying that some babies exhibit in the first few months of age. Unfortunately, as well as identifying this type of behaviour, the word 'colic' also implies an underlying cause. That is, following from the Greek language origins of the word 'colic' (from the Greek 'kolikos', the adjective of 'kolon'), its use implies that a baby's crying is due to gastrointestinal disturbance and the resulting discomfort or pain (Carey, 1984). In practice, as Chapters 3 and 4 will discuss in detail, two major reviews of the evidence have found that only a small minority of babies who cry a lot in the first few weeks have a gastrointestinal disturbance, while it is far from clear that the crying is due to pain.

Similarly, the phrase 'infant sleeping problems' suggests that there is something wrong with the infants involved and that the problem involves defective sleeping – an implication also reflected in the claim that such infants 'fail to sleep through the night'. In fact, the evidence reviewed in Chapter 5 shows that almost all babies wake up during the night. What distinguishes problem cases is not deficient sleeping, but that such babies cry out or otherwise 'signal' their parents when they wake in the night after 12 weeks of age, whereas by this age most babies have stopped doing so.

Parents are correct in judging that a 6-month-old baby who cries out during the night is behaving differently from most other such infants in our society – and there is no doubt about the impact on parents of being kept from sleeping at night themselves. There are, then, good reasons for wanting to understand these differences in how babies behave, but it is not strictly accurate to say that most babies who disturb their parents at night have 'infant sleeping problems'.

These terminological issues are important because the words themselves tell us a lot about the assumptions made by previous generations, some of which have been proved wrong by recent evidence. Indeed, questioning these terms has led to new and different explanations of the phenomena involved.

In an ideal world, it would be helpful to replace the existing terms with more accurate ones but, unfortunately, the terms 'infant colic' and 'infant sleeping problems' are so widely used and ingrained in our culture that it would be an uphill struggle, at best, to change them. Instead, it is more sensible (and realistic) to be aware of the ambiguities and to take them into account. That requires clear distinctions to be drawn between the types of behaviour involved in infant crying and sleeping problems, and between problems for infants and problems for parents.

Key distinction 1: crying or sleeping problem?

Although crying and sleeping problems are not usually distinguished, they are quite different in their features, the ages at which they present, usually involve different infants, and probably have different causes. Infant crying and parental concern about it peak at around 4–6 weeks of age, with most of the crying occurring in the daytime and, particularly, in the evenings (Barr, 1990; St James-Roberts, 1989, 2001a). In contrast, infant sleeping problems occur mainly at night, and after 3 months of age (Adams et al., 2004; Lozoff et al., 1985; Messer & Richards, 1993). Most babies wake in the night for feeding in the early weeks and parents know and expect this. After that age, as noted above, most infants acquire the ability to resettle by themselves when they wake in the night. It is the failure to achieve this milestone, so that infants continue to disturb their parents during the night after 12 weeks of age, which accounts for most infant sleeping problems (Adams et al., 2004; Anders et al., 1992; Goodlin-Jones et al., 2001; Minde et al., 1993).

Emphasizing these distinctions, several recent studies have provided evidence that prolonged 24-hour crying and night waking that disturbs parents usually occur in different infants. But, before examining this evidence, it is helpful to question the preconception involved here, that is, to consider why some writers have assumed that infant crying and sleeping problems are interrelated.

One reason for assuming this relationship is that one type of infant behaviour – crying – is a common denominator. It is often because a waking infant cries out in the night that parents become aware of, and bothered about, infant night waking. Consequently, it is an understandable assumption that a baby who cries a lot generally will be particularly likely to wake and cry in the night. In turn, this involves the inference that some infants are generally irritable or disturbed in the organization of their behaviour. This notion, of a 'difficult infant' and of a general 'regulatory disturbance' is suspect and will receive critical discussion later. For the moment, it is enough to note that the length of crying that occurs when infants wake in the night is typically short – of the order of a few minutes in most circumstances, since the crying usually stops when parents respond.

For example, Marcia Keener and colleagues' (1988) video-recordings showed that fuss/crying during night waking typically lasted for 1–3 minutes. Compared with the 3 or more hours of crying per 24 hours often used to define problematic crying, a few moments of crying in the night-time may not count for much. Indeed, it is probably not the *amount* of infant crying in the night that causes parents to report infant sleeping problems, so much as the fact that their baby's night waking disturbs their own sleep. There is no compelling reason, then, to assume that high amounts of 24-hour crying and signalling parents in the night by crying for a few moments are related. They may be, but that is an empirical matter, requiring evidence, rather than something that is self-evident.

A second reason for believing that crying and sleeping are interrelated is that two early research studies did conclude that infants who cried a lot in the first few weeks of infancy were prone to sleeping problems at later ages (Bernal, 1973; Weissbluth, 1984; Weissbluth et al., 1984) One of these, by Judy Bernal, followed up a group of 77 infants born in Cambridge, England from the newborn period to 14 months of age (Bernal, 1973). At 14 months, 24 infants were considered to have regular night-waking problems based on maternal interviews and behaviour diaries. Looking retrospectively, back to the newborn period, infants in the 14-month night-waking group were found to cry more per 24 hours, and to have more frequent, but shorter, cry bouts as newborns, than infants who did not wake in the night at 14 months. In the second study, Marc Weissbluth and colleagues began with 141 American infants at 4–8 months of age, recruited in this case from paediatricians' clinics (Weissbluth et al., 1984). Looking backwards, 34 of the 141 infants (24%) were reported by parents to have cried for more than 3 hours per day most days in the week at some point in the first 3 months of infancy. These infants had briefer 24-hour sleep durations and more frequent night waking at 4–8 months of age than infants without a history of prolonged crying in early infancy.

These studies do show that some infants who cry a lot in early infancy go on to have sleeping problems at later ages, but they have a major loophole: because they worked backwards, they completely overlooked those babies who cried a lot in the early weeks but did not have night-waking problems later. To address the question properly, the early crying data need to be used to predict the later sleep problems, rather than the other way around. To give a related example, it is now well-known that early retrospective studies gave an inflated impression of the relationship between academic problems in school-aged children and complications during their mother's pregnancy, whereas subsequent analyses that followed up babies who experienced pregnancy complications found that most of them were academically normal at school age (Sameroff & Chandler, 1975). Retrospective analyses can give an exaggerated impression of the strengths of associations. The point is not that there are no infants who have both crying and sleeping problems:

indeed, we will see later that recent studies have identified an important subgroup characterized by this pattern. Rather, the point is that retrospective studies exaggerate the strength of the relationship and, consequently, how many infants have both problem types.

In contrast, recent studies employing more rigorous, longitudinal methods have found that most infants who have crying problems do not have sleeping problems later (and vice versa). Because problematic crying occurs at a younger age than problematic night waking, our main concern is with this *predictive* relationship, but it is worth noting that there are reasons to doubt whether the relationship is a strong one even when the measures are collected at the same age. For example, when Finnish researchers studied sleeping objectively at 6 weeks of age – using polygraphs that measure sleep from brain electrical (electroencephalogram [EEG]) activity – they found no difference in 24 hour amounts of sleeping between infants who cried a lot and other infants (Kirjavainen et al., 2001). These findings are provisional pending replications, but they are already sufficient to question the assumption that prolonged crying is strongly associated with poor sleeping (and vice versa) when both are measured concurrently.

More importantly for present purposes, a substantial number of prospective longitudinal studies have found that amounts of crying at around 4–6 weeks of age (the peak age for crying) are poor predictors of which infants will wake and signal their parents at night at later ages. These findings are important because they show that different infants exhibit these two types of problematic infant behaviour, implying that they have different causes. The role of parenting behaviour, for instance, may be quite different. To throw light on this, a recent report examined the findings from two separate studies, one involving 181 infants, the other 531 infants, and both using validated methods to measure infant crying and to compare this with parent reports of night waking (St James Roberts & Peachey, 2010). Neither of these studies found that infants who cried a lot at 5–6 weeks of age were more likely than other infants to be unsettled in the night just 6 weeks later, at 12 weeks of age. Similarly, Fukumizu and colleagues' (2005) study of Japanese infants found that most infants judged to have colic did not go on to have what they called 'sleep-related night-time crying'. Likewise, but in older infants, Dieter Wolke and colleagues' (Wolke et al., 1995a) epidemiological study of 432 German 5-month-old infants and their parents found that 11% of infants had sleeping problems, 10% crying problems, and just 5% had both types of problems, while sleeping problems, rather than amounts of crying at 5 months, predicted sleeping problems at later ages. Melissa Wake and colleagues' Australian longitudinal study of 483 first-born infants (Wake et al., 2006), too, found meagre associations between early crying and later sleeping problems: in this case the correlations between fuss/cry problems at 2–4 months and sleeping problems at 8–24 months were very weak – of the order of 0.17–0.23. A German study by

Rüdiger von Kries and colleagues (von Kries et al., 2006) found that prolonged crying in the first 3 months was not associated with increased rates of sleeping or feeding difficulties, and Liisa Lehtonen's careful review of crying-baby follow-up studies concluded that most of them slept normally at a later age (Lehtonen, 2001).

Further evidence for the distinctness of crying and sleeping problems comes from two recent randomized controlled trials, both of which found that parenting programmes that reduced infant night waking and signalling at 12 weeks of age did not affect the infants' 24-hour amounts of crying (St James-Roberts et al., 2001; Symon et al., 2005).

To sum up this section, infant crying and sleeping problems are distinct in several important ways. First, infant crying, and parental concern about it, peak at around 5–6 weeks of age, with most of the crying occurring in the daytime and, particularly, in the evenings. In contrast, infant sleeping problems occur mainly at night, and after 3 months of age. Second, in most cases, infants exhibit *either* prolonged crying *or* night waking that disturbs their parents, rather than showing both. Third, a small group of infants exists who are the exception to this rule, that is, who have both crying and sleeping problems that, in this group, persist to older ages. These distinctions are important because they suggest that the three groups have different causal pathways – a proposal that will be examined in more detail in later chapters.

Key distinction 2: parent or infant problem?

As well as this separation of prolonged infant crying as a whole from infant night-time waking behaviour, it is important to distinguish who has the problem. The critical question here is whether infants who cry a lot in the early weeks, or wake and signal at night after 12 weeks of age, are unwell or have anything wrong with them. If not, their behaviour can still be a problem, but it is first and foremost a problem for parents rather than for the infants.

In relation to crying problems, two careful reviews of the evidence have concluded that no more than one in ten infants taken by parents to professionals because of persistent crying have a food intolerance or other organic disturbance (Gormally, 2001; Lehtonen et al., 2000). Parents are often correct in judging that their baby cries more than average amounts, but the vast majority of infants who cry a lot in the first 2 months of infancy are healthy, put on weight normally and do not have long-term disturbances (Crowcroft & Strachan, 1997; Ellett et al., 2005; Illingworth, 1954; Kirjavainen et al., 2004; Lehtonen et al., 2000; St James-Roberts et al., 2001; Stifter & Bono, 1998). Chapters 3 and 4 will examine their crying behaviour and its causes in more detail, but 'infant crying problems' as a clinical complaint are characterized chiefly by parental alarm and concern about their baby's crying, rather than by a pathological infant condition (Crowcroft and Strachan, 1997; Lehtonen et al., 2000; St James-Roberts et al., 2001).

Likewise, most infants who wake and disturb their parents at night beyond 3 months of age have normal weight gain and do not have general or long-term disturbances, other than continuing sleeping problems (Eaton-Evans & Dugdale, 1988; Mindell, 2008; Pollock, 1994; Tikotsky et al., 2010a; Wolke et al., 1995a). To a degree, parental concern about infant night waking reflects Western cultural practices and norms that make it particularly hard for parents to cope with being kept up at night. This does not downplay parental complaints, since parents who work Western office hours need to sleep at night themselves, while it is true that most Western infants over 3 months of age remain settled for long periods at night. Rather, the implication is that most infants who fail to develop this ability are in good health and develop normally in other respects, so that the infant behaviour needs to be distinguished from the, largely parental, problem.

These findings will be reviewed in greater detail later on. For the moment, the point is that they support the conclusion that infant crying and sleeping problems are primarily parental, rather than infant, problems. However, some provisos do need to be taken into account. First, it is clear that a small minority of infants involved in the studies do have organic disturbances, so that it is important to be able to distinguish these cases whenever possible. Second, since it is true that infants who cry a lot or wake their parents at night are behaving differently from most other babies studied, it is legitimate to question why these infant behaviours happen and to consider what can be done about them. Third, prolonged crying or night waking can become a problem for infants, too, if their behaviour disturbs their parents enough to threaten their own care. Indeed, the evidence that infant crying can trigger parental abuse is a major reason why professional services need to focus not just on infant behaviour, but on parents' responses to their baby's behaviour, and any parental vulnerabilities that might affect their responses, as well. This is a theme that will recur throughout this book.

In conclusion, three main points have been made. First, the problem and infant behaviour underlying it both need to be assessed, but they need to be examined separately before an intervention is planned. In particular, parental vulnerabilities, as well as infant behaviour, need to be considered. Second, two main groups of infants, and associated problems, exist: infants who cry a lot in the day and evening in the first 2 months; infants who do not develop the ability to remain settled at night after 3 months of age. Third, recent research has identified a much smaller group of infants who have multiple crying, sleeping and other problems after 3 months of age and has shown that these cases often involve persistent child psychological and family disturbances (Papoušek & von Hofacker, 1998; Rao et al., 2004; Wolke et al., 2002; von Kries et al., 2006). The nature and causes of these three different behavioural pathways, and groups of infants, will be examined in more detail in the next few chapters.

What counts as a 'serious problem?'

As well as an awareness of the terminological pitfalls and distinctions discussed above, anyone involved in this area needs to have a broad grasp of the issues surrounding the question of what counts as a 'real', 'serious' or 'severe' problem. These issues, too, are complex and a source of confusion. Since the pitfalls involved in defining serious crying and sleeping problems tend to be similar, they will be examined together now.

One implication of the evidence presented so far is that the seriousness of a problem depends partly on parental vulnerabilities, as well as on infant behaviours. Indeed, a case can be made that the greatest threat to infant well-being comes from parents who are overwhelmed by infant crying or night waking. Although that argument is difficult to prove conclusively, there is certainly evidence that prolonged infant crying is reported more often by depressed mothers – and fathers – than other parents (Akman et al., 2006; Dennis & Ross, 2005; Kurth et al., 2010; McMahon et al., 2001; Milgrom et al., 1995; Van Den Berg et al., 2009; Wurmser et al., 2006), that prolonged crying predicts maternal depression (Vik et al., 2009), and that prolonged infant crying can trigger depression in vulnerable mothers (Murray & Cooper, 2001). Likewise, there is evidence that infant sleep problems are linked to maternal depression (Armitage et al., 2009; Cronin et al., 2008; Lam et al., 2003; Smart & Hiscock, 2007; Wake et al., 2006), that interventions which reduce infant night waking reduce maternal and paternal depression (Smart & Hiscock, 2007), and that poor outcomes are more likely where parents lack the resources that enable other families to cope (Elliott et al., 1997).

There is also provisional evidence that some parental psychological characteristics, such as a low-frustration threshold, poor parent–infant attachments, low self-confidence or inability to tolerate stress, may make some parents particularly susceptible to infant crying or unsettled night-time behavior (Beebe et al., 1993; Crouch et al., 2008; Donovan et al., 1990; Evanoo, 2007; Groh & Roisman, 2009; Yalçin et al., 2010; Leerkes & Siepak 2006).

Further research is needed to unravel these causal relationships more precisely, but the implication is that cases that combine parental vulnerabilities with infant crying or unsettled night waking are more serious than cases involving infant crying or night waking alone. For practitioners, it follows that there is a need to prioritize cases that involve parental vulnerabilities, including maternal depression and the lack of social supports, in order to improve long-term outcomes. This, in turn involves the need to assess those parental factors, which will be considered further in Chapter 10.

As well as assessing parental vulnerability, establishing problem severity involves assessing the *extent* to which the behaviour of a particular infant is different from the behaviour of most other infants. In principle, both parents and professionals can be helped by this information. Although the 'average' infant may be a myth (or statistical artefact), some degree of variability (or 'individual difference') between infants is generally accepted, so that the issue is whether a particular infant's behaviour is within the normal range, or outside, and whether this is a serious cause for concern. For parents, this information can provide reassurance and, in many cases, may help them to decide that their baby does not have a serious problem, so that they do not need to seek further help. For professionals, this information can help them to distinguish cases where parental guidance and reassurance are all that is needed, and to identify cases that need more extensive investigation and/or referral to specialists. In the all too common situation where health services have insufficient resources, being able to distinguish serious cases can inform decisions about treatment priorities.

Over time, researchers studying infant crying and sleeping have evolved a number of definitions to identify infants whose crying or sleep–waking behaviour lies outside the normal range. Some of the definitions used in these studies are reproduced in Tables 2.1 and 2.2, which also show the percentages of infants in the general population found to have problems when the definitions were used. These percentages are often referred to as problem 'prevalence rates'.

As Tables 2.1 and 2.2 illustrate, the definitions vary greatly and, as a consequence, the resulting prevalence rates vary widely too, so that from 2.2 to 32.1% of infants have been considered to have crying problems or colic in the first 3 months, and from 6 to 64.9% of infants to have sleep problems in the first 2 years. The rates vary for several reasons, one of which is simply that some definitions are more stringent than others. An unfortunate consequence is that the type of infants studied by a group using one definition may be quite different from the type studied by researchers using a different definition, giving rise to conflicting information about causes. For example Sijmen Reijneveld and colleagues (Reijneveld et al., 2002) found that maternal cigarette smoking was associated with infant crying when cases were chosen using some definitions, but not with cases chosen based on other definitions. Clearly, complexity of this sort does not assist professionals or parents trying to work out whether a particular infant has a serious crying or sleeping problem and what to do about it. The use in practice of some of the definitions will be considered in Chapter 10. For the moment the goal is to examine the broader conceptual issues involved in choosing between the definitions – and to develop a workable strategy for employing them.

Table 2.1 Definitions and prevalence rates for infant crying problems or colic (see text for details)

Definition	Infant nationality	Infant age	Prevalence,* %
1 Parent reports infant is 'crying a lot'	Dutch[g]	2–3 months	14
	Dutch[h]	0–1 month	17.8
2 Parent reports infant crying to be a problem	Swedish[d]	0–3 months	8.5
	American[f]	0–4 months	23
	Dutch[h]	0–1 month	14.3
	Australian[i]	2 months	19.1
		4 months	12.8
	German[j]	1–5 months	32.1
	Danish[k]	1–3 months	19
		4–6 months	15
	Finnish[n]	1–3 months	5
3 Parent approach to professional because of infant crying problem	Danish[k]	1–3 months	15
		4–6 months	9
	English[m]	1–3 months	10
		4–6 months	4
4 Colic (undefined) reported by parent	English[l]	0–1 month	18.3
	English[o]	0–12 months	26.3
	Finnish[p]	0–3 months	28.1
	English[q]	0–12 months	16
5 Physician reported colic	American[e]	0–2 months	9.2
6 Basic 'Rule of Threes' for a fussy/colicky infant[a]: *'one who, otherwise healthy and well-fed, had paroxysms of irritability, fussing or crying lasting for a total of more than three hours a day and occurring more than three days in any one week.'*	Swedish[d]	0–3 months	11.7
7 Modified 'Rule of Threes': typically fuss/ crying for 3 hours or more when averaged across the available days, but other variations exist.	Canadian[c]	6 weeks	24
		3 months	6.4
	Dutch[g]	2–3 months	7.6
	Dutch[h]	0–1 month	11.2
	Danish[k]	0–3 months	21
	English[m]	0–3 months	29
		4–6 months	9
	Finnish[n]	1–3 months	14
		3–5 months	7
	Finnish[r]	0–6 months	13

continues

Table 2.1 (continued)

Definition	Infant nationality	Infant age	Prevalence,* %
8 Extended 'Rule of Threes' for seriously fussy/colicky infants[a]: *as for Basic Rule of Threes, except that: 'paroxysms continued to occur for more than three weeks, or became so severe that the pediatrician felt that medication was indicated'.*	German[b] Swedish[d] Dutch[h]	0–3 months >3 months 0–3 months 0–1 month	16.3 5.8 9.3 2.2

* The prevalence is the percentage rate in the population studied given by the authors or calculated from their figures. Rates are typically the proportion of infants who meet the definition at any point in the age-period assessed. No attempt has been made to distinguish between prospectively and retrospectively collected information or to take account of the methods used (see text for some discussion of these issues).
a. Wessel et al. (1954); b. von Kries et al. (2006); c. Clifford et al. (2002); d. Canivet et al. (1996); e. Castro-Rodriguez et al. (2001); f. Forsyth et al. (1985); g. van der Wal et al. (1998); h. Reijneveld et al. (2001); i. Wake et al. (2006); j. Wolke et al. (1995a); k. Alvarez & St James-Roberts (1996); l. Crowcroft & Strachan (1997); m. St James-Roberts & Halil (1991); n. Michelsson et al. (1990); o. Rubin & Prendergast (1984); p. Rautava et al. (1993); q. Hide & Guyer (1982); r. Lehtonen & Korvenranta (1995).

Approach 1: choosing cases on the basis of parental concern or complaint

One approach to this issue, typified by the first few definitions in Tables 2.1 and 2.2, is to regard cases involving parental concern about their baby's behaviour and, particularly, cases where parents have approached health professionals because of their concerns, as serious problems. On the face of it, this approach has some legitimacy, since parents who have taken the trouble to seek help from a professional are likely to have a serious complaint. However, as discussed earlier, the primary issue in this case is to distinguish the parent problem from the infant behaviour contributing to it. For instance, there is evidence that parents are more likely to take first-born babies to clinicians because of problem crying, although first-borns do not cry more than later-borns (St James-Roberts & Halil, 1991; van der Wal et al., 1998). Presumably, this reflects first-time parents' greater anxiety, because of their lack of confidence, knowledge and experience. In addition, many infants selected in this way do not cry more than typical amounts: across the studies that have looked into this question, approximately 40–60% of infants judged by parents to have crying problems do not cry much more than most infants of that age in the general community (Barr et al., 1992; Lehtonen & Korvenranta, 1995; Pauli-Pott et al., 2000; van Sleuwen et al., 2006; Zwart et al., 2007). It follows that, although it is crucial to recognize both parental vulnerabilities and infant characteristics in healthcare practice, parental concern by itself is not a sufficient basis for deciding whether a particular infant's behaviour departs seriously from the norm.

Table 2.2 Definitions and prevalence rates for infant sleeping problems (see text for details)

Definition	Infant nationality	Infant age	Prevalence,* %
1 Parent reports infant sleeping to be a problem	English[b]	13 months	37.8
	Australian[d]	0–38 months	28.6
		7–12 months	36
	Australian[f]	8 months	21.2
		12 months	16.2
		18 months	10
		24 months	12.1
		Across ≥3 ages	6.4
	German[i]	5 months	13.1–14.7
		56 months	7.0–7.7
	Finnish[j]	5 months	23.5–24.9
		56 months	6.5–6.9
2 Parent approach to professional because of infant sleep problem	English[b]	1–13 months	26
3 Did not regularly sleep through the night (6 hours without waking)	English[l]	6 months	10
4 Sleep problem: *sleep latency >30 minutes, or disruptive night wakings*	Italian[g]	<2 years	35
		2–3 years	23
5 Sleep problem: *night waking that involved the parents or bedtime struggles, which occurred ≥three nights/week for the preceding month, accompanied by conflict or distress*	American[c]	0.5–4 years	29
6 Sleep problem: *in last week, infant woke ≥3 times/night, took ≥1 hour to resettle after waking, or any problem causing severe disruption to the mother's sleep*	English[k]	8 months	18
7 Richman criteria for 'night-waking problem'[a]: *waking during ≥5 nights/week*	English[a]	1–2 years	13–20
	German[h]	5 months	21.5
		20 months	21.8
		56 months	13.3
8 Night wakening: *waking regularly and requiring parental attention ≥three times/ night*	Australian[d]	4–12 months	12.7
9 Sleep-related night-time crying ('Yonaki'): *unexplained awakening from sleep characterized by crying that usually occurred every night.*	Japanese[e]	0–6 months	18.8
		0–21 months	64.9
		36–41 months	16

continues

Table 2.2 (continued)

Definition	Infant nationality	Infant age	Prevalence, * %
10 Parent reports sleeping to be a *severe problem*	Internet survey[m]	0–6 months 7–12 months 13–18 months 19–24 months 24–30 months	28.8 36.1 33.3 42.9 34.2
11 Severe sleep problem: *Infant Sleep Questionnaire score* ≥12[b]	English[b]	13 months	18.7
12 Richman criteria for a severe night-waking problem[a]: *night waking ≥5 nights/ week for >3 months, plus one of more of: waking ≥3 times/night; waking for >20 minutes in the night; going into the parents' bed*	English[a]	1–2 years	6–10

* The prevalence is the percentage rate in the population studied given by the authors or calculated from their figures. Rates are typically the proportion of infants who meet the definition at any point in the age period assessed. No attempt has been made to distinguish between prospectively and retrospectively collected information or to take account of the methods used (see text for some discussion of these issues).
a. Richman (1981) (Note that Richman and colleagues (1985) defined a sleep 'disorder' as night waking that persisted for ≥6 months, but during only 4 nights/week); b. Morrell (1999); c. Lozoff et al. (1985); d. Armstrong et al. (1994); e. Fukumizu et al. (2005); f. Wake et al. (2006); g. Ottaviano et al. (1996); h. Wolke et al. (1995a); i. Wolke et al. (1998); j. Wolke et al. (1995b); k. Zuckerman et al. (1987); l. Adams et al. (2004); m. Sadeh (2004).

Approach 2: choosing cases based on quantitative rules to define atypical infant behaviour

This 'behavioural rule' approach involves choosing cases based on measures of infant crying or sleep–waking behaviour, compared with a standard criterion or rule. In principle, this allows the focus to shift from parental subjective concern about a baby to the infant's overt behavioural characteristics. Behavioural rules of this kind offer advantages for research since infants chosen, for example, because they cry for more than 3 hours per day can be selected uniformly by different research groups. In practice, the 'Rule of Threes' definition of a fussy or 'colicky' infant provides a particularly good example of the disadvantages, as well as strengths, of this approach.

Morris Wessel and colleagues' (Wessel et al., 1954) widely cited 'Rule of Threes' defines a fussy or colicky infant as: 'one who, otherwise healthy and well fed, had paroxysms of irritability, fussing or crying lasting for a total of more than three hours a day and occurring on more than three days in any one week' (pp. 425–426).

The first challenge to definitions of this kind is that they are difficult to apply. In principle, the Rule of Threes requires records of crying behaviour to be kept for seven successive 24-hour days, so that infants who do and do not meet the Rule of Threes can be distinguished. Since this is impractical using objective recording methods, researchers and practitioners have had to resort to parent reports, either by asking parents to reflect back over the last week and remember how many days their baby cried for more than 3 hours, or by asking parents to keep continuous records of behaviour using logs or diaries. At the group level, these two methods agree moderately well, so that diaries are often used to validate parent retrospective measures of group differences in crying or sleeping behaviour (Morrell, 1999; Richman, 1981; Wolke et al., 1994b). However, for professionals and parents, the interest is in an individual infant, not a group, while the weakness of the retrospective method for this purpose is that it often exaggerates an individual infant's behaviour. For example, 40% or more infants who meet a version of the Rule of Threes criteria when measured by interviews or questionnaires do not do so when assessed by behaviour diaries (Barr et al., 1992; Canivet et al., 1996; Lehtonen & Korvenranta, 1995; Pauli-Pott et al., 2000; van Sleuwen et al., 2006; Zwart et al., 2007).

In principle, behaviour diary measures are more accurate because they are filled in more or less as infant behaviour occurs and, indeed, there is evidence to confirm their validity (Barr et al., 1988; St James-Roberts et al., 1993a). However, the obstacle in this case is that relatively few parents are able and willing to complete such diaries continuously for 7 days in order to decide whether there is a real problem. Consequently, researchers have been obliged to use 'Modified Rule of Threes' definitions based, for example, on selecting infants who fuss/cry for 3 or more hours when the crying is averaged across the number of diary days available. We have little idea of how many babies would meet the Rule of Threes definition applied accurately, but it would probably be toward the lower end of the prevalences listed in Table 2.1.

In the original article that proposed the Rule of Threes definition for colic cases, Morris Wessel and colleagues also identified a subgroup of 'seriously fussy infants' whose 'paroxysms continued to occur for more than three weeks, or became so severe that the pediatrician felt that medication was indicated' (p. 427). To this author's knowledge, no study so far has asked parents to keep the 21 successive 24-hour diaries needed to use this definition. Instead, the studies in Table 2.1 that sought to use it depended on parental estimation and memory. The point, noted by Michael Rutter (1977) more than 30 years ago, is that definitions used to select atypical cases have to be accurate and convenient to use for those who routinely employ them – while this is an issue for the Rule of Threes and, more or less, for all current behavioural rule definitions of infant crying and sleeping problems. In turn, the difficulties researchers face in translating the definitions into reliable measurements are probably part of the reason for the huge variations in rates of problems apparent in Tables 2.1 and 2.2.

As Ronald Barr (2000) has eloquently pointed out, the second obstacle to the Rule of Threes definition for problem cases is that this rule is arbitrary. There is no evidence or reason for assuming that an infant who cries for only 2 hours 55 minutes per day is different from one who cries for 3 hours 5 minutes, or that one has a problem the other one lacks. It is remarkable in some ways that a definition devised by a single clinical study more than half a century ago – in 1954 – has stood the test of time at all. That it has done so is probably due more to its easy to remember formula, and to the lack of a superior alternative, than to its validity in identifying a distinct group of infants with serious problems.

Similar reservations apply, for instance, to Naomi Richman's definition for severe infant sleep problems (see Table 2.2). Like the Rule of Threes, the logic underlying the Richman criteria seems to be to require the behaviours in question to occur on the majority of days in a week, and over a sustained period of weeks of time. That makes intuitive sense, but there is no particular reason for choosing five rather than four nights per week: indeed, the Rule of Threes definition of a crying problem effectively requires it to occur during 4 days in a week. Similarly, there is no particular reason for choosing three awakenings per night, or 20 minutes of waking, as the rule for a serious sleeping problem. In fact, Richman herself employed a different definition for choosing problem cases in a later publication (see Table 2.2 footnote).

The third challenge to using the Rule of Threes and similar behavioural rules for selecting problem cases is that recent research has shown that the average amounts of crying and sleeping per 24 hours vary substantially between different cultures and countries, probably partly as a function of different parenting practices (Alvarez, 2004; Jenni & O'Connor, 2005; St James-Roberts et al., 2006). Similar issues arise in relation to other aspects of infant sleeping. For example, the Richman definitions of sleep problems and 'severe' sleep problems in Table 2.2 include bed-sharing as a criterion for identifying problem cases, but recent studies have emphasized that bed-sharing is normal practice in many cultures in the world, rather than something considered to be problematic (Ball, 2002; Jenni & O'Connor, 2005). Oskar Jenni and Bonnie O'Connor's fascinating review of the interplay between cultural and biological influences on children's sleep argues that separate sleeping arrangements reflect cultural pressure towards autonomy, which American families value and emphasize more than Japanese families. Likewise, Stephan Valentin (2005) has written about German parents' 'cult of independence' in making arrangements for their infants' sleeping. Jenni and O'Connor (2005) argue persuasively that Western concerns with training children to have set bedtimes and enough sleep are historically recent and reflect twentieth century preoccupations with healthy living, and they quote an American paediatric member of the Public Health Committee in 1910 as stating that 'the American child is kept on a starvation ration of sleep'. In keeping with this claim, American 3-month-old infants were reported to sleep 2 hours less per 24 hours than their Dutch equivalents in the 1990s (Super et al., 1996), perhaps because of Dutch concern for rest, regularity and cleanliness (Jenni & O'Connor, 2005). On the other hand, some societies simply allow children to fall asleep when they get tired (Jenni & O'Connor, 2005). For instance, Italian pre-school children were reported to go to bed later, and to sleep less at night than American children during the 1970s and 1980s, because Italian children often stayed up to participate in social activities with adults in the evening (Ottaviano et al., 1996). Chinese children, too, have been reported to go to bed later, and to sleep an hour less per 24 hours, than American children (Liu et al., 2005), while Swiss 1-year olds went to bed later, and slept approximately 30 minutes less per 24 hours, in the 1980s and 1990s than the 1970s (Iglowstein et al., 2003).

We will return to these interesting cultural differences in later chapters. For the moment the point, as Dieter Wolke (2001) has noted, is that they mean that the number of problem cases will vary between societies by definition, if a single rule, such as the Rule of Threes, is applied universally. For instance, the *average* (median) amount of infant crying in Berry Brazelton's 1962 study of Boston 6-week-olds was 2¾ hours, so that many more Bostonian infants would have problem crying using the Rule of Three definition than infants in Copenhagen in 2004, where the average daily amount of crying at 6 weeks was 1 hour 20 minutes (Alvarez, 2004). We do not know whether many parents in Brazelton's study considered their babies' crying to be severely problematic but that seems unlikely, since the families involved in it were from a routine general practice. The point is that what seems normal in one society may not be so in another.

Approach 3: choosing cases based on population norms

As Dieter Wolke (2001) proposes, a partial solution to this issue is to use each society's figures to define the normal range and delineate atypical cases statistically. For example, in London where the average amount of infant fussing and crying per 24 hours at 6 weeks is around 2 hours 8 minutes (St James-Roberts & Plewis, 1996; St James-Roberts, 2001a), prolonged crying might be defined as more than 3.3 hours (which is one standard deviation above the mean) and very prolonged crying as more than 4.5 hours (two standard deviations above the mean). This approach has the advantage that the extent of an individual infant's atypical crying or sleep–waking behaviour would be considered in relation to population norms. In addition, it would allow for the wide variability that often exists within a general population. For instance, Ivo Iglowstein and colleagues (2003) found that the normal range in amount of sleeping among 3-month-old

Swiss infants (defined by the 10th and 90th percentiles) varied from about 12 to 17 hours per 24 hours. Allowance can also be made for normal age changes in crying and sleep–waking behaviour by using age-adjusted norms (Iglowstein et al., 2003).

This approach has a lot to recommend it and is, in fact, the method nowadays commonly used in research and practice concerned with older children's behavioural problems, as well as measures of weight. It is, however, only a partial solution. In the short-term, one obvious disadvantage is that we do not yet have normative crying or sleeping figures for many countries and cultures. Another is that the resulting definition assumes that we already know which features of infant behaviour give rise to parental concerns – for instance in the Rule of Threes that it is the total amount of crying which underlies parental problems. In practice, as we will see in Chapter 3, bouts of unsoothable crying are also an important source of parental concern, but these are overlooked by the Rule of Threes, which focuses solely on crying amount. Similarly, the Richman definitions overlook the distinction between night waking and settling-to-sleep problems, although infants vary in the extent to which they show one, or other, or both of these behaviours (Gaylor et al., 2005; Mindell et al., 2006).

Another consideration is that any approach based purely on infant behaviour is likely to identify many infants not considered to cry too much or sleep badly by their parents as problem cases. For instance, Peter Lucassen and colleagues' review found that problem rates based on how many parents sought professional help because of crying problems were often lower than the problem rates based on measures of amount of crying (Lucassen et al., 2001). Similarly, Gordon Scott and Martin Richards (1989) reported that 10% of 1-year-olds who woke during 5 or more nights per week were not regarded by their parents as posing a problem, while Dieter Wolke's group (Wolke et al., 1995a) found reduced parental concern about night waking as children got older. Infant crying or sleeping behaviour that worries some parents does not worry all parents all of the time.

In short, normative information about infant crying and sleep–waking is very helpful in identifying infants whose behaviour lies outside the general population range, but it does not provide a sufficient basis for distinguishing problem cases. Parents' culturally based views, values and expectations also need to be taken into account. That does not mean that parents' accounts alone are sufficient, since individual parents are likely to vary in subjective characteristics, such as knowledge and experience, which may affect their perceptions and judgements. Rather, the implication is that the problem from the parents' point of view needs to be assessed alongside measures of infant behaviour, since cultural values influence the judgements of parents in a society about which behaviours are problematic, and provide the basis for their own parenting behaviour. As noted earlier, it is easy to understand why a baby who wakes parents at night is a greater problem when dual-earning

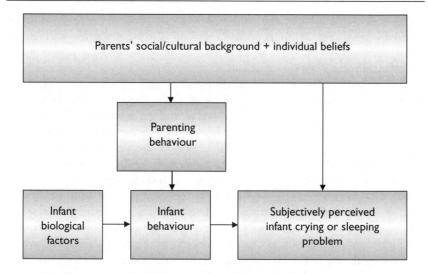

Figure 2.1 Schematic 'dual-pathway' model of the influence of parents' culture and individual beliefs on their reports of infant crying and sleeping problems.

social policies prompt both parents to get up early and work office hours, compared to where parents can adjust their sleep–waking schedules to suit their baby's behaviour. Figure 2.1 represents this principle schematically as a 'dual-pathway' model of the influence of culture both on parents' behaviour and on their judgements that an infant's behaviour is problematic. It follows that infant behaviour needs to be considered in relation to the social context in which it occurs – and that approaches which choose problem cases and intervene based solely on measures of infant behaviour are likely to prove inadequate. This has important implications for practice, which will be revisited in later chapters.

Approach 4: choosing cases based on organic causes

As noted earlier, the word 'colic' was often used in this sense in the past, to refer to problem crying behaviour attributed to an underlying organic disturbance involving gastrointestinal disorder and pain. The disadvantage, since recent research has found gastrointestinal and other organic disturbances in only a small minority of infants who cry a lot in early infancy, is that this approach will overlook most cases with prolonged crying. Yet it is the crying that is the trigger for parents' anxiety and contacts with professionals to seek help. It follows that, while it is important to be able to distinguish cases where prolonged crying is due to an organic disturbance in order to treat them effectively, this is not an adequate approach to the management of infant crying problems as a whole.

Turning to infant sleeping problems, some researchers and practitioners use the phrase 'sleep disorder' to refer to cases considered serious and persistent enough to warrant clinical attention, whereas the term 'sleep problems' is retained for milder and more transient cases. Sleep disorders are also recognized in medical schemes, such as the International Classification of Diseases (ICD-10) published by the World Health Organization (WHO, 1992) and the *International Classification of Sleep Disorders* (Thorpy, 2005).

One way in which the distinction between infant sleep disorders, sleep problems and normal sleeping could be justified is if it is possible to distinguish cases with predominantly organic causation from others. Indeed, the phrase 'sleep disorder' seems to imply a serious underlying organic disturbance not assumed by 'sleep problem'. In contrast to these theoretical distinctions, however, there is currently little empirical basis for distinguishing organic from other cases using measures of sleep–waking behaviour during infancy. This is not to deny that children with neurodevelopmental disturbances are particularly prone to sleep problems, since the evidence shows that to be the case (Kotagal, 2007; Stores & Wiggs, 2001). Rather, the point is that such cases make up only a small minority of the infants with sleep problems, while there is currently no reliable way to distinguish organic cases from others based on measures of sleep behaviour during infancy. Chapter 6 will discuss this in more detail.

As others (Mindell et al., 2006; Sadeh, 2005) have pointed out, another impediment to the sleep 'disorder' versus 'problem' distinction, is that agreement about which criteria define sleep disorders is no better than agreement about how to distinguish problems from non-problems. Nor do researchers in general use the categories proposed in the international classification schemes. Rather, as Jodi Mindell and colleagues noted (Mindell et al., 2006), what appears to be shared is: (1) that measurements are based on parental reports; (2) that definitions of sleep problems include some combination of the *frequency of behaviours* (such as number of awakenings per night, or nights per week containing waking), the *extent of behaviours* (such as the duration of night waking), and the *chronicity of behaviours* (such as the number of weeks or months the night waking has lasted). Each researcher then gives different weights or emphases to these elements.

Given that the severity of sleep problems is assessed in research studies using three different dimensions, each of which allows behaviour to vary more or less continuously, the question is how the resulting measurements can be combined to assign infants to one of three categories and groups (sleep disorder, sleep problem, normal sleeping) any more effectively than into two categories (sleep problems, no sleep problems). Or, put more sceptically, the question is whether these attempts to divide infants into discrete categories based on their sleeping and waking behaviour reflect the reality of infant behaviour. For instance, if we follow some studies and define 'sleeping through the night' as remaining settled without disturbing parents between midnight and 6 am, babies are likely to vary in how many nights of the week they do so (from zero to seven), rather than dividing cleanly into individuals who always do, and always don't, 'sleep through the night'. It is also far from clear why 6 hours is the appropriate rule for identifying a normal length of sleeping, or whether the period between midnight and 6 am is correctly designated to be the 'night'. The implication is that measures of sleep variations and problems are likely to be more continuous in degree than is allowed for by the three categories of sleep disorders, sleep problems and normal sleeping. To some extent, too, the answer to questions about how often a behaviour has to occur before it becomes a serious problem, and what constitutes the night-time, will depend on parental and cultural factors.

In summary, although the distinction between organic and non-organic causes of problematic infant sleep–waking (and crying) behaviour warrants further research, it does not provide a practical basis for distinguishing between serious problems and other cases at the present time. In the longer-term, progress is likely to be made in distinguishing between social-cultural and biological effects on infant behaviour and in improving our definitions and measurements of problematic crying and sleeping. What is less obvious, given the complexities discussed above, is whether the pursuit of a simple set of rules for dividing cases into serious, mild-problem and non-problem categories is likely to bear fruit. Instead, an approach based on the lessons learned about assessing problem behaviours in older children seems more likely to prove worthwhile.

Approach 5: use of a 2-step, screening then diagnostic, procedure

The discussion above highlights the challenges involved in delineating serious crying or sleeping problems, but does not accomplish the positive step of providing methods that professionals and parents can use to distinguish serious cases. However, the same theoretical and practical issues are encountered in studies of older children with behaviour problems, while more progress has occurred in developing workable approaches to definition, assessment and management within that age range. The aim in this section is to clarify the resemblances that exist between these areas and to outline a workable approach applicable to infant crying and sleeping problems.

Like infant crying and sleeping problems, the terms 'behaviour problems', 'behaviour difficulties' and 'conduct problems' refer to behaviour in social situations that is outside the normal range and challenging for others (J. Hill, 2002; Pennington, 2002). In older children, these behaviours include overactive and impulsive behaviour, aggression, non-compliance with instructions, failing to follow rules and other behaviours that violate social conventions. Like sleeping problems, these behaviours are described in international medical schemes, including the ICD-10 published by WHO (1992) and the *Diagnostic and Statistical Manual* (DSM-IV) published by the American Psychiatric Association (1994). Unlike most diseases, though, behaviour problems are not defined by an underlying illness and its symptoms and causes. Behaviour problems are defined by social rules about unacceptable behaviour.

As with infant crying and sleeping problems, the issue of whether child behaviour problems are categorical, all or none, entities or normally distributed 'matters of degree' entities has been a longstanding source of debate. Traditionally, medical thinking has been based on the notion of disease, so that people fall naturally into two groups – ill or well. Illness is identified by its symptoms that, in general, map more or less directly onto an underlying physical cause. There are exceptions – the example usually given being blood pressure, which varies more or less continuously. Even so, blood pressure is relatively simple to measure and divide into two or three categories, such as high, medium and low risk. In contrast, behaviour does not need to map directly onto an underlying physical disturbance – it is possible to learn atypical behaviours with a normal nervous system. Moreover, many children exhibit occasional problematic behaviours from time to time. Identification of serious behaviour problems involves assessing how far they differ from normal (i.e. extent or degree) and how long they have lasted for.

It needs to be admitted that these issues remain contentious. In this older age group, however, it is now widely, if not universally, accepted that most of the child behaviours listed in the paragraph above vary continuously in extent or degree, rather than falling naturally into discrete problem and non-problem categories and groups (J. Hill, 2002; Moffitt, 2008; Pennington, 2002; Sonuga-Barke, 1998). The resulting dilemma, as Edmund Sonuga-Barke (1998) has pointed out, is that the process of identifying cases for professional intervention involves some conflict between two different purposes: the aim of understanding children accurately and the aim of professional practice. In particular, the need to divide cases into two categories (problem and non-problem cases), follows to a considerable extent from the professional need to decide who is to receive treatment and who is not. That decision requires somewhat arbitrary 'cut-off' scores to be set at points on the normal distribution, such as at one or two standard deviations beyond the average for the population as a whole. Exactly where the cut-offs are set depends partly on the resources, including professional resources, available – so that the cut-off will have to be higher, and fewer cases will receive treatment, if there is a dearth of professional services (Pennington, 2002). Likewise, the cut-off can be set lower, and more cases can receive help, if resources are plentiful and treatment cost is low. In effect, the issue of the 'seriousness' or 'caseness' of a particular child is determined relative to a society's investment in resources for such problems, rather than in absolute terms by a single, universally applicable, cut-off rule about child behaviour. The cost-effectiveness of treatments based on alternative cut-offs is a key consideration. Similar issues about balancing treatment effectiveness against cost affect health service decisions about interventions for infant crying and sleeping.

Another parallel between infant crying and sleeping and child behaviour problems concerns their common interest in organic versus social–environmental causation of atypical behaviour. In the older age range, however, debates about the importance of organic or social environmental causes have given way to interest in how they sum and interact over age (J. Hill, 2002; Rutter, 2006). There is substantial evidence that most behavioural differences between children have genetic predispositions, but equally that most problematic behaviours are the result of accumulations of organic and environmental risk factors.

For present purposes, perhaps the most important parallel is that studies of infants and older children both make use of reports of parents in identifying problems. In older children, these can be supplemented by the reports of teachers and others who see children regularly in their everyday environments, but there are no definitive 'tests' for behaviour problems. As with infant crying and sleeping, the reliance on parents' reports with older children is partly due to pragmatic factors, including the challenges and costs involved in assessing child behaviour repeatedly in different situations and over time. But, the use of parent reports reflects, too, the acceptance that child behaviour becomes problematic when it impinges on a social partner, so that measures which seek to separate children from their contexts are of limited value. It follows that measures of children's behaviour problems are partly reflections of the cultural contexts of the parents and others providing the reports (J. Hill, 2002; Pennington, 2002).

This is not, of course, to say that parental reports of child behaviour problems are accepted uncritically. Instead, a distinction between 'screening' and 'diagnostic' assessments has been developed. As their name implies, the primary aim of screening assessments is to select out cases that need more detailed scrutiny. Parents and others who see children in everyday contexts are in the best position to provide screening reports. As a consequence, standard rating scales such as the Child Behaviour Checklist (Achenbach et al., 1987) and Strengths and Difficulties Questionnaire (Goodman, 1997) have been constructed to allow parents and others to identify children's behaviour problems. These instruments come together with normative population information and evidence of their reliability, validity, sensitivity and specificity in identifying problem cases that allow them to be used with a good degree of confidence for screening purposes.

While rating scales such as the Strengths and Difficulties Questionnaire are useful for screening purposes, it is important that they are not assumed to have greater accuracy than they actually possess. In effect, they provide a carefully collected opinion of an informant, such as a parent, expressed in a standard form. This is a particularly important limitation where a single report by a parent about a single child is the only information available. At that point, the parental measure indicates that there is a problem, but does not identify its nature or where it resides. A second stage, of diagnostic assessment then continues in order to clarify the screening information. Diagnostic assessment is likely to involve a process over time, which includes the accumulation and synthesis of information from multiple sources to clarify the nature and extent of the problem and allow remedial steps to be taken.

Returning to infant crying and sleeping problems and the goal of distinguishing the severity of cases in a way that can be used by professionals and parents, this two-stage, screening then diagnostic, assessment framework has a good deal to recommend it. It assumes that clinical involvement in problem cases will usually start with a parental report. It requires inexpensive, easy to use, reliable and valid measures of infant behaviour, together with normative information that allows the extent of an infant's atypical crying, sleeping and other behaviour to be evaluated. This information is likely to be sufficient and to provide reassurance in a substantial number of cases. Where further assessment is called for, information from other sources and methods can be collected, to provide more specialized evidence about infant or parental features that need to be considered in planning an intervention. Because this is likely to be needed in only a small minority of cases that come to professionals' attention, the overall approach promises to be cost-effective.

Chapter 10 will include recommendations for applying this framework for dealing with infant crying and sleeping problems when they are presented. Before turning to treatment, though, prevention needs to be considered. Primary health surveillance and sharing guidance information with parents that *prevents* infant crying and sleeping problems, so far as possible, is at least as important a part of professional practice as treating problems after they have arisen. Moreover, the maxim 'prevention is better than cure' is widely endorsed. Since prevention depends on an understanding of causation, the evidence about the origins of problematic infant crying and sleeping behaviours will be considered in detail in the next few chapters.

Summary and conclusions about the nature and identification of infant crying and sleeping problems

1   Although they are not commonly distinguished, infant crying and sleeping problems are substantially different in the ages and times of the day when they present, often occur in different infants, and may well have different causes. Infant crying, and parental concern about it,

peak at around 4–6 weeks of age, with most of the crying occurring in the daytime and, particularly, the evenings. Infant sleeping problems occur mainly at night, after 3 months of age.

2   As well as distinguishing between infant crying and sleep–waking behaviours, it is important to distinguish between infant and parental problems. Most infants who cry a lot in early infancy, or wake and disturb their parents at night after 12 weeks of age, are in good health and do not have anything organically wrong with them, so that their behaviour is first and foremost a problem for their parents.

3   Many parents find prolonged infant crying or night waking challenging, but some are particularly vulnerable to these stresses. In extreme cases, this can lead to abuse, causing infant brain damage or death in some instances. For these reasons, healthcare services need to approach the problems as involving both infant and parental parts. Interventions need to be based on assessments that distinguish infant from parental elements, but consider these in relation to each other, rather than assuming that the problem involves an infant disturbance.

4   In addition to the two main groups (infants who cry a lot in the first 12 weeks of infancy; infants who are unsettled at night after 12 weeks of age) a third, much smaller, group of infants has organic disturbances. These cases need to be distinguished, wherever possible, for specialist attention. Recent research has identified a group of infants who have multiple crying, sleeping and other problems after 3 months of age and has shown that these cases often involve extensive child psychological and family disturbances. Because of their often poor outcomes, these cases need particularly careful attention.

5   Research and practice have been hampered by inaccurate and ambiguous terminology. Terms such as 'colic' and 'infant sleep problem' are used inconsistently, with the consequence that different infant groups, and different causes of crying and sleeping problems, are identified. This is confusing for professionals and parents trying to understand whether a particular infant has a serious crying or sleeping problem and decide what to do about it.

6   A number of definitions have been put forward for identifying more serious or severe crying or sleeping problems or disorders, but there is little consensus in the use of these. This issue is complex, because infant crying and sleeping behaviours vary continuously along a number of dimensions, rather than falling into discrete, severe-problem, mild-problem and non-problem categories. The complexity is increased by cultural variations in infant behaviour, which depend in turn on cultural factors.

7   Similar issues have confronted research and practice concerned with older children's behaviour problems, but more progress has been made in developing workable strategies for assessing and managing that

age range. As with infant crying and sleeping problems, measures of children's behaviour problems depend on parent reports. This reflects pragmatic issues and the acceptance that child behaviour becomes problematic when it impinges on a social partner, so that measures which seek to separate children from their contexts are of limited value. Since, too, the threshold set to identify serious problems reflects a society's healthcare resources, problems need to be defined in relation to each society rather than by a set of universal rules.

8 Following the approach adopted for children's behaviour problems, a two-stage, screening then diagnostic, framework is proposed as the basis for assessing infant crying and sleeping problems. This assumes that clinical involvement in problem cases will usually start with a parental report or complaint. The screening stage requires simple, reliable and inexpensive assessments, that are likely to be sufficient and to provide reassurance in a substantial number of cases. Where further assessment is called for, information from other sources and methods can be collected, to provide more specialist, diagnostic information about infant or parental features that need to be considered in planning an intervention. This framework will be applied in greater detail in Chapter 10.

9 Primary health surveillance and sharing information with parents that prevents crying and sleeping problems, so far as possible, is at least as important a part of professional practice as treating problems after they have arisen. Since prevention depends on an understanding of causation, the evidence about the nature and origins of infant crying and sleeping problems will be considered in detail in Chapters 3–8, and their implications for prevention in Chapter 9.

Chapter 3

What do we know about the infant part of infant crying problems?

The term 'infant colic'

The phrase 'infant colic' is often used by parents and healthcare professionals to describe cases where a baby's crying is considered to be excessive, problematic or worrying in some way. Some of the confusions surrounding this term were introduced briefly in Chapter 2 and are considered in greater detail in Box 3.1. As this indicates, the difficulty with this term is that it has evolved over time to take on a number of rather different meanings, some of which conflict with others or raise logical or practical confusions. For example, the phrase 'I don't think her crying is due to colic' makes perfect sense if the word colic is used to refer to the presumed cause (for instance, to gastrointestinal pain), but it is nonsense when 'colic' refers to the amount of crying, as in the Rule of Threes definition (see Box 3.1).

The word 'colic', then, is responsible for a great deal of confusion – but is so much a part of everyday language that it is difficult to avoid it altogether. Instead, the approach adopted will be to clarify which of the meanings given in Box 3.1 is being referred to when the word colic is used. The broad phrase 'infant crying problems' corresponds with the first of the definitions in Box 3.1, while the aim in this chapter is to distinguish the precise features of infant crying behaviour that give rise to parental concerns. In the process, the aim will be to move from the vagueness inherent in the word 'colic' to a more specific understanding of the infant crying behaviours involved. Most of the available research comes from studies of infants and parents in Western industrialized societies but, wherever possible, reference will be made to studies from other cultures to provide a background for the Western findings.

Infant crying behaviours

Infant crying is one of the earliest occurring, most iconic and universally recognized human behaviours, but is not simple to describe or measure. In everyday use, the words 'cry' and 'crying' bring vocalization to mind, and

Box 3.1 The confused (and confusing) notion of 'infant colic'

The confusion surrounding the term 'colic' stems from the use of this word to denote a number of different meanings, some of which conflict with others or raise logical or practical difficulties.

1   In its broadest sense, the word 'colic' is used to refer to cases involving problematic infant crying and its impact on parents. This use does not distinguish between infant and parental parts of such cases, although there is evidence that parental and infant factors can each be involved.

2   A variation on the use above involves cases where parents have complained to a health professional about a baby's troublesome crying. As would be expected, this is the approach typically adopted by medical studies, which are based on cases where parents have sought out professional help. Here, too, the infant crying and parental concern about it are confounded.

3   Because of its etymological roots (from the Greek word 'kolikos', the adjective of 'kolon'), the word colic is often used to refer to the presumed cause of the crying, that is, that it is due to gastrointestinal disturbance and pain. This use involves two inferences: (a) that the infant is in pain; (b) that the pain is caused by a digestive disorder. It also excludes cases involving prolonged crying due to other causes.

4   Maurice Wessel and colleagues' widely cited 'Rule of Threes' defines a fussy or colicky infant as: 'one who, otherwise healthy and well fed, had paroxysms of irritability, fussing or crying lasting for a total of more than three hours a day and occurring on more than three days in any one week' (Wessel et al., 1954, pp. 425–426). This definition of colic refers directly to the total *amount* of infant crying (including fussing and irritability) per 24 hours. The difficulties involved in translating this definition into measurements are discussed in Chapter 2 (section on 'What counts as a "serious problem"').

The misunderstanding that can follow from these different uses becomes apparent if the phrase 'I don't think her crying is due to colic' is contemplated. That makes perfect sense if the word colic is used to refer to the presumed cause (that is, to gastrointestinal disturbance and pain), but it is nonsense when 'colic' refers to the amount of crying, as in the Rule of Threes definition. Note, too, the words '. . . otherwise healthy . . .' in the Rule of Threes definition. This stipulation of healthiness is helpful in ruling out cases with fever or illness but, rather perversely, has the consequence that an infant with an organic disturbance should not be said to have colic.

One way out of this terminological maze would be to regard only cases with a gut disturbance as 'true' instances of colic, while cases identified because they cry a lot (for instance, using the Rule of Threes definition) are not considered 'true' colic cases. The disadvantage is that only a small minority of infants who cry a lot in early infancy have gastrointestinal or other organic disturbances (see main text), so that confining the word colic to such infants will neglect most cases with a crying problem. Yet it is troublesome crying that is the chief source of parents' concerns. In any case, the crucial consideration is that terms should not refer simultaneously to two things: to measures of behaviour and to an underlying physiological condition. To use one word to refer to several different things is simply confusing.

Note, too, that many infants selected using one definition (such as 1 or 2) will not be selected by a more stringent definition (such as 3 or 4), so that researchers can end up studying different types of cases (see the text for further discussion).

dictionary definitions, too, tend to start with vocal signals (Harper & Collins, 1991). But crying behaviour also involves facial expressions, body movements and sometimes tears, each of which may tell us something about the mental and physical state of the child producing them. Crying also varies in vigour or intensity. For example, researchers often distinguish between 'crying' and 'fussing' or 'fretting', where these last two terms are used to identify intermittent vocalizations and other behaviours, while 'crying' is confined to more continuous and energetic behaviours. Lastly, variations in infants' readiness to start crying ('reactivity'), and to quieten once crying has begun (cry 'regulation'), can be measured. In particular, infants' inability to stop crying in response to soothing manoeuvres ('incon-solability' or 'unsoothability') has proved to be especially important. These specific terms will be explained where they are used below. Otherwise, to avoid cumbersome language, the word 'crying' will be used throughout this book as a generic term to refer to all forms of infant behaviour considered to reflect underlying psychological or physical distress, discomfort or pain.

Which infant crying behaviours give rise to parental concern?

Infant crying amount

Although it may seem obvious, it is worth noting that there is substantial evidence that the amount a baby cries is a key source of parental concern. For example, objective, 24-hour audio-recordings of babies' crying have

confirmed that parents who contact health professionals about their babies crying are often correct in reporting that their baby cries more than average amounts (Barr et al., 1988; Barr et al., 1992; St James-Roberts et al., 1993b). The proviso, as we have already noted in Chapter 2, is that this is not true of every parent or robust enough for clinical purposes: it is not possible to depend on parental reports alone. Nevertheless, as a generalization it is true that prolonged amounts of crying are often one reason for parents' concerns.

The unexplained nature of the crying

As well as a prolonged amount, another feature of early infant crying responsible for many parents' concerns is its unexplained nature. This is reflected in the Rule of Threes definition of 'colic' crying, which requires both a set amount of crying (over 3 hours per day) and a baby who is '. . . otherwise healthy and well fed . . .' (Wessel et al., 1954, pp. 425–426). The importance of the lack of an explanation as a defining feature of problematic crying was also recognized by a recent textbook entitled: *New Evidence on Unexplained Early Infant Crying: Its Origins, Nature and Management* (Barr et al., 2001). It seems likely that the lack of an explanation for their baby's crying increases parents' helplessness and anxiety that something is wrong with their baby.

Infant cry quality and type: does the crying sound abnormal or signal pain?

Inserting the word 'colic' into an internet search engine will generate material about gut disturbance in adults and there is a long-standing assumption in the clinical and research literature that problematic crying in early infancy is due to gastrointestinal disturbance and associated pain (see Box 3.1). Although it is not clear where this 'gut pain' interpretation of prolonged crying in young babies came from, the first English language paediatric textbook, Thomas Phaire's *The Boke of Chyldren*, published in 1544 (Phaire, 1544/1957), listed 'Colyke and Rumblying in the Guttess' as a common childhood ailment. The implication is that this perplexing phenomenon has existed for around 500 years. More recently, the influential British paediatrician, Ronald Illingworth published a review in 1955 (Illingworth, 1955) which referred to 'three month colic' as crying that was probably caused by 'a localised obstruction to the passage of gas in the colon' (p. 173) and returned to it in 1985 (Illingworth, 1985) as 'pain that is obviously intestinal in origin' (p. 981).

In spite of Illingworth's confidence, it is not self-evident that the features of the crying he (and many others since) wrote about are really symptoms of gut pain. For instance, it is entirely possible that a bout of fierce and prolonged crying could give rise to flatulence, rather than the other way around. The strength of recent research has been to put Illingworth's hypothesis to the test. The 'gut pain' assumption has been challenged: (1) by a critical re-examination of the evidence that it is possible to tell the cause of crying from its sound; (2) by studies that have examined the quality of crying bouts directly; and (3) by studies that have sought evidence of gastro-intestinal disturbance in infants who cry a lot.

Can you tell the cause of crying from its sound? The myth of 'cry types'

To consider, first, the broad question of what sort of information is contained in the sound of cries, we are fortunate to have a careful review of the research from an American team led by Gwen Gustafson (Gustafson et al., 2000). This analysis of the evidence is of immense importance in its own right, because of the longstanding popular belief that infants have different cry 'types' that reflect their underlying psychological conditions (such as hunger, anger and pain) reliably. As a result, generations of parents have probably been made to feel inadequate and guilty because they cannot work out the reason for their baby's crying from the cry sound.

The origin of the belief that babies have different cry 'types' can be traced back to research from a Scandinavian group led by Ole Wasz-Höckert in the 1960s (Wasz-Höckert et al., 1968). This pioneering group is rightly celebrated for helping to put cry research on the map for researchers and clinicians alike. However, the methods they used in their ground-breaking research did not permit the conclusions they drew about cry types. As Gustafson and her colleagues point out, the essential flaw in the Wasz-Höckert group's method was in the pre-selection of the cries they asked listeners to identify. Rather than collecting representative sets of cries from the various situations they wished to sample (i.e. birth, hunger, pain, pleasure), the researchers carefully chose six cries they considered to be typical of each of these four sorts, giving 24 cries in total. Listeners were then asked to choose which of the four categories (birth, hunger, pain or pleasure) each cry corresponded to, rather than being given a free choice in identifying the cries. The consequence is that variations in how a given baby cries on separate occasions when she is (for instance) hungry, and the variations between different babies in how they do so, are removed from the listener's task: the task is made artificially easy. The point is not that there are no prototypical cries – for instance, the exemplary 'pain' cry is familiar to many people. Rather, as Ronald Barr has noted, the point is that it is much easier to identify pain cries reliably when you see the needle going into the baby's foot than when all you have available is the sound of the cry (Barr, 1998). In fact, of the 24 cries Wasz-Höckert and colleagues selected as exemplars, only 16 were identified correctly by their listeners.

Since they did not report which of the four cry types were identified, it remains possible that some distinctions were easier than others. In Gustafson and colleagues' (Gustafson et al., 2000, p. 9) words:

> . . . we cannot assess the likely possibility that one or two of the categories were particularly distinct (e.g. the birth cry of the newborn, whose respiratory tract still contains a great deal of fluid, or the contented coos and babbles that constitute the 'pleasure cries' of the older infant).

It is worth pointing out that findings discrepant with Wasz-Höckert and colleagues' conclusions appeared as early as 1927, when Mandel Sherman (1927) reported listeners' inability to distinguish between newborns' hunger, shock (sudden drop from a height of 2–3 feet), anger (restraint of head and face) and pain cries in the absence of information about the eliciting stimulus conditions. Several more recent studies, too, have confirmed how difficult it is for adults, and even parents listening to their own babies' cries, to tell the cause of cries from their sounds (Grunau et al., 1990; Gustafson & Harris, 1990; Hadjistavropoulos et al., 1994; Muller et al., 1974).

In place of the 'cry type' view of early infant crying, Gustafson and colleagues' conclusion is that the crying is a 'graded signal' which conveys the infant's degree of distress, but not the particular cause. Debra Zeifman (2001) draws a similar conclusion. Having detected a cry signal and evaluated its urgency, caregivers have to work out the cause using experience and contextual information. For example, knowing that it is four hours since a baby last fed makes it a reasonable assumption that a bout of crying is due to hunger. As Heather Hadjistavropoulos and colleagues (1994, p. 490) concluded in the report of their 1994 Canadian study:

> Adult concern is no doubt increased by crying even when the adult is closely attending to the cry, but cry also serves an important role as a biological imperative or a 'biological siren' that attracts caretaking from afar. Thereafter, the adult would be expected to attend directly to the baby and would have multiple sources of information available concerning the specifics of the infant's well-being.

In other words, there is no evolutionary reason why the sound of cries would need to convey the precise nature of their cause, since telling the caregiver to come urgently is all that is needed. With later sections of this book and interventions in mind, one of the best pieces of guidance healthcare professionals can give to parents is to disabuse them of the idea that they are inadequate parents because they cannot work out the cause of their baby's crying from the sound of the cry. Professionals cannot do so reliably either.

Other audible and visible features of the cries

If, then, the bouts of unexplained crying in early infancy do not tell us that a baby is in pain, what is it about the crying that disturbs parents so much? One way to address that is to examine the crying bouts themselves directly, by recording them and analysing their audible and acoustic properties, or by observing infant crying behaviour as it happens. Both methods have been used. The cry-recording/audible analysis approach is not for the faint-hearted. After recording infant vocalizations constantly over 24 hours using voice-activated recorders, researchers have to listen to the recordings, using standard definitions to distinguish amounts of fussing, crying and intense crying. Fortunately, because the equipment only records when sound-activated, a typical 24-hour recording lasts only about 4 hours (St James-Roberts, 1992). The audio-recordings can then be compared with parent-kept diary measures of the same 24-hour fuss/crying. Because the audio-recordings used in these studies had a 'speaking clock' recorded on a second channel, it was also possible to find, and examine separately, the cry bouts judged by parents in their diaries to be 'colic' bouts. For this purpose, parents were asked to mark colic crying bouts on the diaries, where these were defined as crying bouts that involved 'intense unsoothable crying and other behaviour, perhaps due to stomach or bowel pain'. For clarity, these will be referred to here as 'parent-judged colic crying bouts'.

The London researchers using this method compared a group of 67 infants reported by parents to fuss/cry for 3 or more hours in 24 hours on average with two moderate crying groups (St James-Roberts et al., 1996). Their finding was that the infants reported to fuss/cry for ≥3 hours by parents did cry more per 24 hours, and their crying had a higher cry:fuss ratio, compared with infants in the other groups, in the audio-recording measures as a whole. However, most of the crying in all three groups was intermittent 'fussing' rather than continuous or intense crying. Where infants were reported to have 'parent-judged colic crying bouts', the audio-recordings showed that these particular bouts were longer, but not more sudden in onset or intense than bouts of crying judged not to be colic bouts by other parents (St James-Roberts et al., 1996). The 'parent-judged colic crying bouts' were not distinct in their sound.

Acoustic analysis, where computers analyse the acoustic sound properties of cries, are even more accurate than listening studies, although they are limited at present to being able to analyse relatively short periods of up to a few minutes of crying. The two main acoustic parameters examined in such studies are fundamental frequency (audible pitch) and dysphonation (audible harshness). Using this method, the London researchers who carried out the listening study examined the acoustic properties of 'parent-judged colic crying bouts' compared with the most intense segments of pre-feed cries of other infants that stopped when the infants were fed (St James-Roberts,

1999). The question, then, was whether bouts of crying some parents judged to signify colic differed acoustically from 'hunger' cries. The finding was that the parent-judged colic bouts were not higher in fundamental frequency or dysphonation than the 'hunger' cries.

It needs to be recognized that these findings have so far been reported by only one group, whereas others have presented evidence that at least some infants who meet Rule of Threes criteria have distinct cry sounds. For instance, Barry Lester and colleagues' American study found higher frequency and more dysphonated cries in 16 Rule of Threes infants than in 16 comparison infants when crying was elicited by electrode removal (Lester et al., 1992). However, some of their infants were born prematurely and this could have affected their crying – we will see later that prematurely born infants' crying is sometimes high pitched. In a subsequent study by the same group, no difference in fundamental frequency or dysphonation was found between Rule of Threes and other infants, although in this case the mean resonant frequencies were higher (Lester, 1997). Philip Zeskind and Ronald Barr found no overall differences in the acoustic properties of cries before or after feeds of 11 Rule of Threes infants, compared with 22 moderately crying infants (Zeskind & Barr, 1997). In this case, when the 'most vehement' cry utterance (lasting about 1 second) was selected, the most vehement utterances of Rule of Threes infants did not decline in fundamental frequency and dysphonation after a feed, whereas these features of the most vehement utterance of comparison infants did decline.

It may be apparent that there is little agreement in-between these studies about the distinct acoustic features of the cries of infants who meet Rule of Threes criteria for colic, while the significance of indices such as 'mean resonant frequency' and 'most vehement utterance' remains unknown. It certainly remains feasible that some infants who cry a lot have acoustically abnormal cries and the possibility that these are specific to cases with organic disturbances is intriguing. However, the evidence in support of these possibilities is weak. To be clear, there is no doubt that acoustic features such as high pitch do alarm parents, or that cries elicited by painful procedures are often intense (Crowe & Sanford Zeskind, 1992; Dessureau et al., 1998; Lehr et al., 2007; Lester et al., 1992; Wood & Gustafson, 2001). What is lacking is clear evidence that the cries of infants selected by parents or researchers because of prolonged crying in early infancy have a distinct or abnormal sound, or that it is possible to tell the specific cause of the cries from their sound.

Another way of examining infants' cry type directly is to observe their behaviour in the home or clinic. This approach, which allows measures of visible as well as audible behaviour, has been used both by North American and English research groups. The addition of information about visible behaviour turned out to be important. In the first study of this type, after identifying a group of modified Rule of Threes babies, the London researchers observed the infants at home during 4-hour home visits timed to coincide with the time when infants were expected to cry most (mainly in the evening) (St James-Roberts et al., 1995). After recording the infants' spontaneous behaviour, the researchers intervened (with the parents' permission) when the infants continued to cry for more than 5 minutes in spite of their parents' efforts to soothe them. The researcher interventions employed a 'standard consolability procedure', such that the amount of soothing given was gradually increased in seven standard steps, from just talking, through to picking the baby up and rocking while also giving a pacifier, to a score of seven where the baby could not be soothed. The finding was that infants selected because their parents reported ≥3 hours of fuss/crying were sometimes resistant to researchers', as well as parents', attempts to stop them crying. The evidence obtained from clinical assessments is similar. In this case, after selecting modified Rule of Threes and comparison cases, researchers 'blinded' to the infants' group administered height, weight and other standard, mildly stressful neurobehavioural tests involving handling and undressing. Two studies of this kind both found that infants reported by parents to fuss/cry ≥3 hours per 24 hours at home were more inclined to fuss and cry when handled by researchers (Prudhomme White et al., 2000; St James-Roberts et al., 2003). It may be helpful to think of this as an individual disposition some babies have during this early stage of infancy to fuss/cry more than most babies, although it needs to be borne in mind that this disposition does not usually continue to later ages (Barr & Gunnar, 2000).

Based on these findings as a whole, it is thought that the chief features of early crying that disturb parents are the prolonged length of the cry bouts, the crying's relative intensity (a relatively high cry:fuss ratio), and the resistance of the babies to soothing techniques that usually stop infants from crying (Barr et al., 2005; St James-Roberts et al., 1996). The inconsolability or 'unsoothability' of the crying, in particular, is thought to be its most salient feature, since this makes parents feel helpless, frustrated and powerless (St James-Roberts et al., 1995; Barr et al., 2005). The impact of the crying on parents is due, then, to the fact that they cannot control it, rather than to its distinct sound. Given the terminological complexity of this area, it would be unhelpful to add to the confusion by proposing yet another definition of colic to those included in Box 3.1. However, it is an interesting possibility that these long and unsoothable crying bouts may be the core basis for most cases of infant colic as a parent-identified and clinically presented problem.

Summary and conclusions about the infant crying behaviours which give rise to parental concerns

To sum up, the research examined in this chapter has led to a revised understanding of what it is about the crying of some babies that upsets many parents so greatly. Although the crying is sometimes relatively intense, it is more often fretful or 'fussy', and it is not clear that it sounds abnormal or provides information that the baby involved is in pain. Instead, the prolonged and unsoothable nature of the crying, the lack of an explanation for its occurrence, and consequently parents' inability to control it, have emerged as the key features responsible for their concerns. The obvious question is what causes this puzzling behaviour in young infants – and why some infants show these characteristics much more than others?

Chapter 4

What do we know about the causes of prolonged, unsoothable crying in early infancy?

Having identified the sorts of infant behaviour that give rise to parental concerns and complaints to professionals about infant crying, the aim below is to evaluate the evidence in support of different causal explanations for the occurrence of these crying behaviours.

Explanations involving an organic disorder: gut disturbances

There is evidence that organic disturbances, in general, can cause prolonged crying in early infancy. For example, Barry Lester and colleagues documented prolonged crying in the baby of a breast-feeding mother who took the antidepressant fluoxetine hydrochloride (the active ingredient in Prozac) and showed that the baby's crying reduced as the levels of maternal fluoxetine declined (Lester et al., 1993). Other organic disturbances leading to prolonged crying in early infancy include sepsis (Ruiz-Contreras et al., 1999), 'anomalous left coronary artery' (Mahle, 1998), and urinary tract infections (Freedman et al., 2009). However, organic disturbances of these kinds are rare. In a study of all the infants who were presented to a Canadian paediatric hospital because of crying or irritability over a period of 1 year, just 12 of 237 (5.1%) were found to have a serious underlying organic aetiology (Freedman et al., 2009). The critical question, then, is not whether organic disorders *can* cause crying, but how often this happens in practice and, consequently, how many cases involving prolonged infant crying are caused by organic disturbances.

Turning specifically to 'gut disorder' explanations of prolonged crying, there is carefully collected evidence that infants selected using modified Rule of Threes criteria for prolonged crying can have feeding problems, including disorganized feeding behaviour and discomfort after feeding (Miller-Loncar et al., 2004). However, these cases, too, involved a high degree of selection and are unlikely to be typical. Two thorough reviews of the evidence have concluded that food intolerance and all other organic disturbances added together account for no more than 1 in 10 cases taken to clinicians because of excessive crying, or about 1 in 100 infants as a whole (Gormally, 2001; Lehtonen et al., 2000). Put the other way round, 90% of infants seen by healthcare professionals because of their problematic crying do not have an organic disturbance so far as it has been possible to determine. A more recent review (Douglas & Hiscock, 2010) proposed that this rate is nearer to 95%.

The second point about gastrointestinal causation is that, although there is sufficient evidence to conclude that physical disturbances can sometimes cause infants to cry, the evidence about the main organic conditions believed to do so – food allergy and gastro-oesophageal reflux (GOR or GER) – is far from clear or easy to act upon.

Starting with GOR, there is evidence that a small minority of babies have clinical reflux, that is, that they frequently bring up feeds from their stomach into their throat and oesophagus (Heine, 2006; Treem, 2001). Reflux of acidic digestive contents into the oesophagus could well be an unpleasant experience, particularly if the oesophagus becomes irritated, offering a potential explanation for crying. In practice, about 50% of babies regurgitate some feeds and there are no tests to distinguish GOR reliably, so that GOR is far from easy to diagnose (Heine, 2006). It is, though, possible to ask whether GOR identified as accurately as possible is linked to prolonged crying in early infancy. Gastro-oesophageal reflux could be a symptom of food sensitivity but not give rise to repeated bouts of prolonged crying. In the largest and most up to date study to address this issue, Ralf Heine and his Australian colleagues (Heine et al., 2006) followed up 151 babies selected for persistent crying, using cry charts and parental questionnaires to measure crying and regurgitations and 24-hour oesophageal pH monitoring to detect reflux acidity. They found no significant association between GOR (measured as number of reflux bouts, or proportional reflux time) and amount of crying per 24 hours. In another study, the same research group examined the effectiveness of anti-reflux medication as a treatment for prolonged crying, compared with a placebo, using a randomized controlled trial (Jordan et al., 2006). They found no difference in crying reduction between the medicated and placebo group.

Although this Australian work is the most substantial study of GOR to date, it comes from a single research group. However, two reviews of the overall evidence by paediatric gastroenterologists, while reaching somewhat different conclusions, have both noted the lack of consistent evidence that GOR causes crying in 1 to 3-month-old infants (Heine, 2006; Treem, 2001). In his review, William Treem (2001) acknowledged the contradictions in the findings, but concluded that 'Taken together, these studies suggest that pathologic GOR is a significant factor in approximately 5% of infants under 3 months of age who have colic' (p. 170). In contrast, Ralf Heine, reviewing the evidence as a whole up to 2006, concluded that 'a direct causal relationship between acid reflux and infantile colic therefore appears unlikely' (2006, p. 222). More recently, a Dutch review concluded that medication for GOR reduced stomach acidity, but had no effect on infant crying (Blokpoel et al., 2010). Clearly, the jury is still undecided on this issue. Returning to the criteria for robust evidence listed in Chapter 1 of this book, GOR remains a possible, but currently unproven, source of prolonged crying in a small number of babies during early infancy.

There is more support for the idea that prolonged crying in early infancy can be related to adverse reactions to food contents, and particularly to intolerance of cow's milk protein (Forsyth, 1989; Lothe & Lindberg, 1989; Lucassen et al., 1998), but this evidence, too, is far from straightforward. For the most part, large-scale, community studies have found that breast-fed and formula-fed infants are about equally likely to cry for prolonged amounts of time (Clifford et al., 2002; Crowcroft & Strachan, 1997; Lucassen et al., 2001). However, cow's milk protein can be present in both these forms of milk and could give rise to food intolerance, or to allergic reactions, in susceptible infants. The research up to 2001 was reviewed by the Irish paediatrician Siobhan Gormally (2001), who concluded that there was 'strong' evidence for cow's milk protein intolerance as a cause of infant crying, but only in a small minority of the 1 to 3-month-olds presented to clinicians with prolonged crying. More recent studies have continued to indicate that food intolerances and allergies have a minor part to play, but the picture remains perplexing. In a prospective study of 116 infants who were at familial risk of atopy because of their parents' history of allergy, Finnish researchers led by Marko Kalliomäki (Kalliomäki et al., 2001) found that those infants who later showed eczema or asthma fussed (but did not cry) more at 7 weeks, and cried more at 12 weeks, than infants who did not develop eczema or asthma, suggesting that allergy might be involved. In contrast, José Castro-Rodriguez and colleagues' (2001) prospective study of a large American community sample found no association between physician-reported colic in early infancy and markers of atopy, eczema, allergic rhinitis, wheezing or bronchial constriction from 9 months to 11 years of age. Nor were rates of parental asthma or allergy raised where infants had colic. Lucassen and colleagues' (1998) systematic review, too, found no association between a family history of atopy and parental reports of infant colic.

As Heine (2006) noted, prolonged crying is not usually associated with raised immunoglobulin levels in skin-prick or food-specific allergy tests. It follows that the primary way to test for food allergy is to change the infant's diet, by changing to a hypo-allergenic formula where babies are bottle fed, or by restricting their mother's diet where they are breast-fed. Because breast-feeding is recommended for babies' health, restricting maternal diet is indicated as the intervention of choice, although the restrictions on maternal dietary intake needed to implement this method are challenging for families to manage. The most rigorous, randomized controlled trial of the effects of a low-allergen diet for breast-feeding mothers (D. Hill et al., 2005) found a significantly greater reduction in diary-measured infant fuss/crying in the week after 47 mothers started a low-allergen diet than occurred in 43 control group infants. However, the groups did not differ at outcome in the proportions of infants whose fuss/crying per 24 hours equalled or exceeded 3 hours. Moreover, neither mothers' ratings of their infant's amount of crying at outcome, nor of whether colic behaviour was 'improved, the same or worse', differed between the treatment and control groups – implying that the low-allergen diet did not resolve the problem for parents.

In principle, the most robust evidence that crying is due to food intolerance should come from a dietary 'challenge test', so that the food in question is reintroduced after its withdrawal has led to a reduction in crying. In practice, even fewer studies of this sort have been carried out, perhaps because parents are reluctant to allow re-introduction of the suspect food in order to be sure that it causes crying. One study of this type (Forsyth, 1989), had a high rate of parental drop-out and finished with just 17 cases. Half these infants were fed a cow's milk formula first, followed by a hypo-allergenic formula, then a cow's milk formula, while half used the opposite rotation. Careful controls were employed and the parents were unable to detect which formula was which. The overall finding was that infant crying and parent-reported colic reduced upon introduction of the hypoallergenic formula, and worsened after the cow's milk formula was introduced. However, there was substantial variation between infants and inconsistency over time. In the author's words: 'These results demonstrate that, in some instances, colic improves with elimination of cow's milk formula. However, the effect diminishes with time, and only infrequently is the effect reproducible' (Forsyth, 1989, p. 521).

In view of these mixed findings, and how difficult it is to eliminate dairy products from the diet of breast-feeding women, it is not surprising that some reviewers have expressed doubts about the practicality of this approach to the treatment of prolonged infant crying (Wolke, 2001). The conclusion reached by a Cochrane systematic review (Osborn & Sinn, 2006a) is that the evidence about food intolerance as a whole does not support changing wholly breast-fed infants to a hydrolyzed formula. However, where infants at high risk for allergy are unable to be completely breast-fed, they concluded that there was limited evidence that feeding with a hydrolyzed formula reduces allergies in babies and children, compared with a cow's milk formula. They did not recommend substituting soy-based alternatives for cow's milk formula, since soy-intolerance can occur in some cases (Osborn & Sinn, 2006b).

In the last few years, a number of studies have found that adding probiotic bacteria to infant feeds has led to reductions in crying, re-opening the debate about digestive disorder of some sort as a cause of prolonged crying during early infancy. The first, a randomized controlled trial by Francesco

Savino and colleagues in Italy, found that probiotic bacteria fed to 41 breast-fed Rule of Threes infants aged 21 to 90 days reduced their 24-hour crying from a median of 197 minutes at baseline to 51 minutes a month later, while infants in their placebo control group changed much less, from 197 to 145 minutes per 24 hours (Savino et al., 2007). In the treatment group, 95% were considered by the researchers to have benefitted from the probiotic bacteria, compared with a 7% improvement in the placebo control group. A second randomized trial by the same group obtained similar findings (Savino et al., 2010). In addition a study, led by Marc Rhoads in the USA (Rhoads et al., 2009), collected measures of gastrointestinal physiology from 19 7-week-old infants who were referred for problematic crying and met Rule of Threes criteria for crying amount, compared with 17 controls. They found that faecal calprotectin levels (an index of intestinal inflammation in adult studies) were twice as high in the criers than in the control infants. The Rule of Threes infants also had more restricted gut bacterial diversity, while Klebsiella bacteria, previously associated with intestinal and other infections, were found in 47% of Rule of Threes infants, compared with 5% of controls.

The implication of these new studies is to rekindle interest in the possibility that disturbances of gastrointestinal function may contribute to infant crying more often than currently supposed. However, the probiotic claim is not a new one: Illingworth's 1955 review lists a 1920 recommendation by Grulee that babies should be given a 5 ml liquid culture of active lactic acid bacilli in the morning and evening (Illingworth, 1955). Moreover, at almost the same time as these new reports, three other randomized trials have failed to find that adding probiotic bacteria to infants' feeds had any effect on their crying (Coccorullo et al., 2010; Rinne et al., 2006; Weizman & Alsheikh, 2006). Another study, too, has failed to find an association between amount of crying and atopy, while the infants' crying amounts reduced greatly, to normal levels, simply as a result of hospital admission (Zwart et al., 2007).

Inconsistent findings of this sort emphasize the importance of independent replication and the other criteria listed in Chapter 1. Time will tell. To sum up the findings in this area as a whole, the overwhelming majority of infants with prolonged crying in early infancy – 9 out of 10 – do not have a gastrointestinal disturbance and put on weight and develop normally. There is little or no evidence that prolonged infant crying is due to GOR, or that medications that reduce GOR are effective in reducing crying. There is no clear evidence that adding probiotic bacteria to feeds reduces the amounts that infants cry. There is some evidence that cow's milk intolerance causes crying in a small minority of infants. However, where infants are breast-feeding, it is not clear that restricting the breast-feeder's diet to eliminate dairy products is likely to prove effective, while the challenges involved in implementing this form of treatment are considerable. Where infants at high risk for allergy are unable to be completely breast-fed, there is limited evidence that feeding with a hydrolyzed formula reduces allergies in babies and children, compared with a cow's milk formula. Soy-based alternatives to cow's milk formula, however, are not recommended.

For practitioners, one implication of this complex picture is that cases where prolonged crying is due to food intolerance can be expected to be rare. To allow them to be targeted and treated, methods are needed to identify food intolerance and allergy. Since changes to an infant or mother's diet can produce adverse consequences, specialized medical services are needed to advise families about these changes and to monitor their results. A set of guidelines for this purpose developed by an expert international multidisciplinary panel will be presented in Chapter 10, which also provides guidance for the other, 90%, of cases where infants are healthy.

Non-nutritive 'organic disturbance' explanations of prolonged infant crying

As an alternative to digestive disorders, a number of other 'organic disturbance' explanations have been put forward to account for prolonged crying in early infancy. In particular, because the crying peak occurs a few weeks after childbirth, several reports have attributed the crying to exposure to adversities during pregnancy or the perinatal period. The three main causal factors of this type suggested are: (1) maternal cigarette smoking; (2) obstetric complications during pregnancy and the perinatal period; and (3) maternal prenatal stress.

Sijmon Reijneveld and colleagues examined the relationship between ten alternative definitions of 'excessive crying' and four possible 'risk factors' (maternal cigarette smoking, an adverse obstetric history, parents unemployed and urban living) in a sample of 3179 infants (Reijneveld et al., 2002). They found that maternal smoking was the only risk factor that emerged in the majority of (6 out of 10) analyses carried out. Equally, it might be said that smoking was not a risk factor in 4 out of 10 analyses. Other research groups, too, have produced inconsistent findings, with maternal smoking emerging as a predictor of crying in some studies (Søndergaard et al., 2001), but not in other studies, even from the same research group (Søndergaard et al., 2003).

As well as the unreliability of the findings linking maternal cigarette smoking to crying, two other considerations affect the interpretation of the evidence from this research. The first is that, even if maternal cigarette smoking is involved, it does not account for many cases of prolonged infant crying, since most mothers of such babies do not smoke. For example, Charlotte Søndergaard and her Danish colleagues studied 1820 babies and mothers, finding that 21% of mothers who smoked 15 or more cigarettes per day during pregnancy reported problematic infant crying, compared with 10% where mothers did not smoke (Søndergaard et al., 2001). However, the total number of women who smoked 15 or more cigarettes per day during pregnancy was quite small: 6.4% (116 women). Since just 21% of their babies had problematic crying, only 24 of 197 infants in total who had problematic crying could have done so due to maternal smoking. It also follows that in 79% of instances the maternal smoking did not lead to problematic crying.

The second doubt about maternal cigarette smoking as a cause of infant crying stems from the confounding of smoking during pregnancy with other maternal, and paternal, variables that could increase infant crying and/or parental reports of crying problems. Since women who smoke often do so both before and after childbirth, one such confounding is that of a possible effect of cigarette smoke on growth prenatally with the result of a smoky environment postnatally. The evidence about this is controversial, with some reports suggesting that prenatal maternal smoking, and others that postnatal smoking, are the contributing factors (Søndergaard et al., 2001; Reijneveld et al., 2002). At least as important is the extensive evidence that maternal cigarette smoking is linked with social class, education, and a variety of other maternal and parenting variables that could well be the true causes of the infant crying (Maughan et al., 2001; Tong & McMichael, 1992).

It is worth noting that this issue of un-confounding cigarette smoking from the large number of maternal and family variables that go with it is not specific to studies of infant crying. We will encounter it again in relation to infant sleeping, and similar controversies surround attempts to link maternal smoking during pregnancy to other infant and child behavioural and psychological outcomes (Maughan et al., 2001). It is certainly plausible that maternal cigarette smoking could interfere with foetal growth or postnatal metabolism and make infants irritable (Schuetze & Eiden, 2007; Shenassa & Brown, 2004), but whether that causes prolonged amounts of crying around 5–6 weeks of age, why it does so, and how long this lasts for, are all matters for further research.

Turning to the possible link between prolonged infant crying and obstetric complications and/or maternal stress, the picture is similarly unclear. For obstetric complications, some studies have found that factors such as respiratory distress or medication during childbirth predict infant crying (de Weerth & Buitelaar, 2007; Keller et al., 1998; St James-Roberts & Conroy, 2005; Woodson et al., 1979), but others have not, even in some cases when the same methods were employed (Hogdall et al., 1991; St James-Roberts & Conroy, 2005). Similarly, maternal antenatal stress or anxiety have emerged as a predictor of infant crying in some studies (de Weerth et al., 2003; Søndergaard et al., 2003; St James-Roberts & Conroy, 2005; van der Wal et al., 2007; Wurmser et al., 2006), but the findings have not been replicated in others (St James-Roberts & Conroy, 2005; Søndergaard et al., 2001).

The difficulties involved in un-confounding these factors from other prenatal complications and postnatal parenting variables are similar to those noted above for maternal cigarette smoking (St James-Roberts & Conroy, 2005).

Evidence from studies of prematurely born infants

Because prematurely born babies ('pre-termers') are more likely than infants born at full term to have neurological disorders, studies of this group provide another strategy for assessing the link between organic disturbances and crying. Three points need to be kept in mind in evaluating this research. First, although the interest is in premature birth, infants are usually selected primarily for low (or very-low) birth-weight because weight is easier to measure accurately than the length of gestation at birth. Most infants born with low birth-weight are, though, prematurely born. Second, because pre-termers are by definition immature at birth, allowance for the number of weeks of prematurity needs to be made when they are compared with infants born at full term, since otherwise the pre-termers are at a maturational disadvantage. This is referred to as 'corrected age'. Third, an important distinction in this research is between pre-termers with, and without, evidence of neurological deficits. Studies of healthy pre-termers without neurological deficits can be used to examine how maturity affects crying. Here, the interest is in the crying of pre-termers with evidence of brain damage or neurological disorder.

Starting with the most robust evidence, there is a long tradition of research linking neurological deficits with the *quality* or *sound* of infant cries (as opposed to the amount of their crying). Early studies of infants with congenital disorders reported a syndrome known as 'cri du chat', where the crying sounded high pitched and seemed to the researchers to resemble a cat's cry (Vuorenkoski et al., 1966; Wasz-Höckert et al., 1985). Recent studies have used more precise terminology, but the link between neurological deficits and the sound of infant cries, particularly their high pitch, has been repeatedly confirmed (Espositoto & Venuti, 2010; Lester & Boukydis, 1985; Rautava et al., 2007; Zeifman, 2004). Studies of infants with confirmed brain damage have also found longer delays in their cry onset after painful stimulations, such as those involved in inoculations, compared with full-term born infants (Fisichelli & Karelitz, 1963; Karelitz & Fisichelli, 1962).

Some studies of pre-termers without evidence of brain damage, too, have found them to have cries with a higher pitch and more variability in amplitude and pitch than full-term born infants (Rautava et al., 2007). Rather less clear is precisely why their cries should have these features, that is, whether the explanation involves undetected neurological disorders, deficits or immaturities of the vocal tract apparatus involved in cry production, or some other cause. For instance, Liisi Rautava and her Finnish colleagues (Rautava et al., 2007) examined the cries of 21 very-low birth-weight ($\leq$1500 g at birth) infants when they reached 18 months of age, compared with the cries of 54 full-term born control infants. The very-low birth-weight infants had received ultrasound and magnetic resonance imaging (MRI) brain scans, allowing relationships between brain structure and cry acoustics to be examined. Fifteen of the 21 very-low birth-weight infants had MRI evidence of brain pathologies, such as cysts, white matter injury, or abnormalities of the corpus callosum, cerebellum or brain ventricles. The cries of both groups were elicited by routine inoculations carried out at 18 months of age, with the cries being recorded and subjected to acoustic analysis. The main finding was that the very-low birth-weight infants' cries were higher pitched – they had a higher minimum fundamental frequency and fourth formant than the cries of the full-term born infants. However, the differences between the full-term and prematurely born infants' cry acoustics were not accounted for by brain pathology, so that the authors were unable to conclude whether the high-pitched crying was due to brain damage, brain immaturity or neurological factors at all, as opposed (for instance) to the infants' vocal apparatus. For present purposes, the implication of the studies to date is that there is evidence of a relationship between neurological disorder and cry quality, and between premature birth and cry quality, including high pitch, but the nature of this relationship is poorly understood. Professionals who encounter abnormal-sounding cries may wish, then, to look further into an infant's background and we will return to guidelines for doing so in Chapter 10.

Returning to our main focus on amounts of unsoothable crying, it is instructive to ask at the outset whether our expectation is that brain damage will increase, or decrease, the amount a baby cries? Increased crying could happen if the effect of neurological damage is to heighten responsiveness and increase irritability, but equally a seriously unwell infant might be expected to be weak and reluctant to cry. Indeed, early studies produced evidence of both kinds (Karelitz & Fisichelli, 1962; Maunu et al., 2006; Rautava et al., 2007; Wolf et al., 2002).

In more recent research, the most extensive and meticulous studies of the relationship between premature birth, brain damage and amount of infant crying have been carried out by a multidisciplinary team in Turku, Finland, headed by Liisa Lehtonen. In their 2006 study (Maunu et al., 2006), they followed up 124 of the 129 surviving very-low birth-weight infants born in Turku University Hospital between January 2001 and July 2004. The infants' crying was measured using validated behaviour diaries to assess spontaneous, 24-hour, crying at home at term, 6 weeks and 5 months of age, corrected for the infants' prematurity. At 5 months, their crying was compared with that of 49 full-term born infants, measured in the same way. To examine the impact of brain damage, the prematurely born infants were divided into three subgroups, according to brain ultrasound and MRI scans: a group with normal brain scans ($n = 34$), a group with intermediate brain scans ($n = 48$) and a group with clearly pathologic brain scans ($n = 40$). Their main finding was that severe brain injuries did not affect the duration of fussing or crying, the frequency of crying bouts or the pattern of the infants' crying over 24 hours. A proviso was that the very-low birth-weight infants had more frequent fussing bouts, and were held more (and taken out in strollers or cars less), at 5 months than the full-term born infants. However, this was true of the very-low birth-weight group as a whole and not different according to whether or not the infants had brain pathology. The daily duration of fuss/crying declined over age in all three very-low birth-weight subgroups and all three showed an increase in the number of fuss/crying bouts from term to 6 weeks corrected age, followed by a decline to 5 months – patterns over age that are broadly similar to those typically found in studies of full-term born infants.

A second study from this group adds a small, but interesting, caveat (Munck et al., 2008). In this case, 117 of the same very-low birth-weight infants were followed up to 2 years of age, when their cognitive development was assessed using Bayley Scales, which provide standardized scores for infants' mental and psychomotor development. Because this study did not include a comparison group of full-term born infants, its findings speak to differences in crying in-between infants who all had very-low birth-weight and the relationship between these differences and their cognitive development. The finding was that very-low birth-weight infants who cried most at term age, and to a lesser extent at 6 weeks (but not at 5 months), had poorer psychomotor development scores at 2 years of age. The correlations between these two measures were not strong (of the order of 0.2) so that, as the authors pointed out, there was a large overlap between the developmental outcomes of infants with lower and higher amounts of crying in the early weeks – and amount of crying alone was not a useful predictor of later development. On one hand, this suggests that high amounts of crying are not always benign signs, but may indicate an underlying disturbance in some cases. On the other hand, these cases seem to be the exception rather than the rule, raising the question of what features other than the crying distinguish the small number of cases where prolonged crying predicts poor outcomes. The message from the Turku group's first study is that this 'other' factor may not be brain damage. For the moment, the overall conclusion from studies of prematurely born infants is that they do not provide any evidence to support the claim that high amounts of crying in early infancy are a reliable indication of neurological disorder.

To sum up the research into organic disturbances as a whole, it is certainly possible that pathological conditions other than dietary disorders increase crying amounts in early infancy, but the existing findings do not provide convincing evidence that this is commonly the case. The research to date does not support the suggestion that this failure to confirm causation is entirely due to how crying problems are defined (Reijneveld et al., 2002), since some of the studies cited above have used validated measures of crying. Further research involving careful measurements and attempts to separate out the various pre- and postnatal risk factors is certainly needed. In the meantime, the evidence in support of this type of explanation of early infant crying does not come anywhere close to the requirements for robust proof set out in Chapter 1.

'Developmental' explanations of prolonged infant crying

Explanations of this type also attribute prolonged crying to endogenous, within-infant, factors, rather than to parental care or other external environmental factors. Unlike 'organic disturbance' explanations, the proposal in this case is that growth and maturational processes that are a normal part of infant development give rise to the crying. It follows that the crying does not mean there is anything seriously wrong with the babies. This approach is at odds with the reactions of many Western parents, who view crying as a self-evident proof that something is wrong with a baby. However, as Figure 4.1 illustrates, crying can be viewed as evidence of good health in some circumstances. In this case, the example is a birth cry, which has traditionally been considered a sign of robust good health in Western cultures, to the extent that our medical conventions at one time sanctioned the use of a slap to the bottom to elicit such a cry. Robust crying in this context, then, is a sign of good health.

Another example sometimes used to make the same point comes from Marten de Vries's (1987) study of 4 to 5-month-old Masai infants in Kenya. He obtained temperament ratings from parents and followed up the ten 'easiest' and ten 'most difficult' infants, according to their parents, after a famine. The Masai are nomadic and he was able to trace just 13 of the 20. He found that five of seven easy infants, but only one of the six difficult infants, had died. He interpreted this as evidence that being an irritable/demanding infant is adaptive at a time of famine – it induces parents to feed you and promotes survival, whereas being quiet gets you ignored. That may be especially true if your parents value a lusty baby – and the Masai are traditionally a warrior people. Methodologically, this isn't a strong study and, in fact the survival rates for the two groups he reported were not significantly different using a statistical test. What the study seems to suggest is that crying is not always a bad thing, so that we need to think of crying not in isolation but in relation to the specific setting or environment in which it occurs.

I suspect that these two examples may not entirely convince a parent whose 5-week-old baby is crying inconsolably that she is in perfect health but, as a part of re-examining our view of early infant crying, they are

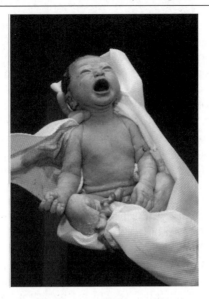

Figure 4.1 A birth cry (reproduced with permission of Wellcome images, © custom medical stock).

certainly food for thought. Health professionals may find it sometimes helps worried parents faced with a crying baby to think of this as a sign of vigour – of a 'Masai baby'. After all, a baby who can cry lustily for prolonged periods is showing signs of vitality that a sick infant may find it hard to manage.

The idea that development affects infant crying has a long history and considerable empirical support. For example, in 1974 – a period before ethical considerations constrained researchers – Vincent Fisichelli (Fisichelli et al., 1974) and colleagues induced crying in infants of different ages using a standard rubber band-snap apparatus to deliver a painful stimulus to the sole of the infant's right foot. The crying was recorded and measures of the latency to response and time spent crying were coded by reliable listeners. The main finding was that crying in response to the band-snap was brief in the first 2 days, increased and stayed similar from 2 days to 12 weeks of age, then showed a gradual falling off in the likelihood and intensity of crying response up to 1 year. At 12 weeks of age, for instance, 90% of infants cried in response to the band-snap, compared with 50% at 16 weeks and 40% at 39–52 weeks. At older ages, the infants who did not cry often grimaced or struggled, suggesting that they had developed alternative behavioural responses to painful stimulation as they got older. Similar evidence that crying responses to painful stimulation diminish with age, in this case following inoculation injections, has been found by Michael Lewis and Douglas Ramsay in the USA (Lewis & Ramsay, 1995a, 1955b, 1999).

As well as diminishing cry responsiveness, development also makes it more self-controlled. For example, Marcy Gekoski (Gekoski et al., 1983) and an American team assessed soothability longitudinally in a group of 13 infants from 60 days to 10 months of age. At each age, the infants were left in their crib until they cried continuously for 60 seconds, following which an unfamiliar female, or their mother, intervened in a more-or-less standard way by picking the infant up, putting her to the adult's shoulder, then patting the infant's back. This was duplicated, so that each infant received both the stranger's and her mother's soothing at each age. These researchers found a reduction in how long the infants took to soothe by both mothers and strangers across age. In particular, the likelihood of 'anticipatory soothing' (the probability that infants would stop crying before being picked up – presumably because they heard or saw the adult approaching) – increased from 40% at 4 months to over 90% by 6 months of age. At 10 months, but not before, the infants were soothed more rapidly by their mothers than the strangers, indicating that they could tell the difference, and use this to inhibit their crying, by 10 months of age. Other evidence of the increasing social–communicative functions that cries acquire with age has been provided by Gwen Gustafson and Jim Green (1991).

Changes in crying amounts at successive ages

Following on from this evidence that development strongly affects infants' ability to control or regulate their crying, the key idea underlying a 'developmental' approach to prolonged infant crying is that normal maturational and psychological changes within infants contribute to variations in the amounts and causes of infant crying at different ages. Infants who cry a lot are, then, considered to be at the extreme of the normal range, rather than unwell. In keeping with this viewpoint, studies that have gone beyond clinically referred groups to include general community samples have found similarities in crying behaviour, such that babies in general have a crying peak in the first 2 months of infancy, with an evening clustering, followed by a marked reduction in crying by 12 weeks of age (Barr, 2001; St James-Roberts, 2001a). This is illustrated in Figure 4.2 by Berry Brazelton's classic 1962 study of 80 infants from a community practice in Boston, USA. One proviso is that not all studies since have found such clear 'peaks': some have found more of a 'plateau', with crying reaching a maximum by about 4 weeks and staying at the same level (Lee, 1994; St James-Roberts, 2001a) while the evening clustering has sometimes been less dramatic than in Brazelton's case (Lee, 1994). Still, even in these studies, the overall amounts of crying have been found to decline substantially, by about 40%, by 12 weeks of age (Alvarez 2004; St James-Roberts, 2001a).

The early crying peaks have been found, too, in Non-Western cultures (Barr et al., 1991b) and in prematurely born infants without medical

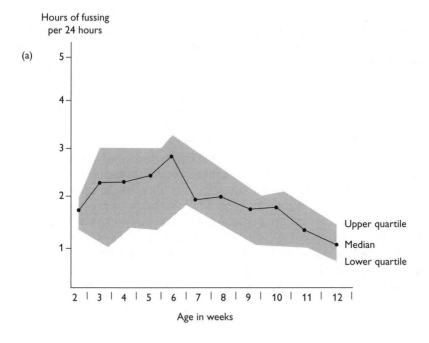

Age in weeks

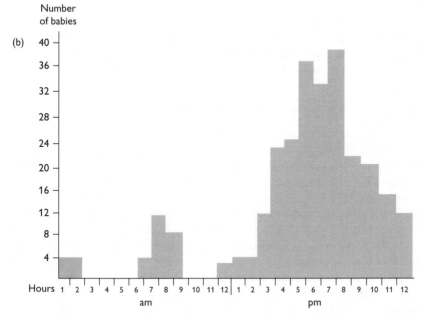

Figure 4.2 (a) The 'developmental crying peak' around 6 weeks of age; (b) the 'time of day crying peak' around 6 weeks of age (redrawn from Brazelton, 1962).

complications at a corrected-age of about 6 weeks (Barr et al., 1996), prompting the suggestion that this crying pattern over age is a 'behavioural universal' of infancy (Barr, 1990). Since most Western clinical cases show this pattern, the argument made is that infants who cry a lot are at the extremes of the normal range in their crying, rather than a separate group with a pathological disturbance (Barr, 1998, 2006; St James-Roberts, 2001b). It is worth noting in passing that a phenomenon that reduces spontaneously, as infant crying typically does, by declining greatly between 1 and 3 months of age, provides the ideal conditions for 'quack' remedies, since the crying is likely to get better providing the remedies are administered at about 6 weeks of age. As we will see below, a matched control group not given the remedy is a minimal requirement for adequate intervention trials.

Recent support for this developmental explanation of prolonged crying in early infancy has been provided by a Canadian study that compared infants who did and did not meet a modified Rule of Threes definition on diary measures of crying at 6 weeks and 5 months of age (Barr et al., 2005). Data were analyzed for 77 infants at both ages. The conclusion was that long and unsoothable crying bouts were specific to the 6-week assessments and virtually disappeared by 5 months of age. Both groups showed these bouts at 6 weeks, but they were more common, and lasted longer, in infants who met the modified Rule of Three definition than the comparison cases. These findings indicate that the long and unsoothable crying bouts that so distress parents are probably linked to processes of infant growth and development that occur in the first 3 months of age, and are found in infants to a lesser or greater degree, rather than being confined to just a subgroup with a pathological organic disturbance.

The neurodevelopmental 'shift' at 2 months of age

Why, then, should normal development give rise to prolonged crying in early infancy? Several researchers have proposed that prolonged crying bouts at this age are caused by the maturational re-organization of brain systems that normally occur at around 2 months of age as reflex mechanisms are replaced by systems involving control of behaviour by the cerebral cortex (Lester, 1985; Barr, 1990). This is sometimes referred to as the 2-month neurodevelopmental or neurobehavioural 'shift' (Emde et al., 1976). In particular, the long and unsoothable nature of the bouts has been attributed to a deficit in neurological control of behaviour during this transition, so that infants are temporarily hyper-reactive (they respond quickly and strongly) – or are unable to regulate (stop) crying once it has started (Barr & Gunnar, 2000; St James-Roberts et al., 2003). The idea that babies at this age may be poor at stopping crying, rather than inclined to start crying more often, offers a radically different way of thinking about their crying from the traditional colic 'gut' view. Unfortunately, there is little direct evidence to support this hypothesis at the present time. For one thing, inability to stop crying should produce longer cry bouts, rather than more frequent bouts. That is precisely what Ronald Barr and team (2005) found in their recent study, but they and others have found evidence that 1 to 3-month-old infants who cry a lot have more frequent crying bouts as well as longer ones (Barr et al., 2005; St James-Roberts et al., 1996). It may well be that accurate separation of cry bouts requires more precise measurements than those used so far, but this remains uncertain.

A further challenge for this explanation is that the 2-month neurodevelopmental 'shift' involves changes to several brain systems, including those responsible for visual-sensory, attention, circadian and social capacities (such as the emergence of social smiling) (Kagan & Herschkowitz, 2005), as well as changes in brain electroencephalographic activity (Salzarulo et al., 2002). In a study of 31 Italian infants, Vanna Axia and colleagues (1999) found that the durations of facial distress elicited by inoculation injections correlated significantly with subsequent measures of visual fixation, suggesting that an infant's ability to switch attention may help to control her crying responses. Except for this finding, however, attempts to narrow down the psychological and physiological systems involved have not obtained consistent findings, so that their primary implication is to point to the need for further research.

In summary, there is considerable evidence of a crying peak in early infancy and to show that unsoothable crying bouts are characteristic of this period. This evidence is consistent with a developmental explanation of prolonged crying during early infancy, that is, which attributes at least part of the cause of the crying to changes in infants that are a normal part of development. It is also possible that developmental processes underlie and enhance the impact of a range of other factors, such as digestive reactions, so that the crying peak is the result of their combined effect. The weakness of this explanatory framework lies in the lack of any direct evidence to document the neurodevelopmental processes involved. It is therefore promising and in need of more research, rather than proven. In addition, it is not at all clear how it accounts for the diurnal pattern of the crying, that is, for the evening crying peak.

Contributions of parenting to early infant crying

As an alternative to theories that highlight endogenous infant systems and their development, some explanations of prolonged crying in early infancy have attributed it to inadequate parenting. In particular, early intervention studies showed both that increasing and decreasing parental response to the crying reduced its amount (McKenzie, 1991; Taubman, 1988). These studies have been criticized on methodological grounds (Wolke, 2001), but since intervention sometimes quietens virtually all babies, reducing overall crying by a statistically significant amount is not particularly difficult to demonstrate – or the point. Unless changes in parenting prevent the prolonged unsoothable crying bouts and 24-hour totals that are the source of parents' concerns, they are unlikely to account for, or resolve, the problem. We need, in effect, two kinds of evidence: that crying has reduced when measured by accurate methods, and that the reductions are sufficient and of a type that resolve the problem for parents.

In principle, the most robust research method for tackling this issue involves randomized, controlled trials, where groups are assigned arbitrarily to alternative forms of parenting and their effects on crying and its impact on parents are measured. In practice, three obstacles have been encountered. First, these intervention studies have been able to achieve only modest changes in parental behaviour, perhaps because Western parents are reluctant to make substantial changes to their care just because they are randomized to do so. Second, the findings have proved inconsistent. For example, supplementary carrying by parents introduced in the first weeks of infancy as a preventive intervention was found to reduce crying in one study (Hunziker & Barr, 1986), but not in three subsequent replication attempts that achieved similar amounts of carrying (Elliott et al., 2002; St James-Roberts et al., 1995; Walker & Menaheim, 1994). Supplementary carrying also proved ineffective as a treatment once prolonged crying had started (Barr et al., 1991a). Third, some of the trials have not distinguished adequately between benefits of the intervention for parents and effects on infant crying behaviour. For example, a recent randomized controlled trial of the 'REST' nursing regime for helping parents to manage colic was favourably evaluated by parents (Keefe et al., 2006a, 2006b), but used maternal subjective judgements of infant changes rather than validated measures of infant behaviour, so that it is not clear whether infant crying was actually reduced. Furthermore, mothers in the control group, who received much less support than the REST mothers, reported similar improvements, albeit of a lesser degree.

There is evidence from other studies that parents value professional support in coping with crying. For instance, Brigid Jordan and colleagues' (Jordan et al., 2006) Australian randomized controlled trial found that two alternative interventions – an infant mental health consultation for mothers, and anti-reflux medication for infants – were no more effective than an infant placebo prescription in reducing diary-measured infant crying over time: with over 90% of mothers in all three groups reporting that crying reduced. This should not be a surprise since, as noted above, crying typically reduces spontaneously after 6 weeks of age, so that almost any intervention at this point will appear to reduce the crying. However, fewer mothers in the Australian study who received the infant mental health consultation were admitted to the hospital for crying-related stress than those in the other groups. The REST and similar approaches appear to provide valuable support for mothers, and their findings are in keeping with the view that problematic infant crying is a social phenomenon that involves parents as well as infants. However, research to document the effectiveness of such interventions in changing infant crying behaviour, and to show whether the interventions are cost-effective, is still needed.

Comparative studies provide an alternative, but in principle less methodologically robust, means of evaluating the consequences of different forms of parenting for infant crying. Unlike randomized controlled trials, the comparative approach involves assessing already-existing groups of parents and infants in different cultures or societies. In their strongest form, studies of this type are longitudinal, measuring the same groups of infants repeatedly from birth, so that group differences in the development of infants cared for in different ways from the outset can be seen. In such studies, it is important that the same methods are used to measure infant crying in both groups, since methodological variations can give rise to large differences in the amounts of crying measured (Barr et al., 1988; St James-Roberts, 1992). To date, two published studies speak most directly to this set of issues. First, Franz Hubbard and Marinus van IJzendoorn's (1987, 1991) carefully controlled longitudinal home observation study found no evidence that typical variations in how long Dutch parents took to respond to crying predicted the amounts infants cried at subsequent ages. More rapid parental response in the first 9 weeks was associated with small *increases* in crying *frequency* in weeks 9–27, but the associations were modest and did not suggest any effect of early parental responsiveness on the amounts infants cried later on.

By including much greater variations in parenting than usual, a recent cross-cultural study has provided evidence that different parenting approaches can give rise to substantially different amounts of infant crying, and found quite different results for crying overall than for unsoothable crying bouts. The methods used in this study involved comparing three groups longitudinally on measures of parenting and infant crying: London parents; Copenhagen parents (who were expected to be more responsive than London parents); and parents who elected before their babies' birth to practice 'proximal care'. This anthropological term was chosen to describe the key feature of this form of parenting, extensive infant holding, in contrast to the typical Western practice of putting babies down (St James-Roberts et al., 2006). For instance, studies in Germany, Holland and North America have found that parents leave their babies to cry on a quarter or more of occasions (Bell & Ainsworth, 1972; Grossmann et al., 1985; van der Wal et al., 1998). Each of the groups in this cross-cultural study included over 50 infants and infant and caregiver behaviour was measured by validated behaviour diaries (St James-Roberts et al., 2006).

As expected, large group differences in parenting were found when the infants were 10 days and 5 weeks of age. Proximal care parents fed their babies more often than other groups (14, compared with 10–12 times, per 24 hours) and held their babies for an average of 15–16 hours per 24 hours, about twice as much as London parents, while Copenhagen parents fell in-between. Proximal care parents co-slept throughout the night with their babies much more often than both other groups. London parents had 50% less physical contact with their babies than the other groups, both when the babies were settled and when they were crying, and stopped breast-feeding at an earlier age.

These differences in parenting were associated with substantial differences in amounts of overall infant crying. The London babies fussed and cried approximately 50% more per 24 hours than both other groups at 10 days and 5 weeks of age. Fussing and crying amounts declined at 12 weeks in all three groups, but remained higher in London infants. In contrast, unsoothable crying bouts were equally common in all three groups. Likewise, infant Rule of Threes 'colic' crying (defined as ≥ 3 hours fuss/crying per 24 hours), occurred equally often, in 5–14% of infants in each group, at 5 weeks of age.

These recent findings need careful interpretation until they are confirmed by randomized controlled trials. However, the study's longitudinal research method, confirmation of large differences in parenting, and use of validated measures of infant crying, are important strengths. The study's findings are also consistent with a good deal of other comparative evidence. First, Marissa Alvarez's earlier diary study of Danish mothers found high maternal responsiveness to be associated with lower amounts of infant fuss/crying than typically found in Western infants (Alvarez, 2004) and high holding and responsiveness was associated with low amounts of crying in a separate study of Korean infants (Lee, 1994). Second, Ronald Barr and colleagues' (Barr et al., 1991b) observations of African Kung San families found that high amounts of hold/carrying, rapid responses to frets, and frequent breast-feeding were associated with low crying durations. Third, Barry Hewlett and colleagues' observation study of tribes in the Central African Republic found that Ngandu 'farmer' communities were more likely to put infants down, while Aka hunter–gatherers were more likely to hold, carry, feed and maintain proximity to their infants (Hewlett et al., 1998). Ngandu infants were observed to fuss and cry more than twice as much as Aka infants at both 3–4 months and 9–10 months of age.

Individually, each of these studies has limitations to its methods or in the size, or age range, of the infant groups included. However, the combination of these findings with those from the longitudinal results from the cross-cultural study described above provides the best available evidence about the relationship between parenting and infant crying in the first few weeks. Compared with typical London care, parenting that involves substantially higher amounts of hold/carrying and greater responsiveness to infant signals leads to low overall amounts of infant fuss/crying in the first 3 months of infancy. It is not yet certain that the relationship is causal, but the consistency of the findings across different cultural groups and research studies suggest that this is likely to be the case. Lastly, the cross-cultural study finding that variations in parenting do not prevent the bouts of unsoothable crying that occur in early infancy is consistent with the evidence cited above that these are specific to early infancy and linked to normal neurodevelopmental changes in infants at this age.

Effects on infant crying of interventions: holding; rocking; pacifiers/dummies; sweet tastes; massage; swaddling; chiropractic manipulation; non-prescribed and prescription liquids and substances

Judging from their behaviour, many parents believe that picking up, holding and rocking help to calm a crying baby, while the American term 'pacifier' (for what the English call a 'dummy') speaks for itself. The findings from this area are more directly relevant to management than causation, but evidence that simple manipulations like wrapping can help to reduce infant crying could inform our understanding of the relationship between parental care and prolonged infant crying. Indeed, there is considerable evidence that parents are often right in judging that these interventions can help to quieten babies. On the other hand, if things were that simple, there would be no need for a book of this kind.

Before examining the evidence, it is helpful to have three things in mind. The first is that studies of soothing interventions need to begin with a crying baby, so that a prior question is how they brought this about. Since researchers can no longer employ rubber band-snap or other standard apparatus to elicit crying, they nowadays need to depend on routinely occurring stimuli – such as hunger or immunization injections – to produce crying. The resulting question is whether or not the nature of such stimuli has an effect on whether an intervention 'works' in diminishing crying and, consequently, whether the findings from studies of this kind generalize to everyday circumstances. For example, holding might diminish crying in the short term, but it would be surprising if it proved effective over the longer term with a baby who remains hungry. It follows that answers to questions about whether interventions 'work' are likely to be prefaced by 'it depends'.

The second consideration is that our concern is not with crying in selected settings so much as with the prolonged amounts per 24 hours that occur among 1 to 3-month-old babies, and with the prolonged crying bouts that contribute to these 24-hour totals. Evidence that an intervention reduces crying will be inadequate unless these crying behaviours have been assessed. Thirdly, although any strategies that help to manage crying are of some interest, our primary concern is whether interventions prevent prolonged crying cost-effectively over the medium- to longer-term. For instance, it is worth knowing whether buggy or car rides can help to settle crying babies, but the value of this intervention will be limited unless its effects persist once the ride is over, and/or it prevents crying the next day and following week. This apparent remedy might prove too costly if a family comes to depend on car rides as the only way of settling a baby. We will need to know the overall benefits – and costs – of intervention strategies.

Holding, rocking and/or rhythmic stimulation

Many studies have confirmed parents' everyday experience that these strategies are often effective for quieting a crying baby (Ambrose, 1969; Campos, 1989; Gatts et al., 1995; Korner & Thoman, 1972; Ter Vrught & Pederson, 1973). There is also evidence that picking up and rocking is more effective in soothing babies than picking up and holding alone (Byrne & Horowitz, 1981), and that lifting up and holding a newborn vertically at the shoulder is a more effective soothing manoeuvre than holding alone (Korner & Thoman, 1972). Many auditory, tactile and visual stimuli can also assist soothing, particularly if they are rhythmic and sustained (Campos, 1989).

To take one example, Ruth Elliott and her colleagues (Elliott et al., 1988) employed a motorized baby carriage to rock 12 6 to 8-week-old Canadian infants selected for prolonged 24-hour crying, compared with 12 comparison infants with low crying totals, at either 40 or 57 rocks per minute. Crying was initiated by leaving the babies in the carriages until they cried moderately or vigorously for 60 consecutive seconds. The researchers found that less crying (and more settled-awake behaviour) occurred during the 4-minute rocking period compared with the 4 minutes afterwards when the infants were left in the carriages without rocking. The rate of rocking made no difference and the effects were the same in both groups of infants. Because the infants' breathing became 'entrained' to the rocking, the authors speculated that rhythmic external stimulation may help infants to regulate their physiological systems. However, since the crying increased immediately when the rocking was withdrawn, rocking appears to have provided a short-term means of management rather than a long-term remedy. It is also not clear from this study whether or not rocking produced any changes in 24-hour crying, any longer-term difference, or had particular benefits for prolonged criers. These seem unlikely, given that the crying recurred once the rocking was stopped.

Similar reservations apply to the studies of rocking while holding as those listed above. Although these strategies often do help to soothe a crying baby temporarily, there is little or no evidence that rocking and holding prevent recurrence of the prolonged crying bouts that characterize problem cases.

This limitation applies, too, to the use of a mechanized cradle to soothe babies (Gatts et al., 1995) – a study that will be reviewed in more detail in Chapter 6. Perhaps surprisingly, there appears to be no systematic evidence to support the common belief that car rides help to settle babies, including those who cry prolonged amounts. Only one study, which included a condition that sought to mimic car rides, seems to have examined this possibility at all, finding no difference between the simulated car ride and control group (Parkin et al., 1993). It is uncertain whether this artificial attempt to reproduce the conditions of a car ride was successful and it would be helpful to know how long car rides have to continue to achieve any effects and whether or not their effects carry over to subsequent days. Dieter Wolke (2001) has cautioned against this practice on the basis that babies often wake up once the engine is switched off, while also noting that this strategy might turn into an unwelcome habit. The evidence about rhythmic stimulation listed above is consistent with the first of these claims and he may well be right about the second, but it would be helpful to have some robust evidence.

In view of the beneficial, if short-term, effects of holding and rocking, it seems puzzling that a series of carefully conducted studies by Michael Lewis and Douglas Ramsay (Lewis & Ramsay, 1995a, 1995b, 1999) found no effects of maternal soothing on infant crying, quieting and hormonal (cortisol) response following routine immunization injections. Cortisol, sampled from saliva, is widely employed as a measure of stress, so that by comparing cortisol before and after the injections these researchers were able to assess whether maternal soothing lessened infant physiological stress caused by this painful procedure, as well as measuring whether the soothing affected infant behaviour. By employing a longitudinal design, with measurements at 2, 4 and 6 months of age, they were also able to examine the role of development. The studies included adequately sized groups of infants, accurate measures of the same infants' behaviour from video-recordings at successive ages, and measures in the more naturalistic setting of the waiting room as well as during the inoculation procedures. The most striking finding was that neither the quantity nor quality of maternal soothing influenced how long infants took to quiet or stop crying at any age. Infant response to the inoculation was affected by age, with more rapid quieting, and reduced cortisol response to the inoculations, at older ages. Across the three ages, the only significant correlation between soothing and crying was positive – infants who took longer to quieten at 2 months received more soothing from their mothers at later ages, suggesting a possible effect of infant on maternal behaviour.

Because these findings are surprising, replication evidence is important. Although they are not entirely in agreement, Italian studies by Vanna Axia, Sabrina Bonichini and colleagues (Axia & Bonichini, 2005; Axia & Weisner, 2002) have confirmed Lewis and Ramsay's most controversial finding that amount and quality of maternal soothing does not lessen infant distress following inoculation injections. Indeed, in the Italian studies soothing was concurrently associated with longer infant quieting, providing further evidence that longer maternal soothing was a function of longer infant crying, rather than acting to reduce crying. Across the two sets of studies, one apparently inconsistent finding was that closer, more proximal soothing at 3 months was associated with quicker infant quieting subsequently, at 5 months of age, in one of the Italian group's analyses (Axia & Bonichini, 2005). However, this finding was not repeated in any of the other analyses carried out by the Italian or American researchers, suggesting that it is in need of confirmation.

Perplexingly, then, these studies provide no support for the claim that parental soothing lessens infant crying caused by the pain of inoculation injections. Although we cannot be certain, one possible resolution of this puzzle lies in the way the studies were carried out. In particular, the infants were placed on tables during the inoculations and, although their mothers and the nurse administering the injections both touched them during the procedure, the mothers were only free to pick up, hold and carry the infants after the needle was withdrawn. Furthermore, for ethical reasons, there was no 'control group' of infants who did not receive any soothing at all.

The implication is that variations in amount and quality of soothing *following* painful injections do not affect quieting, but it remains possible that holding, introduced before and during the injections, would diminish crying and produce more rapid quieting, compared with injections given without holding. Indeed, there is considerable evidence to support this proposal. Using randomized control trial methods, American research by Larry Gray and his colleagues (2000) found that skin-to-skin contact between mothers and newborns reduced crying by 82% and grimacing by 65%, as well as lowering the heart rate substantially, during and following inoculations, compared with newborn infants who were swaddled in a crib during the injections. Similar findings have been reported by others (Castral et al., 2008; Gormally et al., 2001), while Gray and his team (Gray et al., 2002) later found that body contact plus breast-feeding during inoculation reduced crying by 91% compared with a control group without body contact.

As these researchers point out, these findings have important practical implications for medical care, since they provide simple, non-intrusive strategies for reducing infant distress during routine inoculations. In both their studies, Gray and his colleagues noted that 10–15 minutes of skin-to-skin 'settling' between mothers and newborns was needed before the injection took place in order to achieve effective infant quieting. This may explain why Lewis and Ramsay, and Axia and Bonichini, were unable to show that soothing after inoculation reduced crying, since any contact in these studies was much briefer and limited to the post-inoculation period. In turn, this raises the question of how bodily contact achieves such dramatic effects. One possibility is that the mechanisms are thermo-regulatory, so that the warmth of prolonged body contact is analgesic (Blass, 1991). In any case, these findings allow the conclusion that body contact helps infants to reduce their distress upon painful stimulation, so far as the contact is established before the stimulation occurs. These findings are consistent, too, with the evidence given above that prolonged holding and body contact is associated with low 24-hour amounts of crying in 1 to 12-week-old infants although, as noted, this does not prevent the unsoothable crying bouts that occur at this age (St James-Roberts et al., 2006).

Infant pacifiers/'dummies'

Pacifiers/dummies have also been found to reduce crying during inoculations, relative to controls, by several research groups (Blass & Watt, 1999; Campos, 1989; Blass & Camp, 2003). Rosemary Campos (1989) found that pacifiers given during an inoculation were more effective than swaddling in soothing crying and heart rate at both 2 weeks and 2 months of age. However, like the cessation of rocking in the study described above, removal of the pacifier caused crying to increase back to the baseline level. Other studies, too, have found pacifiers to be effective in reducing crying during inoculations, with even greater effects when the pacifiers were combined with a sweet taste (Carbajal et al., 1999). The 'sweet taste' findings will be reviewed below. Although pacifiers help infants in general during painful procedures, there appears to be no evidence that their use is effective in reducing 24-hour crying totals, or prolonged crying bouts, among infants selected for prolonged crying.

Because the use of pacifiers to calm babies has been controversial due to concerns about dental deformities and infections, it is worth noting that pacifiers have recently been found to be effective in reducing the risk of sudden infant death syndrome (SIDS) (Hauck et al., 2005; Mitchell et al., 2006). In a meta-analysis of seven different studies, Fern Hauck and other members of a United States (US) Preventive Services Task Force found that routine use of pacifiers reduced the risk of SIDS, while routine use prior to sleeping, in particular, reduced the SIDS risk by more than 50% (Hauck et al., 2005). The mechanism remains unclear, since these findings applied in spite of evidence that most babies dislodge pacifiers soon after sleep onset. However, the Task Force was clear in recommending pacifier use, particularly during sleeping, up to a year of age, since this should lessen the risk of SIDS without increasing the potential disadvantages of pacifiers. Where infants were breast-feeding, the Task Force recommended delaying pacifier use until this became established (up to a month of age), while they did not recommend adding sweet substances to the pacifier for routine use. It would be helpful to know how and why pacifiers reduce the risk of SIDS but, in the meantime, the Task Force's recommendations seem to have benefits and are unlikely to cause harm, so that parents may wish to consider them. It is not known how many infants refuse to use pacifiers, however.

Sweet tastes

In a series of studies of both human and animal infants, Elliott Blass and his colleagues have led a substantial and important body of research documenting the effects of sweet tastes on infants' responses to painful, or otherwise unpleasant, stimulation (Blass, 1991; Blass & Camp, 2003). The archetypal method involves administering a concentrated sweet taste (typically a solution of sucrose or glucose) to an infant's tongue before a painful injection is given for immunization purposes. Infants randomly assigned to receive the sweet solution are compared with other infants randomized to receive water. The infants are video-recorded and researchers blinded to their group derive reliable measures of crying onset, intensity and duration from the video records. In a variation of this approach, some studies have given the same infants sweet solutions on one occasion, and water on another, with the order randomized between infants.

The findings have been remarkable, both in consistently demonstrating that sweet tastes reduce crying during painful stimulation very substantially and in showing that the effects persist for several minutes of time after the taste is administered. Typically, a sweet taste given 2 minutes before an injection reduces crying during the injection by 50% (Blass & Smith, 1992) and the reduction is maintained for 3 or more minutes afterwards, suggesting that the sweet taste has a sustained analgesic effect. As well as reducing crying, sweet tastes also lessen physiological indices of distress, such as heart rate (Blass & Smith, 1992). There is evidence, too, that this effect is not specific to painful stimulation. Ronald Barr and colleagues (Barr et al., 1999a, 1999b) found that sucrose reduced crying that occurred before feeds (and was presumably therefore due to hunger) by 80% within 10 seconds of the sucrose delivery, with persistence of the reduction for more than 4 minutes afterwards. Because the effect was so rapid, these researchers argued that it was due to the oral sweet taste, rather than to nutritive, mechanisms. Other studies have found a lessening of the effect with age, so that higher sucrose concentrations were needed, and were less effective in producing quieting, at 6 or 12 weeks compared with the newborn period (Allen et al., 1996; Barr et al., 1994; Blass & Camp, 2003). The combination of sucrose with a pacifier, and sucrose with holding, has proved to be more analgesic than sucrose alone (Carbajal et al., 1999; Gormally et al., 2001). Such a simple and effective way of reducing newborn distress has led to recommendations that sweet taste analgesia should be routinely employed during medical procedures involving pain (Carbajal et al., 1999; Harrison et al.,

2010; Stevens et al., 2010). Infant formula milk, too, has been shown to quieten crying newborn infants and to be as effective in doing so and maintaining quieting as sucrose, although in this case the newborns were crying spontaneously 1.5 to 2 hours after a feed (Blass, 1997). The time since last feeding does not diminish the calming effect of sucrose (Blass, 1997) but it is not clear whether it affects the quieting effect of formula.

The effectiveness of sucrose in stopping crying among young infants generally led Barr and colleagues to investigate whether it would be as effective when administered to infants selected for prolonged 24 hour amounts of crying (Barr et al., 1999b). Nineteen Canadian infants who met Modified Rule of Threes criteria for high amounts of crying at 6 weeks of age, and 19 comparison infants with moderate crying totals, were given sucrose or water before and after feeds, with each infant randomized to receive sucrose, then water, or vice versa, at successive feeds. Their key finding was that, compared with the moderate criers, the sucrose calming effect in the high criers was diminished and more short-lived. Initially, this finding under carefully controlled conditions appeared to indicate a difference in neurobehavioural functioning between 6-week-old infants who cried a lot and their peers, as well as pointing to a deficient ability to stop crying as the critical behavioural phenomenon. Unfortunately, however, a study designed to replicate these findings by the same group of researchers was unable to do so, so that sucrose responses in high criers resembled those of other infants in this second study (Ghosh et al., 2007).

This second study's finding also receives some support from a minimally controlled field-trial of 19 Norwegian infants who met Rule of Threes criteria for prolonged crying by Trond Markestad (1997). In this case, parents were asked to administer sucrose, or water from an unlabeled bottle 'when the infant continued to cry after attempts of consoling by feeding, changing the nappy, or by carrying had failed' (p. 356). The bottles were alternated, so that each infant received sucrose first then water, or vice versa, for 2–3 days. No attempt was made to measure crying objectively, but parents were asked to rate the degree of improvement after each administration on a five-point scale. Based on the parents' ratings, 12 of 19 infants were judged by the researchers to have 'experienced a specific ameliorating effect of sucrose judged from consistent improvements on sucrose with relapses on placebo' (p. 356). Obvious concerns include the subjectivity of the parental reports, likelihood that parents would be able to detect the taste of the two solutions, and lack of 24-hour measures. Still, this study does set the scene for more controlled attempts to examine the effect of sucrose on unsoothable bouts and 24-hour crying totals among infants with prolonged crying. In the meantime, it is currently unclear whether or not sucrose affects prolonged criers more or less than other infants, whether it has a practically important effect on their crying, and whether or not any benefits of its use for this purpose outweigh any disadvantages.

Infant massage

A helpful review of the evidence up to 2005 about the effects of massage on infants under 6 months of age was carried out by members of the Cochrane Collaboration, led by Angela Underdown (Underdown et al., 2006). Their review focused on the use of massage for promoting infant mental and physical health in general, but infant crying and sleeping were included among its measures of outcomes. The Cochrane review included only randomized controlled trials involving full-term infants, with each study categorized on methodological quality. A proviso is that the studies varied in the massage techniques and oils used, the length and number of massage sessions, and who carried them out, complicating the interpretation of the findings. We will focus here on the crying findings and examine those for infant sleeping in Chapter 6.

The Cochrane reviewers considered just two crying studies to have a low risk of bias, one of which found that massage reduced crying, while the second study did not. The latter, by Ruth Elliott and colleagues (Elliott et al., 2002) assessed 22 Canadian infants who were randomized in the first week of infancy to receive 10 minutes of massage daily from their mothers, compared with 20 infants who did not receive any intervention, until 16 weeks of age. Mothers in the massage group were trained in its delivery and this was confirmed during the study. These researchers found no differences in daily crying between the massaged and control infants at 2, 4, 6, 12 or 16 weeks of age.

The single methodologically robust study showing that massage reduced crying was carried out by Tiffany Field and her colleagues in USA (Field et al., 1996) and involved 20 1 to 3-month-old infants of depressed mothers who were massaged by staff for 15 minutes a day twice a week for 6 weeks, compared with 20 comparable infants who were rocked by staff for the same amounts of time. During their treatments, the researchers found that the massaged infants were more alert and cried more, while the rocked infants spent more time in Quiet Sleep (the distinction between Quiet and Active Sleep is discussed in Chapter 6). The infants continued to be observed for 15 minutes after the massage (or rocking) ended. During this immediate post-treatment 15 minutes, the massaged infants increased in Quiet Sleep, relative to their sleep during the massage period, although they did not spend more time asleep after the treatment than the rocked infants. Rocked infants became more actively awake and crying when the rocking stopped, which is in keeping with the findings about rocking more generally summarized above. These findings from Tiffany Field's group indicate that infants are more alert and cry more while being massaged than rocked, but are less alert and less inclined to cry immediately afterwards. Specifically, massaged infants spent 2.5% of the post-treatment period crying, compared with 10.7% of this period among rocked infants. Over the 6 weeks the study lasted, the massaged infants gained 1.1 pounds more weight, while the staff administering the treatment judged that the massaged infants improved more in their emotionality, sociability and soothability (although it is not clear that the staff making these judgements were unaware of the infants' group).

Tiffany Field is the head of the Touch Institute at the University of Miami and she and her colleagues have published other studies showing the benefits of massage for both infants and adults that were not included in the Cochrane review. In 2004 (Field et al., 2004), they showed that moderate-touch massage was more effective than light-touch massage in diminishing crying and increasing alertness in the period immediately after the massage. This study involved a group of low socioeconomic status (rather than depressed) mothers and their infants, while the mothers (rather than professional staff) administered the massage for 15 minutes per day from soon after birth until 1 month of age. Compared to light-touch massage, moderate-touch massage increased infant weight gain slightly more (by 0.1 pound) and crying behaviour increased over the month in the light-touch massage group (from 1.7 to 5.2% of the 45-minute observation period), while the amount of crying in the moderate-massage group stayed the same (3–4% at the two ages). The moderate-massage group were also more alert in orienting to visual and auditory stimuli, and less excitable, during a standard behavioural test (the Brazelton Neonatal Behavioral Assessment Scale) at 1 month of age.

For our purposes here, the most important feature of these studies from Tiffany Field's group is that they assess only the period during and immediately after massage and do not involve infants selected for high amounts of crying. They do not tell us whether massage is effective when a baby is already crying when massage begins, whether it helps with the unsoothable bouts that concern parents during early infancy, or whether it reduces crying per 24 hours. Since this group's first study showed an increase in crying during the massage itself, parents who wish to use it should be alerted to this possibility, as well as to the failure of some other research groups to confirm any benefits of massage. Moreover, although massage may well be an enjoyable activity in many cases, parents should expect modest improvements, at best, in their babies. For example, when translated into minutes, the massaged group cried 1.2 minutes less during 15 minutes in the first study, and 1.6 minutes less during 45 minutes in study two.

Two further studies not included in the Cochrane review are of particular relevance here, because they each used randomized control trial methods to evaluate the effects of massage on infants selected specifically for high amounts of crying. The first, carried out by Virpi Huhtala and her colleagues in Finland (Huhtala et al., 2000), involved 58, 3 to 7-week-old infants judged by parents to fuss/cry for more than 3 hours per day. They assigned 28 infants at random to receive massage, and 30 to a crib vibrator-device condition, chosen as a control condition because prior research had shown the vibrator-device to have no effect on crying in such infants. The vibrator condition was designed to act as a placebo–control treatment, to guard against the possibility that involvement in the study by itself might bias parents' reports of infant crying. During the baseline week, parent-kept behaviour diaries confirmed that 83% of the infants did fuss/ cry for 3 or more hours/day, suggesting an unusually high degree of accuracy in these Finnish parents' reports and a high amount of crying in their infants. The intervention (massage or crib vibrator-device) was administered twice daily by parents over a 3-week period, and the behaviour diaries were used to confirm implementation. The study found a similar decline in infant crying amounts over the study period and no difference between the groups, with both groups showing a pattern of reduction similar to the decline typically found in longitudinal studies without any intervention. To quote the authors:

> We did not find any difference in the reduction of colicky crying between infants receiving massage and those with a crib vibrator over a 3-week intervention. We consider that the decrease of crying in our study reflects more the natural course of early crying and colic than a specific effect of the interventions. Thus, infant massage cannot be recommended for treatment of infantile colic.
>
> (Huhtala et al., 2000, p. 5)

The second study, by Duygu Arikan and a Turkish team, selected 175 infants judged by parents to fuss/cry for 3 or more hours per day (Arikan et al., 2008). The infants were assigned at random to one of four intervention groups: massage, sucrose solution, herbal tea, a hydrolyzed formula (designed to minimize food reactions) or to a control group. Parents in the massage group were asked to administer it twice a day for 25 minutes, especially when the infants were irritable. The researchers found that all five groups reduced in crying during the week of the intervention, following the typical pattern in non-intervention studies of the normal course of crying. Compared with the baseline crying amounts, the massage intervention was least effective in obtaining a reduction in crying.

To sum up these studies of infant massage, there is limited evidence from one group that regular massage can have modest short-term benefits when used with infants in general. Parents considering whether to implement a massage programme will need to appreciate that this finding has not been confirmed by other researchers, as well as being aware of the provisos about the effectiveness of massage noted above. In particular, two studies have produced consistent evidence that massage is not effective in reducing crying when used as an intervention with infants selected for prolonged amounts of crying.

Swaddling

Swaddling babies by wrapping them tightly has traditionally been practised as a part of baby care in a variety of cultures. Women who habitually swaddle their babies report that they will not sleep unless swaddled and there is some evidence that swaddling does affect infant sleeping behaviour. These findings will be examined in Chapter 6. The question here is whether swaddling reduces infant crying.

Arguably the best-controlled piece of research to date, carried out by Shohei Ohgi and colleagues (Ohgi et al., 2004) employed a randomized controlled trial to assess the use of swaddling, compared with massage, to treat 25, 11 to 12-week-old Japanese infants with cerebral palsy and 'troublesome crying' during a 3-week period. Thirteen infants received swaddling and 12 a massage intervention. The researcher collecting the outcome data was blinded to the intervention given and validated behaviour diaries completed by parents were used to measure crying. The researchers found that swaddling reduced crying substantially, by a total of 3 hours per 24 hours, while massage did not produce a significant change. They also found that scores on an infant neurobehavioural test were improved when infants were swaddled, suggesting that the infant improvements could be detected by researchers using standardized methods. The infants' parents were more satisfied with the swaddling than massage intervention and it led to a decline in parental anxiety level. Although this study is particularly well controlled, it is not free of caveats. One obvious issue is that we do not know whether similar findings would occur in infants without brain damage. Another is that the amount of time infants spent swaddled (4.2 hours/day) was much greater than the time spent in massage (0.8 hours/day) confounding the difference in type of intervention with a difference in amount. A third proviso is that the study lacked a no-treatment, control, group so that we do not know what would have happened if these children with cerebral palsy had not been treated at all. Still, this study found consistent evidence that swaddling was more effective than massage in leading to lower crying amounts in infants with neurological damage, as well as being preferred by their parents.

Although Ohgi group's study is helpful in providing some evidence under 'laboratory' conditions, it does not tell us what happens in a 'real world' setting, such as when habitual swaddling is used to care for normal infants in a traditional or modern Western cultural environment. To date, only two randomized controlled trials seem to have attempted to address this question. The first, by Bregje van Sleuwen and her colleagues in Holland (van Sleuwen et al., 2007), recruited 496 healthy infants <13 weeks of age who were judged by parents to fuss and cry for 3 or more hours per 24 hours during at least 3 days per week. Forty-seven were excluded because they reduced their crying following dietary changes. After assessing the infants' crying amounts by validated 24-hour diaries, 204 were randomized to receive a 'structured' form of parenting and 194 to receive structured parenting plus swaddling. It should be noted at this point that this study did not include a control group that received only routine care, so that it can only tell us whether swaddling produced added benefits, over and above those due to structured parental care.

Like other studies we have looked at, this study's first finding was that parental retrospective estimates exaggerated the amounts their babies cried, so that only 32.3% of infants claimed to cry >3 hours per 24 hours actually did so according to the baseline diary measures. The two groups were, though, similar in amounts of crying at this baseline point. After introducing the alternative treatments, diaries over the next 7 days were used to compare their outcomes. During the first 24 hours, the structured-care-only group increased their daily crying by approximately 20 minutes, but this then declined subsequently by approximately 11 minutes per 24 hours. In contrast, infants in the structured care + swaddling group reduced their crying by approximately 30 minutes per 24 hours in the first day, increased their crying on day two, and then declined each subsequent day. As a result, there was no difference between the two intervention groups after 7 days. Further analyses dividing the infants into two age-groups (1–7 weeks at randomization versus 8–13 weeks at randomization) indicated that younger infants assigned to the structured care + swaddling condition tended to cry less, while older infants cried less if assigned to structured care only. However, the group differences within each age category were just 10 minutes per 24 hours. Whether this finding suggests that swaddling has worthwhile benefits over and above structured parenting for 1 to 7-week-old infants is a moot point, since it seems doubtful whether parents would be aware of a 10 minutes per 24 hour reduction in crying. In any case, the over-riding consideration is that, because infants in this study averaged 7.9 weeks at enrolment, we would expect many of them to follow the normal developmental pattern of reducing their crying over the following weeks, which was exactly what the researchers found. Because this study did not include a non-intervention control group to represent the status quo, it cannot rule out the possibility that the changes would have occurred anyway as the infants got older, without either of this study's treatments.

The second randomized controlled trial of swaddling as an intervention to reduce crying was carried out by Jonna McRury and Adam Zolotar (2010). The intervention in this case was a 30-minute videotape demonstrating 'The Happiest Baby' method, a widely promoted set of strategies designed to help parents to calm their baby. Swaddling is a key step in this scheme and the video demonstrates how to swaddle a baby. Additional steps if the baby does not calm with swaddling alone include placing the baby on her stomach while awake, providing a 'shushing' noise to her ear, adding small rhythmic movements and giving a pacifier to suck. McRury and Zolotar's trial administered The Happiest Baby intervention to just 18 parents and healthy newborns, with 17 similar families receiving the control condition – a 30-minute videotape that emphasized a warm and loving caregiving environment and the use of routines. The main finding was of no overall difference between the two groups in 24-hour amounts of crying or unsoothable crying. There was a just-significant difference at one age (8 weeks), but such that The Happiest Baby infants cried more, not less. A parental measure, using the Parenting Stress Index, showed more self-reported stress among The Happiest Baby parents when the infants were 12 weeks of age. The small group sizes are an obvious concern, but The Happiest Baby cases tended to score worse on all the crying and parent stress findings at every age, suggesting that small sample size, alone, is unlikely to have caused the failure to find benefits for The Happiest Baby method. The trial's strengths, apart from random assignment, include confirmation that The Happiest Baby parents did employ swaddling and the use of validated measures of infant crying and parenting stress. Although larger-scale studies are needed, the McRury and Zolotar findings do not provide much encouragement for the use of The Happiest Baby techniques, or of swaddling, as a way of helping parents to reduce infant crying.

As well as the habitual use of swaddling assessed in these two randomized controlled trials, swaddling has been assessed as a short-term 'soothing' treatment for when infants are subjected to inoculation pain. The finding, mentioned above, from Rosemary Campos's careful study of 2-week-old, and 2-month-old, infants was that a pacifier stopped the infant crying more quickly than swaddling at both ages. Interestingly, there was an age-difference, so that swaddling was somewhat more effective at 2 months than 2 weeks of age but, even so, the pacifier remained a more effective soothing intervention at this age.

To sum up the swaddling findings, there is promising evidence that it helps to soothe infants with brain damage involving cerebral palsy, but no evidence that swaddling reduces amounts of crying among infants in general, or is effective as a treatment in cases where prolonged unsoothable crying has already emerged as a problem for parents. Although the evidence is unclear, some studies have raised concerns about the safety of swaddling when infants are asleep. These findings will be examined in Chapter 6.

Chiropractic manipulations

Chiropractors have claimed that manipulation of babies' spines and limbs alleviates prolonged infant crying and there is a long tradition of using spinal manipulation for this purpose in Scandinavian countries, in particular (Klougart et al., 1989; Olafsdottir et al., 2001). The explanation for why this technique should relieve crying is not apparent, but one speculation is that passage through the birth canal sometimes causes compression of a baby's body, which manipulation relieves. Here, too, then, the question is whether this approach is based on evidence, or largely a myth.

In their 1989 study, Niels Klougart and his chiropractic colleagues assessed the results of gentle spinal manipulation by 73 Danish chiropractors upon 316 infants referred by parents for problem crying at an average age of 5.7 weeks (Klougart et al., 1989). One limitation of the study is that almost as many such infants – 253 – were left out of the reported findings, primarily because of past or present illness or poor weight gain. A 44% rate of exclusion for ill health seems to be an unusually high percentage, but its main implication is that the findings apply only to infants selected in the same way. Spinal manipulation treatments were given on an average of three occasions over a 2-week period. Infant crying was initially measured by parental retrospective report, but by behaviour diaries and symptom questionnaires once the trial got underway. The most striking finding, as in the Dutch swaddling study discussed above, was that parents initially overestimated the amounts their babies cried, so that their retrospective judgement that crying lasted 5.2 hours per day on average contrasted with the 2.5 hours per day measured by behaviour diary on the first day of the trial. The authors interpreted this as evidence for a rapid effect for their intervention, but a more likely explanation, as we have already seen, is that overestimation of crying amounts by parents is a common result of using retrospective reports. From the diary figures, the infants' crying gradually reduced from 2.5 hours per 24 hours on day 1 of the study to 0.65 hours on day 14, with parallel improvements in parents' judgements of their baby's symptoms. As we noted earlier in this chapter, a similar decline after 6 weeks of age is typical in infants without any treatment, so that the critical question is whether the change in the infants given chiropractic treatment was greater than the change in untreated, control group, infants. The answer is that there was no control group, so that we do not know whether the infants would have cried less over the study's 14 days without chiropractic manipulation. This study's implication, then, is to point to the need for more careful measurements and controls.

Fortunately, a study that meets this requirement using randomized, controlled trial methods was reported by Edda Olafsdottir and her team in Norway in 2001 (Olafsdottir et al., 2001). Here, too, unhealthy infants were excluded from taking part, while infants who responded positively to dietary treatments were also excluded. In this study, 100 infants reported by parents to meet the extended Rule of Threes criteria for crying (>3 hours/day for >3 days/week, for >3 weeks) were selected and assigned at random to receive three chiropractic spinal manipulations over a period of 8 days, or to a placebo control condition where they were partially undressed and held by a nurse for equivalent periods of time, but did not receive spinal manipulations. The chiropractic manipulations were approved by an expert panel of chiropractors. Both parents and researchers were blinded to which condition the babies received, so that knowledge of whether or not spinal manipulations had taken place could not influence their reports. Of the 100 infants, 86 (46 in the treatment and 40 in the control group) completed the study. Results were obtained from parent-kept 24-hour diaries before the intervention was introduced and on three occasions afterwards, and by parent judgements of improvements on a five-point scale. The study found no difference in outcomes between the treatment and control groups. The diaries of both groups showed crying reductions from the baseline of just over 5 hours to 3.1 hours per 24 hours during the 8 days the study lasted. Parents reported that 69.9% of the chiropractic-treated group and 60% of the placebo control group improved, which was not significantly different. This study's group sizes were smaller than in the Danish study described above, but similar sizes are typical in studies of infant crying and it is unlikely that sample size could explain the lack of group differences. The placebo control infants clearly did reduce in crying as much as the chiropractic-treated infants so far as parents were concerned, while the use of a 'blinded' control group was a major strength. Since this is the best study of chiropractic treatment so far, it follows that there is no reliable evidence that chiropractic treatment is effective in reducing infant crying.

Non-prescribed and prescription liquids and substances

The belief that prolonged crying in early infancy is due to digestive disturbances and/or reactions to feeds was examined earlier in this chapter and will not be revisited here. It is worth noting, though, that changes of diet continue to be recommended by magazines, websites and other sources of information aimed at parents, in spite of the absence of evidence that these are common reasons for infant crying. It follows that informing parents of these issues can be an important part of professional practice (Catherine et al., 2008).

A wide variety of non-prescribed, over-the-counter, substances and liquids covered by the generic terms 'colic drops' and 'gripe water' are advertised as remedies for crying and widely used by parents. For example, gripe water was used by 13% of parents, and simethicone (for treatment of flatulence), by 16% of parents in the population-based Avon Longitudinal Study of Parents and Children in South-West England (Headley & Northstone, 2007). As well as their possible practical benefits, these remedies are of importance because of their implication about the causes of crying. Evidence that a substance that changes gastric activity reduces crying, for example, could implicate gastrointestinal disturbance as a cause of the crying, while evidence to the contrary queries this explanation.

Fortunately, these remedies are particularly suitable for randomized controlled trials and there are many studies of this type, and reviews of the resulting evidence. The almost universal conclusion is that colic drops and gripe water are no more effective in reducing crying than placebo controls (Daniellson & Hwang, 1985; Lucassen et al., 1998; Rogovik & Goldman, 2005; Savino et al., 2007; Wade & Kilgour, 2001). To take one of the best-controlled examples, Bernt Daniellson and Philip Hwang (1985) assessed 27 infants with an average age of 4.8 weeks, selected because their parents had sought help for unexplained infant crying in and around the city of Gothenburg in Sweden. The infants were assigned feeding bottles containing simethicone or placebo in random order, with each bottle being used for a week. The bottle contents were controlled so that they did not differ in colour, smell, taste or viscosity. Simethicone was chosen because it breaks down and disperses gas bubbles in the intestine, and had proved effective in treating flatulence and indigestion in adults. Infant crying was measured by 24-hour behaviour diaries kept by parents, by parental ratings of whether improvements had occurred, and by 3-hour observations made by researchers in the infants' homes at the times when the infants usually cried most (often the evenings). Their finding was that most infants reduced in crying over the 2–3 week course of the study, but simethicone did not produce any benefits over and above the placebo control solution.

Rather different reservations apply to the use of herbal extracts and teas, which are commonly employed by parents in some cultures to calm crying babies (Abdulrazzaq et al., 2009). Two studies have found the use of fennel to be associated with reduced crying (Alexandrovich et al., 2003; Weizman et al., 1993). A third found that a herbal remedy that incorporated several plant extracts (including fennel) was more effective than a placebo control in reducing crying (Savino et al., 2005). A fourth study found that fennel tea reduced crying (compared with the control), but was less effective in doing so than a hydrolyzed formula (Arikan et al., 2008). These findings are provocative and indicate a need for further, carefully controlled, research. However, as a recent review of this evidence concluded (Rogovik & Goldman, 2005), herbal remedies raise safety issues that have not yet been addressed, so that they cannot be recommended for use with infants until there is an adequate evaluation of their safety, appropriate dosages and effectiveness in use. With this last point in mind, it is appropriate to end this section by pointing out that the single prescription medicine proved to be effective as a treatment for prolonged crying in randomized controlled trials – dicyclomine hydrochloride – was withdrawn as an infant treatment by the manufacturer because a minority of infants treated with it showed adverse side effects, including breathing difficulties, asphyxia, seizures and coma (Lucassen et al., 1998; Rogovik & Goldman, 2005; Steinherz, 2004; Wade & Kilgour, 2001).

To sum up the findings on interventions for crying as a whole, arguably the most important advance has been to identify the analgesic effects of simple techniques, including holding, feeding and delivering sweet tastes, in ameliorating the effects of painful inoculation injections on infants generally. Providing they are introduced before the injections, these techniques reduce infant crying substantially and, since inoculations are routinely given by health services, their use in such circumstances is ethically desirable, inexpensive and, to date, without any known disadvantages. The only proviso is that the analgesic effects of sweet tastes reduce with age, so that they are likely to be less beneficial after the first few weeks of infancy. Pacifiers/dummies too are effective in lessening crying due to injections in young infants, particularly if they are combined with a sweet taste. Routine use of pacifiers without sweet solutions is advocated as a means of preventing SIDS by an American task force, providing simple guidelines are adhered to.

There is also substantial evidence that holding, rocking and rhythmic stimulation are often effective in soothing spontaneous crying in the short term. A feature of these studies is that crying tends to recur once the stimulation is withdrawn, so that benefits are short lived. Because the studies to date have not assessed differences in the length of interventions of this sort, we do not know whether or not persistent stimulation of this type leads to more prolonged quieting, or the conditions under which this does, and does not, apply. As noted above, there is evidence that prolonged holding and carrying – which presumably provide rhythmic, as well as thermo-regulatory stimulation – reduces 24-hour crying, although it does not prevent unsoothable crying bouts. Because of the widespread belief that rhythmic stimulation, such as buggy and car rides, can soothe infant crying for sustained periods, studies that describe these conditions systematically – and consider their disadvantages, as well as their benefits – are needed. In the meantime, the evidence is inadequate, so that parents and practitioners will need to make up their own minds about the value of these particular techniques.

As well as these somewhat positive findings about sweet tastes, holding and rhythmic stimulation, a number of intervention strategies commonly used to reduce crying in infants generally have been found to have little or no practical value. These include chiropractic manipulations and colic drops. Compared with rocking, regular infant massage appears to increase crying during the massage, but to reduce crying in the period immediately afterwards. However, the evidence for this comes from one research group, the reductions in crying were modest, and other studies have found massage to be less effective than alternatives. Parents who wish to implement a massage programme may like to weigh up the costs and benefits of this approach. Swaddling, too, has been found to have minimal effects on crying in normal babies, and to be less effective than a pacifier in one study, whereas some studies have raised concerns about the safety of swaddling when used to enhance sleeping, which will be examined in Chapter 6. Herbal extracts and teas, too, raise safety issues.

Lastly, what are the implications of the findings in this area for infants who cry a lot per 24 hours? There is no reason to suppose that the benefits of sweet tastes during immunization injections apply any less in this group. Since, too, not all their crying is unsoothable, strategies that help to quieten infants generally may sometimes prove helpful in these cases. In contrast, the available research provides no evidence that any of the interventions examined in this section are effective in reducing the amounts such infants cry per 24 hours or in preventing or ameliorating bouts of unsoothable crying during the first 3 months of infancy.

Summary and conclusions about the origins of problematic infant crying

Using the criteria outlined in Chapter 1, what does the evidence reviewed in this chapter allow us to say that we know with a good degree of confidence about prolonged crying and its causes in early infancy?

1   Infants in general peak in their crying in the first few weeks after birth, with much of the crying clustering in the late afternoon and evening. Their crying declines by about 40% by 12 weeks of age. Most infants taken to professionals for crying problems share these features, so that they are probably at the far end of the normal range, rather than a distinct group with a pathological condition.

2   Prolonged amounts of infant crying and the lack of any explanation for why the crying occurs are central features underlying parental concerns. In particular, some crying bouts during this period are prolonged, relatively intense and objectively hard or impossible to soothe, making parents feel helpless and powerless.

3   These unsoothable crying bouts appear to be distinct from infant fuss/crying in general, in the sense that they are specific to this early-age period and are not affected by cultural variations in parenting. It is believed, but not proven, that the bouts may be caused at least partly by neurodevelopmental changes that are a normal part of development. Since crying of this sort cannot be prevented, methods are needed to help parents to contain it and cope with its impact.

4   In contrast, 1 to 3-month-old infants fuss and cry substantially less overall per 24 hours when parents adopt methods of care that involve more physical contact and greater responsiveness than is currently typical in London and other societies with 'Western' methods of parenting. Randomized controlled trials are needed to show conclusively that this relationship is causal, but the evidence from multiple comparative and longitudinal studies indicates that this is the case. These methods of care can be recommended to parents who wish to minimize overall crying in 1 to 3-month-old infants, with the proviso

that they will not prevent the unsoothable crying bouts that are a feature of this age period and need to be managed in a different way.

5   Prolonged crying in the first 3 months can be due to food intolerance and other organic disturbances, but this provides the explanation in only a small minority of cases. The best estimate is that at least 90% of infants taken to professionals because of their crying are healthy, put on weight normally, and have normal development. Methods are needed to identify and treat the small minority of cases with organic causation wherever possible.

The implications of these findings for clinical practice designed to prevent and manage infant crying will be revisited in Chapters 9 and 10.

Towards a coherent theory: parenting as an 'external regulator' of infant physiology and crying

Chapter 1 of this book included a critical evaluation of expert opinion, on the grounds that speculations are only as good as the evidence they rest on. Since the evidence about early infant crying reviewed in this chapter is more in line with the 'infant-demand' approach to baby care recommended in Jean Liedloff's book *The Continuum Concept* (Liedloff, 1975/1986) than the structured-care approach advocated in *The New Contented Little Baby Book* (Ford, 2002), it is worth returning at the end of this chapter on crying to the broader question of why this might be. As noted earlier, Jean Liedloff believes that parents can avoid crying and sleeping problems by following natural instincts to respond quickly, feed in response to babies' cries, and to hold and sleep with them, rather than adopting care that is convenient in an industrial society.

Although this proposal strikes an intuitive note for many people, and is supported to some extent by the evidence reviewed above, it is not very satisfactory from a scientific point of view. For one thing, the idea that some parental approaches are instinctive and 'natural' appears to imply that others are 'unnatural', which is unfortunate and flies in the face of the evidence of the diversity of approaches to childcare documented in anthropological studies. It is most unlikely that one approach is superior to others in all cases, respects and situations and more likely that the different approaches provide alternative adaptations to particular settings, or 'niches', so that each approach has different strengths and weaknesses, rather than one being more 'natural' than others. This, then, highlights the question of which care strategy is the best for parents within modern Western society, which will be tackled, once other considerations have been examined, in Chapter 9.

The second concern about Jean Liedloff's concept of a 'continuum' is that it is more of an abstract and almost spiritual notion than a scientific concept that is capable of being tested. On one hand, the continuum idea seems to refer to the link between children and society and the belief that society can be adapted to make children fit in seamlessly. Rather differently, however, the continuum concept seems to refer to the continuity between contemporary parent–child relationships and our evolutionary origins. The limitation here is that, although this idea is common to many evolutionary theorists, Liedloff does not develop it enough to provide a researchable theory about the processes involved. Infant crying behaviours are presumably regulated by the physiological and psychological systems that underlie them. What is needed is a detailed and explicit theory that makes specific predictions about the way evolution has crafted the neurological, mental and environmental processes involved, so that this can be tested in order to generate evidence and enlarge our knowledge.

Although Jean Liedloff does not provide such a theory, others have set out to do so. In particular, the American psychobiologist Myron Hofer has developed an intriguing theory that proposes that early infant crying evolved as a reflex behaviour to serve dual functions: a communicative function, which encourages parental contact, and a homeostatic function by preventing infant hypothermia (Hofer, 2001; Hofer & Shair, 1992; Hofer et al., 2001). Parental body contact, then, provides an 'external regulatory environment' for homeostasis in immature infant physiological systems. Hofer has developed and tested his ideas using animal (particularly rat) studies, raising the question of whether it is possible to generalize his findings to human infants. That this generalization is in some degree legitimate is indicated both by studies of our more immediate evolutionary relatives, rhesus monkeys and chimpanzees, and by recent human research.

The idea of parenting as an external regulatory environment for infant physiological function can be traced back to Harry and Margaret Harlow's studies, which showed that infant rhesus monkeys chose to cling to a cloth rather than a wire surrogate parent, indicating that the infants preferred some types of environments over others (Harlow & Harlow, 1962). In a study of chimpanzees, Kim Bard observed the behaviour of mothers and infants kept in indoor–outdoor enclosures in Yerkes Regional Primate Center of Emory University in North America. The methods used involved detailed, highly reliable observations of maternal–infant interactions at successive ages in the first 3 months of infancy. A limitation of the study is that the numbers observed were very small. Bard (2000) reports data for just ten infants and mothers, although she supports these detailed findings with more extensive, but less detailed, observations of other cases. Unlike in most Western human studies, Chimpanzee mothers and infants keep in almost constant body contact. Bard did not find an infant chimpanzee crying peak – indeed the infants fussed and cried very little: the average fussing was 1 minute 12 seconds per hour and crying four seconds per hour. However, the amount of time mothers spent soothing their infants peaked at 6–8 weeks of age. Bard also assessed the amounts of fuss/crying of 20 chimpanzee infants reared in nurseries employing non-maternal care, who received much less body contact with their, human, caregivers. Compared with mother-reared infant chimpanzees, who were held almost constantly, much higher levels of fuss/crying were found in nursery-reared infant chimpanzees. Bard interprets her findings as evidence of a cross-species peak in infant fretfulness at around 6 weeks of age and of the importance of parent–infant body contact in mitigating this fretfulness.

Analogous ideas about parenting as an external regulator of infant physiology have emerged from human studies involving infant pain and SIDS. As discussed early in this chapter, research into infant inoculation has shown that young human infants cry less if they are held during the injection, presumably because body contact helps them to regulate their response to pain. Studies into SIDS have found that childcare environments that involve placing infants on their backs, rather than prone, to sleep reduce the number of infant deaths by around 50%, leading to the successful 'back to sleep' campaign for SIDS prevention (Fleming & Blair, 2007). Other environmental factors that may affect SIDS, including parental movements while co-sleeping, parental cigarette smoking and alcohol consumption, and variations in the nature of infants' sleeping surfaces, are also under scrutiny (Fleming & Blair, 2007).

Hofer's (2001) ideas about 'environmental regulators' are valuable because they enable vaguely couched evolutionary ideas to be translated into, and tested, at a physiological and behavioural level. We are familiar with the idea that infants provide environmental regulation for maternal physiological function, by sucking to encourage breast-milk production, while breast milk conveys benefits for infant health. But, it is only recently that this concept of environmental regulation has begun to guide research on parent–infant interaction more generally. Its importance here is to highlight the idea of parental care as an external regulator of the infant physiology that underlies crying behaviour during the early weeks of infancy. Given the care parents nowadays take to ensure that babies do not get cold, it is unlikely that low temperature, by itself, is the stimulus for unexplained crying in contemporary babies. However, it may be, as the American researcher William Greenough puts it, that some infant brain systems are 'experience-expectant' (Greenough et al., 1987). That is, because they have consistently been exposed to such environmental conditions throughout evolution, infant brain systems have adapted to expect these conditions. As Greenough points out, this is likely to be true of only the most universal environmental features. Whether those include body contact between parents and young babies, and how the lack of body contact gives rise to crying, are questions for ingenious researchers to answer in the future. In the meantime, there is already evidence that body contact with caregivers helps to reduce infant distress greatly during the first 3 months of age. In contrast, as we will see in the next two chapters, quite different features of the parenting environment help infants to develop the ability to remain settled during the night-time after 12 weeks of age.

Chapter 5

What do we know about the infant part of infant sleeping problems?

Following the logic of Chapter 3, the initial aim here will be to understand the particular infant sleep and waking behaviours that give rise to parents' concerns.

It is worth remarking that this focus relegates two other sources of information about infant sleeping – physiological and self-report studies – to a supporting role. The reason for overlooking subjective, self-report measures of whether or not someone is asleep is clear, since these reports are not available, by definition, to those who assess infants. The word 'infant' comes from the Latin for 'unable to speak' (Oxford Dictionary). It follows that research in this area faces obstacles that are easily overcome with children or adults, where ambiguity about whether someone is awake or not can often be resolved simply by asking. Many sleep researchers consider physiological measures, for example using electroencephalographic (EEG) indices of brain and muscle activity, to be the gold standard for measuring sleep and waking. Instead, the focus here on behaviour reflects the fact that parents are usually aware of infant behaviour, not EEG. Furthermore, although physiological measures have advantages so far as objective measurement of brain function is concerned, there is no particular reason for prioritizing them, since sleep exists at behavioural, psychological consciousness and physiological levels.

The conceptual approach to be adopted here is to regard physiological, behavioural and psychological approaches as assessing different aspects of infant sleep–waking as a whole. While physiological measures may have advantages for the study of what might be called 'biological sleep', each of the levels can be assessed to provide complementary, but partially distinct, information. Physiological data will be included so far as they help to illuminate what is happening in infants' brains, which may affect their behaviour, that then has an impact on parents.

The main focus throughout this chapter will be on Western family settings, since most of the research comes from studies in Western industrial societies – and it is chiefly in these contexts that infant sleep–waking behaviour has emerged as a problem for parents. However, a few cross-cultural studies have appeared recently, while interest in sudden infant death syndrome (SIDS) has led to a surge in research into bed-sharing as a possible cause of SIDS and this, in turn, has generated studies of sleeping arrangements in non-Western cultures. This comparative research into sleeping arrangements will be examined because of the importance of SIDS, and because it helps to clarify the role played by culture in framing infant sleeping problems and influencing parenting behaviour. We will then turn in Chapters 6 and 7 to the causes of infant sleeping problems.

Which features of infant sleep–waking behaviour disturb Western parents?

Night waking and 'signalling'

For many Western parents, the cessation of their baby's night waking at around 12 weeks of age is an important and much anticipated developmental milestone, to the extent that a popular phrase, 'sleeping through the night', has been coined to celebrate its achievement. As noted earlier (Chapter 2), this phrase is not strictly accurate, since infra-red video-recordings have shown that almost all infants continue to wake in the night (Anders et al., 1992; Goodlin-Jones et al., 2001; Minde et al., 1993; Sadeh, 2004). Indeed, as Box 5.1 indicates, the popular notion of 'sleeping through the night' is misleading in a number of ways. Nevertheless, parents are correct in reporting that most Western infants stop crying or otherwise attracting parental attention during the night, by about 3 months of age (Anders et al., 1983; Jenni & Carskadon, 2007; Moore & Ucko, 1957). This infant behaviour, called 'night waking and signalling' by Tom Anders and his colleagues who first described its specific nature (Anders et al., 1992; Keener et al., 1988), is the earliest emerging component of infant sleeping problems and remains the most commonly reported constituent at older ages (Jenkins et al., 1984; Morrell, 1999; Sadeh & Sivan, 2009). In a recent large Canada/USA survey, the number of times 1 to 3-year-olds woke in the night was the strongest predictor of parent reports of infant/child sleep problems (Sadeh et al., 2009).

Anders and colleagues' choice of the phrase 'night waking and signalling' rather than 'night waking and crying' conveys a subtle, but important, message. Although infant fussing or crying may be the usual trigger for parents' night-time interventions, we currently understand the particular behaviours involved rather poorly, while they are likely to depend on a family's sleeping arrangements. For example, an infant murmur or movement may be enough to arouse a parent's attention where they share the same bed, whereas a much more vigorous signal may be needed where an infant sleeps in a separate room down the corridor. It seems likely, too, that a given infant signal will be more successful in obtaining a response from some parents than others, depending on parents' sensitivity to arousal

Box 5.1 The confused (and misleading) concept of 'sleeping through the night'

1   Almost all infants wake in the night during the first few weeks of age. We say that they 'wake up for feeding', implying that the waking serves a nutritional purpose. The plausible assumption is that infants need to feed frequently at this early point in development and that night waking allows this to happen.

2   By around about 3 months of age, most Western infants stop waking and fussing during the night. Western parents refer to this milestone as 'sleeping through the night'. In fact, infrared video-recordings have shown that almost all infants continue to wake for brief periods during the night.

3   Rather than 'sleeping through the night', most Western infants acquire the ability to resettle back to sleep by themselves without crying out by around 3 months of age. About a third of infants do not achieve this milestone, so that they continue to cry out or otherwise 'signal' their parents when they wake in the night. The critical question is why these infants continue to signal when they wake up, while other infants stop doing so.

4   Where infant night waking and signalling continues past 6 months of age, this is often referred to as an 'infant sleeping problem'. This phrase is misleading since it is not clear that there is anything wrong with their infants' sleeping, other than needing help to resettle upon waking in the night. Most of these infants are in good health.

5   The phrase 'sleeping through the night' also implies a set division between the 'day' and 'night' and that infants suddenly switch from waking to sleeping during the night at a particular age. The evidence indicates that the process is more incremental, so that lengths of periods without signalling, and the number of nights per week containing such periods, accumulate gradually with age. Although evidence is lacking, the process may often also involve fits and starts, rather than a smooth progression.

from their own sleep. Nor should we assume that the signal stays the same across age, as the toddler who gets out of her own bed, walks into her parents' room and shakes her mother's shoulder, can demonstrate. The importance of the phrase 'night waking and signalling', then, is to recognize that the problem is triggered by infant behaviour, but can involve a variety of communicative forms. The terms 'night waking and signalling' and 'unsettled night-time behaviour' will be used interchangeably here to refer to this set of infant behaviours.

In some of their reports, Anders and his colleagues have referred to infants who settle back to sleep without signalling their parents as 'self-soothers', while those who signal are called 'non-self-soothers' (Goodlin-Jones et al., 2001; Keener et al., 1988). This use of the word 'soothing' is different from the use earlier where reference was made to 'unsoothability' as a feature of problematic crying in early infancy. In that usage, the defining situation begins with crying and involves attempts to stop it, while in Anders' usage the situation begins with waking and the issue is whether waking leads the infant back to sleeping without signalling, or results in a signal to parents. 'Self-soothers' in Anders's terminology do not get to cry in the night.

Following this concept of 'self-soothing', a distinction can be drawn between 'sleep maintenance problems', where an infant sleeps for a short while and wakes often, and 'sleep resettling problems', where the difficulty is with settling back to sleep autonomously after waking up during the night. Each of these elements could well have distinct causes. Unfortunately, although it is helpful to keep these distinctions in mind, they have not been widely studied in infant sleep research so far. An exception is Beth Goodlin-Jones and colleagues' (Goodlin-Jones et al., 2001) night-time video study of 80 American infants, divided into 4 groups of approximately 20 infants at 3, 6, 9 and 12 months of age. In keeping with other findings, almost all infants woke during the night and there was no difference in waking frequency between those who resettled back to sleep autonomously ('self-soothers') and infants who received a parental intervention ('non-self soothers'). Collapsed across the age groups, infants who self-soothed back to sleep spent more time asleep in total during the night and their longest sleep periods lasted an hour longer than those of infants who did not self-soothe back to sleep, suggesting that ability to maintain sleep and to resettle are interrelated. An earlier study (Keener et al., 1988) obtained similar results. These findings provide some initial insight into the processes involved. For the moment, though, their main implication is to highlight that, in progressing from the notion of 'sleeping through the night' to the concept of 'night waking and signalling' we have gained a clearer understanding, but not yet completely worked out the infant behaviours involved.

A concept sometimes used together with night waking is 'sleep fragmentation'. This phrase implies that sleep is being 'broken' and that this is harmful to the individual involved. It owes part of its origins to the syndrome of adult sleep apnoea, which involves repetitive waking due to breathing difficulty, and part of its origin to laboratory studies involving the deliberate frequent waking of adults to assess whether this led to daytime sleepiness and psychological impairment (Walsh & Lindblom, 2008). If the waking is frequent enough it does impair subsequent functioning (Walsh & Lindblom, 2008), adding to the evidence that sustained sleep – or, at least, freedom from frequent external waking – is important for well-being. However, the deliberate frequent arousal that characterized these studies is very different from the spontaneous waking at intervals of several hours that is common among young infants. Arguably, the concept of fragmentation is not applicable (or at least needs very precise delineation) at an age where the natural tendency is to have multiple periods of sleep across 24 hours.

Age of occurrence and persistence

Although Western infants in general wake and signal in the night until about the third postnatal month, we do not know with any great certainty the age at which parental concern about infant sleeping problems peaks. Whereas studies of infant crying have tracked crying and parental concern about it over age, this has seldom happened for sleeping problems. Instead, many studies of sleeping problems have targeted infants who are 6 months or older (Acebo et al., 2005; Hiscock & Wake, 2001; Minde et al., 1993; Richman, 1981) and some have excluded infants below 6 (Acebo et al., 2005) or even 12 months of age in defining serious problem cases (Gaylor et al., 2005; Seymour et al., 1989; Tikotzky et al., 2010b). This focus after 6 months may reflect the understandable assumption that such cases are persistent and, consequently, more serious, but it appears to be arbitrary and to reflect researcher preconceptions more than empirical evidence. On one hand, it does seem reasonable to suppose that most parents will recognize the importance of individual differences in development and allow some leeway, so that a baby who wakes at night, for instance, at 4 months of age is not considered a serious source for concern. On the other hand, 74% of parents of 4 to 9-month-old infants reported discussing infant night waking and fussing with paediatricians in a recent American survey of community healthcare services (Olson et al., 2004). All of those were less than 10 months, and many were less than 6 months, of age.

Table 5.1 presents some evidence about this issue from one of few studies to have assessed infant sleeping problems from birth through early childhood. The findings are from a study of 3269 infants and young children in Queensland, Australia reported by Kenneth Armstrong and colleagues in 1994 (Armstrong et al., 1994). These researchers asked parents to report their children's sleep–waking behaviours and to rate whether these behaviours were problematic for them.

The Table 5.1 findings support the assumption that parents are particularly likely to find infant night-time sleep–waking behaviour to be problematic at around 7 to 12 months of age. Other studies, too, have noted this finding (Moore & Ucko, 1957; Scher, 1991). Still, about a quarter to a third of Australian parents reported infant sleeping problems at each age point in the Armstrong study. Even allowing for the possibility that the smaller sample sizes at some ages make those figures less reliable, the findings

Table 5.1 Australian parents' reports of whether their child's sleep–
waking behaviours were considered problematic, from birth to
38 months of age

Infant/child age (months)	Infants included, n	Infants considered to have sleep problems, %
<1	159	27
1–3	846	23
4–6	740	27
7–9	500	36
10–12	364	36
13–18	205	28
19–24	104	32
25–38	351	28

Source: Redrawn from Armstrong et al., 1994.

do not support the idea of a sudden onset in sleeping problems at 6, or 12, months of age so far as parents are concerned. Presumably, some of those parents are unrealistic, since most Western babies wake and signal parents in the night until about 3 months of age. Normative information should help such parents, but the more critical question is what guidance to give to parents after 3 months, when most infants stop waking and signalling in the night.

A limitation of the figures in Table 5.1 is that they were collected from different groups of infants at each age. The alternative, but more time consuming, method is to assess the same group of infants repeatedly at successive ages. This, longitudinal, approach has important advantages. In particular, this method makes it possible to identify different developmental courses over age. It is then possible to distinguish cases who establish settled night-time routines at an early age from those who never establish them, and both of these from cases with a sporadic history of night-waking problems that start and stop intermittently at successive ages. As well as revealing different developmental pathways (and different causes), these distinctions are likely to be important in understanding the impact of infant night-time behaviour on parents. For instance, a short stretch of night waking may well be tolerated, particularly if there is some reason to think that an infant is unwell, whereas waking in the night that persists for weeks or months, or recurs unpredictably, is likely to be more challenging for parents.

Figure 5.1a illustrates the way in which longitudinal sleep problem data are sometimes presented, following statistician Ian Plewis's (1980) recom-mendation, in the form of a 'probability tree' over successive ages. The starting point can be at any age, but ideally should be at birth or as soon after that as possible. At each step, the number (and proportion) of infants with-out a sleeping problem is given in the top branch, while those with a problem are represented on the bottom branch. By following the developmental

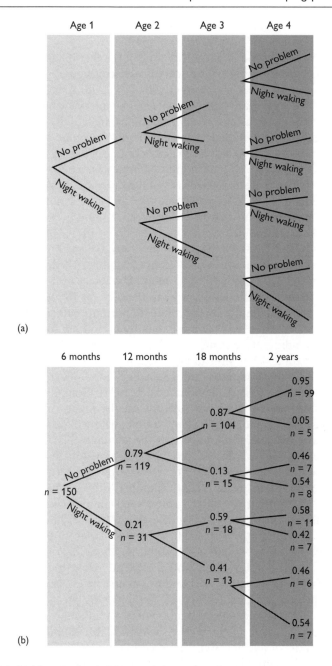

Figure 5.1 (a) Use of a 'probability tree' diagram to illustrate continuity, or discontinuity, in infant night wakings and signalling at successive ages (redrawn from Jenkins et al., 1984); (b) longitudinal sleep problems data shown as a probability tree (redrawn from Jenkins et al., 1984).

course from left to right, the number of infants moving into and out of the sleep problem group can be tracked over age.

Figure 5.1b displays the findings from one of the first longitudinal studies of infant and child sleeping – Sue Jenkins and colleagues' (Jenkins et al., 1984) London study – as a probability tree. The information about the infants' and children's behaviour was collected by interviewing parents from the general community, using standard questions, including ones that asked about infant/child night waking. Problematic night waking was defined by the researchers as waking in 4 or more nights per week (rather than by asking for parental judgements), so that infants/children who woke during 3 nights per week, or fewer, were classified as non-problem cases. As Figure 5.1b shows, of 150 infants first assessed at 6 months and successfully followed up, 79% did not have a night-waking problem at 12 months, while 21% were 'night wakers' at 12 months. At 18 months, most (87%) of 'non-wakers' stayed that way, but 13% of infants who did not wake at 12 months became night wakers. Of the 31 infants who woke in the night at 12 months, just over half (59%) then stopped doing so by 18 months, whereas 41% of the 31 night wakers at 12 months continued to wake in the night at 18 months of age.

These longitudinal figures make three important points. First, many infants develop settled sleep–waking habits by 6 months, so that approximately 80% who did not wake and signal in the night at 6 months remained settled in the night at 12 months of age. Similarly, infants who did not wake in the night at 12 or 18 months had a 90% likelihood of remaining a non-waker at 24 months of age (Jenkins et al., 1984). Second, a substantial number of individuals moved into, or out of, the night-waking group at successive ages. Approximately half the infants who woke and signalled in the night at any one age did not do so at the next age. 'New' night-waking cases occurred, though, at each age so that, in terms of raw numbers, the number of infants with a problem at any one age (but no problem at the preceding age) was often greater than the number with a continuing problem. Within this 'intermittent problem' group, some infants were particularly prone to recurrent problems. For instance, two-thirds of children who were night wakers at 12 months were night wakers at 18 *or* 24 months of age. Third, the number of individuals with a stable night-waking problem at every age was quite small – just 5% of infants persistently woke in the night at 12, 18 and 24 months in this study of London infants (Jenkins et al., 1984).

Support for Jenkins and colleague's findings was provided by Dieter Wolke and colleagues' epidemiological study of infants and parents in South Bavaria a decade later (Wolke et al., 1995b). Infants entered this study at 5 months of age and were followed longitudinally afterwards until 56 months. Although this approach does not provide a full history of sleep–waking behaviour, it is reasonable to assume that most infants with sleeping problems at 5 months of age had never acquired settled night-time behaviour. Consequently, this study provides evidence for the hypothesis that failure to develop settled behaviour at night in the early months is a precursor of long-term sleep–waking problems.

Longitudinal night-waking data for 671 full-term infants were provided by parents at 5, 20 and 56 months of age (Wolke et al., 1995b). Severe night waking was defined by the researchers as waking at least once per night during 5 or more nights per week. Based on this definition, 25% of infants had a night-waking problem, and 75% did not have a night-waking problem at 5 months of age – rates that are very similar to the London figures given above. Also like the London infants, Bavarian infants who did not wake in the night at 5 months were highly likely to remain stable non-wakers, with 85% remaining non-wakers at 20 months. Similarly, 90% of non-wakers at 20 months remained non-wakers at 56 months. Tracking the Bavarian 5-month night-waking group, most (70%) had stopped waking in the night at 20 months of age, while 83% of the night wakers at 20 months then ceased to be night wakers at 56 months. Although infants in this study, too, moved in and out of the sleep problem group, 5-month-old infants with night waking were twice as likely as other infants to wake at night at 20 months of age (although only 14% of 5-month night-wakers remained night-wakers when 56 months old). Unfortunately, Wolke and colleagues do not say what percentage of infants had night-waking problems at all three ages. Melissa Wake and colleagues' Australian study (Wake et al., 2006) found, though, that most sleep problems in the first 2 years were transient, so that just 6.4% of infants had a problem at three or more age points (a figure which closely resembles the London rate of 5% noted above). In longitudinal regression analyses, persistent, rather than transient, problems predicted serious long-term child and parental disturbances – a point we will return to in Chapter 8.

The findings from these English, Bavarian and Australian studies are impressively similar and have important implications for parents and health professionals, since they identify three main developmental pathways for infant night waking and signalling after about 5 months of age.

Pathway 1

This is a stable pathway without night-waking problems, shown by many infants. The percentage depends on the criteria used, but this pattern occurred in the majority of infants in the Wake et al. (2006) study. The implication is that 'good' sleeping habits – from the point of view of Western parents and cultural expectations – are established in many infants by 5–6 months of age.

Pathway 2

This pathway involves intermittent problems and is moderately common. Infants in this group stop night waking and signalling at one age, only for this to recur as they get older. The proportion depends on the ages meas-ured and the interval involved, but between 9 and 15% of infants fell into this group in the research described above (Jenkins et al., 1984; Wolke et al., 1995a, 1998) and higher figures have been reported when the follow-up spans several ages (Moore & Ucko, 1957). Because this 'intermittent' pattern is far more common than cases with continuous night-waking problems (see Pathway 3 below), this group is particularly important. In particular, most 'sleep problems' cases identified in cross-sectional surveys are likely to be of this type. An associated question is what causes re-onset of unsettled night waking, and whether this group includes several different patterns. The Jenkins et al., London study described above, for instance, identified a subgroup with a persistent sequence of 'on–off' night waking at successive ages. These cases may be quite different from infants who settle but relapse only once, for instance following a change in routines.

Anat Scher (Scher, 1991; Scher et al., 2005) has proposed that transitions in psychological development, such as the onset of fear of separation, or abilities like crawling, may sometimes trigger problems at particular age points. There is some evidence of a peak in reported sleep problems at around 6–9 months of age, which might reflect this, in the Australian figures in Table 5.1 and in some other studies (Moore & Ucko, 1957; Scher, 1991). However, this has not always been found and it is not clear what proportion of cases involves re-onset. The proposal that fear of separation or the dark triggers recurrence of night-waking problems at 6–12 months of age will be discussed in Chapter 6. What is clear is that this 'intermittent night-waking and signalling' group, and the causes of recurrent unsettled waking in the night, need to be much better understood. This group's existence is also relevant for studies that treat sleeping problems, since unless the treated infants are followed up repeatedly they may give the mistaken impression that the treatment has proved effective. An untreated, control group of comparable infants with repeated follow-ups is an essen-tial requirement. It is possible, too, that the unpredictability of these cases is a particular source of parental anxiety.

Pathway 3

This pathway includes infants whose night-waking problems are stable at every age, at least in the pre-school period. This occurs in only a small minority of infants, around 5–6% according to the Australian and London studies. Ten percent of infants 'never settled completely at any time in the first year' (p. 335) in an early London study (Moore & Ucko, 1957). It remains possible that these figures are slight underestimates for sleep prob-lems as a whole, since some children may develop other types of sleep difficulties when they cease night waking. Unfortunately, there are no figures to show how often this happens, but since night waking and other sleep difficulties often occur together, the underestimate may not be large. Underestimation of stabilities may also be due to the arbitrary cut-offs used to define problems since, for instance, a child who woke 5 nights a week could move into the non-problem group at a later age if waking only 3 nights per week at that point. Yet he or she would still be a 'night waker' albeit of a lesser degree. It is also worth noting that some other researchers have reported persistence of sleeping problems that appears greater than described here. Jon Pollock (1992), for instance, found that night-wakers at 6 months were three times as likely to remain night-wakers at 5 years of age than non-wakers were to become night wakers. However, the 6-month data in that study were collected retrospectively, so that parental recall may have exaggerated the continuities.

Taken as a whole, these figures suggest that only about 5–10% of children have stable night-waking problems during the pre-school period, whereas a pattern of intermittent problems occurs in at least two or three times as many. The studies also show that infants who become settled in the night by 5 months of age are likely to retain this habit, while many (but not all) infant sleeping problems have their onset in the first 5 months of infancy. It follows that the processes taking place in this early period of development provide the prelude to sleeping problems in many cases.

Settling difficulties

As well as night waking and signalling, both the International Classification of Sleep Disorders (ICSD, American Academy of Sleep Medicine, 2005) and reviews of the research (M. Moore et al., 2007) have identified a second type of problematic sleep–waking behaviour during early childhood: difficulties with initial settling to sleep (sometimes referred to as bedtime 'struggles' [Iglowstein et al., 2003], or 'refusals' [M. Moore et al., 2007]). These problems, which involve taking a long time to fall asleep, often together with infant protests and bedtime delaying tactics, typically start to occur at a later age than night-waking problems, although they may occur in the same infants (Armstrong et al., 1994; Jenni et al., 2005; Jenkins et al., 1984; Wolke et al., 1995a). They are rarer than night waking (Jenni et al., 2005; Jenkins et al., 1984; Wolke et al., 1995a) with 10–15% of 1 to 8-year-olds reported to have difficulties with settling to sleep (Sadeh, 2000). Problems of this kind are thought to reflect both the increasing autonomy of toddler and pre-school children and parenting factors (Gaylor et al., 2005; M. Moore et al., 2007). For instance, Ivo Iglowstein and colleagues (Iglowstein et al., 2003) have argued that bedtime struggles are sometimes due to unrealistic parental expectations about children's sleep needs and bedtimes, so that parents put children to bed before they are sleepy.

In principle, the idea of 'settling problems' involves a distinction between occasions when an infant has difficulty falling asleep at the start of the night and those when she settles readily but wakes up and signals later in the night ('night waking and signalling'). The two types of sleep problems might well have different causes and this seems to be implied by the phrases 'bedtime struggles' and 'bedtime refusals' used by some researchers: these problems appear to involve social conflict, rather than difficulties with maintaining or resuming sleep. In keeping with this notion of distinct problems, night waking and signalling typically precedes 'bedtime struggles' in age at onset, while there is evidence that some infants have one or other type of problem, rather than both (Gaylor et al., 2005). However, it is also the case that many infants and young children with sleep problems have both types (Jenkins et al., 1984; Wolke et al., 1995a). Anders and colleagues' description of infants who resettle themselves after waking in the night as 'self-soothers' suggests that difficulties in settling to sleep autonomously could provide a common denominator and explain why one type of sleep problem sometimes leads on to the other type. Here again, the implication is that we need a more fine-grained understanding of the infant behaviours involved than we currently possess.

After about 9 months of age, difficulties in settling alone are sometimes attributed to toddler separation anxiety (DeLeon & Karraker, 2007; Sadeh, 2005; Scher, 2001), reflecting the evidence from research into emotional development and attachment that children begin to fear separation and to use parents as sources of security from about this age (DeLeon & Karraker, 2007; Scher, 2001). Since fear of separation or the dark is one type of explanation for settling difficulties, it will be considered in Chapter 6. For the moment, the implication is to point to the need to consider child age when infant settling and night-waking behaviours are under scrutiny.

Deficits in amounts of sleep

Worries that children are not getting enough sleep to meet biological needs and that sleep deficit reduces alertness, learning and well-being are a central feature of sleep problem research with children of school age (Owens, 2004, 2007; Owens et al., 2003; Tikotzky et al., 2010b). For instance, night-time sleep decrements have been associated with daytime behaviour problems, irritability and cognitive impairments in children and teenagers (Owens, 2004; Sadeh et al., 2007). Chinese schoolchildren have been reported to go to bed later, and sleep an hour less per 24 hours than American children (Liu et al., 2005), which the authors attributed to cultural factors, in particular the need to study in the evenings and the early start of the Chinese school day. Deficits in sleeping amount have also been reported in some studies of infants. For instance, Salvatore Ottaviano and his colleagues included 1 to 5-month-olds in a 1996 study of Italian children, concluding that 'Comparison with other studies showed that children in this study had a later sleep onset time and slept less than children of the same age living in some other countries' (Ottaviano et al., 1996, p. 1). These researchers speculated that this finding might reflect '. . . certain social habits of Italian families, such as allowing their children to participate in the family's evening life, including a late dinner' (Ottaviano et al., 1996, p. 2). American 3-month-old infants slept 2 hours less per 24 hours than Dutch 3-month-olds during the 1990s according to a 1996 study (Super et al., 1996). More recently, a 2010 internet survey of 17 countries found substantial differences in infant sleeping, so that Japanese 0 to 3-year-olds went to bed later and slept 1.7 hours less per 24 hours than same-aged New Zealand infants (Mindell et al., 2010). There is also a possibility that children's sleep amounts have changed across successive generations. Ivo Iglowstein and colleagues (Iglowstein et al., 2003) found that Swiss 1-year-olds went to bed later, and slept approximately 30 minutes less per 24 hours, in the 1980s and 1990s than in the 1970s.

If it is true that infants' sleep–waking amounts differ from one culture or generation to another, this could be important in understanding cultural diversity, documenting the flexibility of biological constraints on sleeping behaviour, and suggesting that social learning plays a part in setting up sleep habits. Such a finding could also inform the debate about young children's sleep 'needs' and the claim that children in some cultures suffer from a chronic shortage of sleep (Jenni & O'Connor, 2005). The implication could then be that parents in some cultural groups might wish to consider changing their parenting behaviour in order to resolve their children's sleep deficits and improve their well-being.

Unfortunately, although these questions about sleep deficiency are potentially important, the data we have available to answer them are not up to the job. There are two key shortcomings. The first is reliance on parental reports and failure to distinguish between time in bed (which parents can record fairly accurately) and time spent asleep (which parents are less aware of). Parents have been found to overestimate infant sleep, by as much as an hour per night in some studies (Minde et al., 1993; Sadeh, 1996). Ironically, this exaggeration may be greatest where infants are settled at night, since parents will be less aware of waking in those cases than when infants signal (Minde et al., 1993).

The second pitfall is failure to distinguish sleep pattern from sleep amount. Because some cultures take a 'siesta' in the afternoon – and most young children take 'naps' – it is necessary to separate the number and timing of sleep periods from the overall, 24-hour, total amount. For instance, careful scrutiny of Salvatore Ottaviano's study reveals that although the totalled amounts of daytime and night-time sleep of Italian infants and young children reported by parents did seem to be comparatively low (for instance 12.55 hours for 1 to 5-month-olds; 11.88 hours for 6 to 12-month-olds), times spent in naps were tabled separately. Why the data were presented in this way and what distinguished 'naps' are not explained in this brief report, but if the time spent in 'naps' is added to the time spent asleep, the 24-hour figures increase to 17.98 hours in the 1 to 5-month-old, and 15.28 hours in the 6 to 12-month-old group, which are not less than amounts in other countries (Iglowstein et al., 2003; Mindell et al., 2010).

Although, then, Italian infants and children may go to bed later than those in some other cultures, it is not evident that they sleep less per 24 hours than other infants and children, or even that they go to sleep later (since it is not clear whether parents distinguished accurately between bedtime and sleep onset time).

Xianchen Liu's study of Chinese children has the same limitation, although these authors did acknowledge that the Chinese school day included a 2-hour lunch break to allow children to have a nap. Perhaps the most persuasive evidence to date comes from Iglowstein and colleagues' (2003) finding that Swiss infants and young children slept less per 24 hours in the 1980s and 1990s than in the 1970s, since that research used the same measurement method in each generation. Even so, their study used parental report based on bedtimes rather than measures of actual infant sleep. As a consequence, a possible interpretation of the findings offered by one of the authors is that Swiss parents in the 1970s put their children to bed too early, while parents in the 1990s adjusted their children's bedtimes appropriately to their children's sleep needs (Jenni & O'Connor, 2005). It is certainly not clear that Swiss children in the 1990s had a 'sleep deficit'.

Summarizing this evidence, the only conclusion it is possible to draw is that we do not know whether infants or young children in different cultures vary in sleep amounts, whether cultural practices give rise to sleep deficits, or whether infants considered by parents to have sleep problems have insufficient sleep. In fact, it is striking that most studies of sleep problems in the first year do not report infants' 24-hour sleep totals at all. Avi Sadeh's (2004) internet survey is a notable exception and, in this study, infants and young children considered by their parents to have sleep problems were reported to sleep less both in the day and night-time than their peers without sleep problems. Even so, these findings were based on parents' questionnaire reports, while Sadeh's objective studies have not found that infants with sleep problems sleep less during the night than their peers (Sadeh et al., 1991). Rather, his actigraphy studies, which assess body movements to distinguish sleep from waking objectively, confirm that such infants have shorter sleep periods and wake and signal more often, but not that they sleep less at night. Unfortunately, Sadeh has not reported 24-hour actigraphy figures and, to this writer's knowledge, we do not have any objective evidence to confirm whether infants with night-time sleep–waking problems actually sleep less per 24 hours than other equivalently aged infants.

This remarkable oversight may reflect Western parents' perception that babies sleep a great deal throughout the 24-hour day, so that sleep deficiency concerns them less than night waking at this age. A more parsimonious explanation is that infant night waking and signalling is troublesome for parents mainly because it disrupts their own sleep. In any case, the implication is that, to address this issue, we need to supplement parental reports with objective measurements that distinguish infant bedtimes from sleeping times, sleeping amounts from sleeping patterns, and daytime from night-time sleep–waking behaviour. One intriguing by-product of such research will be to establish whether infants and children in Mediterranean cultures follow their parents in assigning part of their sleep to a regular 'siesta' in the afternoon and, if so, the age at which this pattern becomes discernibly different from non-siesta norms.

Before leaving this topic, it is important to mention recent research linking short sleep lengths to child obesity. Taveras et al. (2008), for example, found that children who typically slept less than 12 hours per 24 hours between 6 months and 2 years of age were more likely than other children to be overweight at 3 years of age. Most of this research has involved older children, but one recent study has found some evidence that this association exists at 6 months of age (Tikotzky et al., 2010a). Although this issue is not a common source of parental concern at the moment, it may become one.

The first point to make is that the evidence is not consistent across studies since, although several have found differences in weight gain between long- and short-sleepers (Bell & Zimmerman, 2010; Taveras et al., 2008; Tikotzky et al., 2010a), some careful large-scale studies have not (Jenni et al., 2007). The second is that, on existing evidence, the relationship is weak during infancy. The Tikotzky et al. (2010a) study of 96 healthy first-born 6-month-old infants assessed sleep using an objective method (actigraphy) and by parental report. Measures of weight included the commonly used weight-to-length ratio (which allows for height), and 'weight above expected weight for length' (which allows for gender). As would be expected, birth-weight predicted the 6-month weight measures, as did whether or not the infant was breast-feeding at 6 months. Controlling for these factors, sleep length at 6 months was not associated with weight. However, the percentage of the night-time spent asleep at 6 months was negatively associated with the two weight-to-length measures – although this accounted for only 10% of the variation in the 'weight above expected weight for length' measure and 6% of the infants' weight-to-length ratio. Recalling our interest in infant night waking and signalling, night waking was not associated with any of the weight measures.

The final point to make about this new area of research is that the reason for this possible association between low sleep amount and above-typical weight is unknown – in particular, it is certainly not clear that short-sleeping causes weight gain. A third factor, possibly genetic or environmental, may be the underlying cause. A recent American study of the factors that predict maternal reports of short-sleeping in 6–24 month-olds (Nevarez et al., 2010) found that maternal depression during pregnancy, early introduction of solid foods, infant television viewing, racial/ethnic minority, and attendance at daycare, were associated with shorter infant sleep duration. Early introduction of solid foods appears to be a factor that could also account for increased infant/child weight, but this has not been tested so far. Understandably, there is concern that contemporary children's lifestyles, including staying up late playing computer games or watching television, and poor diet and lack of exercise, might be responsible for the findings. If so, this may be more important at older ages. In any case, the implication of the evidence so far is to point to the need for careful research, to understand the findings better.

Other sleep–waking problems that are common at older ages

As well as deficient sleep amounts, it is instructive to distinguish other aspects of children's sleep–waking behaviour that are problematic for parents at later ages, but seldom reported during infancy. The first of these involves difficulties surrounding daytime 'napping', which seems to emerge as a problem more often after about 1 year of age (Mindell & Owens, 2003). This type of problem is rarely reported during infancy, perhaps because almost all infants have daytime sleep periods, so that the presence or absence of naps is not an issue, or because conflicts around settling refusals during the daytime are uncommon at this age. Ferber (2006) reports that giving up daytime naps can be troublesome for some children.

Second, the *timing* or *phase* of sleep and waking periods during infancy is less of an issue than with older children and, particularly, adolescents, when staying up late and getting up late are a common concern (Carskadon, 2002; Ferber, 2006; Jenni & Carskadon, 2007; Mindell & Owens, 2003; Wyatt, 2007). Unless they are forced to get up early, sleep deficit may not be the issue in such cases, so much as the antisocial nature of such sleep–waking patterns. There is an apparent conceptual link between bedtime struggles in toddlerhood and staying up late in adolescence, but whether the same individuals display both features is not clear.

Lastly, classification schemes for sleep disorders, such as the ICSD (American Academy of Sleep Medicine, 2005) distinguish between 'dysomnias' (which include night waking and other difficulties in settling or maintaining sleep), 'parasomnias' (which are unusual behaviours during sleep, including sleep-walking, restless legs syndrome, nocturnal enuresis and bruxism), and sleep disorders due to medical conditions. Most parasomnias are absent in infants, but sudden infant death syndrome (SIDS, listed as a parasomnia in ICSD) is especially important and will be discussed in Chapter 6. Sleep disordered breathing, which is common during infancy (Sadeh & Sivan, 2009), will also be discussed in Chapter 6.

'Night-time terrors' are also classified as a type of parasomnia by the ICSD. These are among the most dramatic of sleep disorders (Nguyen et al., 2008), involving waking up feeling highly anxious or afraid and struggling or displaying alarm. Since they typically occur during Quiet Sleep, they are distinct from nightmares, which present most often during rapid eye movement (REM) sleep (Horne, 2006; Stores, 2007) (the distinction between Quiet and Active Sleep is discussed in Chapter 6). 'Night terrors' usually occur in adults or children (Stores, 2007), but have been reported from about 6 months of age (Sadeh & Sivan, 2009), although infants' inability to report their feelings makes it uncertain whether true night terrors exist at this age. In any case, they are usually isolated events and disappear spontaneously with age (Sadeh & Sivan, 2009). Where night terrors seem to occur as sporadic events in otherwise healthy infants, it is usually sufficient to reassure parents that these are benign events that will resolve by themselves.

Avi Sadeh and Yakov Sivan's (2009) review of clinical practice describes rare cases where night terrors occur regularly at about the same time of night. There is some evidence, albeit from clinical case studies, that scheduled brief awakenings of the child prior to the anticipated time of the terrors can prevent them from happening and resolve the problem within a few nights (Durand & Mindell, 1999; Petit & Montplaisir, 2010). The scheduled awakening method will be described in Chapter 10.

It may seem perverse to have devoted space to aspects of sleep–waking that are rarely problematic in infancy, but the reason for this will become clear later, since an intervention that simply increases the amount an infant sleeps is not necessarily a good thing. If the infant already sleeps enough and the 'extra' sleep replaces alert interactions with the social and physical environment, increasing sleep amount may not be desirable at all. It is partly for this reason that it is important to be precise about the type of infant behaviours that underlie parents' reports of problems.

Summary and conclusions about the infant sleep–waking behaviours that disturb Western parents

To sum up this chapter, infant night waking and signalling is the earliest emerging type of infant sleeping problem and remains the most common problem at later ages (Jenkins et al., 1984; Morrell, 1999). There is some evidence of a small peak in parents' concerns about infant night waking at around 7–12 months of age, but this appears to trouble a quarter to a third of Western parents in each age period.

The studies also show that many, but not all, infant sleeping problems have their origins in the first 5 months of infancy, while infants who do not have sleeping problems at this point are likely to avoid having sleeping problems at later ages. In turn, this highlights the developmental processes taking place in the first 3–4 months of age, and infants' ability to resettle autonomously after waking in the night, as key phenomena.

The critical question is not what causes the onset of sleeping problems but why some infants do not follow the typical Western pattern of stopping night waking and signalling at around 3 months of age.

Towards toddlerhood and the pre-school period, conflicts around settling and sleep onset at bedtime become troublesome for some parents. These sleep onset problems are rarer and may occur in conjunction with night waking, although they sometimes occur in isolation. Because sleep onset/ settling problems have received little research attention in their own right, the primary goal below will be to understand the causes of night waking and signalling, which remains the most common sleep–waking problem throughout infancy and the pre-school period. Problems with settling to sleep at bedtime will receive consideration so far as the studies allow, particularly in relation to the idea that they are due to difficulties with infant separation or fear of the dark.

Chapter 6

What do we know about the causes of infant night waking and signalling?

Organic disturbance explanations 1: evidence from studies of prenatal adversities and exposure to stress

The idea that infant and child sleeping problems reflect organic disturbances can be traced back to the early studies of Naomi Richman and others, who noted that infants and toddlers selected because of parental reports of night waking were more likely than other infants and toddlers to have histories involving adversities during pregnancy or childbirth (Richman, 1981). More recently, high alcohol consumption by mothers during pregnancy has been linked with frequent night waking in their 6 to 8-week-old infants (Troese et al., 2008) and 8-year-old children (Pesonen et al., 2009). Maternal consumption of cocaine and other drugs during pregnancy, and maternal cigarette smoking (leading to exposure of the foetus to nicotine), too, have been implicated as causes of infant sleep–waking disturbances (Galbally et al., 2009; Schuetze & Lawton, 2006; Stone et al., 2009, 2010). A Cochrane review (Osborn et al., 2010) noted that newborns exposed to opiates before birth can suffer from postnatal withdrawal symptoms, including sleep–waking problems.

One obvious caveat to this evidence is that adversities such as prenatal opiate exposure are rare, so that they are unlikely to account for many cases involving infant night waking and signalling. Since around a quarter to a third of infants in general communities in many countries are unsettled in the night, the question is how many of these are caused by pre- and perinatal adversities in practice. It is important to bear in mind, too, the associational nature of the available evidence. Because it is clearly not possible to run experimental studies, that is, where putative adversities are added in a controlled way, establishing causation involves accumulating evidence from a variety of less effective research designs. These include controlled animal studies, so far as the addition of adversities can be sanctioned, and the use of statistical controls for possible confounding factors in human studies.

The interpretative difficulties that arise are well illustrated by Naomi Richman's (1981) original study. Her study reported that 30% of infants and toddlers with night waking had a history of severe adverse perinatal events, compared to 16% of infants/toddlers without night waking. This was a statistically significant difference but, even so, 70% of the cases with night-waking problems did not have adverse perinatal histories. Furthermore, the well-established association between pregnancy adversities and demographic factors (Sameroff & Chandler, 1975) allows the infant night-waking findings to be explained just as readily in terms of parenting and family environment ('psycho-social risk') variables. Indeed, Richman (1981) herself reported that maternal psychiatric disorder and family tension were more prevalent where infants/toddlers woke at night than in other cases. Other studies, too, have repeatedly documented an association between infant sleeping problems and maternal depression, marital conflict, and family psycho-social risk factors (Goodlin-Jones et al., 2000; Hiscock & Wake, 2001; Lozoff et al., 1985; Meltzer & Mindell, 2007; Seifer et al., 1994a, 1994b; Zuckerman et al., 1987). In particular, there is firm evidence from recent randomized controlled trials that specific parenting behaviours do affect whether or not infants wake and signal in the night. These will be examined later in the chapter. For our purposes here, the point is that studies of whether or not pre- or perinatal adversities cause unsettled night-time behaviour will need to control for these postnatal parenting behaviours – whereas that has not been achieved so far.

Research since Richman's early study has continued to find associations between exposure to adversities during pregnancy and birth and the infant's subsequent sleep–waking. These findings, though, have not provided a clearer picture. For example, the USA Maternal Lifestyle Study, the largest longitudinal, multisite investigation of the effects of prenatal cocaine exposure on child development, has published two recent reports on sleep problems among the infants and children involved (Stone et al., 2009, 2010). Because cocaine is often taken in conjunction with other drugs, Kristen Stone and her colleagues compared three groups: (1) a group of children with prenatal exposure to cocaine, either alone or in combination with other drugs (where the other drugs included opiates, marijuana, alcohol, or nicotine); (2) an 'other drug' group of children exposed prenatally to opiates, marijuana, alcohol, or nicotine but not to cocaine; (3) an 'unexposed' group of children with no prenatal drug exposure. Infant and child sleeping was assessed longitudinally at 18 and 30 months, and at 3, 5, 7 and 9 years of age, using maternal reports of the children's sleep–waking behaviours. Because women who take drugs while pregnant are likely to experience social adversities, the study measured a variety of postnatal social risk factors, including the mother's socioeconomic status, marital status, physical abuse, prenatal medical care and depression, as well as postnatal cigarette smoking. Multivariate statistical analyses were then used to examine the association between maternal prenatal drug use and the subsequent infant and child sleep–waking outcomes, controlling for the postnatal risk factors.

The finding was that cocaine did not predict whether or not the children had sleep problems. Instead, of the five drugs examined (cocaine, opiates, marijuana, alcohol, nicotine) prenatal nicotine exposure was the only unique predictor of infant/child sleep problems. This finding was at odds with previous human and animal evidence about the effect of cocaine, requiring an explanation for the inconsistencies. It is possible that the apparent evidence of effects of cocaine in previous studies was a consequence of less effective controls than achieved by the Maternal Lifestyle Study, or that this study's measures of infant/child sleep were not precise enough, but the reason is not known.

In a Norwegian study (Sarfi et al., 2009) pregnant women with opiate dependency were put on a methadone or buprenorphine maintenance treatment and given a pre- and postnatal educational programme to help them to prepare for motherhood. Although 47% of the prenatally drug-exposed newborns showed withdrawal symptoms, there was no difference between them and control infants in sleep–waking at 3 months of age. Pamela Schuetze and Desirae Lawton (2006) found that prenatal cocaine exposure was related to infant sleep problems at 7 months of age, but this association disappeared once maternal anxiety was included in the analyses. Where infants were in non-maternal care at 7 months, they had fewer sleep problems.

The Maternal Lifestyle Study finding (Stone et al., 2009, 2010) that prenatal exposure to nicotine predicts infant sleep–waking is of importance in its own right. This association also points to the large body of evidence that implicates maternal cigarette smoking as a 'risk factor' for SIDS. However, R. Horne et al.'s (2004) review concluded that inability to arouse from sleep may be the risk factor underlying SIDS – which is almost the opposite of the phenomenon of excessive infant night waking and signalling that is our primary interest here.

To be clear, the point is not to be overcritical of these painstaking studies but to emphasize the complexity of the phenomena being researched. Individual prenatal, perinatal, and postnatal adversities interrelate and accumulate in complex ways. Although studies using statistical controls can throw some light on the factors and processes involved, they are a limited tool and many such studies will be needed before the causal factors and their timing and potency are uncovered. Instead, studies that assess the physiological mechanisms involved may prove more informative. Recent research by Bill Fifer and colleagues (2009), for example, has found that newborns with prenatal exposure to alcohol and/or cigarette smoking have lowered autonomic nervous system responsiveness to challenges, suggesting a possible physical mechanism for infant sleep disturbance. This is in keeping with the R. Horne et al. (2004) review mentioned above about the causes for SIDS, but again highlights the difference between sleep problems involving deficient arousal and excessive night waking and signalling. There is also evidence that postnatal cigarette smoking affects the nicotine content of breast-milk and shortens the subsequent sleep period of breast-fed infants (Mennella et al., 2007). Postnatal alcohol consumption, too, affects breast-fed infants' sleep, but in this case by reducing the amount of active sleep (Mennella & Garcia-Gomez, 2001). These studies offer the promise of distinguishing between different types of sleep–waking problems and their specific causes. It may well be that the greater precision possible with studies of this sort will allow more rapid progress than has been possible so far.

To sum up, findings in this area reveal complex associations among pre-, peri- and postnatal adversities and between these and infant sleep–waking. It is certainly plausible that exposure to one or other of these adversities, or to an accumulation of them, could cause infant night waking and signalling beyond 3 months of age. However, the existing research is some way from being able to prove whether or not that is the case while, if so, it seems likely to account for only a small number of cases. It follows that the primary implication of the evidence is to identify the need for further research to resolve these ambiguities. In the meantime, the uncertainty in this area does have some implications for how practitioners approach infant sleep problems and the parents involved, which will be considered at the end of this section.

Turning to prenatal stress, there is firm experimental evidence from animal studies that environments that stress pregnant females can hamper the postnatal development of their offspring (Clarke et al., 1996; Schneider, 1992). The hypothesized mechanism is that prenatal stress produces high levels of maternal glucocorticoids ('stress hormones'), which cross the placenta and impair growth of the foetal hypothalamic–pituitary–adrenal system (the HPA axis) that regulates the infant and child's responses to stress (O'Connor et al., 2007). Associated questions are whether the sorts of stressors used in the animal studies generalize to human conditions and whether human foetuses are less vulnerable to such prenatal impairments because of species differences in the nature and timetabling of brain growth.

Because prenatal stress cannot be studied experimentally in humans, studies in this area, too, have employed multivariate statistical methods to control for potential confounding variables. Several studies of this sort have been published in the last 10 years, showing poorer developmental outcomes among children of mothers who reported stress during pregnancy (Huizink et al., 2003; O'Connor et al., 2007; van den Bergh & Marcoen, 2004). Most of these have assessed children's daytime emotional, behavioural, cognitive or motor abilities, but Tom O'Connor and his colleagues have recently reported evidence of sleep disturbances among infants whose mothers reported anxiety and depression during pregnancy (O'Connor et al., 2007). Since this study is large scale, carefully conducted and most relevant to infant sleep problems, it warrants detailed consideration.

The methods used involved anxiety and depression questionnaires completed during weeks 18 and 32 of pregnancy by around 10,000 women in the Avon Longitudinal Study of Parents and Children (the ALSPAC study, O'Connor et al., 2007). Infant and toddler sleep problems were measured, again by maternal questionnaire, at 6, 18 and 30 months of age. The most pertinent finding for our purposes is that no significant relationship was found between the mothers' prenatal reports of anxiety or depression and infant sleep problems at 6 months of age. Analyses controlling for several possible confounding factors did find that high maternal prenatal depression and anxiety levels predicted the mothers' reports of whether or not their infants had overall sleep problems at 18 and 30 months of age, but still did not predict their reports, specifically, of infant night waking at these ages. This last finding is most relevant to our purposes, but these results also illustrate the limitations of research that depends solely on maternal reports.

Arguably, whether an infant wakes and signals parents in the night is a relatively factual event, whereas a broad maternal judgement of whether a child has a sleeping problem is more vague and subjective. In the ALSPAC study case, this measure incorporated parent reports of infant/toddler bedtime refusals, difficulties falling asleep, nightmares, and early waking in the morning, as well as night waking. The consequence is to highlight the need to be precise about the infant or toddler behaviour in question and for evidence that it has been measured accurately. Otherwise, it is understandable that many women who live in stressful environments find infant care to be challenging, but not at all clear that prenatal stress impairs the growth of their babies in a way that disrupts their ability to remain settled at night.

Although it is important not to be excessively critical of studies of stress and other pre- and perinatal adversities, the burden of scientific proof for these potential causes of infant night waking and signalling is the same as for any other putative causes. The difficulties faced by researchers are a challenge to design methodologically ingenious studies, not a reason for accepting evidence of associations as proof of causes. Perhaps because of the traditions in this area, some writers may have been more willing to accept the 'organic deficit' explanation of infant sleep problems than should be the case. The emergence of evidence that parenting behaviours contribute to whether or not infants over 3 months of age signal upon waking in the night, examined later in the chapter, may begin to redress the balance. More important still will be studies that examine how infant vulnerabilities and parenting interact over time to predict outcomes, but research of this sort is only beginning to get underway.

Although the overall result is uncertainty, this in itself has implications for how practitioners approach parents and infants with infant sleep problems. Where history taking suggests that pre- or perinatal adversities could be involved, infants may take longer to develop settled sleep–waking routines, and need more support in developing them, than other infants. We will see below that even infants with known neurodevelopmental disturbances can be helped by particular parenting strategies, so that discussing these with parents may prove to be helpful. Another point is that the existing evidence, particularly of the association with SIDS, may be considered sufficient for public health programmes designed to minimize drug, alcohol and cigarette use by pregnant women. Yet, a more common challenge for professionals may be how to advise parents, for instance, with occasional maternal alcohol consumption during pregnancy or commonplace childbirth complications who are worried that they are the cause of their infant's night waking. In such cases, it may be helpful to reduce any self-blame by emphasizing the distinction between associational evidence and proof of causation. Clarifying the lack of proof, and helping parents to focus on things they can change that are of proven effectiveness, may be particularly helpful.

Organic disturbance explanations 2: studies of infants with a low birth-weight

Another strategy for evaluating the importance of organic disturbances for infant night waking involves studying children who are born prematurely or with low birth-weight. Since very prematurely born children, particularly, suffer from a wide variety of organic disturbances, including neurodevelopmental disorders, they would be expected to have a high rate of sleeping problems if the organic approach to explanation is correct. Here, we are fortunate to again have evidence from the large-scale epidemiological studies carried out by Dieter Wolke and colleagues in Germany and, in this case, in Finland as well (Wolke et al., 1995a, 1998). The first of these studies involved four groups: (1) 284 very pre-term children (born before 32 weeks of gestation); (2) 1419 pre-term children (32–36 weeks of gestation); (3) 2724 full-term children (>36 weeks) who had been admitted to special care baby units because of concerns about their health; and (4) 689 full-term control children without health concerns. Each child was assessed longitudinally at 5, 20 and 56 months of age, using parental reports of how many nights per week, and number of times per night, the child awoke. In addition, a night-waking 'severity' index and measure of whether or not parents were distressed by their child's waking were obtained.

The results were complex because a great many comparisons were carried out, but they are simple to summarize. No evidence was found that very pre-term infants, pre-term infants, or full-term infants with neonatal health concerns, had more sleeping problems than the healthy full-term control infants. Indeed, at 5 months of age the pre-term infants woke less often and for shorter periods, during the night. Nor were the parents of pre-term infants, or full-term infants with neonatal health concerns, more upset about their infants' night waking. Analyses of the relationship between the number of prenatal and perinatal medical complications experienced by the infants and their night waking found no significant associations. Rates of night waking at least once per night during 5 or more nights per week in the full-term control infants were 23% at 5 months, 18% at 20 months, and 12% at 56 months, which are similar to the rates in other community studies. Significant, but moderate, stability over age in which infants had night-waking problems was found in each group. In keeping with the literature generally on children's sleep problems, children often fell out of, or entered, the sleep problem group at each successive age.

In a second study, Wolke and his colleagues went on to compare these German infants with groups in Finland selected in the same way (Wolke et al., 1998). The Finnish study included the same group types and methods as the German study, as well as large group sizes. The Finnish findings for night waking and signalling replicated the German findings. Both prematurely born groups and the full-term group with neonatal health concerns were reported by parents to be less likely to wake at night than the full-term control infants at 5 months. No group differences in rate of night waking were found at 20 and 56 months. In both Finnish and German samples, the single most important predictor of night waking at 5 months was the existence of breast-feeding at this age. We will return to this particular, and widely replicated, finding about feeding method below. Further support for Wolke and colleagues' findings comes from a recent Swiss longitudinal study of 130 pre-term and 75 full-term children (Iglowstein et al., 2006), which also found no difference in sleep–waking behaviour between these groups, in this case from birth to 10 years of age.

Organic disturbance explanations 3: studies of children with neurodevelopmental disorders

A third argument for attributing infant night waking to organic disturbances stems from the evidence that children with neurodevelopmental disorders are more likely than other children to have sleeping problems (Dahl & Harvey, 2007; Kotagal, 2007; Stores & Wiggs, 2001). In particular, children with autistic-spectrum disorders and hyperkinesis/attention deficit hyperactivity disorder (ADHD) are often reported by parents to have sleeping problems (Cortese & Yateman, 2006; Dahl & Harvey, 2007; Sadeh et al., 2006; Kotagal, 2007). Sleep–waking problems appear to be particularly prevalent among children with autistic-spectrum disorders, with 40 to 80% of such children reported to have sleep problems (Kotagal, 2007). As Ronald Dahl and Allison Harvey (2007) point out, one issue, particularly with the studies of children with ADHD, is that the evidence from studies based on parental measures of settling and night waking is much stronger than the evidence from objective measures comparing sleep–waking behaviour in children with ADHD with those without. This does not invalidate the parents' reports, since they may concern bedtime resistance or other child behaviours at night not measured adequately by objective assessments of sleep–waking. If so, this suggests that the effects of ADHD on children's sleep–waking may not be direct so much as mediated by parent–child interactions and conflicts. The use of stimulant medications to treat ADHD is a further complication.

The evidence for objectively measured sleep disturbances in children with autistic-spectrum disorders is stronger, with some studies also documenting disturbances in the release of melatonin, which plays a part in sleep–waking regulation, in autistic children (Kotagal, 2007; Wirojanan et al., 2009). There is also recent evidence that melatonin-based treatments improve sleeping in children with autism (Wirojanan et al., 2009). These findings make it likely that autistic children's sleep problems are sometimes directly due, at least in part, to a disorder of the organic systems that regulate sleep–waking. In addition, they illustrate the type of evidence needed in order to substantiate an organic causation. It is necessary both to have accurate measurements of the type of sleep–waking behaviours at issue and to be able to document the underlying physiological mechanisms involved.

For present purposes, however, the evidence from studies of children with autism and ADHD highlights three considerations of a rather different kind. The first is that it is not yet possible to diagnose these disorders accurately during infancy (Luyster et al., 2009), while there is no evidence at present that the sorts or severities of sleep problem behaviours shown by these children during infancy are distinct from those of other children. It follows that it is not possible to distinguish these cases during the infant period. The second consideration arises from the rarity of neurodevelopmental conditions of these kinds. Compared with the rate of around 25% of Western infants and young children reported to have sleeping problems, the rate for ADHD of around 5% (Polanczyk et al., 2007) and autistic-spectrum disorder of 0.06% (Kotagal, 2007) mean that few infants could have sleeping problems because of these conditions. In contrast, studies that have selected cases primarily because of sleeping or night-waking problems (rather than neurodevelopmental conditions) have found that most such children are healthy and do not have other disorders, except for persistent sleeping problems (Eaton-Evans & Dugdale, 1988; Ferber, 2006; Goodlin-Jones et al., 2001; Keener et al., 1988; Lozoff et al., 1985; Sadeh, 2006; Sadeh et al., 1991; Sadeh & Sivan, 2009; Wolke et al., 1995a). In short, because neurodevelopmental conditions such as autistic-spectrum disorder and ADHD are rare, they can account at most for only a small minority of cases where infants wake at night or have other sleeping problems.

Returning to our core concern with the implications of the research for professional practice, the third consideration is that behavioural methods, involving changes in parenting practices, are the most effective methods of treatment for sleep problems, even where children do have neurodevelopmental disorders. This conclusion, which emerged from a major review of the evidence about sleep problems among children with neurodevelopmental disorders by Gregory Stores and Luci Wiggs (2001), points to social interactions as an element in maintaining child sleep–waking behaviours and problems, even in cases where organic disorders are known to exist.

In summary, the research evidence about the contribution of organic disturbances to infant sleeping problems indicates that these are directly causal in only a small minority of cases. The clearest evidence for a direct effect of a physiological disorder on sleep–waking comes from studies of children with autistic-spectrum disorder, but these make up about 1% of the child population as a whole, compared with the 25% or greater prevalence rate for night waking and settling problems typically found in Western studies. A further consideration is that it is not usually possible to diagnose autism, ADHD or other neurodevelopmental disorders reliably in the infant period (Luyster et al., 2009), while there is no evidence as yet that they have distinct types or severities of sleep–waking problems that would allow them to be distinguished during infancy. It follows that, although healthcare professionals should be aware of the existence of such cases, they should expect them to be rare, and should keep in mind that it is not currently possible to identify them with any confidence during the infant period. Finally, although due allowance can be made where developmental disorders are suspected, the most suitable treatments for such cases are the same as those which are effective for infants and children in general. Chapters 9 and 10 translate this research evidence into recommendations for prevention, and treatment, respectively.

Organic disturbance explanations 4: asthma, eczema, allergies and intolerances

This set of medical conditions have in common that the child symptoms are considered to be due to endogenous susceptibilities but triggered or exacerbated by environmental factors. The conditions often run in families, but there is a good deal of controversy about their definition, prevalence, the extent to which they are due to internal factors, and the role of the environment in causing, and protecting against, their symptoms. For present purposes, an important distinction is between causation that involves a disturbance of the physiological systems that regulate sleep–waking versus the disruptive effects of disordered breathing, coughing or itching skin upon sleeping. In principle, the first of these involves a type of sleep disorder, while in the second case the sleep–waking problem is caused by (secondary to) the symptoms of a medical condition, such as asthma. The conditions have been included together in this section because there is evidence that they are a cause of persistent settling and night-waking problems in a minority of infants. Several studies have found that dermatitis is associated with parental reports of delayed infant and child sleep onset and inadequate sleep (Beattie & Lewis-Jones, 2006; Chamlin et al., 2005; Ferrer et al., 2010; Fukumizu et al., 2005; Ricci et al., 2007), while treatments that reduce dermatitis symptoms improve children's and parents' sleep and quality of life (Beattie & Lewis-Jones, 2006; Ferrer et al., 2010). Asthma, too, has been associated with poor sleep quality and frequent night waking (Owens, 2007).

Because asthma involves breathing difficulties, it is sometimes included in the broad category of 'sleep-disordered breathing' (SDB), which ranges in severity from snoring and wheezing through to 'obstructive sleep apnoea syndrome' in severe cases (Ferber, 2006; Sadeh & Sivan, 2009; Schechter, 2002). Sleep-disordered breathing has been linked with both concurrent and chronic sleep impairment (Gottlieb et al., 2003; Kozyrskyj et al., 2009; Neto et al., 2007; Sadeh & Sivan, 2009) and is found more often in prematurely born children than those born at term (Holditch-Davis, 2010). Since breathing can be disturbed by viral infections, as well as by atypical airway and respiratory anatomy or physiology, the syndrome probably involves a diverse set of causes, symptoms and severities (Bloomberg, 2009; A.L. Wright, 2002). Most studies are of children and adults, but SDB has been identified in infants (Montgomery-Downs & Gozal, 2006). Several studies have found that breast-feeding during the first 2–5 months reduces the prevalence or severity of SDB symptoms (Just et al., 2010; Klinnert et al., 2001; Montgomery-Downs et al., 2007; Tarazona et al., 2010; Thygarajan & Burks, 2008; A.L. Wright, 2002). Estimates of its prevalence depend on whether individual or multiple symptoms, and isolated or recurrent episodes, are counted. Surveys indicate that up to 40–50% of infants have occasional wheeze, reducing to around 20% for recurrent cases (Ly et al., 2006; Neto et al., 2007) and just 3% for 'frequent wheeze' (Ly et al., 2006). Snoring during 2 or more days/week was reported by 12% of parents of 944 infants and toddlers in Kentucky, USA (Montgomery-Downs & Gozal, 2006). Treatments in severe and chronic cases of SDB may involve supplemental oxygen (Sadeh & Sivan, 2009) and surgery, including adenoid/tonsillectomy, which is usually delayed until older ages (Benninger & Walner, 2007; Ivanhoe et al., 2007; Sadeh & Sivan, 2009; Schechter, 2002). Continuous positive airway pressure masks and nebulizer hoods during sleep have also proved helpful (Ferber, 2006; Saskin, 2008).

The inclusion of sleep apnoea and various types of SDB in sleep classification systems attests to their importance as a set of medical conditions that can disrupt sleeping. One proviso is that the evidence about SDB links it to sleep impairment in general, rather than to persistence of night waking and signalling after 3 months of age. We do not know what percentage of night-waking cases is due to this cause, but in principle it is likely to be rare and cases should be apparent because of their symptoms. Virtually all studies, too, depend on parental report and there is a striking lack of objective measurement of infants' sleep amounts, patterns and quality in this area. One exception, a study comparing 40 asthmatic 8 to 15-year-olds with non-asthmatics on objective measures, found no differences in amounts of sleep, but the asthmatic children were more active during sleep and had a lower percentage of Quiet Sleep (Sadeh et al., 1998). Within the asthmatic group, severely asthmatic children's longest sleep periods were shorter and they awoke more often, suggesting a greater disruption to their sleep (Sadeh et al., 1998).

For primary healthcare professionals, these findings imply a need to be alert to infants who show SDB symptoms, as well as to cases involving eczema. Where cases are identified, the variations that exist in symptom severity and persistence, as well as simple explanations such as respiratory tract infections, need to be looked into. Specialist referral may be warranted where symptoms are severe and persistent.

Organic disturbance explanations 5: teething

Both parents and medical staff believe that 'teething' causes infant sleep and other disturbances (Wake et al., 2000; Zuckerman et al., 1987). Although teething could be considered a normal 'developmental' process, it is included in this section because this explanation assumes that an organic condition, involving painful penetration of the gums by emerging teeth, is a cause of some infants' sleep problems.

Based on parental reports, the commonest age for the emergence of first teeth is approximately 7–8 months of age (Baykan et al., 2004; Tighe & Roe, 2007), with the period around 12–15 months being the peak for reported teething symptoms (Tighe & Roe, 2007). In the most careful study to date, 21 children in suburban day nurseries were followed from 6 to 24 months of age, with daily gum inspections, temperature measurements and health symptom checklists being completed by staff and parents (Wake et al., 2000). Altogether, the assessments included the eruption of 90 teeth, and comparison of 236 'tooth days' with 895 'non-tooth days'. The study found no evidence of a relationship between tooth emergence and sleep problems, temperature increases, or any symptoms of poor health. In spite of this, all the parents reported retrospectively that their infants had suffered from teething symptoms.

Other studies with larger numbers of infants, but less well controlled measurements, have found associations between teething and infant night-waking problems and other ailments (Macknin et al., 2000). Even so, the relationships were weak and no particular symptoms occurred more than 20% more often during teething than non-teething days. In a helpful review of these studies, Tighe and Roe (2007) pointed out that there is no pattern of symptoms that can reliably distinguish teething from any other potential cause of the symptoms, while even the associations that have been reported do not link teething with serious problems. Similarly, Sadeh and Sivan (2009) concluded that, if teething disrupts sleep at all, it usually does so for no more than a day or 2 around about the emergence of a new tooth. There is a need for larger-scale studies and more careful measurements, but the implication of the evidence so far is that teething is unlikely to be a factor in cases of persistent night waking and signalling.

Individual differences in infants' constitutional dispositions and vulnerabilities

The findings reviewed in previous sections of this chapter make it unlikely that infant night waking and signalling is commonly a direct result of an organic disturbance in the child. That does not mean that individual differences in infant's make-up have no part to play. Studies of children's development in general have made it abundantly clear that the biological make-up of children almost always contributes to variations in their behavioural characteristics (Rutter, 2006). In most cases, however, these contributions have proved to be subtle, indirect and interactive, rather than direct effects that are sufficient to explain the behaviours in question (Rutter, 2006).

Infants' biological predispositions are likely to affect their sleep–waking behaviour in at least two ways. First, studies in older children have begun to produce robust evidence that children's genotypes influence their behavioural characteristics (Arseneault et al., 2003; Kochanska et al., 2009; Plomin et al., 1990; Rutter, 2006). In many cases, these genetic dispositions are thought to make some children 'resilient' or 'vulnerable' to environmental adversities and resources, so that problems develop as a result of interactions between child and environmental factors, rather than either of these in isolation. To some extent, this way of thinking is akin to the notion of 'temperament', except that the notion of temperament is more static and permanent, whereas vulnerabilities and resiliencies need not be stable. These concepts focus attention on interactions and developmental processes in a more dynamic way (National Scientific Council on the Developing Child, 2010) which is why these terms, rather than the concept of temperament, have been used here. For our purposes, problematic infant sleep–waking behaviours could arise from a cumulative process of interaction between child vulnerabilities and the parenting environment, rather than directly from a disturbance of infant sleep–waking physiology.

As well as genetic influences, physical adversities in the prenatal uterine environment or early postnatal environment may interfere with growth, delaying or interfering with developmental processes. The possibility that prenatal stress might operate in this way was considered earlier. Similarly, a prenatal nutritional deficiency or drug or alcohol exposure might impair foetal growth, but the original deficiency would have ceased to exist at the time of the problematic sleep–waking behaviour, which occurs at a later age. This is sometimes referred to as an effect on the *programming* of growth. In such cases, the effect might be to delay or restrict normal developmental processes, rather than to lead to a permanent organic deficit in sleep–waking physiology.

Both genetic and growth programming explanations require a distinction to be made between the factor that originally *initiated* the causal sequence and the factors involved in *maintaining* the sleep–waking problem over age. The outcome, in our case infant night waking and signalling, could be mediated by the postnatal environment, including the cues provided by the parenting environment and by the infant's ability to detect and learn from these cues.

At older ages, 1–3% of children have been estimated to have sleep problems due to organic 'bio-maturational disorders' and organic para-somnias, compared with a prevalence of 15–35% for 'psychosocial cases' (France & Blampied, 2004). These figures are best estimates, rather than based on precise evidence. Nevertheless, it is reasonable to expect that a variety of dispositional factors and developmental processes will also con-tribute to night waking in early infancy. For instance, Beth Goodlin-Jones and colleagues (Burnham et al., 2002) found that infants who resettled by themselves had higher levels of Quiet Sleep than infants who signalled to parents in the night. Since Quiet Sleep increases with maturity, this finding suggests that individual differences in infant neuromaturational charac-teristics might have a part to play.

Models of children's sleep development that involve cumulative interactions between the infant's biological dispositions and the parenting environment have recently been put forward (Goodlin-Jones et al., 2000; Sadeh et al., 2010) and are likely to prove important in guiding research. However, because so few studies have tackled this issue, the main impli-cation of this (dearth of) evidence is to point to the need for fine-grained, longitudinal research. In the meantime, there are two important implica-tions for professional practice. The first is the need to keep in mind that individual vulnerabilities and resiliencies are likely to affect infants' ability to respond to the environment, including the parenting environment, so that some infants will take longer, and require more support, than others. The second is the need to focus on developmental processes and the infant–parent interactions that guide them.

Developmental contributions to infant sleep–waking problems

Chapter 5 concluded that 'The critical question is not what causes the onset of sleeping problems but why some infants do not follow the typical Western pattern of stopping night waking and signalling at around 3 months of age.' Here, we return to this question and to its implication that most cases of infant night waking are the result of individual variations in normal developmental processes rather than the direct consequences of organic disturbance. Although our focus is on infancy, it is helpful to begin with a brief summary of the evidence about adult sleeping, since this is the end-point for infant sleep–waking development and much of this process is accomplished in early childhood. More is known, too, about the neurological basis for sleep–waking in adults than infants, much of which is relevant to babies.

Except for those in 'siesta' cultures, most adults have one long sleep period per 24 hours, which usually occurs during the darkness of night. There is extensive evidence that the brain's suprachiasmatic nucleus provides the biological 'clock' upon which this sleep–waking cycle and other circadian rhythms are based (J. Horne, 2006; Jenni & Carskadon, 2007; Rivkees, 2007). As those of us who cross time zones and experience jet-lag know, the clock is slow to adjust, but can be reset by regularly occurring environmental stimuli. In particular, light plays a central role in resetting the clock and our eyes contain photoreceptors that are specialized for this purpose, quite separate from those involved in vision (J. Horne, 2006; Rivkees, 2007; van Gelder, 2004). Other environmental stimuli are less well understood, but a dynamic interplay between a variety of external and endogenous regulatory influences is probably involved. Italian research by Piero Salzarulo and his colleagues (Salzarulo et al., 2002), for example, has identified rising body temperature and rapid eye movement (REM) sleep as precursors of spontaneous waking in adults.

The most widely accepted theory about endogenous regulation of sleep–waking is Alexander Borbély's two-process model (Borbély, 1982; Jenni & Carskadon, 2007), which was later elaborated by Borbély and his colleagues to include three processes (Borbély & Achermann, 1999). As well as the circadian mechanism described above, which regulates *when* sleep and waking occur, this theory includes the following.

1   A homeostatic process involving sleep need, which mediates the rise of sleep propensity during waking and its dissipation during sleep. Evidence for this mechanism includes the much replicated finding that sleep deprivation results in a 'rebound' increase in sleep during subsequent, unrestricted, 24-hour periods (J. Horne, 2006; Walsh & Lindblom, 2008). This mechanism influences sleep length and amount and is presumed to be particularly important during early childhood, since infants sleep a great deal.

2   An ultradian process occurring within a sleep period and responsible for the alternation of the two main sleep states, REM and non-REM sleep. In adults, these REM and non-REM sleep states alternate through the night, with each cycle lasting for about 90–110 minutes (Hirshkowitz et

al., 1997; Jenni & Carskadon, 2007; Lozoff & Zuckerman, 1988). The cycles involve variations of sleep depth and brain and body activity, so that adults do not remain soundly asleep at night for continuous periods of 8 or more hours of time. Rather, adult sleep involves brief arousals, awakenings and re-settlings, so that continuous periods of settled sleep do not usually last more than a few hours (Goodlin-Jones et al., 2000; Halász et al., 2004; Montemitro et al., 2008). As Péter Halász and his Hungarian colleagues put it, 'Spontaneous arousals are natural guests of the sleeping brain' (Halász et al., 2004, p. 14). For our purposes, an important finding is that adults arouse more often and readily during REM sleep than deeper, non-REM, sleep states (Halász et al., 2004; J. Horne, 2006; Salzarulo et al., 2002).

Under naturalistic circumstances, these three endogenous systems work together to modulate sleep and waking lengths and patterns. Although the effects of light on the circadian mechanism have been studied most, the length of sleeping is known to also be influenced by other features of the external environment. However, there is a debate among adult sleep researchers about the extent to which sleep is moulded by the environment and, correspondingly, about the limits of biological flexibility. For instance, the eminent sleep researcher Jim Horne has argued that adults often sleep longer at weekends not to make up for a sleep deficit but because they can lengthen sleep self-indulgently, just as it is possible to eat or drink more on some occasions than others (Harrison & Horne, 1995; J. Horne, 2008). He supports this argument with historical evidence that, before the availability of electric light, Inuit adults in the Arctic Circle used to sleep up to 14 hours per 24 hours in the dark winter months, compared with around 6 hours in the summer time (J. Horne, 2008). Similarly, there is evidence that domesticated cats and enclosed farm animals sleep much more than their freeranging counterparts (J. Horne, 2008). Horne argues that, given the right environment, adults can learn to increase their settled sleep periods considerably beyond the statistical norm of 7–7½ hours per 24 hours that has emerged from epidemiological studies of adult sleeping. The implication is that usual adult sleep length need not reflect sleep 'need' directly – and that adult sleep amounts are strongly influenced by the environment and involve learning. Not all sleep researchers accept Horne's arguments, but they are food for thought when considering the influence of nature and nurture on sleep period length.

Returning to the early stages of development, truly remarkable changes in the organization of children's sleep–waking behaviour take place during the first year of age. These features have been described in many studies, albeit in most cases involving Western infants and based mainly on parental reports, which tend to inflate amounts of sleep (Iglowstein et al., 2003; Sadeh, 1996). Keeping those limitations and the adult findings in mind the changes – and ages when the changes are typically accomplished by Western infants – are as follows.

1 Variations in 24 hour amounts of sleep

Perhaps the most obvious difference between adult and infant sleep–waking lies in the amount of sleep taken, with newborn infants sleeping around 16 hours/24 hours, about twice as much as adults (Heraghty et al., 2008; Kleitman & Engelmann, 1953; Parmelee et al., 1961, 1964; Sadeh, 1996). In practice, this particular developmental process is gradual and spread across infancy and childhood, so that the mean 24-hour sleep amount reduces to about 14 hours by 1 year and 11 hours by 5 years of age (Heraghty et al., 2008; Iglowstein et al., 2003). As a consequence, the variability between infants is more striking than the variability in their average sleep amounts over age. For example, the range of individual difference in 24-hour sleep amounts found in a community sample of 6-month-old Swiss infants (between the 2nd and 98th percentile) was between 10.5 and 18 hours per 24 hours (Iglowstein et al., 2003) and similar variability has been reported for American and Canadian infants (Sadeh et al., 2009).

This variability between individuals remains substantial but lessens with age (Iglowstein et al., 2003). Following Borbély's model, it is usually assumed that the high amount of sleep in young children reflects a high sleep need. Why this should be the case is poorly understood, as is the function of sleep generally. Explanations often infer that sleep is necessary for physiological and psychological processes involved in growth and development and there is firm evidence that sleep enhances some types of memory trace and learning in adults, children and infants (Bernier et al., 2010; J. Horne, 2006; Kopasz et al., 2010; Roth et al., 2010). Sleep probably serves both psychological and physiological needs, but why so much more time is occupied by sleep in infants than adults, and why this amount varies so greatly between infants, are not at all clear.

2 Reduction in the frequency, and increase in length, of waking and sleeping periods

During the first few weeks of age, most babies wake frequently during the day and night-time. As newborns, they typically sleep for 3 or 4 hours at a time, then wake for shorter periods, but with a great deal of variability in the length of both sleeping and waking periods (Kleitman & Engelmann, 1953; Parmelee et al., 1961, 1964). With increasing age, the sleep and waking periods lengthen and frequencies decline (Bamford et al., 1990; Jacklin et al., 1980; Kleitman & Engelmann, 1953). By 1 year of age, infants typically have one long sleep period, together with one or two shorter 'naps', per 24 hours (Anders, 2004; Heraghty et al., 2008; Mindell, 2008).

3 Reduction of feed frequency, including loss of the midnight to 6 am feed

Because they appear hungry and take feeds readily, we say that infants 'wake up for feeding', implying that the waking serves the nutritional purpose of enabling growth. Growth is assumed to be a baby's priority, while the immaturity of the infant digestive system leads to the need for frequent feeds. Most parents expect 1-month-old infants to wake for night-time feeds (Klackenberg, 1968). Intervals between feeds increase with age (Glotzbach et al., 1994; Kleitman & Engelmann, 1953). Most Western infants develop the ability to remain settled for periods of 5 or more hours without feeding, with this longer fast typically occurring during the night-time, by 12 weeks of age (Kleitman & Engelmann, 1953; Wright, 1993).

4 Circadian organization of sleep–waking

This involves a consolidation of sleep into long periods in the night-time, with waking being concentrated into the daytime. It is sometimes said that newborn babies entirely lack a circadian organization in their sleep–waking, but this conclusion goes beyond our current knowledge, since several studies have found more sleeping during the night than daytime in the newborn period (Kleitman & Engelmann, 1953; Sadeh et al., 1996). It is, then, possible that newborns have a rudimentary day: night difference in sleep–waking. In any case, clear signs of a circadian organization have repeatedly been observed by about 6 weeks of age (Bamford et al., 1990; St James-Roberts et al., 2001) and this has been reliably reported by 12 weeks of age in studies spanning several generations and a variety of societies (Henderson et al., 2010; Jenni & Carskadon, 2007; Moore & Ucko, 1957; Parmelee et al., 1964).

For infants, this is an amazing achievement in just a few weeks of time. Indeed, the transition from sleep–waking that is more or less evenly distributed across the day and night-time to a circadian cycle involving consolidation of sleep into prolonged periods at night (and waking in the day) is among the most remarkable achievements of early childhood. It is illustrated in Figure 6.1, which shows data from the 'COSI' (Crying Or Sleeping Infant) study, a randomized controlled trial that invited parents of newborn infants to adopt one of three forms of infant care: a limit-setting 'behavioural' programme designed to promote settled infant night-time behaviour; an educational leaflet programme; or a control group involving routine services (St James-Roberts et al., 2001). There are differences between the three infant groups in this study after 6 weeks of age, which will be discussed in detail later in this chapter. However, the group similarities are much more remarkable. At 3 weeks of age, only about 20% of infants had long settled periods during the night (defined as 5 hours or

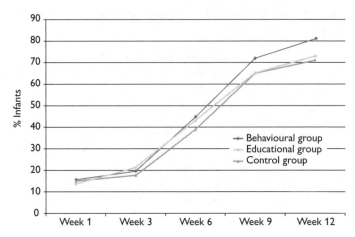

Figure 6.1 Crying Or Sleeping Infant (COSI) study data showing the percentages of infants in each group with night-time sleep periods >5 hours. It can be seen there is a rapid increase in long settled sleep periods at night in the first 3 months of age (redrawn from St James-Roberts et al., 2001).

more in this study), whereas the proportion of infants with these long periods without waking and signalling increased to around 70–80% in all three groups by 12 weeks of age.

The graph in Figure 6.1 includes average figures and some infants are likely to show this change somewhat earlier, or later, while it is also important to bear in mind that the results come solely from UK babies. Still, the reliability of curves of this shape across most babies in many studies suggests that Figure 6.1 reflects a strong developmental propensity among infants in general, at least in Western societies. Many writers have speculated that this process has evolutionary origins, permitting infants to coincide their social interactions and learning periods with those of their parents. Mirroring this process, at least in part, the amount of daytime sleep declines markedly by 6–8 months of age (Sadeh et al., 2009). Most toddlers continue to have a daytime nap: in Iglowstein and colleagues' Swiss cases, 94.6% had a nap at 18 months, declining to 35.4% at 4 years of age (Iglowstein et al., 2003).

5 Establishment of moderately stable individual differences in sleep habits

A number of well-known public figures have claimed to need very little sleep, and we are familiar with the idea that some adults are early wakers who shine in the morning ('larks'), while others are at their best at the end of the day ('night owls'). More controversially, a number of researchers have claimed that individual differences in sleep habits are established in early infancy. As we have seen, there is some truth in these claims, in that many infants who acquire the ability to remain settled for long periods in the night by 5 months of age continue to be 'good sleepers'. However, the pattern over age is often more complicated than this generalization implies, and we do not have enough evidence to know whether infant patterns predict adult habits to any substantial degree.

6 Changes in qualitative aspects of sleep: sleep subtypes, bodily movements and arousals

The two main adult sleep substates – REM and non-REM sleep, are not clearly discernible in newborns, so that researchers use a combination of behavioural and electroencephalogram (EEG) criteria to distinguish between Active Sleep (considered an immature form of REM) and Quiet Sleep (which is analogous to non-REM), with a proportion of sleep time labelled 'indeterminate' sleep state (Heraghty et al., 2008; Peirano et al., 2003). Newborns have proportionately more Active Sleep (and less Quiet Sleep) than older children and typically begin sleep periods with Active Sleep, while older children and adults usually do so with non-REM sleep (Anders, 2004; Burnham et al., 2002; Fagioli & Salzarulo, 1982; Heraghty et al., 2008; Hoppenbrowers et al., 1982; Jenni et al., 2004; Mindell et al., 1999; Peirano et al., 2003).

The reason for the preponderance of REM sleep in early infancy is unclear, but has been attributed to REM's importance for establishing neuronal connections (Peirano et al., 2003; Roffwarg et al., 1966). Sleep usually begins with non-REM sleep by about 3 months of age (Heraghty et al., 2008; Peirano & Algarin, 2007) and REM gradually moves later in sleep periods. The REM and non-REM sleep states alternate through the night, with each cycle lasting around 50–60 minutes in infancy, giving way to the adult length of 90–110 minutes by school age (Hoppenbrowers et al., 1982; Jenni & Carskadon, 2007).

The inhibition of muscle tone that characterizes adult REM sleep is deficient in early infancy and becomes apparent by around 6 months of age. In keeping with this, studies of spontaneous body movements have shown a marked reduction over the first 6 months (Coons & Guilleminault, 1982; Montemitro et al., 2008). Infant spontaneous arousals, and 'arousability', during sleep also change with age (Kato et al., 2006; Montemitro et al., 2008; Richardson et al., 2008). Arousals and brief waking periods continue and are normative throughout childhood, just as in adulthood (Sadeh, 2000; Tikotsky & Sadeh, 2001). In one study of 5-year-olds, only 3 of the 59 children assessed by objective, actigraphy, methods did not wake at least once per night (Tikotsky & Sadeh, 2001).

Some of these changes, such as those involving REM and non-REM sleep are subtle, so that parents may be unaware of them. Since, though, it can be difficult to distinguish a sleeping infant showing robust REM from one who is awake during early infancy, parents may find that this information helps them to avoid picking up an infant who is still asleep by mistake (Ferber, 2006). Parents may find it helpful, too, to know that infants reduce their limb and body movements while asleep during the first 6 months of age, particularly if they bed-share with their baby. One other reason for the importance of this evidence is that infants, like adults, arouse more readily in REM than non-REM sleep states (Don & Waters, 2003; R. Horne et al., 2002; Lozoff & Zuckerman, 1988; Montemitro et al., 2008; Mosko et al., 1996). Because the amounts and arrangement of REM and non-REM sleep undergo such major transformations during infancy, individual differences in the development of these endogenous cycles might make some infants particularly easy to arouse and wake up. Aspects of the sleep environment, such as bed-sharing, may enhance this tendency, as discussed below.

The division of our knowledge about sleep–waking development into the six sections above is somewhat arbitrary and should not be taken to mean that six distinctly different processes or phenomena exist. It is likely that some of the changes overlap and reflect common mechanisms, so that, for instance, processes two to four above are often drawn together under the general rubric of 'sleep consolidation'. In fact, we do not know yet whether one process or a number of quite separate systems are involved, while we will see below that the causal links between feeding, nutrition and sleep–waking remain controversial. The intended value of this six-category description lies in capturing the extraordinary complexity of the changes that take place in so short a time and indicating the developmental processes that may contribute to the occurrence of night waking and signalling. We now turn to the role of the environment in mediating these changes.

Environmental contributions to infant night waking 1: feeding and nutritional factors

Following what has been learned in adults, it is likely that both endogenous infant and external, environmental, factors influence how the process of infant sleep–waking development described above takes place. Since infant night waking prior to 3 months of age is thought to reflect the need for frequent feeding, nutritional processes are probably involved. For instance, infants' stomachs may need to be large enough to contain sufficient milk before they can sustain a long period without feeding – which may explain the finding that heavier babies at birth sleep through the night at a younger age (Adams et al., 2004).

The idea that feeding contributes to infant sleep–waking behaviour is also supported by the consistent evidence that formula-fed infants remain settled for sustained periods at night, and stop having a feed between midnight and

6 am, at an earlier age than breast-fed infants (Anuntaseree et al., 2008; DeLeon & Karraker, 2007; Eaton-Evans & Dugdale, 1988; Elias et al., 1986; Goodlin-Jones et al., 2001; Hiscock & Wake, 2001; Klackenberg, 1968; Lee, 2000; Lozoff & Zuckerman, 1988; Sadeh et al., 2009; Schmid et al., 2010a). For example, Marjorie Elias and colleagues followed 16 infants whose mothers were La Leche League members and breast-fed their babies up to 2 years of age, compared with 16 'standard-care' infants who were weaned off breast-feeding at a median age of 13 months. Both groups received supplementary foods and the researchers discounted this as a variable. According to sleep diaries kept by the mothers, the standard-care group increased their maximum night-time sleep bouts to a median length of 8 hours at 4 months, and 9 hours at 24 months, of age. In contrast, the persistently breast-fed infants' maximum sleep bout length was maintained at 3–5 hours, and was just 4.8 hours at 24 months of age.

The most obvious explanation of this finding is nutritional. That is, breast-fed infants are assumed to wake more often at night until a later age because of nutritional differences in the content of breast milk, compared with bottle-fed formula milk. Parents, particularly, often attribute night waking to the constituents of feed types (Crocetti et al., 2004), believing that a dense or heavy feed helps infants to remain asleep – the so-called 'gravity theory' of infant sleeping. Although this remains controversial, some studies have found an association between the introduction of weaning foods and a reduction in number and increase in the length of sleep periods (Bamford et al., 1990). Varying formula-feed composition between the day and night, too, has been found to increase the night-time consolidation of sleep (Cubero et al., 2006). In keeping with this nutritional perspective, Nicholas Blurton-Jones pointed out in 1972 that animal species that have long feed intervals tend to feed their young on milk with a high fat and protein content, whereas frequent feeders have a lower fat/protein composition in maternal milk. Humans, like other primates, have comparatively low fat/protein content breast milk, which Blurton-Jones took to imply a need for frequent breast-feeding (Blurton-Jones, 1972).

Although nutritional mechanisms may well explain why babies wake often in the first few weeks, it is less clear whether they can account for the *changes* in sleep–waking and feeding behaviour that occur as they get older. Scottish research by the psychologist Peter Wright (Wright, 1993) found that the amount of breast milk taken at each feed was similar from birth to 4 weeks of age, but infants typically showed a circadian pattern by 8 weeks, taking the largest feed at the beginning of each day. Teresa Pinilla and Leann Birch (1993), too, found that the early morning feed increased progressively in the first 8 weeks, suggesting that this was due to the increase in night-time feed intervals. If so, this suggests an effect of sleep–waking interval on amount of feeding, whereas it is more difficult to understand how a larger feed at the start of the day would lead to a longer inter-feed interval the following night. Furthermore, by 4 to 6 months of age a second change takes place, with the largest feed now occurring at the end of the day (Wright, 1993). Wright explained this finding by suggesting that infants have adapted by this age to anticipate the coming fast (Wright, 1993). The implication is that an additional process over and above nutrition itself – anticipatory learning – may exert an effect on the organization of feeding behaviour by 4–6 months of age.

The question these findings give rise to is whether nutritional needs continue to drive sleeping and waking, or whether sleeping and waking are controlled by other, non-nutritional, influences (such as the circadian and homeostatic mechanisms contained in Borbély and his colleagues' model) with increasing age. In support of this possibility, Igino Fagioli and colleagues (1988) found a normal development of day:night sleep–waking cycles in infants over 4 months of age even when they were fed by continuous intravenous drips. In multivariate analyses, the Elias study of persistently breast-fed babies described above found that sharing a bed was the most important single predictor of sleep bout length, concluding that bed-sharing and breast-feeding added together to predict sleep bout length (Elias et al., 1986). Unfortunately, the small number of cases in this study and overlap of bed-sharing with breast-feeding prevented the two from being satisfactorily disentangled. What the findings do imply, however, is that nutritional needs alone cannot account satisfactorily for the changes in sleep–waking and feeding patterns that occur after the first few months of infancy. Instead, it is necessary to look elsewhere – to growth and maturational processes and to non-nutritional aspects of the care-giving environment – in order to understand how infant sleep–waking develops. Many researchers have highlighted the social–environmental differences that exist between breast and bottle feeding, as distinct from the nutritional differences in the milk provided by these two approaches. Several lines of evidence suggest that, after the first few weeks, these other environmental factors may be more important sources of sleep–waking organization than milk constituents.

Environmental contributions to infant night waking 2: studies of sleeping arrangements, SIDS and limit-setting care

During the 1980s and 1990s, a simple change in the arrangement of infants' sleeping environments proved hugely important in reducing the rate of SIDS in countries all over the world. The 'Back to Sleep' campaign and studies associated with it showed that putting infants down to sleep on their backs (rather than stomachs) reduced the rate of SIDS by almost 50% (Blair et al., 2009; McKenna, 2005; American Academy of Pediatrics, 2005). In addition, this set of findings provided a highly compelling message about the importance of the external, caretaking environment for infants' regulation of their physiology. Evidence accumulated that infants often sleep longer and more soundly, and arouse less often, when prone on their stomachs than when supine on their backs, and it seemed likely that some parents become aware of this and put infants down to sleep in a prone position to facilitate sleep, inadvertently increasing the risk of SIDS (R. Horne et al., 2002; van Sleuwen et al., 2007). More recently, attention has shifted to other risk factors, including the possibility that sharing a bed with a parent or parents increases the likelihood of SIDS. This more recent literature is complex, contentious and only partly relevant to our main focus on infant sleeping. We will need to return to it later, since it is clearly vital that any recommendations about parenting methods designed to prevent problematic infant night waking should not increase the risk of SIDS. For the moment, though, the importance of this research into the risks and benefits of bed-sharing has been to provide a rich source of evidence about cultural differences in family sleeping arrangements and their consequences for infant sleep–waking behaviour.

As others have pointed out, bed-sharing between parents and children has been the normal arrangement for much of human history and continues to predominate in many countries of the world (Jenni & O'Connor, 2005; Owens, 2004; Yang & Hahn, 2002). The shift towards infants sleeping in separate beds or cots in the same room as parents, or in separate rooms, seems to be a feature of Western industrial societies and to be the outcome of a variety of economic and social-ideological factors. For example, a city-dwelling family's income may affect the number of rooms their home contains, or increase the number of individuals living together, placing constraints on their ability to provide separate rooms and/or beds (Lozoff et al., 1996; Vemulapalli et al., 2004). If so, this seems likely to affect low-income families most and to increase room and bed-sharing in modern societies more than to reduce it.

Other authors have argued that separate sleeping arrangements are largely the results of cultural beliefs and customs. Contemporary American and German societies, for example, emphasize individual autonomy, leading to separate sleeping locations and parenting practices that encourage infants to settle by themselves. In contrast, Japanese, Korean and Mayan traditions emphasize familial bonds and interdependence, leading to more proximal sleeping arrangements (Jenni & O'Connor, 2005; Morelli et al., 1992; Valentin, 2005; Yang & Hahn, 2002).

The English anthropologist Helen Ball (2007) has provided evidence that bed-sharing facilitates breast-feeding at night and is associated with per-sistence of breast-feeding beyond the first few weeks of infancy, which is considered desirable by medical authorities. The bed-sharing mothers questioned by Hauck et al. (2008), too, reported that bed-sharing made breast-feeding easier, as well as helping mother and baby to sleep better. If so, this may help to explain some reports that bed-sharing is gaining in popularity in Western societies (Goldberg & Keller, 2007; McKenna & Volpe, 2007; Willinger et al., 2003). Exclusive breast-feeding until 6 months of age reduces rates of infant gastrointestinal infection and results in more rapid maternal weight loss and delayed return of menstrual periods (Kramer & Kakuma, 2009). Whether bed-sharing is good because it promotes breast-feeding, which contributes to infant health, or bad because it increases the likelihood of SIDS, remains a contentious question (McKenna & Gettler, 2010).

Returning to our central concern with infant night waking, the SIDS-related research on bed-sharing has added to the rather sparse cross-cultural literature on sleeping to provide extensive evidence that routine bed-sharing through the night is associated with infant night waking and signalling beyond the first 3 months of age (Adams et al., 2004; DeLeon & Karraker, 2007; Elias et al., 1986; Fukumizu et al., 2005; Hiscock & Wake, 2001; Jenni et al., 2005; Kelmanson, 2010; Lee, 1992; Louis & Govindama, 2004; Lozoff et al., 1996; Lozoff & Zuckerman, 1988; Sadeh, 2003; Santos et al., 2008; Zuckerman et al., 1987). In order to interpret these findings, though, several distinctions need to be made. First, it is important to distinguish the term 'co-sleeping' (which is sometimes used to refer to sleeping in the same room, or side-by-side on separate mattresses) from bed-sharing, and to distinguish occasional bed-sharing for short periods (for instance for feeding) from bed-sharing that occurs regularly and through the night. It is the latter that shows the clearest association with persistence of infant night waking and signalling (Adams et al., 2004; St James-Roberts et al., 2006). Second, since many Western parents respond to their infant's night waking and signalling by taking her into their bed, it is necessary to distinguish 'reactive' bed-sharing of this sort from planned bed-sharing that was initiated from birth (Lozoff et al., 1984; Gaylor et al., 2005). Otherwise, the direction of causation is obscured. Third, since bed-sharing often occurs in conjunction with breast-feeding and may help to sustain it, it is important to distinguish between the effects of nutritional and non-nutritional aspects of feeding and care.

With these distinctions in mind, the combined findings from two different sorts of study provide evidence that parenting methods that include bed-sharing maintain infant signalling in the night beyond 3 months of age, while limit-setting parental care encourages infants to stop signalling. The first type of study, which uses comparative methods, can be illustrated by the three-group (London, Copenhagen and proximal care) cross-cultural study of parenting and infant crying and sleeping that we first encountered in Chapter 4. In this study, both proximal care and Copenhagen babies were breast-fed more often than London babies, but proximal care babies (the group who shared a bed with their parents throughout the night), were more likely to wake and signal their parents during the night at 12 weeks of age (St James-Roberts et al., 2006). Since the parental care differences were adopted at birth, this suggests that something about bed-sharing through the night, rather than solely the content of breast milk, might be responsible for the continuation of night waking and signalling.

Unfortunately, this study did not collect night-waking data after 12 weeks of age. However, many other comparative studies have found associations between bed-sharing and infant night waking at older ages (Elias et al., 1986; Fukumizu et al., 2005; Latz et al., 1999; Lozoff et al., 1996; Mao et al., 2004; Mindell et al., 2010; Louis & Govindama, 2004; Ramos et al., 2007; Santos et al., 2008). Many studies, too, have found that limit-setting parenting methods, including those that encourage autono-mous infant settling, lead to settled infant behaviour during the night, (Adair et al., 1992; Kerr et al., 1996; Mindell et al., 2010; Pinilla & Birch, 1993; St James-Roberts et al., 2001; Symon et al., 2005; Sadeh et al., 2009; St James-Roberts et al., 2006; Wolfson et al., 1992). In contrast, parenting methods that involve high amounts of parental contact and intervention at infant bedtimes are associated with increased infant night waking (Adair et al., 1991; Anuntaseree et al., 2008; Cronin et al., 2008; Mindell et al., 2010; Sadeh et al., 2010). The consistency of these findings across separate studies of sleeping arrangements is remarkable. However, it needs to be kept in mind that comparative studies of this type do not allow the control of extraneous factors needed in order to establish causation. By themselves, they do not rule out the possibility that uncontrolled factors, such as the nutritional characteristics of breast-milk, influence bed-sharing infants to continue night waking and signalling.

The evidence in this regard comes from four separate randomized con-trolled trials of the effect of limit-setting, 'behavioural' parenting pro-grammes on infant night waking and signalling. Parenting programmes of this type might be considered the antithesis of proximal care, since they involve introducing clearly defined limits on infant behaviour, rather than responding to infant demands. In all four cases, these studies found that infants whose parents adopted 'limit-setting' methods of care were more likely than other infants to remain settled at night by 12 weeks of age (Pinilla & Birch, 1993; St James-Roberts et al., 2001; Symon et al., 2005; Wolfson et al., 1992). Two of the studies found that limit-setting parenting reduced night waking and signalling among breast-fed infants (the Symon and Wolfson studies did not report feeding methods). The largest of these studies, a UK trial called COSI, included some 200 infants in each group, was carried out in a health service setting, and included measures of parental approval as well as infant behaviour, adding to the evidence that this approach is effective in practice (St James-Roberts et al., 2001).

The advice given to parents who received the limit-setting guidance in the COSI study is summarized in Box 6.1 and given in full in Appendix II. As can be seen, it involves introducing a structured environment designed to help infants to distinguish between day and night and does not involve

> **Box 6.1 The three parenting steps found to help infants to 'sleep through the night' by 12 weeks of age (see text for details)**
>
> - Settle a baby thought to be sleepy in a cot or similar place, and avoid feeding or cuddling a baby to sleep at night-time.
> - Reduce the light and minimize social interaction at night.
> - Once the baby is at least 3-weeks-old, healthy and putting on weight normally, begin to delay feeding for a few moments when the baby wakes at night. The short delay means that waking is not immediately rewarded by feeding. This is done gradually, using handling or diaper/nappy changing to add a short delay, but does not involve leaving the baby to cry for a long time.
>
> *Appendix II includes a more detailed version of this guidance.*

changes to feeding method or contents. Indeed, the COSI study also found that this limit-setting approach was particularly effective in promoting settled night-time behaviour at 12 weeks among infants who had a large number of breast-feeds (>11 per 24 hours) in the first postnatal week (Nikolopoulou & St James-Roberts, 2003). These infants continued to breast-feed frequently, but did so during the daytime and reduced their feeding frequency at night. The limit-setting approach was equally affective with breast- and formula-fed infants and their weight gain was normal. At a 9-month follow up, parents who had used the limit-setting approach were more satisfied with it and had made contact with health services less often because of infant crying and sleeping problems, compared with the other groups (St James-Roberts et al., 2001).

In combination, the findings from these four randomized controlled trails provide robust evidence that limit-setting parenting methods enable infants to become settled in the night at an early age. In addition, there is evidence, so far from just one randomized trial, that simply introducing a daily routine involving bathing and wind-down activities each evening reduces infant's' night waking and signalling, increases their sleeping, and improves their mood on waking up (Mindell et al., 2009).

Before accepting the findings from these randomized controlled trials, two studies that appear at first sight to have produced discrepant findings need to be considered. One of these studies, by McRury and Zolotar (2010) involved what was called a 'behavioural' intervention, but one which was very different from the 'limit-setting' parenting methods examined in the four randomized controlled trials discussed above. As described in Chapter 4, the McRury and Zolotar trial employed swaddling and other elements of

The Happiest Baby programme, which did not prove to be effective in reducing crying or improving sleeping. The McRury and Zolotar (2010) findings, then, do not assess limit-setting parenting methods or conflict with the findings from the randomized trials examined above.

The second study, by Douglas Teti and colleagues (2010) found that maternal emotional availability at bedtime, not parenting behaviour, was associated with settled infant behaviour during the night. However, the explanation for the apparent inconsistency with the findings from the randomized controlled trials may well lie in the research design used by the Teti et al. (2010) study. Rather than collecting longitudinal evidence, each infant and parent was assessed only at one age point, while the measures of infants and parents were collapsed across a wide age range (from 1–24 months of age). As a result, the study can identify associations, but not causation. Because of this, as Teti et al. (2010) themselves point out, their first finding can be interpreted as evidence that infant sleep problems at night caused some mothers to reduce their emotional availability as the infants got older. Their second finding, that parenting behaviours were not associated with infant night-time sleep–waking behaviour, does appear to conflict with the evidence summarized above. However, their analyses (Teti et al., 2010, p. 310) explicitly excluded a measure of parental 'structuring' behaviours (which they defined as 'a parent's capacity for appropriately scaffolding child activity and setting appropriate limits') because their observers were unable to code it reliably. This is a methodological limitation, but since this was their only measure of limit-setting parenting, this aspect of parenting was simply not assessed in their study. The Teti et al. (2010) study is, then, important in drawing attention to parental 'emotional availability' as a factor to be examined in future studies.

However, even if we accept that infant night waking and signalling reduces emotional availability in some parents, we should not assume that parents who adopt limit-setting methods from the outset are emotionally unavailable to their babies. In older infants and children, parenting methods which combine warmth with limit-setting have repeatedly emerged as effective in supporting child development (Cole & Cole, 2001; Ding & Littleton, 2005). Such methods, referred to as 'authoritative' parenting methods in child development research, fall in-between 'permissive parenting' at one extreme and 'authoritarian' parenting at the other, to support child independence by providing both affection and guidance. It may well be that many parents who choose to use limit-setting methods are warmly attached to their babies. Further research is needed to throw light on that question, but for present purposes the main implication of the Teti et al. (2010) findings is to highlight the superiority of longitudinal research designs, and randomized controlled trials, as methods for establishing causation.

In conclusion, then, the combined findings from four randomized controlled trials provide compelling evidence that non-nutritional, environmental factors contained in parenting are important sources of individual differences in infant night-time waking and signalling behaviour by 12 weeks of age. This conclusion is consistent, too, with the evidence from a large number of comparative and longitudinal studies. Limit-setting parenting methods enable infants to become settled in the night at a young age, while infant-demand parenting methods, particularly those involving bed-sharing and a high amount of parent–infant contact at bedtimes, maintain infant night waking and signalling. This conclusion is important in its own right, since it can be used to guide healthcare practice and help parents who wish their babies to remain settled at night at a young age. Maintaining our focus on causation, it is worth noting, though, that the studies so far have not distinguished precisely *how* these parenting approaches influence infants' night-time behaviour.

The issue, as Box 6.1 illustrates, is that the broad category of 'limit-setting' includes several different parenting behaviours, while this is equally true of 'infant-demand' parenting and 'bed-sharing'. As a consequence, at least five different aspects of the parenting environment could, in principle, be involved (St James-Roberts, 2007a). First, James McKenna and colleagues found that bed-sharing mothers and infants aroused more frequently (often as a result of the other's movement or sound), and spent significantly more time in lighter stages of sleep, and less time in deeper non-REM stages of sleep, compared to infants sleeping alone (McKenna, 2005). The implication is that bed-sharing could cause infants to wake more often. As we saw earlier in this chapter infant 'arousability', and the endogenous and environmental factors that lead some infants to arouse from sleep more readily than others, have emerged recently as important issues and are the focus for a good deal of current research.

Second, the proximity of co-sleeping infants and parents may simply lead parents to detect and respond to infant signals more readily. Indeed, there is some evidence that waking infants often spend time making low noises before a full cry (Quandt, 1986).

Third, the limit-setting approach to care described in Box 6.1 asks parents to maximize day:night differences in light:darkness, as well as in social stimulation and play. It may be that these environmental cues help infants to set up a circadian sleep–waking organization, as happens with adults. Y. Harrison (2004), for example, found an association between settled night-time behaviour and greater exposure to light in the early afternoon. If, as suggested earlier, infants are biologically predisposed to consolidate sleeping into the night and waking into the day-time, the environmental cues contained in the limit-setting approach to care may support this biological propensity.

Fourth, settling infants while awake could be important, since this may enable them to resettle autonomously on waking, while infants who fall asleep in their parents' arms may require this in order to resettle later in the night (Adair et al., 1991; Anuntaseree et al., 2008; DeLeon & Karraker, 2007; Goodlin-Jones et al., 2001; Louis & Govindama, 2004; Sadeh, 2003).

Finally, co-sleeping may facilitate immediate feeding when babies awake, rewarding the waking, whereas separate sleeping arrangements may delay feeding. An American study by Melissa Burnham and colleagues (Burnham et al., 2002) found that delayed parental response to night waking at 3 months predicted autonomous re-settling at 12 months. Delaying feeding for a few moments to break the bond between waking and feeding is the third element of the limit-setting programme described in Box 6.1.

The existence of these five different possibilities emphasizes the complexity of the processes involved in developing the ability to remain settled at night – and goes some way towards explaining why this phenomenon is not yet fully understood. The five potential mechanisms are not mutually exclusive and several may be involved. Several of them assume the existence of learning and it is plausible that infant learning is involved in the development of settled night-time behaviour (and cessation of night-time signalling). This hypothesis is consistent with the adult evidence, cited earlier, that sleep–waking habits involve learning, while it is also supported by the evidence that behavioural methods (which ignore signalling and reward settled behaviour), provide the most effective treatments for sleeping problems at older ages (Mindell et al., 2006; Ramchandani et al., 2000). In effect, such methods teach alternative patterns of learned behaviour.

This hypothesis, then, attributes the predominant form of infant sleeping problems – infant night waking and signalling – to a delay in learning to inhibit signalling behaviours upon waking in the night, rather than to a deficit or disturbance of sleep–waking physiology. The maintenance of signalling is attributed, at least partly, to aspects of the parenting environment. This explanation holds out the promise of being able to distinguish cases involving learning from cases that involve an organic disturbance. It will be important to examine these possibilities in future research. Fortunately, although research is needed to uncover the relative importance of learning and the various mechanisms posited above, the existing evidence-base is sufficient to guide clinical practice and will be revisited in Chapters 9 and 10.

Finally, following on from the point made earlier that infant sleep problems are primarily problems for parents, several recent randomized trials have found that behavioural programmes that reduce infant night-waking problems have benefits for parents' own well-being, self-confidence and sleep (Hiscock et al., 2007; Mindell et al., 2009; Smart & Hiscock, 2007; Stremler et al., 2006; Wolfson et al., 1992). For example, a Canadian intervention study by Robyn Stremler and her colleagues used a randomized controlled trial to evaluate the effectiveness of a behavioural–educational intervention programme introduced from birth for enhancing parental and infant sleeping, compared with a control condition. Their finding was that infants whose mothers received the programme woke and signalled less often at night and their longest settled night-time sleeps were 46 minutes longer, on average, than those of control group infants. In addition, the mothers who received the behavioural–educational programme averaged 57 minutes more sleep per night themselves, and fewer reported their sleeping as a problem, compared with the control group. It is important to note that this study was small-scale, with just 15 cases per group, and did not include a long enough follow-up to show whether effects were sustained. However, larger-scale trials both in Australia and the USA have shown that intervention programmes that reduce infant night waking and signalling have knock-on benefits for maternal, and paternal, well-being (Hiscock et al., 2007; Mindell et al., 2009; Smart & Hiscock, 2007; Wolfson et al., 1992).

Environmental contributions to infant night waking 3: evidence from other interventions – massage; swaddling; prescribed and non-prescribed liquids, and substances

Chapter 4 examined the use of interventions involving touch, movement, chiropractic manipulations and substances such as sucrose to reduce infant crying. Here, the focus is on the effects of manipulations of this sort on improving infant sleeping. Most studies of their use have measured day-time crying, but not infant sleep or night-time behaviour, so that evidence about these is much thinner on the ground. Two exceptions are the Hunziker and Barr (1986) study of effects of supplementary carrying on crying, which found no effect of this on sleep duration, and James Gatts and colleagues' (1995) randomized controlled trial of the effect of a mechanized cradle. This provided rocking and rhythmic sound, together with some containment of infant movements, while lessening the amount of infant stimulation in the night versus the day and over age. The result was to increase the amount of time infants spent in the cradle (compared with a control group). More mothers using the cradle reported that their babies slept for 7 hours at night during at least 5 nights/week at 11 weeks of age (92%) than mothers of control infants (68%). Audio-recordings, which detected less waking and signalling during the night-time in the mechanized cradle group, supported this conclusion. These findings were carefully collected, but are limited by the uniqueness, unavailability and potential cost of the mechanized cradle, as well as by the lack of replication evidence. Another concern is whether reducing infant–parent contact and interaction is beneficial for infant development.

Below, the two interventions used to improve infant sleeping and evaluated by more than one study – massage or swaddling – are assessed first. The use of prescribed and non-prescribed substances is then discussed in the last part of this section.

Infant massage

The Cochrane Collaboration's 2006 review of the evidence about the benefits of massage for infants under 6 months of age included infant sleeping as one of the outcomes (Underdown et al., 2006). Only randomized controlled trials involving full-term infants were examined, with each study classified on methodological quality. The reviewed studies differed in how often and how long infants were massaged for, the method of massage, and who provided it (e.g. mother or researcher), thus complicating the findings. Three studies, all Chinese, reported that massage increased amount of infant sleeping, but none of these was considered to have adequate controls for bias. Just two studies that reported sleep measures were considered to have a low risk of bias (Agarwal et al., 2000; Field et al., 1996). One of these, a study of 6-week-old Indian infants by Agarwal and colleagues, found that the length of their sleep period immediately after the massage (given in the morning), increased. However, there was no difference between the massage and control groups in overall sleep amount per 24 hours or in the day or night-time.

The second methodologically robust study, carried out by Tiffany Field and her colleagues in North America, compared massaged with rocked infants (Field et al., 1996). The infants were 1–3 months old and received massage (or rocking) from a researcher twice per week for 6 weeks. They were found to spend more time in inactive-alert and active-awake states during the massage than during rocking. Rocking was more effective than massage in inducing sleep while it continued, but the rocked infants cried more than the massaged infants during the 15 minutes after the rocking was stopped. We have already encountered this 'rebound' phenomenon (see Chapter 4, the section on 'Effects on infant crying of interventions'). The massaged infants spent more time than rocked infants in an inactive-alert state during the 15 minutes after their massage, but there was no group difference in amount of Quiet or Active Sleep during this period. Unfortunately, infant sleeping was not assessed at greater length in this study, so that it is not known whether any differences in infant night-time sleep, or waking and signalling, occurred between the groups.

In a more recent study, Field and colleagues observed two groups of infants for a single 45-minute period after their mothers had massaged them once per day during a period of 1 month (Field et al., 2004). The two groups differed in whether the massage was moderate in intensity (which was expected to be beneficial) or just light-touch. No differences were found in amount of infant deep or light sleep, but the moderately massaged group spent less time in REM sleep than the lightly massaged group. This difference was, however, small (7.9% versus 11.6% of the 45-minute observation), while it is not clear whether less REM sleep is desirable. Still more recently, this group has reported that 15 1-week to 2-month-old infants bathed using lavender bath oil spent more time after the bath in deep sleep than infants bathed with an aroma-free bath oil (Field et al., 2008). This was not true, though, of 15 older infants (2–4.5 months of age) bathed in the same way. A recent American study by Jodi Mindell and colleagues (Mindell et al., 2009) found that combining a massage and bathing with the introduction of a regular daily routine increased both infants' and toddlers' sleep, and reduced waking and signalling during the night. Whether this was due to the routine, bathing or massage is not known.

These findings clearly warrant replication and separation of the inter-vention elements. For the moment, the findings as a whole are mixed, but they do not provide clear evidence that massage or associated practices such as bathing with aromatic oil increase infant sleeping, or reduce waking and signalling, during the night. In addition, there is no evidence that massage provides an effective treatment for night waking and signalling that is already a problem. That said, as the Cochrane Collaboration pointed out (Underdown et al., 2006), there is no evidence that massage and associated activities cause harm, while they may be pleasurable for parent and baby. Consequently (Caglayan et al., 1991; Lipton et al., 1965) they can be recommended to parents who wish to use them, particularly if combined with a daily routine, on the understanding that there may not be any lasting effect on infant night waking and signalling.

Swaddling

Swaddling babies by wrapping them tightly is a longstanding tradition in a variety of non-Western cultures, and many mothers in these countries believe that their babies are more settled and sleep better if swaddled (Caglayan et al., 1991; Lipton et al., 1965). Anthropological studies, too, have provided evidence that swaddled infants tend to be more settled and spend more time sleeping (Chisholm, 1983), although studies of that type cannot tell us whether the swaddling is the causal factor. As James Chisholm (1983) pointed out, swaddling is typically confounded with other cultural practices that make it difficult to isolate the particular effects of swaddling.

Fortunately, as well as anthropological findings, there are controlled studies of the effect of swaddling on infant sleep–waking. In a 2002 study, Claudia Gerard and colleagues (2002) studied 26 healthy North American infants ranging in age from 24 to 180 days. The infants were alternately swaddled and not-swaddled while placed supine during daytime nap periods, so that they served as their own controls. While swaddled, the infants were found to have less frequent awakenings during Quiet Sleep, and 'startles' during Quiet Sleep were less likely to progress to full arousals. Swaddling also increased the amount of time spent in REM sleep, but not Quiet Sleep. Patricia Franco and colleagues (2005) studied REM and non-REM sleep in 16 healthy European infants aged between 6 and 16 weeks. These infants, too, served as their own controls, but in this case the measurements were collected at night. The researchers found that swaddling while supine reduced the amount of time infants spent awake by 6% and increased the proportion of time spent sleeping during the observation period from 93.3% (un-swaddled) to 97.8% (swaddled). Swaddled infants spent proportionately more time in non-REM sleep (51.9%) than non-swaddled infants (44.8%), but with no difference in REM sleep. Less intense auditory stimuli were able to arouse the infants during REM sleep when they were swaddled than un-swaddled, which was considered to guard against the danger that swaddling would increase the risk of SIDS.

These studies provide more or less consistent evidence that swaddling produces modest increases in amount of sleep and modest reductions in infant arousals and waking under carefully controlled conditions in the day and night-time. These findings are also consistent with the anthropological evidence noted above and with a systematic review of the evidence about swaddling carried out by Bregje van Sleuwen and colleagues (2007). The mechanism is not entirely clear, but it may be that swaddling confines arm and other bodily movement in a way that reduces startles and waking (Chisholm, 1983).

Also unclear, but more important, is whether these findings as a whole support the use of swaddling in everyday circumstances. For one thing, there is a shortage of evidence as to whether swaddling reduces infant night waking and signalling when used routinely in home settings. It is possible that infants get used to it, so that any effects are short lived. Furthermore, there is a longstanding debate about the safety of swaddling and some evidence of a link between swaddling and SIDS (Blair et al., 2009; van Sleuwen et al., 2007). Interpretation of these findings is complicated by the confounding of swaddling with other SIDS risk factors, such as prone sleeping and parental alcohol consumption, so that it is not known whether swaddling directly contributes to SIDS. Indeed, some studies have found lower SIDS rates among swaddled babies sleeping supine, but relatively high rates where swaddling and prone sleeping were combined (Franco et al., 2005; van Sleuwen et al., 2007). As a consequence, one review has cautioned against swaddling where infants are old enough to roll from supine to prone positions, which some may be able to do as early as 3 months of age (van Sleuwen et al., 2007).

Another consideration is whether it is desirable, in general, to increase infant sleep. As Chapter 5 discusses, it is infant night waking and signalling, not an infant sleep deficit, which is the problem for parents. Potentially, an overall increase in sleep with reduced alert waking could reduce infants' ability to interact with and learn from their environment. This then raises questions about the best time of day to use swaddling. Other complications are about the best form of swaddling to use and whether or not it has to be introduced at an early age for infants to tolerate it (Gerard et al., 2002). Whether infants become familiar with swaddling and adjust their sleep–waking, is another possible confounding factor (Richardson et al., 2010). There is a great deal more to learn. In the meantime parents may want to be aware of these controversies and the associated uncertainty as to whether swaddling has benefits that outweigh the potential risks.

Prescribed and non-prescribed liquids and substances

Naomi Richman's (1985) early study of the sedative drug trimeprazine tartrate as a treatment for severe night-waking problems in 22 2-year-old children found that it reduced the frequency of night waking in most, though not all children initially, but the improvements were short-lived. On average, the children woke and signalled parents during 3.7 nights per week while taking the drug, and most were still waking at least 5 nights per week (and had returned to baseline levels) 6 months after the drug treatment was finished. Richman concluded that drug treatment of sleep problems was of limited clinical value and this finding led her and others to examine behavioural methods, which proved more effective. These are examined in Chapter 10.

Richman's conclusions have since been echoed by other researchers, who have found that drug treatments are less effective and less acceptable to parents than behavioural treatments, which also have fewer adverse side effects (Ferber, 2006; France & Hudson, 1993; Mindell et al., 2006; Simonoff & Stores, 1987). The sole exception to this picture involves special groups of children with medical conditions, where there is some evidence that prescribed medications may help children with autism (Wirojanan et al., 2009) or allergic conditions (Ferrer et al., 2010). However, these findings involve older children, not infants, while their newness suggests a need for caution. Overall, the findings add to general concerns about the effects of medication on the growth, development and well-being of infants and young children, the quality of the resulting sleep, and the development of dependency on sleep medication (Ferber, 2006; France & Hudson, 1993). Except in cases where medications are employed to treat insomnia due to specific medical conditions, or where behavioural programmes prove ineffective, they are not recommended as treatments for infant sleep–waking problems (Mindell et al., 2006; Sadeh & Sivan, 2009).

The use of non-prescribed, 'over the counter', herbal and other substances such as valerian, chamomile and antihistamines for child insomnia has been examined by a number of expert multidisciplinary groups (Mindell et al., 2006; Owens et al., 2003, 2005). The main tenor of their findings has been to emphasize the lack of evidence that these substances are effective, highlight concerns about safety, and indicate the need for evidence and a safety-conscious approach to their use. There are likewise few systematic studies of the results of treating adult insomnia with herbal and complementary remedies, and they too emphasize safety worries and the lack of evidence for efficacy (Meolie et al., 2005; Stojanovski et al., 2007). For present purposes, the implication is that parents can be advised about the lack of evidence that medications and herbal remedies provide effective treatments for infant sleep problems, as well as concerns about their safety. Behavioural methods, which are the treatments of choice, will be described in Chapter 10.

Environmental contributions to infant settling or night-waking problems 4: fear of the dark and separation from parents; infant–parent attachments

Fear of being alone at night is common among young children (Marks, 1987; Muris et al., 2000, 2001), and a child's fear of separation from parents, or of isolation in the dark, could well provide an explanation for some young children's reluctance to settle quietly at night, or need for parental attention upon waking. In keeping with this proposal, two books for parents about infant sleep problems, by Dilys Daws (1993) and Avi Sadeh (2001) have highlighted bedtime separations of infants and parents as a key issue.

Explanations of this type have been categorized as 'environmental' here because they concern particular settings, but they could equally be said to be developmental in origin, since they attribute the infant behaviours in question to psychological processes – fear of separation, isolation or darkness – which commonly have their onset after about 6 months of age (Marks, 1987; Rutter, 1972; Schaffer & Emerson, 1964). Explanations of this type often also employ ideas from attachment theory, which emphasizes the importance of emotional bonds between infants and parents for the long-term psychological health and well-being of the child (Ainsworth et al., 1978; Bowlby, 1969, 1988; Morrell & Steele, 2003; Scher et al., 2000). According to this theory, originally formulated by John Bowlby (1969, 1988) and developed by Mary Ainsworth and colleagues (1978) and many others since, separation from the attachment figure – usually a parent and often the mother – is a major stressor that activates fear systems which evolution has built into the infant mind to maintain proximity between infant and parent and ensure infant safety. In healthy relationships, the attachment figure provides a 'secure base' for exploration and comfort during times of threat (Bowlby, 1988). Darkness and aloneness are considered to be 'natural clues to danger' (Bowlby, 1973; Cassidy, 1999). When contact with the attachment figure cannot be achieved under conditions of threat, infant separation anxiety, proximity seeking, and contact maintaining behaviours such as crying are triggered by the attachment system to attract and maintain parental proximity, reduce distress and provide comfort (Ainsworth et al., 1978).

The assumption is that it is biologically 'natural' for young children to feel anxious, insecure or fearful when put to bed alone, especially in a darkened room. Often, too, it is assumed to be 'natural' for parents to want to maintain close proximity with their baby. The unfortunate implication of the word 'natural' that there is just one correct way of behaving – and the contrary evidence from anthropological studies that parents in different cultures care for infants in a variety of ways – were highlighted in Chapter 4.

Before examining the evidence on infant attachment and sleep–waking behaviour in particular, it is helpful to focus on progress in attachment theory research more generally. This theory has been hugely valuable in generating studies, including longitudinal follow-up investigations of children exposed to social privation and studies comparing children adopted out of institutions with those remaining inside (Nelson et al., 2007; Smyke et al., 2010). It is not possible to do justice to this enormous body of research here, but there is a *Handbook of Attachment*, now in its second edition (Cassidy & Shaver, 2008) and excellent reviews exist elsewhere (Barret, 2006; Rutter et al., 2009). Three findings from this research are, though, particularly relevant for our purposes.

The first concerns parental sensitivity to infant signals and needs, considered by Bowlby and Ainsworh to provide the primary basis for secure infant attachments (Ainsworth et al., 1978; Bowlby, 1969). The research on this issue is summarized in a meta-analysis of 21 separate studies (involving 1099 infants) by Marianne De Wolff and Marinus van IJzendoorn (1997). Parental sensitivity was defined as 'the ability to respond appropriately and promptly to the signals of the infant' (De Wolff & Van IJzendoorn, 1997, p. 584), while infant attachment security was measured in most of the studies using Ainsworth and colleagues' 'Strange Situation' procedure, which is the 'gold standard' for measuring attachment. The Strange Situation involves deliberate separation of a parent and 12 to 18-month-old infant and the introduction of a stranger in an unfamiliar room, followed by reunion with the parent (Ainsworth et al., 1978). Attachments are categorized as secure or insecure mainly according to whether the infant seeks comfort from, and is reassured by, the parent on reunion (Waters, 1978; Waters et al., 2000). The finding from De Wolff and van IJzendoorn's (1997) meta-analysis is that sensitive parenting during early infancy does predict infant attachment security, but only to a moderate degree. The effect size is equivalent to a correlation of 0.24, so that sensitive parenting accounts for only a minority of the variation in infant attachment security. The implication is that factors other than parental sensitivity, including other parenting characteristics, infant features and contextual factors, influence whether or not infants show secure attachments.

The second finding from attachment research relevant here is that Bowlby's original ideas about the extent and directness of the effects of a lack of early attachment bonds on children's development have not been borne out. Instead, the findings have shown considerable plasticity in child development, so that recovery from even truly awful early privation can be substantial where adoption into supportive family environments takes place. Research is continuing, but only 'disinhibited attachment' (or 'indiscriminate friendliness') has been consistently found to be a direct consequence of early social privation (Nelson et al., 2007; Rutter et al., 2009; Smyke et al., 2010; Tizard & Hodges, 1978; Tizard & Rees, 1975; van IJzendoorn & Juffer, 2006; van Zeiji et al., 2006). Poor outcomes, such as emotional and behaviour problems or cognitive impairment, are generally the consequence of persistent and multiple adversities (Rutter, 2006; Rutter et al., 2009; van IJzendoorn & Juffer, 2006). Although emphasizing the importance of caregiver–child relationships for later development, these findings imply that early trusting relationships do not themselves influence outcomes directly so much as by providing a framework within which children learn to understand and regulate their emotions and behaviour (Rutter, 2006; Rutter et al., 2009; van IJzendoorn & Juffer, 2006). Recent studies have begun to document how this works (Kochanska et al., 2009). The point is not, of course, to condone inadequate parenting or social experience, but to highlight the need to avoid a rigid and exclusive focus on infant–parent bonds.

The third finding relevant for our purposes involves a distinction between mild and overwhelmingly strong stressors (called 'toxic stressors' by Gunnar et al., 2009). There is a large body of evidence that frequent exposure to overwhelming stressors is harmful, but mild stressors in early childhood can encourage infants to make autonomous adjustments that are beneficial for development because they increase resiliency (Gunnar et al., 2009; Marks, 1987; Rutter, 2006). The implication is that the stress of separations is not necessarily harmful – providing they are managed thoughtfully as part of a caring environment they can be beneficial. Indeed, a distinction often made is between affectionate and 'over-dependent' relationships, where the latter involve an excessive dependence on parental support and failure to develop autonomous coping (Rutter, 1972; Rutter et al., 2009; Scher, 2001). It is important, then, to distinguish between the event of separation of an infant and parent, the manner in which it is managed, and the quality of the care environment the young child experiences before and after the separation (Rutter, 1972). There is no doubt that separation from a parent is often highly upsetting for older infants and young children. Indeed, the standard measure of attachment, Ainsworth and colleagues' 'Strange Situation', described above, involves deliberate separation of a parent and infant, plus the introduction of a stranger in an unfamiliar room, in order to stress the infant. However, the Strange Situation focuses less on the resulting infant stress (which is assumed to be more or less universal) than on the infant's response to the re-union on the parent's return. Insecure attachments are measured by whether the infant seeks comfort from, and is reassured by, the parent (Waters, 1978; Waters et al., 2000). In effect, secure attachment is defined by the infant's maintenance of an affectionate bond in spite of the stress of a separation.

The point, as Michael Rutter recognized over 30 years ago (Rutter, 1972), is that it is normal and commonplace for affectionate bonds to survive separations, so that it is necessary to distinguish between the separation and the attachment. There is a great deal of evidence that attachments survive separations, such as those involved in a mother's hospital admission or trips away from home (Rutter, 1972; Sagi et al., 1994). Some degree and frequency of separation of child and parent is an almost inevitable feature of everyday life – and will become a major part of normal experience by school age. Children need to be prepared to cope with separations from parents, so that they do not become over-dependent. It is not the separation itself which is the crucial issue so much as how and when it happens, how long it lasts for, and whether the child receives support in learning to manage it (Rutter, 1972). This principle is reflected in one of the methods used to treat infant sleeping problems (called 'checking' or 'graduated extinction'), examined in Chapter 10.

Turning from Attachment Theory in general to studies of relationships between parenting, infant attachment and sleep–waking problems, it is to be expected, as Higley and Dozier (2009) have found, that many securely attached infants will have mothers who respond sensitively when they are distressed in the night. However, it is not self-evident what the theory predicts about the relationship between infants' attachment security and unsettled night-time behaviour. Attachment bonds are commonly measured at around 12 months because they are considered to be consolidated by this age. If we assume that separation activates attachment feelings directly, infant distress upon separation could be a sign that attachment bonds have been securely formed. The prediction in this case is that infants who show distress at bedtime or on waking alone in the night should be securely attached, while insecurely attached infants should not show distress.

Another possibility, and perhaps the main concern for parents, is that parenting strategies that employ 'limit-setting' methods to enforce separations – such as putting a child down to sleep alone – will damage their infant's trusting attachment relationship. Since methods of this kind seem likely to increase infant crying somewhat (relative to staying in contact), the prediction is that infants who are distressed at separation or on waking in the night are exhibiting signs of insecure attachments to their parents. Or, it could be that feelings of insecurity prevent settled sleeping, so that infants who are unsettled in the night are insecurely attached.

A third possibility is that distress at separation, or signalling in the night, are the results of an infant's over-dependence on parents for regulation of her fear: they reflect dependence more than attachment. In this case, infants who are distressed at separation or upon waking alone should be securely attached in the Strange Situation, but also show signs of over-dependence, such as clinginess, at times when they are not separated. Finally, infants may be able to maintain secure attachments in spite of separations at night. In this case there should be no association between measures of distress at bedtime or in the night and secure or insecure attachments. Otherwise, although the precise prediction is not clear, children who differ in settling or night-waking behaviour are expected to differ in attachments in some way.

Seven studies speak to this question. Because the answer is particularly important for parents, and the findings are not straightforward, each of the studies will be examined in some detail. Studies measuring parental (rather than infant) attachments will be examined in Chapter 7.

The first infant study, from Abraham Sagi and colleagues (1994), involved Strange Situation measures of attachment in 23 14 to 22-month-old children sleeping at night in a communal nursery in Israeli kibbutzim, compared with 25 same-aged kibbutzim infants who slept at home with their parents at night. Of the home sleepers, 80% were securely attached to their mothers, compared with only 48% of the infants who slept communally. This finding indicates a clear relationship between communal night-time sleeping arrangements and infant attachments, but its implication for our understanding of infant settling and night-waking behaviour is much less clear.

One of several possible confounding variables examined by the researchers was the frequency and amount of infant–parent separation, which did not mirror the difference in night-time sleep arrangements because mothers of home-sleeping children were away from the kibbutz more often, for instance on short holidays. These separation measures did not predict the infants' attachments, making the point that the home-sleeping children were able to maintain secure attachments to their mothers in spite of their separations.

Since all the children spent their daytimes in kibbutzim nurseries (9 hours/day for 6 days/week), it is notable that 80% of the kibbutzim infants who spent their daytimes (but not night-times) in nurseries from 3 to 4 months of age were securely attached to their parents. The mother–infant separations themselves, then, did not predict insecure infant attachments. Unfortunately, it is not clear why the communal night-time sleeping arrangements did affect the infants' attachments. Sagi and colleagues speculated that this might be due to the frequent changes in night-time caregivers, so that nobody familiar was available if infants became distressed at night. In any case, it is uncertain whether these findings would generalize to non-communal sleep arrangements. Most importantly for our purposes, we do not know whether these arrangements affected infant sleep–waking, since this study did not measure infant settling behaviour, or night waking and signalling, at all. This study tells us that communal night-time sleeping arrangements led to insecure infant attachments, but not whether they affected infant sleep–waking. It is worth noting that Israeli kibbutzim no longer utilize communal sleeping (Aviezer et al., 2002).

Two other Israeli studies, both carried out by Anat Scher and colleagues (Scher, 2001; Scher & Asher, 2004), do address the relationship between attachment and infant sleep–waking directly. Both measured infant sleep–waking using an objective method – actigraphy – as well as by maternal reports. The first study, of 94 1-year-old infants from a general community background, used the Strange Situation to measure attachment, while the second, of a different group of 57 similar infants, used a procedure that required mothers to choose statements about attachment behaviours that applied to their infants. The main finding from both studies was that the infants' night-waking behaviours were not related to their attachment security, irrespective of whether objective or maternal measures of sleep–waking were used. Rather, night waking and signalling was common across the infant groups. For instance, 55% of securely attached and 60% of insecurely attached, infants were reported by mothers to be night wakers in the Scher (2001) study.

One subsidiary finding is also of interest. In further analyses, infants who were reported by mothers to have difficulties with settling at bedtime were more likely to be rated 'secure but dependent' during the Strange Situation procedure because they spent more time close to their mothers throughout this procedure, suggesting clinginess or high dependence (Scher, 2001). This was not true of infants with insecure attachments: they were reported to settle well at bedtime. Scher and Asher's (2004) study, too, concluded that dependency, rather than insecurity, explains why some infants have difficulty in settling to sleep. In any case, the main implication of the Scher group findings is that infant distress at bedtime separations, and night waking, are not related to secure, or insecure, attachments to their mothers.

A similar study, but involving 44 12-month-old American infants and their mothers, was carried out by Elizabeth Higley and Mary Dozier (2009). The infants' attachments were assessed using the Strange Situation. Of the 44 infants, 27 (61%) were classified as securely attached and 17 (39%) as insecurely attached to their mothers. Infant and parental behaviours at night were measured both by maternal reports and from infra-red video-recordings in the infants' bedrooms at home, which were coded by trained observers who did not know the infants' attachment status. The main finding was that there was no difference between secure and insecure infants in how often they woke in the night, the number of times the infants signalled in the night, the number of times infants had settling difficulties, or the number of infants who remained settled without signalling through-out the night. There was a non-significant tendency for secure infants to be 'clear signallers', that is, to fuss or cry clearly upon waking, as opposed to infants who remained settled or signalled quietly when they awoke. The importance of this non-significant association is unclear, but so far as it is interpretable it suggests that secure infants are more likely to cry loudly when waking in the night than insecure infants. This study is limited by its small group sizes, but its main finding is consistent with that of the Scher studies in showing no association between infants' night-time settling and waking behaviours and their attachment status.

The fifth study relevant to this topic (McNamara et al., 2003) compared two subgroups of infants with insecure attachments ('insecure resistant' and 'insecure avoidant') on maternal reports of sleep problems at 6 and 15 months of age. Because no securely attached cases were included, this study cannot address the question of whether or not infant security is related to high (or low) rates of night waking. Instead, it assesses whether the two types of insecure attachment have different links with infant sleep–waking problems. The study's strengths include Strange Situation measures of insecure attachment and large sample sizes (193 insecure-avoidant and 143 insecure-resistant infants) obtained as part of a national USA cohort study. In the Strange Situation, insecure-avoidant attachments involve failure to greet the mother, together with active infant avoidance of proximity or interaction with her, while insecure-resistant (or ambivalent) attachments are shown by infant behaviours that involve anger or ambivalence in the relationship, including pushing away, dropping or hitting toys offered, and body movements in resistance to being held, together with signs of inability to be comforted by contact with the parent (Waters, 1978; Waters et al., 2000). The McNamara et al. (2003) finding of most direct relevance here is that the two insecure groups did not differ in proportions of cases with reported night waking at either age. Instead, mothers' subjective ratings of infant sleep problems identified these more often in insecure-resistant than insecure-avoidant infants at both ages (66% versus 53% at 6 months, and 56% versus 44% at 15 months, respectively). As noted earlier, the inter-pretative difficulty with such findings is to know whether they are a measure of infant or maternal characteristics. In this regard, the findings from the Scher (2001) and the Higley and Dozier (2009) studies are far more robust.

In contrast to the studies examined above, the sixth study of this issue did find higher rates of reported night waking in insecure, than securely attached, infants (Morrell & Steele, 2003). This study recruited 100 mothers and their 14 to 16-month-old infants in UK vaccination clinics, using the Infant Sleep Questionnaire to select 40 with sleeping problems and 60 without. Attachment security was measured using the Strange Situation and all 100 mothers returned a second Infant Sleep Questionnaire at a follow up by post 1 year later. Arguably the most important finding was that the majority of infants – 65% of those with sleeping problems and 77% of control cases – were securely attached. The main difference between these groups was that more infants with sleep problems than control infants were ambivalently attached (12.5% versus 1.7%). However, these figures look more substantial than was actually the case. Because the original group size was just 100 cases and insecure attachments are uncommon, these per-centages of ambivalent attachment involve just 5 of 40 infants with sleep problems, and 1 of 60 infants without sleep problems, querying the robustness of the difference. Even in Morrell and Steele's own analyses, infant ambivalent attachment explained just 4% of the variation in infant night-waking problems. In contrast, mothers' reports that they found it difficult to set limits in responding to their child at night explained far more of the variation in problematic infant night waking (36%). We will examine this last finding, together with other evidence about relationships between parental characteristics and infant sleep–waking, in Chapter 7.

The last and most recent study (Keller & El-Sheikh, 2010) involved 176 children with a mean age of 8.7 years, 142 of whom were followed up 2 years later (mean age 10.7 years). At both ages, sleep was measured by actigraphy and child self-report, while attachments were measured by child reports using two questionnaires: the Inventory of Parent and Peer Attachments and the Emotional Security about Marital Relationship scale. The latter obtains children's view of whether their parents' relationship is secure. Cross-lagged statistical methods were employed to examine predictive associations between the measures over the 2-year period. Just one significant association was found between the attachment measures at age 8 and the actigraphic sleep measures at age 10: girls who felt insecure about their parents' marital relationship at age 8 took longer to settle to sleep at age 10. This was not true of boys and none of the age 8 attachment measures predicted the actigraphic measures of night waking at 10 years of age. There were more associations between the subjective, child-report, measures over age. The children's reports of a secure mother–child relationship at age 8 predicted less subjective 'sleepiness' at age 10 in both boys and girls, even after controlling for sleep measures at age 8. In boys, but not in girls, insecurity about their parents' marital relationship at age 8 predicted increased subjective sleepiness and reported night waking at age 10.

Although intriguing, these findings are not simple to interpret. As well as the lack of evidence for any effects of attachment on objectively measured night waking, the associations over age between the subjective measures, although significant, were not strong (the standardized path coefficients ranged from 0.15 to 0.30). It is also much more difficult to measure attachments validly in 8 to 10-year-olds – there is no equivalent of the Strange Situation measure at this age. Overall, the findings may be best interpreted as provisional evidence that children's worries about their relationships with their mothers, and relationships in-between their parents, have a disruptive effect on their sleeping. If so, one implication would be to highlight the distinction between children of that age, who are capable of worrying about their relationships and their parents' marriage, and infants – who seem unlikely to be aware of these concerns. On balance, these findings appear to be less directly relevant than the Scher and the Higley and Dozier studies in assessing the links between infants' attachments and their sleep–waking behaviours.

To sum up, what can we conclude about explanations that attribute infant settling difficulties, or night waking and signalling, to infant attachments? As usual, there is a need for more research. In particular, we need to know whether infants who can self-settle by 5 months of age are less likely to have problems with separating, or waking and signalling, at later ages. Since fear of separation and the dark usually starts after about 6 months, it is possible that early-onset self-settling becomes a familiar habit that prevents infants from being afraid of separation and the dark at older ages. Unfortunately, we do not have the detailed evidence we need to answer that question satisfactorily. It is certainly possible that night waking recurs more often at around 9 months than at other ages, but here too the evidence is inadequate.

The existing evidence is, though, enough to help parents faced with a child who is distressed in the night. First, it certainly does not show a clear link between night-time settling or waking problems and secure or insecure infant attachments. Many securely attached infants are upset at separations and signal when they wake in the night, so that these behaviours do not indicate anything wrong with infant–parent attachment relationships. It may reassure many parents to know that it is normal for children to be stressed by being left alone in the dark after about 6 months of age and that this is probably due to psychological development. They can be reassured, too, that there is no evidence that careful use of limit-setting parenting methods to enable separations, and encourage autonomy, during early infancy are likely to damage their infant's trusting attachment relationship with them. Parents may find it helpful to anticipate these developments in infant attachment and fear of separation and the dark at around about 6 months of age and to have a clearly thought-through strategy for managing separations.

The second point for parents is that the distinction between separation and attachment relationships made by Rutter (1972) remains a critical one. Children's emotional bonds with their parents can certainly survive overnight separations, while separations are an almost inevitable part of growing up. The critical question, then, is when and how to manage separations so that children are not unduly upset, acquire autonomous self-soothing abilities and avoid becoming over-dependent.

For professionals, the implication is that issues around managing separation and being alone in the dark need to be raised and discussed with parents. We will return to the strategies available in Chapters 9 and 10, after we have considered two other issues which affect these decisions. The next section will evaluate the effectiveness of aids designed to reduce children's night-time anxiety, such as night-lights and 'security' objects. Since parental decisions may depend on their own feelings in response to their child's distress, Chapter 7 will then examine the other side of the attachment coin: whether parents' own anxiety about separations from their young children affect whether they adopt methods of care that maintain infant separation distress and night waking and signalling.

'Sleep aids': use of attachment/security objects and night-lights to facilitate settling

Whether because of cultural traditions, personal preferences or medical advice about sleeping arrangements that minimize the risk of SIDS, many Western parents choose to put their infants down to sleep in a cot in their own bedroom, or in a separate room. Current SIDS-prevention guidance from the American Academy of Pediatrics (2005) and UK National Health Service (NHS, 2010) is that the safest place for infants to sleep is in a separate cot in their parents' bedroom. This guidance will be discussed in more detail in Chapter 9.

To help infants and young children to settle alone at night, many Western parents use 'sleep aids' such as soft toys, cloths or blankets. These are often referred to as 'attachment' or 'security' objects, or as 'comforters' – sharing the inference that they help to reduce infant anxiety due to separation and darkness at night. The idea that they can help to promote autonomy is common to a number of theorists. Donald Winnicott (1953) called them 'transitional objects' because he thought they helped to bridge the gap between the infant's sense of inner-self and the outer world. Pauline Mahalski (1983) argued that they provide an aid that infants can use to reduce arousal and distress during the transition from waking to sleeping states. As well as the key issue of the effectiveness of these 'sleep aids' in enabling infants to settle at bedtime and resettle upon waking, it is also important to know whether they have any unhelpful outcomes, including setting up habits that become troublesome and difficult to change at later ages.

Sleep aids are used in many, possibly most, Western families – depending on the definition used, the cultures involved, and the age of the children included. In a largely retrospective study of 390 Swedish children aged from 18 months to 16 years based on parental reports, Ekecrantz and Rudhe (1977) found that 74% of these children had used an attachment object at some time. Richard Passman and colleagues reported that as many as 60% of US children used attachment blankets, with a peak in use at 30 months of age. Mothers reported that 57.5% of North American 3-year-olds used blankets, 3–8% pacifiers and 20% hard objects, as attachment objects (Passman & Adams, 1982; Passman & Halonen, 1979). In New Zealand, Mahalski (1983) found that 90% of 1 to 5-year-olds took an object to bed, but only half of those were reported by their mothers to be strongly attached to them, in that the object helped them to settle. Boniface and Graham (1979) interviewed mothers of 702 UK 3-year-olds, using a more specific definition of attachment objects: 'A lot of children have a special cloth or rag, or something like that, that they take to bed with them or like to hold if they are tired or upset. Does your child have anything like this, or has he/she ever used anything like this?' (Boniface & Graham, 1979, p. 218).

On that basis, only 16.4% of the children were currently using an attachment object, 2% had used one previously but not at the current time and 82% of UK mothers reported that their 3-year-old had never used an attachment object.

For our purposes, Melissa Burnham and colleagues' (2002) study of 3 to 12-month-old USA infants is particularly relevant. In this case, the definition of a 'sleep aid' used was: 'any object (including parts of the child's own body) that a child uses in his/her sleep environment to facilitate sleep without requiring parental assistance' (Burnham et al., 2002, p. 595).

This definition of a 'sleep aid' is broader than Boniface and Graham's but has the advantage for our purposes of focusing specifically on objects used for settling to sleep, as well as including behaviours such as thumb-sucking likely to be common at this age. This study also appears to be the only one that has directly assessed sleep aid use by video-recording infants at home at night, rather than depending solely on parental reports. Approximately 20 infants in California, USA were recruited into each of four age-groups: 3, 6, 9 or 12 months of age. All the infants were sleeping separately from their parents, either in cots in their parents' bedroom or in separate rooms, and sleep-aid use did not differ between these locations. Each infant was followed up over a 3-month period, with 2 nights of video-recording at the recruited age, 2 weeks later and after 3 months. The six videos were supplemented with a parental questionnaire about sleep-aid use, defined as an infant's volitional holding, touching, and/or sucking on an object during wakefulness. As well as monitoring the use of spontaneous or parent-provided sleep aids, the study introduced a novel sleep aid – a knotted T-shirt previously worn by the mother and infused with her odour – at the 2-week follow up recording of each age group. The subsequent recordings assessed whether its use was maintained or other sleep aids substituted.

The main finding was that sleep-aid use was common, so that 95.2% of infants used some sort of sleep aid at the peak of 6 months, reducing to 68.4% at 12 months of age. The concept of an attachment or security object seems to imply some consistency in which object is used, but in practice the preferred objects varied with age and about half of the infants used a different object at later recordings within each 3-month period. Sucking thumbs, fingers or hands was most common at 3 months, whereas use of a soft object was most common at 6 months. Some combination of various aids, including the T-shirt, was also common in 6-month-old infants and became most common in 9- and 12-month-olds.

The authors concluded that 3 to 12-month-old infants use sleep aids frequently and interchangeably rather than using a specific favourite object consistently at every age. This finding suggests that the phrase 'sleep aid' (or 'settling aid') may be more accurate than the notion of an 'attachment object' as traditionally defined, at least at night in the first year of age. The reasons for the changes in sleep aids used are unknown, but presumably involve changes in infant cognitive and emotional abilities or in parenting practices. For instance, the authors speculated that 3-month-old infants may not be able to control reaching for external objects, so that they use parts of their body. The idea that parental practices can influence sleep-aid use is supported by their finding that infants of USA mothers who disapproved of the use of pacifiers for settling were much less likely to use them (Burnham et al., 2002).

Because sleep aids are meant to reduce infant or child anxiety due to separation and aloneness in the dark, their use might be expected to be less common in cultures where parents stay with their children during settling or share the same beds. Three studies have found evidence that supports this expectation. Hong and Townes (1976) compared three groups of doctors' children aged from 7 months to 8 years old, employing maternal reports of 50–169 children per group. The rate of security blanket use in the US group (54%) was higher than among the children of Korean-born doctors working in the US (usage rate 34%) and both these were higher than for children of Korean doctors living in their own country (usage rate 18%). Pacifiers were used by 34%, 22% and 14% of the children, respectively. These rates of security-object use mirrored the different cultures' sleeping arrangements, so that 75% of the US children slept in their own room by 3 months of age, whereas almost all the Korean children slept in the same room, and usually on the same mattress, as their mother, with American-resident Korean families having mixed sleeping arrangements. In a study that compared 14 Mayan families from Guatamala with 17 US families, parents reported that the Mayan bed-sharing infants rarely used thumb-sucking or security objects to help with settling (Morelli et al., 1992). Among 126 US infants, Wolf and Lozoff (1989) found that infants who had an adult present as they fell asleep were less likely to use an attachment object or suck their thumbs.

These findings consistently show that parenting practices that involve staying with settling infants, or bed-sharing, reduce infants' use of sleep-aid objects. In effect, these parenting strategies function as infant sleep aids; or sleep-aid objects provide a substitute for parental contact and stimulation. An obvious question is whether parental presence is a more effective sleep aid than sleep-aid objects such as soft toys. The evidence that many Western parents use bed-sharing to help unsettled infants to sleep ('reactive' bed-sharing) suggests that this is a particularly effective settling strategy – and that many infants like it. The finding that parent-settled infants suck their thumbs less, too, might be an indication that they are experiencing less stress. Unfortunately, however, there is a surprising lack of research to establish whether this is the case. It would be helpful to know, for example, whether infants who settle in contact with parents are less anxious or distressed at bedtime, or upon waking in the night, than those who use attachment objects. It is not obvious that this is the case, since both bed-sharing and staying with infants while settling have been consistently found to maintain waking and signalling later in the night (Adair et al., 1991; Anuntaseree et al., 2008; Burnham et al., 2002; DeLeon & Karraker, 2007; Goodlin-Jones et al., 2001; Louis & Govindama, 2004; Sadeh, 2003). Nor do we know whether infants who settle with parental presence do so more quickly than those using sleep-aid objects, or infants without any form of sleep aid.

There is a clear need for research that confirms whether settling infants with a 'parent sleep aid' has advantages that are insufficiently understood. Since the critical question for many parents will be how and when to vary their infant's sleeping arrangements, evidence about different ways of managing the transition, and the best age at which to do so, would be immensely valuable. For the moment, the potential benefits of staying with infants while settling, and of bed-sharing, need to be balanced against their disadvantages, including the maintenance of infant night waking and signalling until a later age and the possibility that these may become habits that are hard to break later on, when parents or child wish to become more independent. Morelli et al. (1992) reported that Mayan infants were typically weaned from their parents' bed at 2–3 years of age, usually to sleep with another member of the family. They suggested that this transition was usually managed without difficulty, but did not provide any evidence to support their claim.

As noted above, there are also concerns about the safety of bed-sharing. It needs to be said that there are concerns, too, that some 'sleep-aid' objects, including pillows, quilts, comforters, sheepskins, stuffed toys and other soft objects might increase the risk of SIDS and the American Academy of Pediatrics (2005) has recommended that they should be kept out of the infant's sleeping environment. It is for this reason that the T-shirt used as a sleep aid in the Burnham et al. (2002) study was tied in a knot, suggesting that it is easier to prevent any risks associated with sleep aids than with bed-sharing.

The question we are left with is whether the use of sleep-aid objects reduces infant distress upon settling or waking (relative to not having any sleep aid) and whether its advantages outweigh its disadvantages. At present, it is possible to give a cautiously positive, but provisional, answer to this question. One reason it is provisional is that there are no randomized controlled trials in this area. In fact, whether such trials are possible is a moot point, given Burnham and colleagues' (2002) finding that nearly all 3 to 12-month-old USA infants spontaneously use thumbs, body parts or materials in their environment as sleep aids. In any case, because the existing studies are comparative, we only know what follows when infants or parents choose to use sleep aids: we cannot be certain whether they are the causal factor that improves infant self-settling, or whether infants and parents in general would use or benefit from them. A further limitation is that none of the sleep-aid studies so far has provided measures that distinguish settling at bedtime from resettling after waking later in the night. Even the Burnham et al. (2002) study overlooked this distinction, perhaps because some of the infants were already asleep when placed in their cots. It follows that we do not know whether sleep aids reduce infant anxiety due to separation at bedtime in particular.

With these provisos, many Western parents have reported sleep aids to be helpful, or that they are often used (Boniface & Graham, 1979; Burnham et al., 2002; Keener et al., 1988; Mahalski, 1983; Newson et al., 1982). A few studies have also measured infant behavioural outcomes among infants with sleep-aid objects, compared with infants without sleep aids. Anders et al. (1992) found that 3-month-old infants who used sleep aids had longer sleep periods, while 8-month-old sleep-aid users were less likely to signal their parents during the night and to be considered problem sleepers by their parents.

Morley et al. (1989) followed up a group of 320 low-birth-weight infants at 9 months of age, finding that just 9% of infants who used a soft object, thumb or fingers as a 'comforter' woke and signalled parents in the night, compared with 29% of those who used a dummy/pacifier or no comforter. Waking and signalling was least common (4%) among infants who used a soft object, either alone or together with another comforter.

In the Burnham et al. (2002) study, 66.6% of mothers felt positive about using soft objects as a sleep aid, 21.5% considered them acceptable and just 11.6% felt negatively about their use by their own child. As noted above, pacifiers were less popular with these mothers. This study found no significant relationship overall between the frequency of sleep-aid use and how often infants self-soothed back to sleep, while the odour-infused T-shirt introduced experimentally did not prove more effective than other sleep aids. However, there was an overall tendency for sleep-aid users to self-settle back to sleep on their own more often than non-users. In particular, 86% of infants who used a soft object as a sleep aid self-soothed back to sleep without parental involvement at the 2-week follow up, compared with 56% of infants who used any other type of sleep aid or nothing, and this difference was statistically significant. The authors point out that this difference was less substantial than found in their own previous studies and by others, possibly because almost all the infants used some sort of sleep aid.

Studies from other research teams and older ages have shown that children who use sleep aids have normal development. Lehman et al. (1992) found that most of the 33 infants who used a soft attachment object at 19 or 30 months were securely attached to their mothers, both in concurrent measures and Strange Situation measures collected at 12 months of age.

Boniface and Graham (1979) found that 3-year-olds with attachment objects were more independent and tended to have fewer sleep problems than other infants. In John Newson and colleagues' (1982) UK study, 4-year-old children who insisted on taking a cuddly object to bed were considered by their mothers to be less likely to be timid or lacking in self-confidence and less likely to show tension under stress. More of them were reported to be forthcoming rather than shy with unfamiliar adults and to enjoy being with other children. As a whole, these findings indicate that non-parental sleep aids can help infants to settle themselves, are considered helpful by parents and do not affect current development adversely.

There are fewer studies of whether sleep-aid objects have any longer-term 'side effects' such as the development of dependencies. Ekecrantz and Rudhe (1977) asked mothers of 77 4-year-olds about their child's use of sleep-aid objects, then re-questioned the mothers when the children were 6.5 years old. They found no significant differences between the children with and without objects in reported independence, creativity, frustration tolerance or general adjustment at the follow up and concluded that the use of such objects did not affect the children's psychological development. John Newson and colleagues (1982) interviewed mothers of 700 UK 4-year-olds about sleep-aid use, then re-interviewed the mothers when the children were 11 ($n = 500$) and 16 years ($n = 260$) of age. At 4 years, 30% of the children were reported to insist on taking a 'cuddly' to bed. At 11 years of age, the children who had used 'cuddlies' were more gregarious, forth-coming in relation to grown-ups, more likely to enjoy solitary play-acting games, more confident and more likely to 'take things as they come' as opposed to being 'worriers'. At 16 years of age, the children who had used sleep aids at 4 were more frequently described as 'tender-minded', more were inclined to show overt affection to their mothers, and fewer had become regular smokers. The last of these findings presumably reflects concerns that sucking a sleep aid might lead to oral fixations, which were topical at that time. These findings need to be interpreted cautiously because of the large array of assessments collected, the methods used, and the difficulty in distinguishing child characteristics from parental subjective appraisals. However, taken together, the evidence does not show any detri-mental long-term consequences of sleep-aid use.

Evidence about the use of night-lights is remarkably sparse. Expert reports consistently recommend the use of dim electric lights with young children to reduce night-time fears (Mindell & Owens, 2003; Valman, 1981; Weiss, 2010). Bernard Valman (1981) proposed that a landing light casting dim illumination through an open door can serve the same purpose and Mindell and Owens (2003) recommend leaving the bedroom door partly open to reassure young children. Weiss (2010) advises that night-lights should be left on all night, presumably so that a child does not wake up in darkness. However, the strategies used to identify evidence for this book (see Appendix I) have not located any controlled studies of night-light use and they are not mentioned in surveys of young children's night-time fears (see for example, Muris et al., 2001).

This lack of evidence is all the more surprising in view of the impression that night-lights are widely used by parents with infants and young children. Marie Hayes and colleagues (2001) reported that night-lights are used less often by young children who bed-share with their parents than those who sleep separately, suggesting that they have some of the same functions as non-parental sleep-aid objects, but did not report on their rate of use or effectiveness. Since the difference between light and darkness may be important in establishing circadian sleep–waking routines (see section on 'Environmental contributions to infant night waking 2'), it is presumably important that any night-lights are dim, which should also prevent any possible risk of damage to the eyes. It follows that parents can be advised that expert paediatricians recommend the use of a dim electric night-lights where children seem afraid of the dark, but that their effectiveness and disadvantages are unknown.

To sum up, findings in this section show that most infants who sleep separately from parents employ sleep aids when settling, at least so far as the definition of sleep aids is broad enough to include sucking or touching the infant's own thumb and other body parts or nearby objects. There is some evidence that infants tend to use a mixture of different sleep-aid objects, with some variation over age, rather than employing a single favourite 'attachment object' when settling to sleep.

Where parents stay with a settling infant, or share a bed, infants are reported to suck their thumbs and use sleep-aid objects less often. In effect, parental presence appears to act as an infant sleep aid, or sleep-aid objects as a substitute for parental presence. It is not known whether parental presence is more effective in settling infants, so that they are less aroused, distressed or settle more readily, than when infants use non-parental sleep aids. It would be helpful to know.

Some parents may choose to stay with their infants while settling them, believing that this is preferable to using non-parental sleep aids. Like bed-sharing, this practice is common in many societies and can reflect cultural values as well as individual preferences. Where parents favour this approach, they need to consider the potential disadvantages and have a plan for coping with them. The disadvantages include an increased likelihood that infants will continue to wake and signal in the night until a later age. Other advantages and disadvantages of bed-sharing will be discussed in more detail in Chapter 9.

Many Western parents approve of the use of sleep-aid objects, including soft objects in particular, and find them helpful. Where parents adopt this approach, there is evidence of improved infant self-settling, compared with cases where no sleep-aid objects were used. Precautions are needed to avoid any risk of SIDS and the American Academy of Pediatrics recommends that soft objects such as pillows, quilts, comforters, sheepskins and stuffed toys which might cause suffocation should be kept out of the infant's sleeping environment. Otherwise, there is no evidence of adverse effects of the use of sleep-aid objects on infants' concurrent or subsequent development.

Summary and conclusions about the nature and origins of infant sleeping problems

Applying the criteria outlined in Chapter 1, what do we know about infant sleep–waking problems and their causes?

1   Most Western infants cease to wake and signal during the night, and develop the ability to remain settled for long periods at night, by about 3 months of age. This is often referred to, inaccurately, as 'sleeping through the night'. In fact, most infants continue to wake during the night. The critical distinction is whether infants acquire the ability to resettle autonomously after waking, or continue to signal their parents.

2   Infants who persist in night waking and signalling past the first 4 months of infancy are more likely than other infants to have sleeping problems in late infancy and in toddler and pre-school periods. Difficulties in settling to sleep at bedtimes (sometimes called bedtime 'conflicts' or 'struggles') become more important as infants become older. Still, the inability to resettle to sleep autonomously after waking in the night remains the most common source of sleeping problems at these ages.

3   Western parents are rarely worried about the amount their baby is sleeping or the effect of insufficient sleep on infant well-being, whereas this becomes a more common concern when children reach school age. In spite of anecdotal claims, there is little firm evidence that parenting or cultural variables affect the overall amounts that infants sleep per 24 hours. The implication is that research using objective measures of sleep–waking is needed to resolve this question.

4   The proportion of infants who wake and signal their parents in the night at every age from 5 months of age through the pre-school period is quite small – about 5–10% – compared with the rate of around 25% found by cross-sectional surveys of infant and child sleeping problems. The implication is that most cases in such studies have 'intermittent night-waking problems'. This pattern probably includes a variety of subgroups, ranging from infants with repeated re-onset to cases with single re-occurrence due, for instance, to a change in routines. It follows that much more needs to be known about the distinction between stable and intermittent cases and the factors that cause stability and recurrence.

5   It is likely that organic disturbances contribute to night waking in a small minority of infants, but there is a dearth of evidence about the nature of these disturbances and how to distinguish them in the infant period. Most infants who wake and signal their parents in the night are healthy, grow normally, and do not have other kinds of problems, so that their night-waking behaviours are unlikely to be caused by organic disturbances. It follows that healthcare professionals should expect organic cases to be rare. Although due allowance can be made where organic disorders are suspected, the most suitable treatments for such cases are the same as those that are effective for infants and children in general.

6   Type of feeding contributes to the likelihood that babies will become settled at night at an early age. Babies bottle-fed formula stop waking and signalling at night, and cease taking a feed between midnight and 6 am, at an earlier age than breast-fed babies. However, it is not clear how long this difference is maintained by the constituents of the milk infants are fed, and there is evidence that other aspects of parental behaviour associated with feeding may be important after the first few months of age.

7   In particular there is firm and consistent evidence from randomized controlled trials and comparative studies that parenting behaviours affect the likelihood that infants will remain settled at night by 3 months of age. This is the case for breast-fed as well as bottle-fed infants. At least five different components of parenting may be involved and we do not know which components (or combinations of them) are important. However, limit-setting forms of parenting combining these components increase the number of infants who remain settled at night by 12 weeks of age. In contrast, care practices that include sustained parental contact during settling and regular bed-sharing through the night increase the likelihood that infants will continue to wake and signal parents beyond 3 months of age.

8   The conclusion that parenting behaviours influence whether or not infants continue to wake and signal in the night after 3 months of age should not be taken to mean that individual differences in infants' make-up have no part to play. There is abundant evidence in other areas that children's biological dispositions and vulnerabilities contribute to their behavioural characteristics and development. There is, too, promising evidence that individual differences in maturity may moderate infants' ability to arouse and wake up during sleep. However, because our understanding of how biological factors regulate infant sleep–waking is so limited, they are a more suitable focus for research than healthcare practice. The implication of this evidence for healthcare professionals is that individual infant vulnerabilities and resiliencies are likely to affect their ability to respond to the parenting environment, so

that some infants will take longer to develop culturally normal sleep–waking patterns, and require more support to do so, than others.

9   Parenting factors have been highlighted because of the robust evidence that they affect infant night waking and signalling, and because these parenting factors are amenable to change, so that parents who want to influence their infant's night-waking behaviours can take steps to do so. This emphasis is also relevant for healthcare professionals who support parents.

10 The implication of the findings in this area as a whole is to recast infant sleep problems in a new, and more optimistic, light. Traditionally, they have often been viewed as disturbances of endogenous sleep–waking regulatory systems: in effect, as medical conditions. Instead, contemporary findings indicate that the most common type of problematic infant sleep–waking behaviour – the maintenance of infant night waking and signalling – is usually a variation or delay in the development of culturally normal sleep–waking patterns, due to interactions between normal developmental processes during early infancy and the care-giving environment.

11 This reframing of infant sleep problems as largely social–developmental in nature highlights the importance of social factors in predicting good and poor outcomes. This emphasis is important for health services and professionals. In addition, this view empowers parents to make choices about infant care that reflect their circumstances, resources and priorities. It is not the case that parenting approaches such as cuddling a baby to sleep are medically 'wrong' or 'right', so that responsible parents do not need to adopt one form of care because the alternatives will harm their baby. Rather, parents need to choose the form of parenting that fits their values, needs and circumstances best. Healthcare professionals can advise parents about the likely outcomes of a particular form of parenting, so that parents can make informed choices about the most cost-effective approach for their circumstances.

Lastly, it may not have escaped attention that the evidence about parenting and infant sleeping considered in this chapter is consistent in some ways with the limit-setting approach to baby care recommended in Gina Ford's *The Contented Little Baby Book* whereas, as noted in Chapter 4, the more permissive, infant-led approach recommended in *The Continuum Concept* is associated with lower amounts of crying per 24 hours in the first 3 months of age. This conclusion, that neither infant-demand nor limit-setting parenting methods is better overall, but rather that they have different benefits – and costs – helps to explain why the debate about strictness versus permissiveness in baby care has continued across so many generations. Each of these approaches to parenting is partly effective, but in a different way. This conclusion depends, in turn, on understanding the difference between infant crying and sleep–waking behaviours and on adjusting parenting to infant age. The question of how best to coordinate these two parenting approaches in order to manage crying and sleeping effectively in contemporary Western societies will be taken up again in Chapters 9 and 10.

Chapter 7

The influence of parents' cultural and personal beliefs on their care-giving behaviour and infant sleeping problems

Throughout this book, a distinction has been drawn between an infant behaviour and a parental judgement that the behaviour is problematic. The two are related, but only partly. The 'dual pathway' model presented in Chapter 2 proposed that parents' culturally influenced beliefs, values and circumstances affect their subjective judgements about which infant behaviours are problematic, as well as influencing the parenting behaviours that contribute to infant night waking and signalling. Having focused on the contribution of the parenting environment to infant sleep–waking behaviour in the preceding chapter, the goal here is to complete the picture by examining how parental psychological characteristics and cultural contexts combine to influence both their parenting behaviours and judgements that infant night-waking behaviours are problematic. Understanding how these work together is needed if the advice given to parents is to meet their needs and circumstances, be accepted, and be acted upon.

Links between parents' psychological characteristics, parenting behaviours and infant night waking and signalling

The first study of whether parents' psychological characteristics might be a factor in young children's sleeping problems appears to have been carried out by Diane Benoit and colleagues in 1992 (Benoit et al., 1992). Twenty mothers who reported night waking and/or settling problems in their 30-month-old toddlers were compared with 21 mothers who did not report toddler sleep problems, employing measures of maternal attachment. The attachment measures in this case were obtained from the mothers' Adult Attachment Interview reports of their attachments with their own parents when they were children. The finding was that mothers who reported insecure attachments to their parents were more likely to report having toddlers with sleep problems than mothers who had secure attachments to their parents. This difference was substantial. All the mothers of toddlers with sleep problems in this study were classified as insecurely attached compared with 57% of the mothers with secure attachments to their parents. Interestingly, there was no evidence that mothers of toddlers with sleep problems had experienced more upsetting or traumatic experiences of separation during their childhoods. Rather, the mothers' current mind-set, involving unresolved insecurities about relationships with their own parents, appeared to be the strongest predictor that their 30-month-old toddlers would have sleep problems.

Following Benoit's path-finding study, subsequent research has sought to clarify the nature of the parental psychological characteristics involved and to understand how these might link with their parenting behaviours, and with infant night-time sleep–waking behaviours. The first study of this sort was carried out by Julian Morrell in the UK in 1999. It involved 157 mothers and their 13 to 16-month-old infants and used the Maternal Cognitions about Infant Sleep Questionnaire (MCISQ) to assess relationships between mothers' MCISQ scores and their reports of infant night-waking behaviours and problems (Morrell, 1999). Mothers who expressed doubts about limit-setting, and favoured responding to infant demand, reported more infant sleep–waking problems, whereas these problems were not associated with maternal worries about infant hunger or safety (Morrell, 1999). The implication is that mothers who believed in infant-demand care methods were less likely to employ limit-setting, increasing the likelihood that their babies would signal on waking in the night. However, because both sets of measures were obtained concurrently from mothers, this study was limited to identifying an association between maternal beliefs and reports of infant night-waking behaviour – it did not provide direct measurements of the mothers' parenting strategies or any information about causation.

More recently, an Australian study by Nikki Johnson and Catherine McMahon (2008) obtained questionnaire reports from 110 parents about their pre-school children's (mean age 3.81 years) sleeping problems, together with parental MCISQ measures of their cognitions and reports of bedtime interactions using the Parental Interactions Bedtime Behaviour Scale, which distinguishes care that encourages child autonomy from care that involves active parental responding to infant demand. Their findings were consistent with Morrell's, although the extent of reported parental interactions at bedtime was a better predictor of child sleeping problems than the MCISQ measures of parental beliefs; but the two were related. This study extends Morrell's finding to an older age range and includes measures of parenting behaviour, but it too has the limitation that all the measures were provided concurrently by parents. Consequently, the findings do not demonstrate a causal link. That requires, at the least, longitudinal research with measures at successive ages, together with objective measures of parenting and infant sleep–waking behaviour in different groups.

Two Israeli researchers, Anat Scher and Avi Sadeh, have produced findings that are consistent with Morrell's London study, provide more robust evidence, and indicate the causal processes involved. Scher's focus is on mothers' feelings of anxiety about separation from their infants (Scher & Blumberg, 1999; Scher, 2008). In her most recent study, 52 mothers recruited in well-baby clinics reported on their anxiety about separating from their babies when they were 10 months of age (Scher, 2008). Infant night-waking and settling time were measured by objective, actigraphy methods as well as by maternal report. Her most robust finding was that infants of mothers with high separation anxiety woke more often during the night when assessed concurrently by objective measures of night waking than infants whose mothers had moderate or low separation anxiety.

Avi Sadeh and colleagues' first study in this area also showed concurrent relationships between parental psychological beliefs and infant night waking (Sadeh et al., 2007). More recently, Sadeh and his colleague Liat Tikotzky have taken the important step of measuring parental beliefs and infant sleep–waking longitudinally in a community sample of 85 infants and parents (Tikotzky & Sadeh, 2009). Crucially, parental beliefs about the reasons for infant night waking were measured before their baby's birth, as well as afterwards. Parents completed the Infant Sleep Vignettes Interpretation Scale plus measures of the strategies they planned to use, or actually used, when settling infants to sleep and when they woke in the night.

The researchers found that maternal beliefs about infant night waking measured prenatally predicted which infants would wake in the night after they were born, that is, at 6 months of age. In particular, pregnant women who believed that infant waking in the night would be due to infant distress and need for parental support were more likely to have 6-month-old infants who woke and signalled in the night, whereas pregnant women who attributed infant night waking to the need to set limits were less likely to have 6-month-olds who woke and signalled at night. The same predictions were possible between 6 and 12 months after birth: after controlling for infant sleep–waking at 6 months, maternal beliefs at 6 months that emphasized concern about infant distress, rather than the importance of limit-setting, predicted increased infant night waking over the next 6 months, measured both by objective and parental measures. Parental beliefs emphasizing concern about infant distress at night also predicted parents' reports of more use of active soothing behaviour, which was related, in turn, to increased infant night waking and signalling. Parental beliefs emphasizing the importance of limit-setting predicted reports of less active soothing by parents, and these were predictive of reduced infant night waking and signalling. More recently still, Janis Baird and her colleagues in England found that General Health Questionnaire measures of women's proneness to psychological distress obtained even before they were pregnant predicted an increased likelihood that their babies would wake in the night at 6 and 12 months of age (Baird et al., 2009).

These studies show striking similarities in their findings, but it is important to note their limitations as well. Only two studies so far have obtained longitudinal measures that show that parental subjective thoughts or feelings about baby care predict infant night waking, and only one of these obtained evidence that parenting behavior mediates this relationship. Even that study did not measure parenting behaviours directly. Another limitation is that the focus so far has been almost exclusively on mothers, but recent research has produced evidence that fathers need to be included: Liat Tikotzky and colleagues (2010b) found that, after controlling for breast-feeding, higher paternal involvement in infant care was associated with fewer infant night wakings according to both maternal and paternal reports. More needs to be known, too, about infant variables. Although these cannot account for the findings as a whole, they may mediate parental actions because parents are influenced by the extent of infant distress and protest upon separation.

The various studies described above are also quite different in the type of parental psychological characteristics they measured. An obvious question is whether 'proneness to psychological distress' (as measured by Baird), parental 'concern about infant distress' versus 'cognitions about limit-setting care' (as measured by Sadeh) and maternal 'separation anxiety' (as measured by Scher) are different things or measures of some common underlying parental psychological characteristic. The term 'belief' has been used here to emphasize the evaluative nature of these parental subjective characteristics and it seems likely that they include an emotional, as well as social-cognitive, element so that some parents are more anxious about infant fragility, distress and separation, leading them to intervene and provide support, whereas other parents are more confident about, and encourage, infants' autonomous abilities. These terms also recall others used elsewhere in this book, for instance in distinguishing parenting that promotes close parent–child emotional bonds versus child autonomy, and parenting that values 'strictness' over 'permissiveness'. Of course, they also recall Attachment Theory, considered in the previous chapter, except that now the focus is on parents', rather than infants', response to separations at night. In older children, the colloquial phrase 'tough love' and more formal term 'authoritative parenting' are used to describe parenting approaches that combine affection with limit-setting and it appears that these psychological characteristics have much in common with those examined here.

These findings do appear to be promising, in that they offer the potential to uncover the origins of the parenting behaviours known to influence whether or not infants continue to wake and signal in the night (see Chapter 6). However, it is important to bear in mind the newness of this area of research and the lack of specificity in the findings. We are some way, for instance, from being able to provide tools that professionals can use routinely to assess the psychological characteristics of parents in general when providing guidance. Nor is it clear that an approach of that kind would be cost-effective. For the moment, the practical implication of this evidence is to highlight the need to ask parents about their feelings and priorities and to take them into account when discussing the advantages and challenges involved in limit-setting parenting methods. Because, too, parents in some cultures believe that it is cruel to leave babies to settle and sleep alone by themselves (Jenni & O'Connor, 2005; Morelli et al., 1992), parents' cultural traditions and values will need to be included in these discussions.

Links between parents' cultural backgrounds and judgements that infant night waking and signalling is problematic

A recent large-scale international website-based survey found that parents in all 17 countries that took part reported infant/toddler sleep problems (Mindell et al., 2010). Extraordinarily wide variations between countries were found in the percentages of parents who reported the problems, ranging from 10% (in Vietnam) to 76% (in China) (Mindell et al., 2010). The reason for the remarkably high rate in China is unclear, but internet survey methods of this kind are susceptible to sampling biases. Interestingly, measures of sleep proximity (room-sharing and bed-sharing) were not associated with parents' subjective judgements of whether their infant/toddler had sleep problems. In a representative study of 3907 Brazilian mothers and their 12-month-old infants, Ina Santos and colleagues (2008) found that 46% of Brazilian infants habitually shared the bed with their parents during the night, 46% of infants habitually woke their parents in the night, but only 16% of Brazilian mothers reported that their child's sleep habits interfered with their own well-being.

In a study of Korean mothers, 98% shared their bed with 3 to 24-month-old children, 83% of the children woke and signalled, and 28% cried more than once per night, but just 16% of mothers reported that their child's night waking was a problem (Lee, 1992). These findings suggest that parent reports of infant sleeping problems may be the result of parental cultural and lifestyle factors as much as a consequence of infant night-waking and signalling behaviour. In Santos and colleagues' words (2008, p. 119): 'It is possible that waking is being perceived differently by the mothers who co-sleep than by the mothers of those who do not.'

Although that seems entirely plausible, it is also possible that the nature of bed-sharing infants' actual night-waking behaviours, and consequently their parents' experiences during the night, are different from those of other families. For example, Sarah Mosko et al. (1997) found that maternal awakenings were shorter but more frequent when bed-sharing with their babies than when the infants were in cots, while Sally Baddock and colleagues (2006) observed that bed-sharing mothers checked on their babies more often, but more briefly, resulting in minimum disruption of maternal sleep. These authors speculated that infant night waking and signalling may be less disruptive for both infant and parents when they share a bed, as well as pointing to other potential advantages, such as enabling breast-feeding and close emotional bonds. Taking this idea a stage further, the implication is that the fit between parents' culturally influenced beliefs and their experiences (including their baby's night-time behaviour) is a critical factor in determining whether infant night waking is considered to be problematic. A cultural belief system that values interdependence could then give rise to proximal sleeping arrangements that promote the detection of infant night waking and signalling but stop some parents from judging that it is problematic. In contrast, cultural values that emphasize autonomous development could influence parents to adopt sleeping arrangements that reduce infant night waking or its detection by parents.

Support for Santos and colleagues' proposal has been provided by a number of other studies. Betsy Lozoff and her colleagues (1996), for example, assessed 186 urban American families of 4 to 48-month-old children subdivided by ethnicity and socioeconomic status. In keeping with the other studies, co-sleeping was associated with parent-reported night waking: in this case the proportion of co-sleeping infants waking during 3 or more nights per week was approximately double that of non-co-sleeping cases. However, among families who co-slept, white parents were more likely than black parents to consider their child's sleep–waking behaviour to be a problem. Lozoff and colleagues' conclusion that 'one explanation is that different childrearing attitudes and expectations influenced how parents interpreted their children's sleep behavior' (Lozoff et al., 1996, p. 9) is remarkably similar to that of Santos and her team.

As noted in Chapter 6, an important distinction in the co-sleeping literature is between planned or intentional bed-sharing, which starts at birth and follows parental childcare values and beliefs, and 'reactive bed-sharing' that occurs in response to infant sleeping problems. In a recent edition of the journal *Infant & Child Development* devoted to the co-sleeping literature, Kathleen Dyer Ramos and colleagues reported that parents of planned co-sleepers detected 2-year-olds' night waking but did not consider it problematic, whereas parents who were reactive co-sleepers did consider infant night waking to be problematic (Ramos et al., 2007). In the same journal issue, Gary Germo and colleagues (2007) found that parents who chose to co-sleep with their toddler children and those who chose not to do so were both satisfied with their sleeping arrangements – whereas parents who co-slept in reaction to their child's night waking were dissatisfied with the outcome. Here, too, the implication is that a mismatch between parents' beliefs, intentions and experiences was a more potent determinant of parental concerns than the nature of their sleeping arrangements by itself.

The obvious missing element in these studies is measures of parenting behaviour and whether these are consistent with parents' cultural beliefs.

Since, too, parents may change their minds after trying out a form of care, longitudinal studies that plot these changes and the circumstances that give rise to them are needed. Because parents in some cultures believe that it is cruel to leave babies to settle alone by themselves (Jenni & O'Connor, 2005; Morelli et al., 1992), it is not hard to imagine that conflicts may occur for such parents if circumstances lead them to work in a Western society that emphasizes infant autonomy, dual earning, the need to work office hours, and the benefits of limit-setting care in helping babies to sleep through the night.

Similar conflicts may occur where two parents have different ideals and child care goals, or where parents change their priorities as infants get older. There is a good deal more to learn about the relationship between parents' social–cultural beliefs, circumstances and parenting behaviours, as well as about the results of cultural practices such as bed-sharing for infant development in the longer-term (Hunsley & Thoman, 2002). In the meantime, the findings in this section are clear enough to draw attention to cultural and personal beliefs as factors that need to be taken into account when parents and professionals discuss plans for infant care, so that the resulting guidance meets parental needs and circumstances and is approved of, so that parents are motivated to act on it.

Links between parental vulnerabilities and infant sleep problems

An association between parent-reported infant sleeping problems and maternal depression has been reported by many studies (Goodlin-Jones et al., 2000; Hiscock & Wake, 2001; Lozoff et al., 1985; Meltzer & Mindell, 2007; Seifer et al., 1994b; Zuckerman et al., 1987). This finding, though, raises far more questions than it answers. For instance (since both measures typically come from mothers) is the relationship between depression and infant night-waking behaviour, or does depression affect mothers' perceptions of how problematic the behaviour is? We need objective measures of infant night-waking behaviour to find out. Equally, the question of the direction of effects (infant on parent, or vice versa) requires clarification. It may well be, as Avi Sadeh and colleagues (2010) have argued, that effects are bi-directional, so that depression influences parenting behaviour, which influences infant night waking and signalling, and that infant unsettled night-time behaviour triggers maternal depression. There is evidence for each of these elements (Cronin et al., 2008; Lam et al., 2003; Smart & Hiscock, 2007; Wake et al., 2006) but it is not yet clear how they affect each other longitudinally over time. Parents' fatigue due to interruptions to their own sleeping may reduce their physical energy and impair their judgements or ability to provide adequate care (Bayer et al., 2007; Dennis & Ross, 2005; Fisher et al., 2004; Kurth et al., 2010; Thomas & Foreman, 2005) and it may be that parental fatigue is a more common cause of adverse parent–child interactions than depression itself. We need to understand more about the role of depression, fatigue and inadequate social support, in predicting poor coping and adverse outcomes.

Although research that addresses these questions is needed, health service practice cannot, and probably should not, wait upon its findings. Arguably, the risk of abuse and poor social interactions where parents cannot cope with disruptions to their own sleep is a greater threat to infant well-being than any direct effects of infant night waking (Chavin & Tinson, 1980; Schwebel & Brezausek, 2008). The implication is that health service professionals need to be skilled in detecting and managing social risk, as well as medical risk. It follows that healthcare staff require tools for assessing both infant and parental parts of this problem and prioritizing cases where the two combine. Methods for this purpose will be examined in Chapter 10.

Summary and conclusions about the influence of parents' cultural and personal beliefs

There is growing evidence that parents' psychological characteristics and beliefs provide the foundations for their parenting behaviours, which are known to influence whether or not infants persist in waking and signalling in the night. It is likely, too, that parents' cultural background, as well as their individual characteristics and circumstances, influence parents' subjective judgements about which infant behaviours are problematic. In extreme cases, parental psychological vulnerabilities, including depression and exhaustion, may hamper parents' ability to cope with their infant's night-time behaviour.

These findings are recent and further research is needed to understand the processes involved more precisely. However, the evidence is already clear enough to suggest two practical steps. First, there is a need to consider parental psychological vulnerability and the availability of social supports in cases where parents report infant sleeping problems. Second, the guidance given to parents in general needs to include asking about their cultural and personal beliefs and priorities, so that these can be taken into account when choosing between infant-demand and limit-setting forms of parenting. By doing so, the likelihood that parents will accept the guidance given, feel motivated to act on it, and find it effective, should be increased. Further research is needed to confirm that is the case. We will return to the collection and use of this information for healthcare purposes in Chapters 9 and 10.

Chapter 8

Multiple infant crying, sleeping and other problems after three months of age

The nature, prevalence and impact of these problems

Almost all studies of Western infants to date have found that amounts of infant crying, and rates of parental concern about it, reduce greatly after about 12 weeks of age (see Chapter 3). However, evidence has begun to accumulate that prolonged crying at older ages, although much rarer, has more serious long-term implications. These cases are distinct from most infants who cry a lot in a number of ways. First, their prolonged crying is reported to occur when they are older than 3 months of age. Second, unlike most infants who cry a lot in the first 3 months, these infants often have multiple (sleeping, feeding and other) problems, as well as prolonged crying (DeGangi et al., 1991; Papoušek & von Hofacker, 1998; Rao et al., 2004; Schmid et al., 2010b; Wolke et al., 2002). Third, the parents of infants in this group have a high rate of psychosocial vulnerabilities or ambivalent parent–child relationships (Papoušek and von Hofacker, 1998; Wolke et al., 2009). Fourth, follow-up studies have found that these infants have serious disturbances, including hyperactivity, cognitive deficits, poor motor coordination, and behaviour problems, that persist until at least school-age (Rao et al., 2004; Schmid et al., 2010b; Wolke et al., 2002).

In short, the defining features of these infants are (1) that they exhibit problematic behaviour in multiple areas; (2) the behaviours occur in older infants, that is beyond the age when these behaviours undergo developmental transitions among infants in general.

In one of the first studies of infants of this kind, Georgia DeGangi and colleagues (1991) identified a group of just 11, 8 to 11-month-old infants who exhibited disturbances of sleep, feeding, state-control, self-calming and irritability. Infants who solely had crying problems, or solely sleeping problems, were deliberately excluded from this group. They referred to the infants they examined as cases of 'regulatory disorder', so that this term was reserved for infants with reported problems in at least two areas of behaviour beyond 7 months of age. Boys predominated in the regulatory-disordered group and their parents reported that most of them were 'difficult'. Compared with 24 normal infants, the regulatory-disordered infants scored significantly lower on the mental development component of the Bayley Scales of Infant Development. The researchers did not find differences in measures of physiological regulation between the groups, but they speculated that the regulatory-disordered infants had difficulty in controlling the activity of their autonomic nervous systems to meet environmental demands.

Since the DeGangi group's path-finding study, much of the clinical research into this group of infants has been carried out by Mechthild Papoušek and colleagues in a university-based clinic in Munich, Southern Germany (Papoušek & von Hofacker, 1998; Papoušek et al., 2001). In addition to the primary presenting complaint of prolonged crying, the infants she and her colleagues studied were characterized by sleeping problems, feeding problems, failure to thrive, excessive clinging and social withdrawal, separation anxiety, excessive temper tantrums and early forms of aggressive behaviours (Papoušek et al., 2001). About two-thirds of the Munich cases presented when infants were between 7 and 30 months old, with only a third before 6 months of age. In diagnostic interviews, 80% of parents reported that their infant's problems had persisted for several months, but information about the age of onset was limited and retrospective, so that its accuracy is unknown. At 30 months of age, the infants were re-assessed as toddlers, in comparison with a similarly aged group without comparable behaviour problems (Papoušek et al., 2001). At this age, the infants with previous crying and multiple problems were reported by mothers to have high rates of aggressive behaviour, anxious/depressed behaviour, social withdrawal, sleep problems, somatic problems and overall emotional and behavioural problems.

More recently, a separate German study by Rüdiger von Kries and colleagues (von Kries et al., 2006) used 1865 telephone interviews to collect maternal reports of infant crying, feeding and sleeping problems between 6 and 47 months of age. The median child age when the mothers were interviewed was 25 months and reports of behaviour before 6 months of age were retrospective. The study found that prolonged crying in the first 3 months was not associated with increased rates of sleeping or feeding difficulties, whereas infants over 6 months of age who cried a lot were 6.6 times more likely than other infants to have sleeping problems and 8.9 times more likely to have eating difficulties, according to parental reports. Similarly, Barry Zuckerman and colleagues (1987) found that English infants who solely had sleeping problems at 8 months did not have later behaviour problems, whereas those with chronic sleep problems continuing to 3 years of age were more likely to have multiple behaviour disturbances. In a longitudinal study of an English group of 64 infants whose parents sought help from the charity *Cry-sis*, Dieter Wolke and his group (2002) followed them up at 8–10 years of age. Their average age as infants was 3.8

months, 56 of the 64 were reported to fuss and cry for >3 hours per day after 3 months of age, and 59 had multiple problems involving sleeping and feeding, as well as crying. At primary school age, the *Cry-sis* cases were 14 times more likely to have pervasive hyperactivity problems than case–control children from the same schools. An important feature of this study was that the hyperactivity was reported by teachers and children, as well as by parents. Similarly, Malla Rao and colleagues' longitudinal study of Norwegian and Swedish children found that prolonged crying after 3 months of age (but not before 3 months), predicted hyperactivity, cognitive deficits, poor fine-motor abilities and disciplinary problems when the children reached 5 years of age (Rao et al., 2004).

Organic disturbance explanations

The nature, persistence and severity of these problems suggest that the individuals in this group are quite different from most infants who solely have crying or sleeping problems, so that the causes of their problematic behaviours are also likely to be different. One possibility is that organic disturbances play a part in at least some of these cases. Indeed, the phrase 'regulatory disorder' used by DeGangi seems to imply that these individuals have a general disturbance in the physiological or psychological systems underlying their behaviour. Whether that is actually the case in practice, though, is far from clear.

One stumbling block to date is that the term 'regulatory disorders' has no agreed definition or meaning, so that some writers have used it, for instance, to refer to atypical patterns of sleep–waking organization. Given a definition of that type, night waking alone could be said to be a 'regulatory disorder' although, as we have seen, most infants who wake in the night do not have problems with other aspects of their behaviour or physiology. Although the concept of regulatory disorders was adopted by the American 'Zero-to-Three' clinical diagnostic classification scheme for problems in the first 3 years of age (Skovgaard et al., 2007), it remains true that it lacks a firm empirical basis. As Martin Maldonado-Duran and Juan-Manuel Sauceda-Garcia (1996, p. 66) put it: 'The concept of regulatory disorders is a clinical one, as yet without firm scientific support in terms of its nature, difference from other behavioural disturbances, and the boundaries between it and other disorders'.

A related issue is that there is limited evidence so far that infants selected for behaviour problems in multiple areas have neurological or other organic disturbances. Indeed, no evidence of neurological disturbances or high exposure to biological risks was found by Rao and colleagues in their study (Rao et al., 2004). Using a neurobehavioural assessment, Mechthild Papoušek and Nikolaus von Hofacker's (1995, p. 218) Munich study did find evidence, in their words, of 'mild to moderate neurological immaturity' in postural control, trunk hypotonia and body asymmetry in half the 61 infants with crying and multiple problems they assessed at an average of 3.6 months of age, compared with 16% of control infants. Whether these neurological signs persisted or were anything more than transitory signs of immaturity is, though, not known. Dieter Wolke and his group found that shortened gestational age and neonatal neurological complications predicted regulatory problems at 5 months and lower scores on cognitive assessments at 56 months in their German cohort study (Wolke et al., 2009). The most recent study from this group (Schmid et al., 2010a) found that records of prenatal complications and very pre-term birth predicted multiple regulatory problems, but not single crying or sleeping problems, at 5 months of age. Overall, these somewhat mixed findings indicate that organic disturbances may play a part in this group's long-term problems, but the findings are far from conclusive.

The longitudinal research methods used in some of these studies are important in identifying the age at onset of the problematic behaviours in question and distinguishing different causal pathways. Since quite large numbers of infants cry a lot in early infancy, or wake at night after 12 weeks of age, an obvious question is whether these develop into more extensive and severe disorders in some cases, or whether their multiple problems have a later onset. If some infants graduate from single into multiple problems, the next step is to understand what distinguishes these infants from the majority who do not develop long-term problems.

Unfortunately, there is a dearth of longitudinal studies that start early enough in infancy to speak to this question. The reasons for this are not hard to find. Since 'regulatory disorders' are expected to be rare, large numbers of infants need to be followed longitudinally over quite long periods from the first weeks of infancy in order to scrutinize the small numbers of cases who develop multiple problems later. This is highly expensive, a daunting prospect for researchers and families, and fraught with practical problems, since the families with most problems are likely to be precisely the cases who are most likely to drop out of the study over time. As a result, to this author's knowledge, longitudinal information of this sort is available from just one study, of 547 Canadian infants from birth to 6 months of age carried out by Tammy Clifford and her colleagues (Clifford et al., 2002). Using a definition of 3 or more hours of fuss and crying a day to define prolonged crying, this study found prolonged crying at 6 weeks in 24% of infants while, in keeping with many other studies, this dropped markedly, to 6.4%, at 12 weeks of age. About half of the infants who cried a lot at 12 weeks had continued to do so since 6 weeks, while in 3% of infants the onset of prolonged crying did not occur until 12 weeks of age or later.

These figures need to be qualified by the methodological limitations of this study, including the use of retrospective parental estimates of crying in

42% of cases, while it is not known how many of the infants had multiple problems at either of the ages reported. Nor does this research provide any insight into the question of whether physiological disturbances are involved in either of the groups of infants, or into the concept of regulatory disorders. What the study does add is a provisional guideline that prolonged crying after 12 weeks occurs in roughly 6% of infants, while about half of these were already crying a lot at 6 weeks of age. A remarkably similar finding – that 5.8% of infants were considered by parents to cry excessively beyond 3 months – was obtained by von Kries and colleagues' (2006) telephone survey of German parents. This survey also found that these older infants were likely to have problems across multiple areas of behaviour. Schmid et al. (2010a) found multiple regulatory problems in 5.4% of 5-month-old German infants. Wurmser et al. (2001) reported that 'excessive crying' occurred in 39.6% of German 1 to 3-month-olds, while it persisted in 21% of these cases, giving a prevalence of 8.4% after 3 months of age.

There are many provisos, but the initial implication of these findings is that the group of infants with crying and multiple problems after 3 months of age contains two subgroups with different developmental profiles: those with early onset and persistent problematic behaviour, and those with problematic behaviour with a late onset. It follows that the 'early onset' cases must be included in the larger group of infants who cry a lot during early infancy, so that the challenge for future research is how to distinguish the small number of cases where problems persist from the large majority where crying problems are transitory. In a promising approach to this question, Cynthia Miller-Loncar and her American colleagues (2004) found disorganized feeding behaviour in a small, highly selected group of 19 6 to 8-week-old infants who were clinically referred for prolonged crying. Approaches of this kind that attempt to subdivide cases at an early age may allow early detection of infants who are likely to have multiple and persistent problems.

Social–environmental adversity

The simplest non-organic causal explanation for multiple behaviour problems in older infants and children is that these are due in large part to family environmental factors. There is evidence that emotional, behavioural, eating and sleeping problems in 18-month-olds are associated with family psychosocial risk factors (Skovgaard et al., 2007). Similarly, Papoušek and her team found that many parents of older infants with crying and other problems had psychosocial vulnerabilities, including a high rate of marital discord and maternal depression (Papoušek et al., 2001), which in turn are known to predict child problems at older ages (Skovgaard et al., 2007; Zuckerman et al., 1987). Wolke and colleagues (2009) found that ambivalent parent–child relationships predicted poor longer-term outcomes in their study of infants with regulatory disorders. In the Papoušek et al. (2001) study, 60 infants recruited because of parent-reported prolonged crying and multiple problems in the first 6 months of infancy were followed up when they reached 30 months of age. At this point their mothers rated themselves as exhausted, depressed, anxious, less efficacious in their maternal role and more dissatisfied with their marital relationships, compared with control group mothers. Strikingly, more than half the mothers of multiple-problem infants reported that their levels of anxiety and depression were already high before their infants were born (Papoušek et al., 2001).

As discussed earlier (Chapter 6), social–environmental 'risk factors' might not act as the sole causes of the problematic infant behaviours, so much as working to maintain, extend or worsen infant behaviours that have another initial cause. With the important proviso that the evidence is far from conclusive, the available research findings suggest the need to take parenting and family variables into account when infants over 3 months of age present with multiple behaviour problems.

Intervention studies

It is important to recognize that the methods used by Papoušek and other similar studies do not allow causation to be determined, a point the researchers themselves acknowledge. A more powerful method for this purpose is to carry out intervention studies that attempt to change parenting in one group, while another receives equal researcher attention that does not target parenting behaviour. Although they did not include such a control group, the Munich team have implemented an intervention programme focusing on sensitive management of infant behaviour. This involved an average of 3.4 sessions each lasting 1–2 hours (Papoušek et al., 2001). Although 93% of parents and infants were rated 'fully or partially improved' at the end of the programme by a psychologist and paediatrician, at a follow-up assessment at 30 months of age the programme infants were reported by parents to be highly difficult, hard to control and to have high rates of emotional and behaviour problems. Furthermore, there were no differences in the rates of these problems between treated and non-treated families.

Dieter Wolke and colleagues (1994a) assessed 48 infants with a mean age of 3.8 months whose parents had contacted the English charity *Cry-sis* because of their infants' crying and other problems and who met criteria for prolonged amounts of crying. With sequential assignment, about half the mothers received a counselling intervention, while half were guided by trained *Cry-sis* staff in how to use a structured behavioural programme. A third, comparable, group of 44 infants received only routine primary healthcare. Most infants in all three groups had multiple problems, including feeding, health and sleeping problems. Unfortunately, it is not known whether the infants' parents had psychosocial risks of the sort found by Papoušek and colleagues. This study found that the structured behavioural programme was more effective in reducing crying than the counselling intervention, but all three groups of infants were still crying substantially more than community norms at an assessment 3 months later. As we have already noted, a later follow-up of 64 of the *Cry-sis*-referred infants at 8–10 years of age found a greatly raised prevalence of pervasive hyperactivity problems, compared with case–control children from the same schools (Wolke et al., 2002).

A further study in this age range is Dymph van den Boom and colleagues' (van den Boom, 1995, 2001) Dutch intervention and follow-up randomized control trial. Cases were selected to include families of lower socioeconomic status and infants who were objectively irritable when 10- and 15-days old, but it is not known whether the infants had crying, sleeping and other problems at later ages, when the intervention took place. For present purposes, the importance of this study is that the intervention programme was delivered after the infants were 6 months of age, while the study included a randomized, non-intervention control group, allowing analysis of the effects of parenting. The intervention programme involved three sessions, each lasting 2 hours, between 6 and 9 months, which provided mothers with advice on adjusting their interactions in response to their infants' cues. Researcher observations on completion of the programme found that it improved maternal responsiveness, attentiveness, contingent stimulation and controlling behaviour. Intervention infants displayed more positive social behaviour, more exploratory behaviour and were less irritable. At 18 months, 72% of the intervention infants displayed secure attachment behaviour in the Strange Situation, compared with just 26% of the non-intervention control infants. Similar improvements in intervention infants, mothers and their relationships were sustained at the final follow up at 42 months of age.

The van den Boom findings are promising in showing that interventions that target parent–infant interactions with older infants can produce worth-while improvements in infant behaviour and development. They are in keeping, too, with extensive evidence that changes in parents' interaction with infants and young children can improve the children's behaviour (Olds et al., 2007; Webster-Stratton & Hammond, 1997). Less clear is whether the sort of benefits found by van den Boom would apply with infants or families with severe and multiple problems of the sort described by Papoušek and her group (Papoušek et al., 2001) or Wolke and colleagues (2009). Equally, it remains unclear whether inadequate parenting in these families is the main cause of behaviour problems in older children, or at least partly a response to the infants' behaviour at a young age.

Summary and conclusions about multiple infant crying, sleeping and other problems after 3 months of age

To sum up this chapter, many of the infants who come to clinical attention because of prolonged crying after 3 months of age are reported by parents to have multiple problems, while some families of such infants also face multiple psychosocial adversities. These combined features are associated with more serious and long-term disturbances than are typical where infants have early crying or sleeping problems alone. Although we do not have accurate prevalence figures, it appears that about 6% of infants fall into this category. The available data indicate that about half such infants start their problematic behaviours earlier, while half have their onset after 3 months of age. The implication is that two different developmental profiles, and subgroups of infants, exist at this age: infants with early onset and persistent problematic behaviour; infants with late onset problematic behaviour.

The findings in this older, multiple-problem, group implicate parenting as a contributing factor in some cases and this is consistent with our under-standing of the importance of parenting as a scaffold for infant learning in this age period and evidence about the origins of children's behaviour problems more generally. Contemporary, transactional, models of develop-ment emphasize the importance of cumulative biological and social risk factors in predicting adverse long-term outcomes (Rutter, 2006; Sadeh et al., 2010). It appears at least possible that the long-term problems encoun-tered in these cases may be the result of child characteristics that hamper interactions with the environment, in combination with parenting factors and social–environmental adversity. Research studies that apply this way of thinking longitudinally to infancy and beyond are likely to be particularly informative.

In the meantime, the implication of the findings as a whole is to highlight the paucity of the evidence about this group of infants and the need to prioritize them for research and clinical work. It follows that professionals who encounter these cases will need to fall back to a large degree on the evidence that exists about managing children's emotional and behaviour problems more generally (Olds et al., 2007; Webster-Stratton & Hammond, 1997). We will return to the question of how best to use this evidence to help families with infants who cry a lot and have multiple problems beyond 3 months of age in Chapter 10.

Chapter 9

Best practice for preventing infant crying and sleeping problems: anticipatory guidance for professionals to share with parents

The assumption underlying this book is that parents will wish to use tried and tested, evidence-based forms of baby care, so far as these fit their circumstances, values and resources. It also assumes that parents generally, and first-time parents in particular, will need expert guidance from a primary healthcare professional in how to apply the evidence to their own individual baby and circumstances. The goal in this and the next chapter is to translate the evidence examined so far into guidelines that support this partnership between professionals and parents.

The guidelines in these chapters are based on the evidence reviewed in Chapters 3–8 and have been developed in workshops with health service professionals in North America and the UK (Barr et al., 2001; St James-Roberts, 2006b, 2007b). An important proviso is that, although they have been designed to take different cultural values into account, they have not yet been fully evaluated under health service conditions or in multicultural contexts. As Olds et al. (2007) emphasize, dissemination research is needed to understand those factors that affect the successful dissemination and implementation of evidence-based interventions. In particular, parents' acceptance of and motivation to implement recommendations are of critical importance. The guidelines below need to be evaluated, and improved, by dissemination research.

Chapter 10 provides guidelines for cases where infant crying or sleeping problems become serious enough to warrant further assessment or action, including referral for specialist treatment. The guidelines in this chapter are designed for routine discussion with parents to provide reassurance and prevent problems – and should be sufficient in most cases. The guidelines can be reproduced as written materials for professionals and parents and adapted as needs be. An example of such a leaflet for parents (*'Night and Day': Helping Your Baby to Know the Difference*) is reproduced in Appendix II.

The goal is to introduce these topics with all parents (often mothers in practice) during routine contacts in the first few postnatal weeks. Research has shown that direct contact and discussion is most beneficial: leaflets by themselves are not sufficient (St James-Roberts et al., 2001). Because of the distinction between infant crying and sleeping problems, and the importance of age, the material is divided into three parts. The initial focus is on the first 6 postnatal weeks and, particularly, infant crying, which peaks at this age. Next, the particular and thorny issue of bed-sharing, which extends across age and raises safety issues, is considered. The third section provides guidance about the consolidation of sleep–waking during the period from 6 weeks to 6 months. This division helps to organize the information into the periods when it is most applicable, but should not be rigidly adhered to.

Preventing infant crying and sleeping problems 1: guidelines for the first 6 weeks (the infant crying peak)

Normal features of infant crying in Western societies in the first 6 weeks

- Parents can be prepared to expect babies to fuss and cry quite a lot during the first few weeks – much more than at later ages. The usual pattern is for crying to increase from birth to around 4–6 weeks, the peak age for crying. Typical babies in Western societies fuss/cry for a total of around 2 hours per 24 hours at this age.
- This is an average figure – some babies cry more, some less. The differences between babies are large and babies vary quite a lot from day to day.
- The crying is not evenly distributed across the day: there is often a peak in the evenings or late afternoons.
- At this age, many babies have occasional periods when they cry for no apparent reason. These crying bouts are long and 'unsoothable' – the crying cannot be stopped by strategies that usually stop a baby's crying, such as feeding or picking up. Trained professionals cannot prevent or stop these bouts either.
- These *unsoothable bouts* occur more or less often in babies generally and are thought to be linked to changes in infants that are a normal part of development. In most cases, there is nothing physically wrong with babies who have these unsoothable crying bouts, and even babies looked after by the most sensitive and responsive parents have them. They are sometimes referred to as 'colic' bouts, but most babies who have them gain weight normally, are in good health, and are not in pain so far as research has been able to tell.
- These three features of early crying – the age peak, evening clustering and unsoothable bouts – are *normal* parts of development. Most infants who cry a lot are towards the far end of the normal range of individual differences, rather than being ill or unwell.
- Parents can be alerted to expect the unsoothable bouts and made aware that this type of crying is normal at this age and not their fault.

The bouts will gradually disappear of their own accord as an infant gets older, and will not affect their baby's long-term development.

- In a small minority of cases – 5–10% of babies who cry a lot (about 1 in 100 babies overall) – prolonged crying in early infancy can be a symptom of an organic disturbance, including a food intolerance. Healthcare professionals and parents should expect these cases to be rare. Symptoms to help identify them, and intervention strategies, are described in Chapter10.

Other messages about babies' crying in the first 6 weeks

- It isn't possible to predict which baby will cry a lot. Gender, birth order and feeding method are poor predictors.
- Parents are sometimes told that they should be able to tell the *cause* of a baby's crying from its *sound*: i.e. that there are different 'hunger', 'anger' and 'pain' cries. This is a myth. Even trained scientists cannot tell the cause reliably based on the sound alone. An intense cry tells us how distressed the baby is, but not the particular cause. Parents need to work that out based on experience: e.g. if baby has not been fed for 4 hours, the cry is likely to be a hunger cry. Parents can be reassured that they should not feel guilty if they cannot tell the cause of a cry from its sound.

Infant crying and parental care

- Parents cannot 'spoil' a baby by holding too much or being too responsive to crying at this age.
- A distinction often made is between *'infant-demand' and 'limit-setting'* parental care.
- Terms like *'infant-demand', 'attachment' and 'natural'* parenting refer to approaches where parents set out to follow an infant's cues:
  - by feeding often on demand;
  - by holding/carrying a lot;
  - by responding quickly to all frets and cries.
- Terms like *'limit-setting'* or *'structured'* parenting refer to approaches where parents impose routines and limits on their babies, by:
  - introducing regular times for sleeps, feeds and other activities;
  - putting babies down, rather than holding them;
  - sometimes delaying responses to crying, rather than always responding immediately to all frets and cries.
- Parents may not worry about the amount their baby cries.
- If parents wish to minimize the overall amount of crying, infant-demand parenting, including lots of holding (rather than putting babies down) is likely to help in the first 6 weeks. In the largest study, where

infants were held for an average of 9.5 hours/day (including feed-times), and parents responded rapidly to frets and cries, the infants cried a third less per 24 hours than UK infants generally. The holding can be shared between adults and some parents find a cloth 'baby-sling' helpful.

- Parents in modern societies often balance baby care with competing employment, financial and social pressures. The supports available to help them, for instance via paid maternity or paternity leave, vary between countries and according to parents' circumstances. Against this background, many parents may find it difficult to employ a highly 'infant-demand' form of care, even if they approve of it in theory. They may find it reassuring that the approach to baby care used by parents in Copenhagen reduced infant crying as effectively as full 'proximal care' in the cross-cultural study described in Chapter 4. Compared with typical London parenting methods, Copenhagen parents put their babies down much less, and seldom left their babies without physical contact, or to cry, during daylight hours. Instead, they held and responded to their babies more. This 'Copenhagen' approach to baby care may be a workable compromise for many parents.

- Although infant-demand parenting methods will reduce the overall amount a baby cries at this age, they will not prevent unsoothable crying bouts. These are a normal part of development at this age. The bouts will gradually disappear of their own accord as an infant gets older and babies who have them will have normal long-term development. If parents find them hard to tolerate, some strategies that help to contain them are given in Chapter 10.

Normal features of infant sleep–waking in the first 6 weeks

- Babies have short periods of sleep and waking at this stage. They wake every few hours for feeding, with not much difference between the day and night.
- Waking in the night for feeding is normal at this age.

Infant sleep–waking and parental care

- Feeding on demand is recommended as best for baby's health and growth, and breast-feeding on demand is especially recommended for these reasons, at this age.
- When babies are put down to sleep, placing them on their backs is recommended for safety reasons. Babies placed to sleep on their backs have a greatly reduced likelihood of sudden infant death syndrome SIDS, where an infant dies for unexplained reasons.

- Babies can be placed on their fronts for interactions and play in the daytime providing they are monitored.
- During the first 6 weeks, a baby's sleep–waking is not affected much by whether parents adopt infant-demand versus limit-setting care. After infants reach 6 weeks of age (but not before), different forms of parenting do start to affect infant night waking. But, decisions about bed-sharing need some early consideration, because arrangements set up in the first few weeks and continued are likely to have consequences at later ages. This is discussed in the guidelines below about bed-sharing.

Preventing infant crying and sleeping problems 2: the pros and cons of bed-sharing with infants

Parents' decision about whether to bed-share with their baby is not a simple matter of right and wrong. The choice involves balancing a number of possible pluses and minuses, as well as safety issues, according to their plans and circumstances. These issues will matter more after about 6 weeks of age, but they will need to be planned from early on because arrangements set up in the first few weeks and continued are likely to have consequences at later ages.

Possible pluses

- Sharing the parents' bed with a baby is common throughout the world and some cultures approve of it because they think it is unkind to require a young child to sleep alone.
- Some parents value the close emotional relationship with their baby that bed-sharing gives them and find that it is convenient for breast-feeding at night. This can help to prolong breast-feeding to an older age, which has advantages for infant and maternal health.
- Bed-sharing works best when it is deliberately chosen by parents from the outset. It is sometimes adopted later on as a way of coping with a baby who is unsettled in the night. In those cases (called 'reactive bed-sharing') it can become a problem for parents where babies get used to it and refuse to settle alone as they get older.

Possible minuses

- Parents who regularly bed-share with babies report that infant night waking continues to an older age than happens where parents do not bed-share. We do not yet know why this happens: it could be that their closer proximity just makes them detect a baby's waking more readily. But, parents need to anticipate whether this would be a problem for them.

- Some infants develop a liking for bed-sharing and refuse to leave the parents' bed and sleep alone at older ages. This does not happen in all cases but, unfortunately, we do not yet know why this happens with some infants but not with others.
- There are safety concerns about bed-sharing. This area is complex, controversial and still evolving over time. Some medical authorities, including an American Academy of Pediatrics Policy Statement (American Academy of Pediatrics [AAP], 2005) have advised against routine bed-sharing, particularly because of the risk that parents may lie on their babies and cause SIDS. This guidance remains controversial, because some countries where bed-sharing is common have low rates of SIDS, while factors often associated with bed-sharing, rather than bed-sharing itself, may be the true risk factors for SIDS (Fleming & Blair, 2007; McKenna, 2005). James McKenna, in particular, has argued that bed-sharing tends to keep infants and parents in a lighter sleep state, which may protect against, rather than increasing the risk of SIDS (McKenna, 2005; McKenna & Gettler, 2010). It is known and generally accepted that infant–parent bed-sharing is dangerous (and should be avoided) where parents smoke, after parents consume alcohol or illicit drugs, or where the sleeping occurs on a soft surface, such as a sofa. There is also evidence that babies who sleep alone in a separate room are more likely to die from SIDS, so that sharing the parents' bedroom, but not their bed, is safer (American Academy of Pediatrics, 2005).

The AAP (2005) report recommended that infants can be brought into a parental bed for nursing or comforting but should be returned to their own crib or bassinet when the parent is ready to return to sleep. Putting infants down to sleep on their sides was no longer accepted as an alternative to supine sleeping, because putting infants down to sleep on their backs is safer. Breast-feeding was recommended because of its overall benefits, but not because it reduced the risk of SIDS. When two SIDS researchers, Peter Fleming and Peter Blair, reviewed the available evidence in 2007, the UK National Health Service (NHS) advice about SIDS drew attention to these risk factors, but fell short of advising against bed-sharing (Fleming & Blair, 2007). At the time of writing this book, this guidance has hardened and the current UK NHS website advice is: 'The safest place for your baby to sleep is in a crib or cot in a room with you for the first 6 months. You should never bring your baby into bed with you' (NHS, 2010). The word 'never' contrasts with the AAP (2005) guidance and it is too soon to know whether parents will comply with this or whether it has overall benefits.

Clearly this is an evolving situation and professional bodies are trying to give advice that is clear and simple to implement as well as safe. The only conclusion it is possible to draw is that professionals and parents will need to obtain the latest guidance from their own medical authorities and countries and to make up their own minds about whether and when to bed-share.

Preventing infant crying and sleeping problems 3: guidelines for the period from six weeks to six months of age (helping babies to distinguish day from night)

This is a period of rapid and remarkable development, much of it taking place between 6 and 12 weeks of age. This rapid development is accompanied by striking variability *between* infants. Babies vary greatly in how much they cry, the age when they stop having unsoothable crying bouts, and in the age at which they are first settled at night. This variability worries many parents. Unexplained crying makes them think something is wrong with their baby. Having a baby who 'sleeps through the night' is an important milestone for many parents. They compare with other parents and worry if their baby still wakes in the night, which they view as a sign that something is wrong. The guidelines below can provide reassurance and help.

Normal features of infant crying, and effects of different forms of parenting, at this age

- Generally speaking, the amount babies cry nearly halves between 6 weeks and 3 months of age (Chapter 10 includes some specific figures).
- The other features of crying described in the guidelines for early infancy (the afternoon/evening peak and unsoothable bouts) usually reduce. Occasionally, periods of prolonged crying continue to 4 months of age, but then diminish.
- These changes in crying happen without any major changes in parenting and are thought to be due to developmental processes taking place in infants.
- Most babies who cry a lot in the first 3 months are normal in their development at that age and in the long-term. Most of them are settled in the night by 12 weeks and not particularly likely to be poor sleepers at later ages. Where unsoothable infant crying bouts distress parents in this age range, strategies for coping are given in Chapter 10.

Normal features of infant sleep–waking during this period

- Sleeping periods get longer, particularly during the night-time. Waking periods concentrate into the daytime and gradually get longer, but the change is slower and more gradual than with sleeping (Chapter 10 includes some detailed sleep–waking figures).

- In Western cultures, two-thirds of infants stop waking up and crying out or otherwise 'signalling' their parents during the night by 3 months of age. A third of infants continue to wake and signal their parents.
- The word 'signal' is used because parents can be alerted by a variety of infant behaviours: a murmur may be sufficient where they are sharing a bed with their infant. Night-time waking and signalling need not involve prolonged crying, because any crying usually stops once parents respond.
- When infants stop signalling in the night, parents call this 'sleeping through the night', but this phrase is misleading. Infra-red video-recordings have shown that almost all infants continue to wake in the night. By 3 months, most babies start to fall back to sleep by themselves. The critical issue is not that some babies have disturbed sleeping. It is why a quarter or more of infants continue to wake and require parental attention in order to resettle, whereas most infants can resettle without parental intervention by about 3 months of age.
- There is nothing physically wrong with most infants who wake up and 'signal' their parents in the night after 3 months of age: they are healthy, put on weight and grow normally, and do not go on to have other developmental problems, with one exception. The exception is that infants who wake and signal parents in the night after 4 months of age are likely to continue to wake and disturb their parents in the night when they are toddlers and pre-school-aged children.
- Where infant night waking and signalling continues past 6 months of age, this is often referred to as an 'infant sleeping problem'. This phrase is misleading since it is not clear that these infants have anything wrong with their sleeping, other than needing help to resettle upon waking in the night. Most of these infants are in good health. Likely sources of parental concern are (1) that their baby is behaving differently from most other babies in their society; and (2) that their baby being awake at night keeps the parents awake and disturbs their own sleep. Strictly speaking, the problem belongs primarily to parents, rather than to infants.

Effects of parenting on infant sleep–waking during this period

- After about 6 weeks of age, parenting strategies and sleeping arrangements do start to influence whether infants stop signalling in the night (and 'sleep through the night' as far as parents are concerned). Some parents may wish to adopt 'limit-setting' parenting strategies that support babies in becoming settled at night at a young age. These are described in Appendix II.
- Not all parents find infant night waking to be a problem or wish to give priority to having a baby who is settled at night at a young age.

For example, Brazilian mothers report a high rate of bed-sharing, a high rate of infant night waking, but a low rate of infant night-waking problems. Parents in other cultures, too, value closeness and having their baby with them more than having an infant who remains settled during the night.

- Because most babies who wake and signal parents in the night are in good health, parents need to choose the form of parenting that fits their aims, values and circumstances best. It is not the case that parenting approaches such as cuddling a baby to sleep are medically 'wrong' or 'right', or that parents should choose one particular form of care because the alternatives will harm their baby. Decisions about these issues are primarily cultural/lifestyle decisions involving balancing pluses and minuses, rather than medical decisions about what's best for a baby's health.

- In Western societies, factors such as whether both parents need to get up in the morning to work (and so find disruptions of their own sleeping to be troublesome) are important in deciding whether being kept up by their baby in the night is a serious problem. This can be less troublesome if parents can adjust their own sleeping to their baby's sleep–waking patterns.

- By asking parents about their cultural and personal beliefs about sleeping arrangements for their baby and the 'limit-setting' methods described below, professionals can help them to work out their priorities.

- If parents wish to help their baby to stop waking and signalling in the night by 3 months of age, there is some evidence that setting up daily routines, such as bathing and wind-down activities at approximately the same time each evening, may help to establish settled infant sleep–waking habits.

- There is particularly firm evidence that the use of *'limit-setting'* parenting from about 6 weeks of age is likely to help to stop babies waking and signalling in the night by 3 months of age. Since no benefits of this approach were apparent before 6 weeks of age, parents can delay introducing it until after this age. An important advantage is that this approach is effective with breast-fed infants and that, unlike 'controlled crying' methods used to treat infant sleeping problems after they have arisen, does not involve leaving babies to cry. The steps proven effective are listed in Appendix II.

- Infant and child night waking and signalling remains the main concern for parents, but other child sleep–waking problems begin to occur at older ages. Difficulties with getting toddlers and young children to settle to sleep (sometimes called bedtime 'struggles') become more common. Difficulties of this kind often occur together with night waking, but the two can occur separately. The evidence is weaker, but bedtime struggles are thought to be partly due to how parents manage their children's bedtimes.

- Separations at bedtime. From around about 6 months of age, many infants become afraid when separated from their parents, and left alone in the dark, at bedtime. The age when this happens and extent of the distress varies from infant to infant.

- Parents, too, vary greatly in how easy they find these separations and some find them upsetting, perhaps partly because of their infant's distress. There may be differences between mothers' and fathers' views of how to manage these occasions. Anticipating this and having a strategy agreed between parents for managing bedtime separations may help everyone involved.

- It may reassure parents to know that this infant response to separation and the dark is common at this age and probably the result of normal psychological development in their child.

- Where infants sleep alone in a cot in their parents' bedroom, or in another room, 'sleep-aid' objects such as soft toys and knotted blankets (sometimes known as 'attachment', 'security', or 'transitional' objects) can help infants to settle themselves to sleep or to resettle upon waking. Infants also often use their thumbs, other parts of their body or materials in their environment, to help to settle themselves. Providing they are safe, these objects can be helpful for infants and parents. Objects such as pillows, quilts, comforters, sheepskins and stuffed toys that might cause suffocation should be kept out of the infant's sleeping environment because they may increase the risk of sudden infant death syndrome (SIDS). Dim electric night-lights and/or leaving the bedroom door partly open may also help to reduce infant anxiety about being alone in the dark.

- Infants and children maintain their loving attachments to parents in spite of separations and there is no evidence that separations at bedtime or overnight damage infants' attachment bonds. On the contrary, separations that children can manage are likely to increase their resiliency. Because separations will be necessary at some stage, the critical question is when and how to manage separations so that children are not unduly distressed, acquire autonomous self-soothing abilities, and avoid becoming over-dependent.

- Parents may judge their baby to be too young to cope with bedtime separations, or find their infant's distress at bedtime separations intolerable. In such cases, staying with an infant while settling and other means of maintaining contact may reduce distress on both sides. These methods are practised in many cultures all over the world and parents may consider that the benefits outweigh the disadvantages. The main disadvantage is that this is likely to become a habit, so that infants will continue to need parental involvement to settle. They will be more likely to need parental contact upon waking in the night rather then resettling autonomously and this may continue until the pre-school age. Parents who adopt this strategy may find it worthwhile to construct a plan for when and how they will introduce limit-setting strategies later on in case they are needed.

- Where parents are able to implement them, parenting methods that prioritize limit-setting will make it more likely that infants will become autonomous in self-settling. If parents wish to use these methods but find their child's distress at bedtime prevents them from being implemented, a method that allows parents to reduce contact gradually (known as 'checking' or 'graduated extinction') may help. It is described in Chapter 10.
- Bed-sharing in this age-period raises the same issues as listed in the guidance for birth to 6 weeks (above) and it may help to re-visit them at this stage.
- In rare cases, infant night waking and signalling can become a problem for infants if parents cannot cope. It can disturb their relationships and interactions and may lead to parental depression. Parental fatigue due to interruptions to their own sleeping may reduce their physical energy and impair their judgements or ability to provide adequate care.
- Single parenthood, lack of social supports, exhaustion, depression or a poor relationship with a baby, may make night waking particularly challenging for parents. Discussing the arrangement of social supports and the use of the 'limit-setting' parenting methods may help parents to cope.
- Chapter 10 provides guidelines for cases where parents are struggling to cope with infant crying or night waking.

Best practice for treatment: guidelines for managing infant crying and sleeping problems after they have arisen

Introduction

The information in the previous chapter is designed to inform and reassure parents and to prevent problems – and should be sufficient in most cases. In a minority, persistent infant crying or unsettled night waking may become sufficiently serious problems to warrant further assessment or action, including referral for specialist treatment. This chapter is designed for use in identifying and managing these cases.

Three distinctions continue to be important.

Distinction 1

This concerns distinguishing between three different groups of infants as follows.

1   Infants who solely have prolonged unexplained crying in the early weeks. This is relatively common, occurring in around 1 in 5 infants (depending on how stringent a definition is used). Most of these infants are healthy, are not likely to have sleeping or other problems when older, and have normal long-term development.
2   Infants who solely wake in the night and disturb parents after 3 months of age. This too is a relatively large group, around a quarter to a third of infants, depending on the definition used. Most of these infants are healthy and have normal long-term development. They are not particularly likely to have other problems, except that their night waking and signalling is likely to persist to toddler and pre-school ages.
3   Infants who *both* (a) have multiple areas of problematic behaviour (crying plus sleeping problems, often together with feeding and other problems); *and* (b) where these multiple problems occur after 4 months of age. This is a much smaller and recently recognized group, estimated to include about 5% of infants as a whole. These infants (but not those with solely crying or sleeping problems) are particularly likely to have

serious disturbances of attention, behaviour and movement control that persist up to school age, making them a priority for healthcare services.

Distinction 2

This concerns distinguishing between infant and parental problems. Because most infants who cry a lot or wake and disturb parents in the night are in good health, the 'problem' belongs first and foremost to parents. Cultural factors, family arrangements and individual vulnerabilities influence how problematic the infant behaviours are for parents. It follows that the problems are inherently social, and that the most serious threat for infants may occur where parents cannot cope, leading to 'shaken baby syndrome' or other forms of abuse. Healthcare services need to be able to assess and distinguish both infant and parental parts of the problem and to target cases accordingly. Cases combining parental vulnerability and troublesome infant behaviour may be prioritized.

Distinction 3

This concerns distinguishing between infants whose problematic behaviour is a consequence of normal developmental processes plus parenting factors versus those where an organic disturbance is involved. Where possible, healthcare services need to be able to distinguish organic cases and refer them for specialist treatment.

   These distinctions lead to the guidelines below.

Guidelines for cases where problematic infant crying is the sole presenting complaint

Assessing problematic infant crying

- Where parents report an established infant crying problem, parental complaint, rather than infant behaviour, is the presenting symptom. Such complaints involve a subjective judgement, while parents vary in their knowledge about and tolerance of crying. It follows that measurements that assess infant behaviour are an essential first step in understanding what the problem is.
- Two methods that collect data about infant crying from parents are convenient to use and sufficiently accurate for this purpose: the Crying Patterns Questionnaire (CPQ) and the Baby's Day Diary. These are reproduced in Appendix III and IV respectively. Both fussing and crying are assessed and usually totalled together, because crying and fretful 'fussing' are often interwoven, making it difficult to distinguish

between them. The CPQ depends on recall of infant crying over the previous day and week, making it less accurate, but more convenient, than the diary (which parents fill in more or less as crying and other behaviour occurs). Because infant crying tends to vary from day to day, parents need to keep the Baby's Day Diary for at least 3 days, making it quite onerous to complete. The CPQ takes about 5 minutes to fill in during an interview and is suitable for initial use; the results will indicate how much time a baby spends crying and whether the crying peaks in a particular time of day. The Diary can be employed to follow up complex cases or where there is doubt about the CPQ figures.

- Completion of the CPQ or diary with a parent is likely to produce benefits on its own. Parents often report that this process provides insight, while in many cases it will be clear that the baby is showing amounts and patterns of crying that are normal at this age, so that this reassurance is all that is needed. For purposes of comparison, figures for amounts of infant crying at different ages are given in Box 10.1. These figures need to be employed with care. They can provide an indication of whether an individual baby is crying more, or less, than most others, but by themselves do not provide any reason for concluding that there is anything wrong with the infant in question.

- As well as infant behaviour, the primary assessment work-up should also consider parental vulnerability. Methods for doing so are given in the section on 'Guidelines for cases involving concern about parent vulnerability', below.

Managing and treating prolonged infant crying

- In around 1 in 10 infants presented because of prolonged crying (and about 1 in 100 infants overall), the crying may be due to an organic disturbance, such as a food intolerance. The 'red flags' for indentifying such cases identified by paediatric members of an international expert group (Barr et al., 2001) are as follows:
  - high-pitched/abnormal sounding cry;
  - lack of a diurnal rhythm (lack of a peak in evening/late afternoon);
  - presence of frequent regurgitations, vomiting, diarrhea, blood in stools, weight loss, or failure to thrive;
  - positive family history of migraine, asthma, atopy, eczema;
  - maternal drug ingestion;
  - persistence past 4 months of age.

- Parental report of these signs of a possible organic disorder indicates a need for referral for expert assessment. Expert medical guidance is also important where parents suspect food intolerance and wish to make changes to their own diet or to introduce or vary infant formulas, since such changes can produce additional difficulties.

Box 10.1 Figures for amounts and forms of infant crying

Measures of the amounts infants cry are usually collected by parents and combine fussing and crying into a single 'crying' figure because infants cycle between these, making it difficult to separate them in everyday circumstances.

Because of variability in the methods used in the studies and the inaccuracy of the methods, the figures below should be viewed as 'rule of thumb' approximations, which provide a helpful, if rough, guide. If interpreted carefully, they should enable many parents to be reassured that their infant is not crying more than most others of an equivalent age – and allow infants who are crying more than most others to be identified. By itself, evidence that an infant is crying a lot does not mean that there is anything wrong with the infant, but may suggest a need to collect further information (see main text).

A Mean or median figures for total 24-hour fuss/crying from infants in the general community in different countries

Infant age, weeks	Canada[a]	Canada[b]	Denmark[c]	Italy[d]	UK[e]	USA[f]	USA[g]
2				148 (90)	138 (77)	105 (30)	
3	102 (15)		90 (58)				
5–6	132 (30)	163 (75)	79 (67)	151 (100)	128 (70)	165 (30)	152 (72)
8				119 (79)			
12	78 (10)		48 (44)		97 (44)	50 (15)	
21							
40					50 (32)		

Figures are mean (SD, standard deviation) values unless otherwise indicated. Figures are from behaviour diaries kept by parents. Group sizes vary from 50 to 1857 cases.
a. Canadian figures are calculated from Figure 1 in Hunziker & Barr (1986); b. Canadian figures for Vancouver from Fujiwara et al. (2011). c. Alvarez (2004); d. Bonichini et al. (2008); e. St James-Roberts & Plewis (1996); f. Brazelton's (1962) figures are median and upper/lower quartile range values from Boston, USA. g. Fujiwara et al.'s (2011) figures from Seattle, USA. Prolonged crying can be defined as >1 standard deviation above the mean for infants of the same age and country. Chapter 2 provides a discussion of definitional issues.

B Bout-based measures

As well as the overall amount an infant cries, recent studies have found that the occurrence of prolonged, 'unsoothable' bouts of crying is particularly stressful for parents (Barr et al., 2005; Fujiwara et al., 2011; St James-Roberts et al., 1995, 1996). In both Seattle and Vancouver the existence, and especially the maximum lengths, of unsoothable crying bouts, were most strongly associated with caregiver reports of daily frustration: even more so than the amounts infants cried (Fujiwara et al., 2011). Since unsoothable crying makes up less than 10% of overall crying (Fujiwara et al., 2011; St James-Roberts et al., 1996), its potency to frustrate parents is probably due to its capacity to make parents feel helpless and guilty. It follows that it is worthwhile to assess unsoothable crying and discuss it with parents. The recommended CPQ assessment allows this (see main text). Chapter 3 provides further information about unsoothable crying bouts.

C The 'Rule of Threes' definition

The 'Rule of Threes' (>3 hours fuss/crying per 24 hours on >3 days/week) is often used by researchers to define prolonged crying or 'colic'. Although this rule is easy to remember, it is more or less arbitrary and difficult to apply fairly because crying amounts differ between cultures, as shown in A above. In consequence, more infants will meet this definition, for instance, in Canada or the USA than in Denmark. This is probably a result of differences in parenting methods. See Chapter 3 for further discussion of these issues.

- The procedures for expert referral depend on local medical and specialist arrangements, set up and coordinated by local services.
- Where no organic disturbances are found, the available evidence provides no basis for advising parents in general that changes in their method of care are likely to resolve crying problems in 1 to 3-month-old infants once the problems have arisen. This conclusion is particularly true of the prolonged, unsoothable crying bouts that are often central to parents' concerns in early infancy.
- Instead, once organic disturbance has been considered, and the infant's healthy growth and development has been confirmed, the focus of intervention should be on containing the crying and providing parents with support. Important elements advocated by an expert international group (Barr et al., 2001) are:
  - discussing the notion that crying means that there is something wrong with a baby of this age and introducing alternatives (e.g. that the crying is a sign of a vigorous baby);
  - viewing the first 3 months of infancy as a developmental transition, that all babies go through more or less smoothly;
  - reassuring parents that it is normal to find crying aversive and discussing the dangers of shaken baby syndrome;
  - discussing ways of containing/minimizing the crying and highlighting positive features of the baby;

- considering the availability of supports and the development of coping strategies that allow individual parents to take time out and 'recharge their batteries';
- empowering parents and reframing the first 3 months as a challenge that they can meet, with positive consequences for themselves and their relationships with their babies;
- continuing to monitor infant and parents.

Guidelines for cases where problematic infant sleeping/ night waking is the sole presenting complaint

Assessing infant sleep–waking problems

- Here too the first goal is to distinguish between infant and parental parts of the problem. The Brief Infant Sleep Questionnaire (BISQ) shown in Appendix V will indicate the type of infant behaviours involved, takes a few moments to complete, and is standardized for 5 to 29-month-old Western infants. Appendix VI includes a sleep diary, which is more suitable for further assessment. In this age-range, infant night waking and signalling is likely to be the predominant complaint. The BISQ will indicate how often this occurs and how long it lasts for.
- Some figures to help to decide how severe the infant sleeping problem is are given in Box 10.2. These figures, too, need to be employed with care. They can provide an indication of whether an infant is more or less unsettled in the night than most infants of a similar age, but by themselves do not provide any reason for concluding that there is anything wrong with the infant in question. As Box 10.2 shows, there is a wide variation in how much normal infants sleep. If there are serious worries about amount of sleeping per 24 hours (as opposed to settling or night-waking issues) and, particularly if other problems with daytime behaviour or medical conditions occur, specialist referral for assessment may be helpful.
- Most cases with established sleep problems will involve older infants or young children. At these ages, fear of separation from parents and of the dark can contribute to bedtime settling and waking problems. History taking with parents that addresses this issue is called for. There is evidence that parents' anxiety about separations increases parental active involvement in settling and prolongs separation periods, which then prevents infants from acquiring autonomous self-settling abilities. Discussing this issue with parents may help them to decide whether to reconsider their approach to bedtimes and adopt limit-setting forms of care (see the Guidelines for 6 weeks to 6 months in Chapter 9 and Appendix II). 'Checking' and other methods for minimizing child, and parental, separation anxiety are described below.

Box 10.2 Figures for infant sleep–waking

Because of variability in the methods used in the studies and the inaccuracy of these methods, the figures below should be viewed as 'rule of thumb' approximations, which provide a helpful, if rough, guide. If interpreted carefully, they should enable many parents to be reassured that their infant is not sleeping less, or waking more, than most others of an equivalent age – and allow infants who wake and signal more than most others to be identified. By itself, evidence that an infant is unsettled in the night does not mean that there is anything wrong with the infant, but may suggest a need to collect further information (see the main text).

A Figures for bedtime, night waking and signalling, and sleep and waking length

Country	Mean (SD)						
	Hour of bedtime[a]	Night wakings, n	Awake in the night, hours	Longest sleep, hours	Hour of rise time[a]	Night sleep, hours	Total 24-hour sleep
Australia	19.71 (1.12)	1.23 (1.21)	0.44 (0.60)	7.93 (2.94)	6.59 (0.99)	10.17 (1.46)	13.16 (1.87)
Canada	20.74 (1.19)	1.24 (1.37)	0.41 (0.58)	7.84 (2.91)	–	9.96 (1.52)	12.87 (1.99)
China	20.95 (1.03)	1.78 (1.28)	0.52 (0.72)	8.11 (2.75)	6.90 (1.01)	9.49 (1.24)	12.49 (1.93)
Hong Kong	**22.29** (1.09)	1.10 (1.10)	0.46 (0.83)	7.81 (2.56)	7.78 (1.38)	9.02 (1.46)	12.16 (2.10)
Indonesia	20.45 (0.97)	1.97 (1.31)	0.68 (0.82)	7.10 (2.90)	**5.93** (1.18)	9.15 (1.36)	12.57 (2.16)
India	22.19 (1.11)	**2.07** (1.57)	**0.72** (1.02)	**5.65** (2.90)	7.19 (1.35)	9.15 (1.35)	11.83 (2.51)
Japan	21.29 (1.07)	1.25 (1.25)	**0.28** (0.42)	8.23 (2.82)	7.13 (0.97)	9.42 (1.09)	**11.62** (1.48)
Korea	22.10 (1.16)	1.50 (1.31)	0.34 (0.65)	7.88 (2.84)	**7.98** (1.21)	9.42 (1.25)	11.90 (1.72)
Malaysia	21.79 (1.10)	1.54 (1.25)	0.47 (0.72)	6.95 (2.84)	7.47 (1.21)	9.19 (1.54)	12.46 (2.38)
New Zealand	**19.46** (0.92)	**0.93** (1.09)	0.33 (0.53)	**8.88** (2.91)	6.66 (0.74)	**10.61** (1.35)	**13.31** (1.84)
Philippines	20.85 (1.30)	1.60 (1.28)	0.54 (0.81)	7.16 (2.77)	6.87 (1.42)	9.15 (1.58)	12.69 (2.37)
Singapore	21.63 (1.20)	1.35 (1.24)	0.41 (0.63)	7.28 (2.72)	7.47 (1.21)	9.26 (1.54)	12.36 (2.23)
Thailand	20.88 (1.19)	1.58 (1.16)	0.33 (0.50)	7.07 (2.73)	6.87 (1.40)	9.90 (1.31)	12.71 (2.06)
Taiwan	22.15 (1.10)	1.33 (1.39)	0.45 (0.80)	7.19 (2.97)	7.70 (1.51)	**8.73** (1.86)	12.07 (2.39)

continues

Country	Mean (SD)						
	Hour of bedtime[a]	Night wakings, n	Awake in the night, hours	Longest sleep, hours	Hour of rise time[a]	Night sleep, hours	Total 24-hour sleep
UK	19.91 (1.09)	1.06 (1.08)	0.37 (0.60)	8.60 (2.96)	–	10.51 (1.56)	13.10 (2.03)
USA	20.87 (1.15)	1.15 (1.13)	0.42 (0.68)	7.79 (2.83)	–	9.74 (1.59)	12.93 (2.09)
Vietnam	21.73 (1.12)	1.54 (1.32)	0.36 (0.47)	5.93 (2.75)	7.18 (1.05)	9.32 (1.12)	12.99 (2.19)

Source: redrawn from Mindell et al.'s (2010) international cross-cultural survey of 0 to 36-month-olds. With permission from Elsevier.
The highest and lowest figures are in bold to indicate the variation between countries. SD, standard deviation.
a. 24-hour clock.

Figures were collected from parents using the Brief Infant Sleep Question-naire, which defines the night as 7 pm to 7 am, the day as 7 am to 7 pm (Sadeh, 2004). In each case, the figures are averaged over 0–36 months of age. Most data were collected through websites, but those from Thailand and Vietnam by interview. This method does not allow the representativeness of the sampling to be controlled. The total sample size was 29,287 cases, ranging from 501 to 4505 per country. Where figures are missing they were not collected in those countries. Within each country, adding and subtracting a standard deviation from the mean will give an approximate guide to the normal range.

B Settling difficulties at bedtime

These tend to occur in later infancy or the toddler period, often together with night-waking problems. They are usually defined by how long an infant takes to settle (e.g. >30 minutes) and/or whether she refuses to settle without parental presence. With some variation according to the stringency of the definition used and infant age at assessment, around 10–20% of infants have been reported to have settling problems in American, Australian, British and German studies (Armstrong et al., 1994, Gaylor et al., 2005; Jenkins et al., 1984; Wolke et al. 1995b).

C The Richman criteria for a serious night-waking problem

The pitfalls involved in the various definitions of sleep problems were dis-cussed in Chapter 2. Although they are more or less arbitrary, the 'Richman criteria' are often used to identify a serious night-waking problem. They are slightly modified below to include the requirement of ≥6 months age (unnecessary for Richman since all her cases were >1-year-old). It is important to bear in mind that there is probably nothing seriously wrong with most infants who meet these criteria. Rather, if used with care, they provide a helpful 'rule of thumb' for identifying cases where night waking is serious enough to warrant further attention, or for reassuring many parents that their infant's sleep-waking problem is not particularly serious.

The Modified Richman criteria for a serious night-waking problem.

- Infant is ≥6 months of age.
- Infant has been waking and signalling ≥5 nights/week for ≥3 months.

Plus

- Waking ≥3 times/night, *or*
- Waking for ≥20 mins/night, or
- Going into the parents' bed*

* This last criterion is nowadays only applied where bed-sharing is used to settle an infant who will not otherwise sleep ('reactive bed-sharing').

Richman estimated that 6–10% of 1- to 2-year-old infants met these criteria for a serious sleep problem.

D Amount of infant sleep

As Chapter 5 discusses, parents of infants are seldom worried about the overall amount their baby sleeps – concerns about insufficient sleep are more typical at older ages, particularly with school-aged children and teenagers. Still, some figures may be helpful, not least to show the extraordinary range that exists between infants in how much sleep they usually take. Infants, like adults, differ greatly from one another in how much time they spend asleep.

The figures from Iglowstein et al.'s (2006) Zurich Longitudinal Study of Swiss infants and children (shown below) illustrate these individual differences between infants very clearly. Figures at each age are from 452–460 children in the general community. As well as the average (mean) figures, the 2nd percentile figure shows how much the shortest-sleeping 2% of infants slept, while the 98th percentile shows how much the longest-sleeping 2% of infants slept. For instance, at 6 months the range was between 10.4 hours per 24 hours (for the shortest 2% of sleepers) and 18.1 hours per 24 hours (for the longest 2%). This study did not report night-waking figures.

Age in months	Night sleep, hours			Day sleep, hours			Total 24-hour sleep, hours		
	2%	98%	Mean (SD)	2%	98%	Mean (SD)	2%	98%	Mean (SD)
6	8.8	13.2	11.0 (1.1)	0.4	6.4	3.4 (1.5)	10.4	18.1	14.2 (1.9)
12	9.7	13.6	11.7 (1.0)	0.2	4.6	2.4 (1.1)	11.4	16.5	13.9 (1.2)
18	9.7	13.5	11.6 (0.9)	0.5	3.6	2.0 (0.7)	11.1	16	13.6 (1.2)
24	9.7	13.4	11.5 (0.9)	0.7	2.9	1.8 (0.5)	10.8	15.6	13.2 (1.2)

Source: redrawn from the Zurich Longitudinal Study of infants and children (Iglowstein et al., 2006).
SD, standard deviation.

- History taking may also include obtaining parental reports of whether unsettled infant night-time behaviour has continued since birth, or is of a more intermittent/recurrent type (see Chapter 5, section on Age of occurrence and persistence). This information does not allow different intervention methods to be chosen, but it may be helpful to discuss which factors trigger re-onset of unsettled night behaviours and whether parenting behaviours maintain them.
- Asking parents about infant health problems, recent illnesses and medical conditions (including asthma or eczema) may be informative. Although the contribution of these factors to infant night-waking problems is controversial, breathing impairments (due to infections or blocked respiratory passages), and itchy skin may hamper settled sleep. It may be helpful to take these symptoms into account when deciding treatments. If these problems are severe and persistent, specialist referral may be indicated. There are currently no evidence-based methods for distinguishing cases where infant night waking and other sleep problems are due to organic disturbance. However, this need not be a barrier to treatment, because the methods that help infants in general to remain settled at night are also effective when used with children with known neurodevelopmental disorders.
- It is likely that individual differences in infants' vulnerabilities and resiliencies make it easier for some infants to become settled in the night than others. Here, too, there is a dearth of firm evidence. But, discussing individual differences in infants' make-up may help parents to understand why their infant has continued to wake and signal in the night. The implication is that such infants can follow the same developmental pathway as other infants if they are given extra support.

- As well as infant behaviour, the primary assessment work-up should also consider parental vulnerability (methods for doing so are given later in this chapter).

Management of infant night waking and signalling, Step 1: discussing the options

Once the nature of the problem is clear, treatments can be discussed with the parents. Reviews of the evidence by researchers in England, Israel, New Zealand and North America are unanimous in concluding that *behavioural programmes* are effective in treating infant sleep problems, and are preferable to treatments involving medication (France & Hudson, 1993; Mindell et al., 2006; Ramchandani et al., 2000; Sadeh, 2005). The most recent review, in particular, concluded that 49 of 52 studies (including those using randomized controlled trials), have found behaviour programmes to be effective (Mindell et al., 2006). A feature of behaviour programmes is that they are forward looking: they involve changing a child's behaviours, rather than understanding what caused them in the first place. In effect, they assume that, irrespective of the original cause, the child's night-time behaviours are now being maintained by the rewards contained in the caregiving environment. Changing those rewards will stimulate the child to learn different behaviours. Behaviour programmes employ limit-setting methods of care to achieve these aims. This approach is supported by the evidence that the methods are effective, but they are not always successful and come with 'costs' which, for some parents, are too much to bear. It follows that, prior to trying them out, parents need to be familiarized with these methods and to discuss the pluses and minuses involved.

Possible minuses of using these programmes

- The two main behaviour programme methods are called '*controlled crying*' (or '*extinction*') and '*positive behaviour*' programmes. The more effective – controlled crying – programmes involve leaving infants to cry at bedtime or when they wake up and signal parents in the night-time. The crying usually lasts less long on the next occasion and eventually the 'signalling' stops and the infant learns to resettle by him or herself. The key drawback is that some parents are unable to leave an infant to cry because they find this stressful or cruel. Unfortunately, half-hearted use of these methods teaches the infant to cry for longer, and so worsens the problem.
- It follows that a full discussion of what parents can manage is a vital first step *before* these strategies are attempted. Parental resources, values and circumstances are key issues. Some parents may prefer graduated, over standard, methods (see below) because they can be less

stressful, while others choose 'positive behaviour methods' (which do not involve leaving an infant to cry), even if they are less likely to prove effective. Alternatively, finding ways of tolerating and coping with their child's night waking may prove less disruptive for the family as a whole than trying to impose methods to stop the night waking that conflict with parents' values and circumstances. Parents can be reassured that most children who wake them in the night are healthy, and that many children will eventually stop doing so on their own. In any case, professionals can describe the alternative approaches and help parents to make choices.

- Although controlled crying methods are usually effective for periods of 6–12 months after they are implemented properly, the benefits do not always last. Few studies include long-term follow-ups (Mindell et al., 2006). One exception, a large-scale Australian randomized controlled trial, found that many infants and young children who initially bene-fitted from a controlled crying programme reverted to unsettled night waking at later ages (Lam et al., 2003). When followed up and reassessed at 3 to 4-years-old, the original treated and control groups showed similar rates of sleep problems: 36% in the behavioural treat-ment group and 26% in the control group, the implication being that some control group infants improved over age without an intervention, while some intervention infants failed to maintain their improvement. As a result, there were no long-term benefits from receiving the behaviour programme. The authors suggested the need for occasional 'booster' sessions to enhance parental use of limit-setting principles. However, there have been no evaluations of sessions of that type to date and we do not know why sleeping problems recurred in so many children, or why they occurred in some cases but not others.

- It is important to bear in mind that these disappointing long-term findings have so far come from just a single study. They are, though, consistent with the developmental evidence in Chapter 5, showing that a pattern of intermittent, on–off, night-waking problems at successive ages is quite common. Parents may wish to take account of these doubts about long-term effectiveness when deciding whether to imple-ment controlled crying or other behavioural programmes to treat infant sleeping problems.

- It has been claimed that controlled crying methods are harmful for infants and children, because they damage children's 'attachment' rela-tionships with their parents, or even because prolonged crying may disrupt infants' breathing and cause damage to their brains. Both these claims lack supporting evidence. The evidence about infant attachments and night waking was examined in Chapter 6 (in the section on 'Environmental contributions to infant settling or night-waking prob-lems') and no association between them was found. One study has found that infants' attachment relationships with parents improved after successful use of a controlled crying programme: using parent reports to measure both parents' affectionate feelings toward their children and the children's secure attachments to their parents, relationships were found to have improved on both sides after the behaviour programme (France, 1992). A recent review found no evidence that behavioural treatments disrupt infant mental health (Črnčec et al., 2010a). More research is needed, but alarmist messages are unlikely to be helpful. Instead, the onus is on those who believe controlled crying methods to be harmful, and the alternatives better, to produce evidence to support their case. As noted in Chapters 6 and 7, it is possible that infant-demand forms of parenting, including bed-sharing and parent-settling, have advantages that are not yet appreciated. In the interim, some parents may consider that the benefits from using controlled crying methods are not justified because of their concerns about these issues.

Possible pluses of these programmes

- Although doubts remain about long-term effectiveness, controlled crying and, to a lesser extent, positive behaviour methods have proved successful in the short and medium term (up to 12 months) in many studies in a variety of countries. At the least, these methods can empower parents to feel that they are taking steps to resolve the problem. If the methods are implemented successfully, they should also provide relief that can be of substantial benefit if the infant night waking has been highly disruptive for the family.
- Other studies have documented benefits for parents' own sleeping and well-being following successful treatment of infant night waking and signalling (reviewed in Chapter 6 in the section on 'Environmental contributions to night waking 2'). These benefits for parents may carry forward to produce better care, with benefits for children as well as parents, although there are no studies as yet to demonstrate this to be the case.

Management of infant night waking and signalling, Step 2: implementing the chosen approach

Following consultations with a healthcare professional about the advantages and disadvantages of the different methods in Step 1 (see above) parents can make informed choices about the most suitable method for their circumstances. The two methods proven to be most effective – controlled crying (or 'extinction') and checking ('graduated extinction') – are described below, together with a variation involving parental presence. Then, the 'positive behavioural methods' are described. Although they are unlikely to produce the rapid reductions in infant sleeping problems produced by controlled crying methods, they may help parents to manage, provide infants with a structured environment and allow time for improvements that are likely with increasing age. It is important that professionals maintain their contact with parents to monitor progress.

Standard, graduated and parent-present controlled crying methods

Using these approaches, the first step is for a professional and parents to agree a suitable and realistic bedtime and length of sleeping for the infant in question. She is then settled in her cot at the agreed time, often following a set of pleasurable activities, such as bathing, designed to promote calming and to establish a routine. Once she is put down, the **standard controlled crying** (or 'standard extinction') approach involves ignoring her crying and other protests that occur during settling, waking or resettling during the night, so that these are not rewarded by parental attention. In effect, the baby is left to cry until the crying stops. On successive nights the crying lessens and then ceases to occur after a few nights, usually within about a week.

If applied consistently by parents, almost all studies evaluating this method have found it to be effective in reducing settling and night-waking problems. The most extensive review (Mindell et al., 2006), for instance, found controlled crying programmes to be effective in 17 of 19 studies that had evaluated them. The studies have found no adverse effect of extinction methods on breast-feeding or infant intake, while reduced levels of maternal depression, improvements in parents' confidence in their ability and enhanced marital satisfaction were found to follow their use in some studies (Mindell et al., 2006). As already noted, the chief disadvantage of this approach is that some parents find it cruel or culturally or personally unacceptable. One other proviso noted by the Mindell and colleagues' (2006) review is the existence of 'post-extinction response bursts', that is, recurrence of night-time distressed or unsettled child behaviour a few weeks or months after a successful initial intervention. Parents are advised to anticipate and avoid inadvertent reinforcement of this 'rebound' child behaviour (Mindell et al., 2006).

Checking (also known as 'graduated extinction') is a more gentle method, designed to minimize distress in infant and parents and so increase implementation. There is some evidence that rates of use and parental acceptance are greater with graduated than standard controlled crying (Reid et al., 1999). Parents who find separating from their children at bedtime difficult may prefer this method. In Mindell and colleagues' review (2006), all 14 studies that examined this approach found it to be effective in improving settling and reducing night waking. Here, too, the first step is to agree realistic goals for bedtime and sleep length, while enjoyable pre-bed activities can be used to help with calming and to set up a routine. In this case, once an infant is settled in a cot, parents can make regular 'checks' to ensure their baby's safety and provide limited comforting and reassurance, but the checks are kept minimal in length and amount of interaction. The checks can initially take place every 5 minutes, but this interval is often set following a discussion of what infant and parents can tolerate. The interval is then gradually lengthened to 10 and 15 minutes, in the same or sub-sequent nights. The goal is to free the child from depending on parents to settle to sleep and to foster the development of autonomous settling and resettling after night waking. The use of 'sleep-aid' objects and dim electric night-lights, as described in Chapter 6 (in the section on 'Sleep aids') may also be considered, although they have not been examined in combination with checking methods. The chief disadvantage of graduated extinction is that this approach, too, exceeds some parents' willingness to implement it. Although it is less abrupt, it may take longer to implement as a result (Mindell et al., 2006; Rickert & Johnson, 1988).

A third variant, **extinction with parental presence**, has not been as extensively evaluated, but found to be effective in a few studies (Mindell et al., 2006). This method is based on the assumption that infant distress at bedtime is primarily caused by anxiety about separation from parents. Some versions involve staying in the child's room during settling, while a version evaluated by Sadeh (1994) required parents to sleep in the infant's room, with minimal intervention (limited to returning her to sleep) if the infant woke and signalled during the night. Sadeh (1994) found that adopting this strategy for 7–10 nights was as effective as graduated extinction in reducing infant night waking and signalling, using both parental and objective measures of infant sleeping. This method was described as 'promising' by Sadeh (2005). The longer-term results are not known, so that it is not clear when and how parents can withdraw from sharing a bedroom with their child if they wish to do so at a later stage.

Positive behaviour methods

This rather loose term has been used in the literature to encompass methods that avoid the need to leave infants to cry. The word 'positive' denotes programmes that involve active steps to support and reward settled night-time behaviour.

The main elements involved are essentially the same as those included in the behaviour programme designed to prevent infant sleeping problems described in Chapter 9 and Appendix II. The chief difference is that these are introduced in response to sleeping problems and, typically, at an older age.

The steps involve introducing a nightly routine of pleasurable, calming activities designed to teach a familiar pre-sleep routine. Feeding or rocking to sleep is discouraged and the infant is settled awake in the same place at approximately the same time, so that autonomous settling is encouraged. Lighting in the baby's sleep environment is kept dim at night and accentuated in the morning, to encourage circadian entrainment of sleep to darkness and waking to daylight. Sleep aids may be helpful.

There is far less evidence that these methods are effective in treating infant sleep problems once they have arisen than in preventing them, and they are not as effective as graduated or standard extinction for treatment purposes (Mindell et al., 2006; Sadeh, 2005). They do not deal directly with separation difficulties, but it is possible that these become less of an issue for child and parents once a familiar routine is in place.

The term **faded bedtime** is used to refer to methods that seek to adjust infant bedtimes (Mindell et al., 2006; Sadeh, 2005). Typically, this is employed when the timing of infant or child sleep periods is problematic, for instance when sleep onset does not occur until the middle of the night. Using this approach, bedtime is first delayed to encourage sleepiness and a set of quiet routine activities is introduced to precede and coincide with sleepiness. Once this association is established as a routine, the time of the routine activities and settling is gradually brought forward towards the desired settling time by steps of 15 to 30 minutes. Mindell and colleagues' (2006) review concluded that faded bedtime is probably effective, but has been evaluated in far fewer studies than graduated or standard extinction and there are no follow-up assessments of this method as yet.

Lastly, **scheduled awakenings** refers to a method whereby parents deliberately wake an infant some time before night waking is expected to occur, then resettle her afterwards. There is some evidence that this leads to more prolonged sleeping, but the mechanisms are unclear, the approach is demanding for parents to implement, and there is only limited evidence of effectiveness in general (Sadeh, 2005; Mindell et al., 2006). This method is also inappropriate where the child's sleeping problems include initial settling difficulties. There is some evidence that it can help to treat regularly occurring 'night terrors' by waking infants before these occur (see Chapter 5, the section on 'Which features of infant sleep–waking behaviour disturb Western parents?').

Guidelines for cases involving concern about parental vulnerability

- There is evidence that persistent infant crying can trigger depression in mothers who are vulnerable to it. Infant night waking and signalling has also been linked with maternal depression, although the direction of causality is uncertain. Both types of problematic infant behaviour can trigger infant maltreatment, so that cases involving both parental vulnerability and problematic crying or sleeping may need to be prioritized.

- Several questionnaires are available, together with normative figures, that provide quick and convenient screening measures where maternal depression is suspected. The method chosen will need to reflect those used in the country concerned. Hewitt et al. (2009) provide an authoritative review of this research. The Edinburgh Postnatal Depression Scale (EPDS) has been widely used for this purpose in the UK and other countries and versions are available in several languages on the worldwide web. In the UK, a score of 12 or above is considered to indicate a probable depression and there is evidence that primary care interventions using this cut-off can be helpful (Morrell et al., 2009). Interpretative care is important, since not all mothers will admit depression, while the EPDS may measure general emotional distress rather than depression alone. With careful use, it will provide some idea of the existence and extent of maternal emotional disturbance.

- Depending on whether infant crying or sleeping problems are the primary problem, the steps described above may help to minimize the impact of these on depressed parents. Črnčec et al. (2010b) found that mild to moderate depression did not prevent parents from being able to implement behavioural programmes to treat infant sleep problems. According to local policies, treatment and support for depression may also be considered.

- Although the evidence is poor, it is likely that other individual and situational characteristics make some parents particularly vulnerable to infant crying or night waking. These may include parental psychological characteristics, such as a low tolerance of frustration, as well as exhaustion, single parenthood and lack of social supports. However, there is no evidence yet that these factors can be measured reliably and cost-effectively under health service conditions.

- It follows that there is a need for further research to establish tried and tested, cost-effective, methods for routine use in identifying parental vulnerabilities other than depression. Where they are suspected as a result of history taking, it may be helpful to discuss the availability of social supports and to follow local policies for supporting needy families.

Guidelines for cases involving multiple problems after 3 months of age

- The guidelines so far concern the most common circumstances, where infants have *solely* crying, or *solely* sleeping, problems. The focus in this section is on infants who both (1) *have multiple areas of problematic behaviour* (crying plus sleeping, feeding or other problems); and (2) *where these multiple problems occur after 4 months of age*. Depending on their age, these infants have been found to have two or more of: prolonged crying, problematic settling or night waking, feeding problems, failure to thrive, excessive clinging and social withdrawal, separation anxiety, excessive temper tantrums, and early forms of aggressive behaviours. They are sometimes referred to as infants with 'regulatory disorders' or 'regulatory disturbances'.

- Until recently, these cases have been hidden among the larger groups with solely crying or sleeping problems. Recent studies have shown that these infants (but not those with solely crying or sleeping problems) are likely to have disturbances of attention, behaviour and movement control that persist up to school age.

- These cases can be expected to be rare. The best estimate is that about 5% of infants fall into this category. About half of these are thought to be cases where prolonged crying and other problems have continued since early infancy, while in half the problems started after 3 months of age. It is not currently possible to distinguish these cases until after 3 months of age.

- Unfortunately, our understanding of this recently recognized group of infants is poor. There is, however, evidence that interventions that target parenting are effective in helping troubled children and their parents, in general, from the early weeks of age through the pre-school period (Olds et al., 2007; van den Boom, 1995; Webster-Stratton & Hammond, 1997).

- Several countries have developed national or regional schemes for supporting families with young children. An important development has been the multidisciplinary nature of these schemes, so that professionals who have traditionally been seen as providing medical and social services work collaboratively together. These 'joined up' services are likely to be particularly suitable for this group of children. There is also growing evidence that specially trained nurses and other primary healthcare professionals are likely to be able to provide guidance that is accepted by parents and effective in helping these families (Olds et al., 2007).

- Primary healthcare professionals are in a strong position to put parents in touch with, and provide guidance about, these schemes. The guidelines listed above may play a part, by helping to reduce the impact of infant crying and unsettled night-time behaviour on these hard-pressed parents.

A last few words

Earlier in this book, it was suggested that infant crying and sleeping problems are issues whose time, historically speaking, has come. I had in mind a number of social processes that seem to be a result of developments in modern Western societies.

1   The growth in dual employment and the need for parents to balance earning and career pressures with parenthood. A baby who cries a lot, or keeps parents awake at night, can be challenging in these circumstances and, particularly, where a parent is isolated from family and community supports.

2   The growth in recognition that health service practice should be evidence-based.

3   The growth of 'risk models' in research, so that biological and social risk factors are examined longitudinally, as they work together, rather than opposed as nature versus nurture.

4   The resulting growth of 'joined up' services, so that medical, social, educational and other services strive to work together.

5   The growth of health-economic research and awareness that common problems are a major concern for health services even where they are not usually life threatening. This body of evidence has highlighted, too, the long-term cost of infant and child behaviour problems for society, education and social services.

The conceptualization of infant crying and sleeping problems proposed here seems to match these developments in reframing the problems as social and family matters rather than solely as infant medical conditions, disturbances or pathologies. This may not seem such a radical departure until we recall the inclination, still, to treat infant 'colic' crying with 'colic drops', or how recently expert advice has recommended the use of behavioural methods, rather than medication, as treatments for infant sleeping problems.

This book began by noting the lack of evidence-based guidelines for professionals who support parents in managing their infants' crying and sleeping – and proposing that the dearth of systematic services for this purpose is at odds with the personal and financial cost of these problems for families, communities and health services. My hope is that the material contained here will help to continue the process of 'joining up' by bringing research and practice together, by helping to give prominence to these earliest challenges for parents, and by supporting the development of cost-effective services that link up to support families from birth through childhood.

Literature search strategy and author disclosure of interests

This book started with a list of approximately 1500 references for studies of infant crying and sleeping accumulated during 30 years of research. To supplement these more systematically, three bibliographic databases (PubMed; PsycINFO; Google Scholar) were searched using 'infant crying', 'infant colic', and 'infant sleep' as keywords. Each search was limited to publications in the English language during the last 10 years (January 2000 to December 2010). The other search parameters varied somewhat from one database to another, according to their criteria. For PubMed, the search was limited to 'human studies' and 'all child (0–18 years)' age; for PsycINFO to 'human studies' and 'birth–12 years'; for Google Scholar to studies in the 'Biological and Life Sciences', 'Medical Sciences' and 'Social Sciences' indexes.

Even with these restrictions, these searches generated a prolific number of references – for instance, the PubMed search for 'infant sleep' generated 2536 references by itself. As would be expected using this method, many of these were of little relevance. Since it was impractical to read them all in full, the method employed was to examine titles, followed by abstracts, then the full publication where the research warranted detailed attention. Otherwise, studies were included according to methodological robustness (see criteria in Chapter 1) and omitted where they duplicated established findings. Where few or no publications on a topic were found by the initial search, further searches of the databases were run using the section headings employed in the book.

The resulting review process involves a degree of subjectivity about which studies are included and cannot be claimed to be comprehensive. However, to include all the studies would need a much longer book and make it more tedious to read. To the best of my understanding, no study has been excluded because of the nature of its findings or because they are inconsistent with a particular viewpoint or opinion. So far as possible, the aim has been to produce a review of the evidence on infant crying and sleeping and their impact on parents that is representative up to the end of 2010.

The references in the text show the material on which the book is based, so that the critical reader can identify any important errors or omissions.

While writing this book I was employed by the Institute of Education, University of London and my research into infant crying and sleeping was supported by a grant from the Wellcome Trust, a UK charitable foundation that funds biomedical research. Neither of these organizations nor any commercial interest has sought to influence the contents of this book.

'Night and day': helping your baby to know the difference

Reproduced from the COSI study (St James-Roberts et al., 2001) with permission

How does your baby know that it's night-time?

At birth, babies have little understanding of day and night. In order to introduce this, you can vary your reaction to them according to whether it is day or night. It is very important to be consistent, so that the differences between day and night can be learned.

The following guidelines are aimed at helping you to develop a plan of care that responds to your baby's needs, but also encourages your baby to adopt a sleeping pattern which you can live with!

Introducing a plan of care

The first 6 weeks

DAYTIME

1   Feed your baby on demand, as often as she/he wishes.
2   When your baby wakes, look at and talk to her/him, smile. Make the time after the feed a pleasurable 'social' event. Take your time and enjoy each other's company.
3   Take your baby out for a walk or better still, encourage your partner, relative or close friend to do this while you have a rest.
4   On the days that you bathe your baby, try to ensure that it is approximately at the same time. This will help your baby to associate certain times of the day with certain activities.
5   Take the time to offer your baby cuddles, playing, love and attention.

NIGHT-TIME

1   Put your baby into her/his 'night clothes' (babygro, nightdress, etc).
2   After feeding, if baby is still awake, try not to hold, rock or nurse her/
    him to sleep. Put your baby in the cot while awake and leave her/him to
    settle. The light levels should be low at night – not dark necessarily, but
    not too bright either.
3   If your baby doesn't settle, check the following:
    a   check her/his nappy/diaper – does it need changing?
    b   try winding her/him;
    c   is baby too hot or too cold – add or remove clothing or blankets
        accordingly;
    d   stroke and talk softly to your baby. If needs be, pick her/him up
        and have a cuddle.
    Give each action a chance to work before trying something else (at least
    10 minutes).
4   Try to distinguish between 'crying' and 'fretting' in order to reduce the
    number of times you pick your baby up. Babies often fret before
    settling to sleep but do not always need further attention.
5   When your baby wakes in the night for a feed, try to keep the light low.
    Respond to your baby's immediate physical needs, nappy/diaper
    change, feed and settle back to bed. (If baby doesn't settle, then work
    through the previous suggestions.)
6   Avoid playing, or 'socializing' at night.
7   If your baby is waking more than 3 to 4 hourly at night, it will not
    always be necessary to go through the ritual of nappy/diaper changing
    unless the need is obvious.
8   Make night-time as uninteresting as possible for your baby. Minimal
    interaction and stimulation. Night time is for sleeping!

Part 2 of the plan of care

Weeks 6–12

The second part of the programme can be introduced after your baby is
about 6 weeks old, as long as she/he is thriving and your health visitor and
general practitioner have no concerns for her/his weight gain or well-being.

DAYTIME

During the daytime, keep to the same methods as during weeks 1–6. Make
daytime an interesting time to be awake.

NIGHT-TIME

It is now time to begin to lengthen the time between night-time feeds.

This does NOT mean leaving your baby to cry unattended for long periods. To break the association between waking and feeding, the aim is to delay feeding when baby wakes at night. For instance, use changing nappy/diaper, resettling back in cot, patting, carrying etc to delay giving a feed.

This will need to be done gradually – perhaps just 5 or 10 minutes of delay at first. After a week or two, the gap between night-time feeds should become noticeably longer and your baby will start to sleep for longer periods at night.

This method should not reduce the amount of breast milk or formula that your baby takes over 24 hours. Instead, she/he will probably take a bigger feed first thing in the morning and increase other feeds during the day. After a while, your baby will also learn to increase the feed in the late evening to help sleep through the night.

The introduction of this plan of care is not designed to alter the length of time that your baby sleeps during the 24-hour period, but to encourage her/him to take more sleep during the night.

REMEMBER – BE GENTLE BUT CONSISTENT. WE HOPE THAT THIS APPROACH WILL ALLOW YOU AND YOUR BABY TO ENJOY THE TIME YOU SPEND TOGETHER.

The Crying Patterns Questionnaire (CPQ, revised)

[Please see notes at the end on how to complete this questionnaire.]

Baby's name: _____ Age: (wks/months) _____ Sex: _____

Person completing CPQ: _____ Informant (e.g. mother): _____

Today's date: _____

SECTION A

1   Amount of fuss/crying in each period of a typical day:

If yesterday's crying times, tick here: ☐

Morning 6 am–midday	Afternoon Midday–6 pm	Evening 6 pm–midnight	Night Midnight–6 am	Total (24 hours)
_____ (hours)	_____ (hours)	_____ (hours)	_____ (hours)	_____ (hours)
_____ (minutes)	_____ (minutes)	_____ (minutes)	_____ (minutes)	_____ (minutes)

2a   What about bouts of unsoothable fretting and crying?

(Periods when your baby fusses and cries and requires constant soothing, or is hard or impossible to settle down.) How many mornings this week have included bouts of this kind? How about afternoons; evenings; nights? (Record number in each period. If none, record '0'.)

Number of mornings	Number of afternoons	Number of evenings	Number of nights
_____	_____	_____	_____

2b If unsoothable bouts are recorded: Is crying type mainly: Unsettled fussing (FUSS); Crying or intense crying (CRY); Mixed fussing/crying (MIX)? (Record FUSS, CRY or MIX in each period):

In mornings	In afternoons	In evenings	In nights

SECTION B (Optional)

3 **During the last week which methods have you used in settling and looking after your baby?** Please go through the list and tick any methods used to show how often you have used them.

Method	Used occasionally	Used about once a day	Used repeatedly each day
Cuddling & rocking			
Swaddling			
Carrying in arms			
Baby sling			
Dummy			
Rocking in cradle/cot/chair, etc.			
Car rides			
Singing or soothing sounds of music			
Extra feeds/drinks			
Taking into own bed			
Gripe water/herbal remedy			
Non-prescribed medicines			
Prescribed medicines			
Other – please describe			

4 **Have you tried leaving your baby to 'cry out'?**

No	Yes, once	Yes, a few times	Yes, frequently

If yes, for how long? Indicate minutes or hours _____

5   Are you finding your baby's crying to be a problem or upsetting?

(If yes, please say how often in the last week.)

No	Yes: how many times?

6   Have you recently approached your health visitor, general practitioner or anyone else because of concern about your baby's crying? What about in the past?

No	Yes, in the last month	Yes, in the past

(Please tick and indicate nature of anyone approached.)

Notes on completing the CPQ[1]

The Crying Patterns Questionnaire (CPQ) is designed to collect information from a mother or other primary care-giver about an infant's fuss and crying patterns. It is suitable for use during the first 9 months of age. The following particulars are recorded.

1   Whether the baby's fuss/crying is usually spread fairly evenly over the day – or whether there is one particular time of day when the baby is especially inclined to cry.
2   The amount of time (in minutes or hours) spent fussing and crying in each period of the day (morning, afternoon, evening, night) and over 24 hours.
3   The frequency and nature of any bouts of unsoothable crying – whether the crying is mainly fussy/fretful behaviour, mainly intense crying, or a mixture of the two.

The questionnaire can be filled in by a parent. More commonly, it is administered as an interview by a researcher or professional, either in person or over the telephone. A suggested format for the interview is included below. In our experience, these are the main queries likely to arise.

1 The CPQ was first used by St James-Roberts and Halil (1991). It exists in two versions: Crying Patterns Questionnaire (CPQ) and Crying Patterns Interview (CPI). The version here combines the two and takes account of recent research findings. The questions in Section A are largely unchanged, except that the wording now refers to 'bouts of unsoothable crying' instead of 'periods of persistent crying'.

1   *'What is meant by "fussing and crying"? For example, if a baby is unsettled but only cries if left alone, is that really crying?'*

The term 'fuss/crying' is intended to include *all* periods of distressed or unsettled behaviour. A mother may have difficulty saying how much time is actually spent crying – for instance because it is made up of stops and starts. Or, she may say that her baby doesn't really cry so long as she carries or otherwise continuously soothes him/her.

In both cases, ask her to estimate the total amount of time spent unsettled, fretting or crying. It is not necessary to be accurate to the exact minute – the difference, for instance, between a total of 2, 5 and 10 minutes of crying in one period of the day is not important. The aim is to distinguish between babies who fuss/cry for just a few minutes, compared with half an hour, compared with 1 or more hours in a given period of the day.

2   *'What if a baby's crying pattern is irregular – it changes from day to day?'*

Babies are highly variable in their behaviour and a degree of day-to-day variability in crying is to be expected. The aim is to record the most common pattern during the last week – in effect, the pattern shown on most days. If a mother is clear that there is no regular pattern – it has been very different each day – note this by ticking the box and record the figures for yesterday.

Format for the CPI interview

This format doesn't have to be adhered to rigidly – it is just to get you started and can then be adjusted until you are comfortable with it.

'I'd like to ask you some questions about (baby's name)'s crying patterns during the last week. There are really two main questions. First, I'd like to find out whether there is one particular time of the day when (baby) is particularly inclined to fuss/cry or be unsettled – or not. Secondly, I'd like to get some idea of how much time – in hours or minutes – (baby) has usually spent fussing and crying in each period of the day – morning, afternoon, evening and night.'

(Mothers will often talk spontaneously about one period, in which case start then. Otherwise:)

'Can we start with the morning – from 6 am to midday – can you add up how many minutes or hours of fuss and crying there usually are in total during that time of day?'

(Enter times on CPQ form. If needs be, ask the mother to talk through a 'typical' morning, so far as there is one, and help her to add up the fuss/crying total.)

'How about:

- in the afternoon – midday to 6 pm?
- in the evening – 6 pm to 12 midnight?
- at night – midnight to 6 am?'

[N.B. If there is no 'usual pattern', ask about yesterday's fuss/crying times (tick to indicate).]

Once these details are recorded, carry on with the remaining questions. Please answer all questions in part A. The questions in part B provide additional information and are optional.

Baby's day diary

Based on the original used by Hunziker and Barr (1986), this version was used in research by St James-Roberts et al. (1993b).

Baby's name: _____ *Baby's age:* _____ *days/weeks* *Today's date:* _____ *Diary completed by* _____

INSTRUCTIONS FOR COMPLETING THE 'BABY'S DAY' DIARY

The diary is designed to enable you to record your baby's behaviour and your activities with your baby over a continuous 24 hour period. As you can see, the day is divided into four blocks of six hours each and each hour is divided into five minute intervals. For example:

MORNING

06.00 06.30 07.00 07.30 08.00 08.30 09.00 09.30 10.00 10.30 11.00 11.30 12.00

The record is filled in by shading on the time rulers. For instance, in the example below, baby:

| Slept until 7.30 | Fussy for 10 mins | Fed from 7.40–8.15 | Awake and content 8.15–9.05 | Slept 9.05–10.20 | Cried for 20 mins | Fed 10.40– 11.00 | Fussy for 10 mins | Awake and content until 12.00 |

MORNING

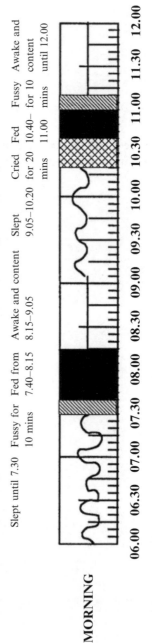

06.00 06.30 07.00 07.30 08.00 08.30 09.00 09.30 10.00 10.30 11.00 11.30 12.00

The length of shading tells us how long the activities and behaviours lasted. Please try to be accurate to the nearest five minutes.

BABY'S DAY DIARY

BABY BEHAVIOURS

SLEEPING

AWAKE & CONTENT

FUSSY *

CRYING **

UNSOOTHABLE CRYING ***

FEEDING

MORNING

6.00 6.30 7.00 7.30 8.00 8.30 9.00 9.30 10.00 10.30 11.00 11.30 12.00

AFTERNOON

12.00 12.30 1.00 1.30 2.00 2.30 3.00 3.30 4.00 4.30 5.00 5.30 6.00

EVENING

6.00 6.30 7.00 7.30 8.00 8.30 9.00 9.30 10.00 10.30 11.00 11.30 12.00

NIGHT

12.00 12.30 1.00 1.30 2.00 2.30 3.00 3.30 4.00 4.30 5.00 5.30 6.00

* FUSSY: your baby is unsettled and irritable, and may be vocalising but not continuously crying

** CRYING: periods of prolonged, distressed vocalisation

*** UNSOOTHABLE CRYING: bouts of hard-to-soothe or unsoothable crying or fussing

How many people looked after the baby during this diary period?

Mum [ ]
Dad/Partner [ ]
Others [ ]
Please write how many others [ ]

The Brief Infant Sleep Questionnaire

Redrawn from Sadeh (2004) with the author's permission.

Please mark only one (most appropriate) choice, when you respond to items with a few options.

Name of Responder: _____ Date: _____

Role of Responder: _ Father _ Mother _ Grandparent _ Other, Specify: _____

Name of the infant: _____ Date of Birth: Day: ____ Month: ___ Year: ____

Infant's Sex: _ Male _ Female; Birth order of the infant: _ Oldest _ Middle _ Youngest

Sleeping arrangement for infant:

__ Infant crib in a separate room   __ Infant crib in parents' room

__ In parents' bed   __ Infant crib in room with sibling

__ Other (specify): _____

In what position does your child sleep most of the time?

__ On his/her belly   __ On his/her side   __ On his/her back

How much time does your child spend in sleep during the NIGHT (between 7 in the evening and 7 in the morning)? Hours: _____ Minutes: _____

How much time does your child spend in sleep during the DAY (between 7 in the morning and 7 in the evening)? Hours: _____ Minutes: _____

Average number of night wakings per night: _____

How much time during the night does your child spend in wakefulness (from 10 in the evening to 6 in the morning)? Hours: _____ Minutes: _____

How long does it take to put your baby to sleep in the evening?
Hours: _____ Minutes: _____

How does your baby fall asleep?

__While feeding __Being rocked __Being held __In bed alone __In bed near parent

When does your baby usually fall asleep for the night: Hours: _____ Minutes: _____

Do you consider your child's sleep as a problem?

__A very serious problem   __A small problem   __Not a problem at all

Sleep diary for keeping by parents

Diary 'log' measures of infant sleeping are kept at the same time as sleep periods, so that they should be more accurate than questionnaire measures, which rely on memory. The disadvantage of diaries is that they take more effort and time to complete. Because of day-to-day variability, they need to be completed for several consecutive 24-hour days (seven is desirable, four a workable minimum) and the resulting figures have to be averaged afterwards. For these reasons, questionnaire measures (such as the BISQ in Appendix V) are more convenient for routine use, while diary measures can be reserved for cases where more detailed or accurate information is needed. The Baby's Day Diary included in Appendix IV can be used to assess sleep, or the diary form below is adapted from Naomi Richman's (1985) sleep diary.

Sleep diary

Infant's Name: _____

	Day 1	Day 2	Day 3	Day 4	Day 5	Day 6	Day 7
Time infant woke in morning							
Mood on waking							

Time of infant's nap(s) in the day:
   Start-time(s)
   End time(s)							

Infant time to bed in evening							
Infant time to sleep in evening							
Time(s) infant woke in night							
What did you do?							
Time(s) infant went back to sleep							
Time you went to bed							

References

Abdulrazzaq, Y. M., Al Kendi, A., & Anagelkerke, N. (2009) Soothing methods used to calm a baby in an Arab country. *Acta Paediatrica*, 98, 392–396.

Acebo, C., Sadeh, A., Seifer, R., Tzischinsky, O., Hafer, A., & Carskadon, M. (2005) Sleep/wake patterns derived from activity monitoring and maternal report for healthy 1- to 5-year-old children. *Sleep*, 28, 1568–1576.

Achenbach, T., Verhulst, F., Baron, G., & Althaus, M. (1987) A comparison of syndromes derived from the Child Behaviour Checklist for American and Dutch boys aged 6–11 and 12–16. *Journal of Child Psychology and Psychiatry*, 28, 437–453.

Adair, R., Bauchner, H., Philipp, B., Levenson, S., & Zuckerman, B. (1991) Night waking during infancy: role of parental presence at bedtime. *Pediatrics*, 87, 500–504.

Adair, R., Zucherman, B., Bauchner, H., Philipp, B., & Levenson, S. (1992) Reducing night waking in infancy: a primary care intervention. *Pediatrics*, 89, 585–588.

Adams, S., Jones, D., Esmail, A., & Mitchell, E. (2004) What affects the age of first sleeping through the night? *Journal of Paediatrics & Child Health*, 40, 96–101.

Agarwal, K., Gupta, A., Pushkarna, R., Bhargava, S., Faridi, M., & Prabhu, M. (2000) Effects of massage & use of oil on growth, blood flow & sleep pattern in infants. *Indian Journal of Medical Research*, 112, 212–217.

Ainsworth, M. D. S., Blehar, M. C., Waters, E., & Wall, S. (1978) *Patterns of Attachment: A Psychological Study of the Strange Situation.* Hillsdale, NJ: Lawrence Erlbaum Associates, Inc.

Akman, I., Kusçu, K., Ozdemir, N., Yurdakul, Z., Solakoglu, M., Orhan, L., & Karabekiroglu, A. (2006) Mothers' postpartum psychological adjustment and infantile colic. *Archives of Disease in Childhood*, 91, 417–419.

Alexandrovich, I., Rakovitskaya, O., Kolmo, E., & Sidorova, S. (2003) The effect of fennel (foeniculum vulgare) seed oil emulsion in infantile colic: a randomized placebo-controlled trial. *Alternative Therapies*, 9, 58–61.

Allen, K. D., White, D., & Walburn, J. N. (1996) Sucrose as an analgesic agent for infants during immunization injections. *Archives of Pediatrics & Adolescent Medicine*, 150, 270–274.

Alvarez, M. (2004) Caregiving and early infant crying in a Danish community. *Journal of Developmental & Behavioral Pediatrics*, 2, 91–98.

Alvarez, M., & St James-Roberts, I. (1996) Infant crying patterns in an urban community in Denmark. *Acta Paediatrica Scandinavia*, 85, 463–466.

Ambrose, A. 1969. *Stimulation in Early Infancy*. New York: Academic Press.

American Academy of Pediatrics, Task Force on Sudden Infant Death Syndrome. (2005) The changing concept of sudden infant death syndrome: diagnostic coding shifts, controversies regarding the sleeping environment, and new variables to consider in reducing risk. *Pediatrics*, 116, 1245–1255.

American Academy of Sleep Medicine. (2005) *International Classification of Sleep Disorders: Diagnostic and Coding Manual*. Westchester, NY: American Academy of Sleep Medicine.

American Psychiatric Association (1994) *Diagnostic and Statistical Manual of Mental Disorders (DSM-IV)*, Washington, DC: Amercian Psychiatric Association.

Anders, T. F. (2004) Sleep-wake states and problems and child development. In: Tremblay, R. E., Barr, R. G., & Peters, R. (eds.) *Encyclopedia on Early Childhood Development*. Montreal, Quebec: Centre of Excellence for Early Childhood Development.

Anders, T. F., Halpern, L. F., & Hua, J. (1992) Sleeping through the night: a developmental perspective. *Pediatrics*, 90, 554–560.

Anders, T. F., Keener, M., Bowe, T. R., & Shioff, B. A. (1983) A longitudinal study of night-time sleep–wake patterns in infants from birth to one year. In: Call, J. D., & Galenson, E. (eds.) *Frontiers of Infant Psychiatry I* (pp. 150–166). New York: Basic Books.

Anuntaseree, W., Mo-suwan, L., Vasiknanonte, P., Kuasirikul, S., Ma-a-lee, A., & Choprapawan, C. (2008) Night waking in Thai infants at 3 months of age: association between parental practices and infant sleep. *Sleep Medicine*, 9, 564–571.

Arikan, D., Alp, H., Gozum, S., Orbak, Z., & Karaca, E. (2008) Effectiveness of massage, sucrose solution, herbal tea or hydrolysed formula in the treatment of infantile colic. *Journal of Clinical Nursing*, 17, 1754–1761.

Armitage, R., Flynn, H., Hoffman, R., Vazquez, D., Lopez, J., & Marcus, S. (2009) Early developmental changes in sleep in infants: the impact of maternal depression. *Sleep*, 32, 693–696.

Armstrong, K., Quinn, R., & Dadds, M. (1994) The sleep patterns of normal children. *The Medical Journal of Australia*, 161, 202–206.

Arseneault, L., Moffitt, T. E., Caspi, A., Taylor, A., Rijsdijk, F. V., Jaffee, S. R., Ablow, J., & Measelle, J. R. (2003) Strong genetic effects on cross-situational antisocial behaviour among 5-year-old children according to mothers, teachers, examiner-observers, and twins self-reports. *Journal of Child Psychology and Psychiatry*, 44, 832–848.

Australian Association for Infant Mental Health (2002) *Controlled Crying: Australian Association for Infant Mental Health Position Paper*. Doublebay, New South Wales: AAIMHI. Retrieved September 21, 2011 from http:// www.earlychildhoodaustralia.org.au/pdf/papers/april2003_aaimhi_controlled_ crying.pdf

Aviezer, O., Sagi, A., & van IJzendoorn, M. (2002) Balancing the family and the collective in raising children: why communal sleeping in kibbutzim was predestined to end. *Family Process*, 41, 435–454.

Axia, G., & Bonichini, S. (2005) Are babies sensitive to the context of acute pain episodes? Infant distress and material soothing during immunization routines at 3 and 5 months of age. *Infant Behavior & Development*, 14, 51–62.

Axia, G., Bonichini, S., & Benini, F. (1999) Attention and reaction to stress in infancy: a longitudinal study. *Developmental Psychology*, 35, 500–504.

Axia, V. D., & Weisner, T. S. (2002) Infant stress reactivity and home cultural ecology of Italian infants and families. *Infant Behavior & Development*, 25 255–268.

Baddock, S. A., Galland, B. C., Bolton, D. P. G., Williams, S. M., & Taylor, B. J. (2006) Differences in infant and parent behaviours during routine bed sharing compared with cot sleeping in the home setting. *Pediatrics*, 117, 1599–1607.

Baird, J., Hill, C. M., Kendrick, T., & Inskip, H. M. (2009) Infant sleep disturbance is associated with preconceptional psychological distress: findings from the Southampton Women's Survey. *Sleep*, 32, 566–568.

Ball, H. L. (2002) Reasons to bed-share: why parents sleep with their infants. *Journal of Reproductive and Infant Psychology*, 20, 207–222.

Ball, H. L. (2007) Bed-sharing practices of initially breastfed infants in the first 6 months of life. *Infant and Child Development*, 16, 387–401.

Bamford, F. N., Bannister, R. P., Benjamin, C. M., Hillier, V. F., Ward, B. S., & Moore, W. M. O. (1990) Sleep in the first year of life. *Developmental Medicine and Child Neurology*, 32, 718–724.

Bard, K. A. (2000) Crying in infant primates: insights into the development of crying in chimpanzees. In: Barr, R. G., Hopkins, B., & Green, J. A. (eds.) *Crying as a Sign a Symptom, & a Signal: Clinical, Emotional and Developmental Aspects of Infant and Toddler Crying*. London: Mac Keith Press.

Barr, R. G. (1990) The normal crying curve: what do we really know? (Annotation). *Developmental Medicine and Child Neurology*, 32, 356–362.

Barr, R. G. (1998) Reflections on measuring pain in infants: dissociation in responsive systems and "honest signalling". *Archives of Disease in Childhood, Fetal Neonatal Edition*, 79, 152–156.

Barr, R. G. (2000) Excessive crying. In: Sameroff, A. J., Lewis, M., & Miller, S. M. (eds.) *Handbook of Development Psychopathology (2nd edn.)*. New York: Kluwer Academic/Plenum Publishers.

Barr, R. G. (2001) "Colic" is something infants do, rather than a condition they "have": a developmental approach to crying phenomena, patterns, pacification and (patho)genesis. In: Barr, R. G., St James-Roberts, I., & Keefe, M. R. (eds.) *New Evidence on Unexplained Early Infant Crying: Its Origins, Nature and Management*. Skillman, NJ: Johnson & Johnson Pediatric Institute.

Barr, R. G. (2006) Crying behaviour and its importance for psychosocial development in children. *Encyclopedia on Early Childhood Development*. Montreal, Quebec: Centre of Excellence for Early Childhood Development. Retrieved September 21, 2011 from http://www.child-encyclopedia.com/documents/barrANGxp.pdf

Barr, R. G., & Gunnar, M. R. (2000) Colic: The 'Transient Responsivity' Hypothesis. In: Barr, R. G., Hopkins, B., & Green, J. A. (eds.) *Crying as a Sign, a Symptom, & a Signal*. London: Mac Keith Press.

Barr, R. G., Barr, M., Fujiwara, T., Conway, J., Catherine, N., & Brant, R. (2009) Do educational materials change knowledge and behaviour about crying and shaken baby syndrome? A randomized control trial. *Canadian Medical Association Journal*, 180, 727–733.

Barr, R. G., Chen, S., Hopkins, B., & Westra, T. (1996) Crying patterns in preterm infants. *Developmental Medicine & Child Neurology*, 38, 345–355.

Barr, R. G., Desilets, J., & Rotman, A. (1991a) Parsing the normal crying curve: is it really the evening fussing curve? *Biennial Meeting of the Society for Research in Child Development*, 18 April, Seattle, Washington.

Barr, R. G., Konner, M., Bakeman, R., & Adamson, L. (1991b) Crying in Kung San infants: a test of the cultural specificity hypothesis. *Developmental Medicine and Child Neurology*, 33, 601–610.

Barr, R. G., Kramer, M. S., Boisjoly, C., McVey-White, L., & Pless, I. B. (1988) Parental diary of infant cry and fuss behaviour. *Archives of Disease in Childhood*, 63, 380–387.

Barr, R. G., Pantel, M. S., Young, S. N., Wright, J. H., Hendricks, L. A., & Gravel, R. (1999b) The response of crying newborns to sucrose: is it a 'sweetness' effect? *Physiology & Behavior*, 66, 409–417.

Barr, R. G., Paterson, J., MacMartin, L., Lehtonen, L., & Young, S. (2005) Prolonged and unsoothable crying bouts in infants with and without colic. *Developmental and Behavioral Pediatrics*, 26, 14–22.

Barr, R. G., Quek, V. S., Cousino, D., Oberlander, T. F., Brain, J. A., & Young, S. N. (1994) Effects of intra-oral sucrose on crying, mouthing and hand–mouth contact in newborn and six-week-old infants. *Developmental Medicine & Child Neurology*, 36, 608–618.

Barr, R. G., Rotman, A., Vamengo, J., Leduc, D., & Francoeur, T. E. (1992) The crying of infants with colic: a controlled empirical description. *Pediatrics*, 90, 14–21.

Barr, R. G., St James-Roberts, I., & Keefe, M. (eds.) (2001) *New Evidence on Unexplained Early Infant Crying: Its Origins, Nature and Management*. Skillman, NJ: Johnson & Johnson Pediatric Round Table Series.

Barr, R. G., Trent, R., & Cross, J. (2006) Age-related incidence curve of hospitalized Shaken Baby Syndrome cases: convergent evidence for crying as trigger to shaking. *Child Abuse & Neglect*, 30, 7–16.

Barr, R. G., Young, S. N., Wright, J. H., Gravel, R., & Alkawaf, R. (1999a). Differential calming responses to sucrose taste in crying infants with and without colic. *Pediatrics*, 103, e68.

Barret, H. (2006) *Attachment and the Perils of Parenting: A Commentary and Critique*. London: National Family & Parenting Institute.

Bayer, J., Hiscock, H., Hampton, A., & Wake, M. (2007) Sleep problems in young infants and maternal mental and physical health. *Journal of Paediatrics and Child Health*, 43, 66–73.

Baykan, Z., Sahin, F., Beyazova, U., Özçakar, B., & Baykan, A. (2004) Experience of Turkish parents about their infants' teething. *Child: Care, Health and Development*, 30, 331–336.

Beattie, R. M., & Lewis-Jones, M. S. (2006) An audit of the impact of a consultation with a paediatric dermatology team on quality of life in infants with atopic eczema and their families: further validation of the Infants Dematitis Quality of Life Index and Dematitis Family Impact score. *British Journal of Dermatology*, 155, 1249–1255.

Beebe, S. A., Casey, R., & Pinto-Martin, J. (1993) Association of reported infant crying and maternal parenting stress. *Clinical Pediatrics*, 32, 15–19.

Bell, J. F., & Zimmerman, F. J. (2010) Shortened nighttime sleep duration in early life and subsequent childhood obesity. *Archives of Pediatrics & Adolescent Medicine*, 164, 840–845.

Bell, S. M., & Ainsworth, M. D. S. (1972) Infant crying and maternal responsiveness. *Child Development*, 43, 1171–1190.

Benninger, M., & Walner, D. (2007) Obstructive sleep-disordered breathing in children. *Clinical Cornerstone*, 9, 6–12.

Benoit, D., Zeanah, Ch., Boucher, C., & Minde, K. (1992) Sleep disorders in early childhood: Associations with insecure maternal attachment. *Journal of American Academy of Child and Adolescent Psychiatry*, 31, 86–93.

Bernal, J. (1973) Night waking in infants during the first 14 months. *Developmental Medicine and Child Neurology*, 15, 760–769.

Bernier, A., Carlson, S. M., Bordeleau, S., & Carrier, J. (2010) Relations between physiological and cognitive regulatory systems: infant sleep regulation and subsequent executive functioning. *Child Development*, 81, 1739–1752.

Blair, P., Sidebothom, P., Evason-Coombe, C., Edmonds, M., Heckstall-Smith, E., & Fleming, P. (2009) Hazardous cosleeping environments and risk factors amenable to change: case-control study of SIDS in south west England. *British Medical Journal*, 339, b3666.

Blass, E. M. (1991) Suckling: opioid and non-opioid processes in mother–infant bonding. In: Friedman, M. (ed.) *Chemical Senses (Vol.4): Appetite and Nutrition*. New York: Marcel Dekker Inc.

Blass, E. M. (1997) Milk-induced hypoalgesia in human newborns. *Pediatrics*, 99, 825–829.

Blass, E. M., & Camp, C. A. (2003) Changing determinants of crying termination in 6- to 12-week-old human infants. *Developmental Psychobiology*, 42, 312–316.

Blass, E. M., & Smith, B. A. (1992) Differential effects of sucrose, fructose, glucose, and lactose on crying in 1- to 3-day-old human infants: qualitative and quantitative considerations. *Developmental Psychology*, 28, 804–810.

Blass, E. M., & Watt, L. B. (1999) Suckling- and sucrose-induced analgesia in human newborns. *Pain*, 83, 611–623.

Blokpoel, R. G., Broos, N., de Jong-van den Berg, L. T., & de Vries, T. W. (2010) Omeprazole of limited value in crying babies. *Nederlands Tijdschrift voor Geneeskunde*, 154, A1850.

Bloomberg, G. R. (2009) Recurrent wheezing illness in preschool-aged children: assessment and management in primary care practice. *Postgraduate Medicine*, 121, 48–55.

Blurton-Jones, N. (1972) *Ethological Studies of Child Behaviour*. Cambridge: Cambridge University Press.

Bonichini, S., Axia, V., St James-Roberts, I., & Decian, S. (2008) Infant crying and maternal holding in the first 2 months of age: an Italian diary study. *Infant and Child Development*, 17, 581–592.

Boniface, D., & Graham, P. (1979) The three-year-old and his attachment to a special soft object. *Journal of Child Psychology and Psychiatry*, 20, 217–224.

Borbély, A. A. (1982) A two-process model of sleep regulation *Human Neurobiology*, 1, 195–204.

Borbély, A. A., & Achermann, P. (1999) Sleep homeostasis and models of sleep regulation. *Journal of Biological Rhythms*, 14, 559–568.

Bowlby, J. (1969) *Attachment and Loss (Vol. I)*. New York: Basic Books.

Bowlby, J. (1973) *Attachment and Loss (Vol. II)*. New York: Basic Books.

Bowlby, J. (1988) *A Secure Base: Clinical Applications of Attachment Theory*. London: Routledge.

Brazelton, T. B. (1962) Crying in infancy. *Pediatrics*, 29, 579–588

Burnham, M. M., Goodlin-Jones, B. L., Gaylor, E. E., & Anders, T. F. (2002) Use of sleep aids during the first year of life. *Paediatrics*, 109(4), 594–601.

Byrne, J. M., & Horowitz, F. D. (1981) Rocking as a soothing intervention: the influence of direction and type of movement. *Infant Behavior & Development*, 4, 207–218.

Caglayan, S., Yaaprak, I., Secklin, E., Kansoy, S., & Aydinlioglu, H. (1991) A different approach to sleep problems: swaddling above the waist. *Turkish Journal of Paediatrics*, 33, 117–120.

Campos, R. G. (1989) Soothing pain-elicited distress in infants with swaddling and pacifiers. *Child Development*, 60, 781–792.

Canivet, C., Hagander, B., Jakobsson, I., & Lanke, J. (1996) Infantile colic – less common that previously estimated? *Acta Paediatrica*, 85, 454–458.

Carbajal, R., Chauvet, X., Couderc, S., & Olivier-Martin, M. (1999) Randomised trial of analgesic effects of sucrose, glucose, and pacifiers in term neonates. *British Medical Journal*, 319, 1393–1397.

Carey, W. B. (1984) 'Colic' – primary excessive crying as an infant–environment interaction. *Pediatric Clinics of North America*, 31, 993–1005.

Carskadon, M. A. (2002) *Adolescent Sleep Patterns: Biological, Social and Psychological Influences*. Cambridge: Canbridge University Press.

Cassidy, J. (1999) *The Nature of the Child's Ties*. New York: Guilford Press.

Cassidy, J., & Shaver, P. R. (2008) *Handbook of Attachment: Theory, Research & Clinical Applications (2nd edn.)*. New York: Guilford Press.

Castral, T. C., Warnock, F., Leite, A. M., Hass, V. J., & Scochi, C. G. (2008) The effects of skin-to-skin contact during acute pain in preterm newborns. *European Journal of Pain*, 12, 464–471.

Castro-Rodriguez, J., Stern, D., Halonen, M., Wright, A., Holberg, C., Taussig, L., & Martinez, F. (2001) Relation between infantile colic and asthma/atopy: a prospective study in an unselected population. *Pediatrics*, 108, 878–882.

Catherine, N. L. A., Ko, J. J., & Barr, R. G. (2008) Getting the word out: advice on crying and colic in popular parenting magazines. *Journal of Developmental & Behavioral Pediatrics*, 29, 508–511.

Chambless, D., Sanderson, W., Shoham, V., Johnson, S., Pope, K., Crits-Christoph, P., Baker, M., Johnson, B., Woody, S., Sue, S., Beutler, L., Williams, D., & Mccurry, S. (1996) An update on empirically validated therapies. *The Clinical Psychologist*, 49, 5–18.

Chamlin, S. L., Mattson, C. L., Frieden, I. J., Williams, M. L., Mancini, A. J., Cella, D., & Chren, M.-M. (2005) The price of pruritus: sleep disturbance and cosleeping in atopic dermatitis. *Archives of Pediatrics & Adolescent Medicine*, 159, 745–750.

Chavin, W., & Tinson, S. (1980) Children with sleep difficulties. *Health Visitor*, 53, 477–480.

Chisholm, J. S. (1983) *Navajo Infancy*. New York: Aldine Publishing.

Clarke, S., Soto, A., Bergholz, T., & Schneider, M. (1996) Maternal gestational stress alters adaptive and social behavior in adolescent rhesus monkey offspring. *Infant Behavior & Development*, 19, 453–463.

Clifford, T. J., Campbell, M. K., & Speechley, K. N. (2002) Sequelae of infant colic: evidence of transient infant distress and absence of lasting effects on maternal mental health. *Archives of Pediatric & Adolescent Medicine*, 156, 1183–1188.

Coccorullo, P., Strisciuglio, C., Martinelli, M., Miele, E., Greco, L., & Staiano, A. (2010) Lactobacillus reuteri (DSM 17938) in infants with functional chronic constipation: a double-blind, randomized, placebo-controlled study. *Journal of Pediatrics*, 157, 598–602.

Cole, M., & Cole, S. R. (2001) *The Development of Children*. New York: Worth Publishers.

Coons, S., & Guilleminault, C. (1982) Development of sleep–wake patterns and non-rapid eye movement sleep stages during the first six months of life in normal infants. *Pediatrics*, 69, 793–798.

Cortese, S., Konofal, E., Yateman, N., Mouren, M.-C., & Lecendreux, M. D. (2006) Sleep and alertness in children with attention deficit/hyperactivity disorder: a systematic review of the literature. *Sleep*, 29, 504–511.

Črnčec, R., Cooper, E., & Matthey, S. (2010a) Treating infant sleep disturbance: does maternal mood impact upon effectiveness? *Journal of Paediatrics and Child Health*, 46, 29–34.

Črnčec, R., Matthey, S., & Nemeth, D. (2010b) Infant sleep problems and emotional health: a review of two behavioural approaches. *Journal of Reproductive & Infant Psychology*, 28, 44–54.

Crocetti, M., Dudas, R., & Krugman, S. (2004) Parental beliefs and practices regarding early introduction of solid foods to their children. *Clinical Pediatrics (Philadelphia)*, 43, 541–547.

Cronin, A., Halligan, S. L., & Murray, L. (2008) Maternal psychosocial adversity and the longitudinal development of infant sleep. *Infancy*, 13, 469–495.

Crouch, J. L., Skowronski, J. J., Milner, J. S., & Harris, B. (2008) Parental responses to infant crying: the influence of child physical abuse risk and hostile priming. *Child Abuse & Neglect*, 32, 702–710.

Crowcroft, N. S., & Strachan, D. P. (1997) The social origins of infantile colic: questionnaire study covering 76 747 infants. *British Medical Journal*, 314, 1325–1328.

Crowe, H. P., & Sanford Zeskind, P. (1992) Psychophysiological and perceptual responses to infant cries varying in pitch: comparison of adults with low and high scores on the Child Abuse Potential Inventory. *Child Abuse & Neglect*, 16, 19–29.

Cubero, J., Narciso, D., Aparicio, S., Garau, C., Valero, M., Esteban, S., Rial, R., Rodriguez, A. B., & Barriga, C. (2006) Improved circadian sleep–wake cycle in infants fed a day/night dissociated formula milk. *Early Human Development*, 18, 151–156.

Dahl, R. E., & Harvey, A. G. (2007) Sleep in children and adolescents with behavioral and emotional disorders. *Sleep Medicine Clinics*, 2, 510–512.

Daniellson, B., & Hwang, C. P. (1985) Treatment of infantile colic with surface active substance (simethicone). *Acta Paediatrica Scandinavia*, 74, 446–450.

Daws, D. (1993) *Through the Night*. London: Free Association Books.

de Vries, M. W. (1987) Cry babies, culture, and catastrophe: infant temperament among the Masai. In: Scheper-Hughes, N. (ed.) *Child Survival*. Dordrecht: Reidel Publishing Co.

de Weerth, C., & Buitelaar, J. K. (2007) Childbirth complications affect young infants' behavior. *European Child & Adolescent Psychiatry*, 16, 379–388.

de Weerth, C., Van Hees, Y., & Buitelaar, J. K. (2003) Prenatal maternal cortisol levels and infant behavior during the first 5 months. *Early Human Development*, 74, 139–151.

De Wolff, M. S., & van IJzendoorn, M. H. (1997) Sensitivity and attachment: a meta-analysis on parental antecedents of infant attachment. *Child Development*, 68, 571–591.

DeGangi, G., Dipietro, J. A., Greenspan, S. I., & Porges, S. W. (1991) Psycho-physiological characteristics of the regulatory disordered infant. *Infant Behavior & Development*, 14, 37–50.

DeLeon, C. W., & Karraker, K. H. (2007) Intrinsic and extrinsic factors associated with night waking in 9-month-old infants. *Infant Behavior & Development*, 30, 596–605.

Dennis, C., & Ross, L. (2005) Relationships among infant sleep patterns, maternal fatigue and development of depressive sympomatology. *Birth*, 32, 187–193.

Dessureau, B. K., Kurowski, C. O., & Thompson, N. S. (1998) A reassessment of the role of pitch and duration in adults' responses to infant crying. *Infant Behavior & Development*, 21, 367–371.

Ding, S., & Littleton, K. (2005) *Children's Personal and Social Development*. Milton Keynes: Blackwell/Open University Press.

Don, G. W., & Waters, K. A. (2003) Influence of sleep state on frequency of swallowing, apnea and arousal in human infants. *Journal of Applied Physiology*, 94, 2456–2464.

Donovan, W. L., Leavitt, L. A., & Walsh, R. O. (1990) Maternal self-efficacy: illusory control and its effect on susceptibility to learned helplessness. *Child Development*, 61, 1637–1647.

Douglas, P. S., & Hiscock, H. (2010) The unsettled baby: crying out for an integrated, multidisciplinary primary care approach. *Medical Journal of Australia*, 193, 533–536.

Durand, V. M., & Mindell, J. A. (1999) Behavioral intervention for childood sleep terrors. *Behavior Therapy*, 30, 705–715.

Eaton-Evans, J., & Dugdale, A. E. (1988) Sleep patterns of infants in the first year of life. *Archives of Disease in Childhood*, 63, 647–649.

Ekecrantz, L., & Rudhe, L. (1977) Transitional phenomena: a review of present theories and a pilot study of the phenomenon's significance for the child's psychic development. *Reports of the Department of Psychology, University of Stockholm*, 502, 1–15.

Elias, M. F., Nicholson, N. A., Bora, C., & Johnston, J. (1986) Sleep/wake patterns of breast-fed infants in the first two years of life. *Pediatrics*, 77, 322–329.

Ellett, M. L., Schuff, E., & Davis, J. B. (2005) Parental perceptions of the lasting effects of infant colic. *American Journal of Maternal/Child Nursing*, 30, 127–132.

Elliott, M. R., Fisher, K., & Ames, E. W. (1988) The effects of rocking on the state and respiration of normal and excessive cryers. *Canadian Journal of Psychology*, 2, 163–172.

Elliott, M. R., Pedersen, E. L., & Mogan, J. (1997) Early infant crying: child and familty follow-up at three years. *Canadian Journal of Nursing Research*, 29, 47–67.

Elliott, M. R., Reilly, S. M., Drummond, J., & Letourneau, N. (2002) The effect of different soothing interventions on infant crying and on parent–infant interaction. *Infant Mental Health Journal*, 23, 310–328.

Emde, R. N., Gaensbauer, T. J., & Harmon, R. J. (1976) *Emotional Expression in Infancy: A Biobehavioural Study*. New York: International University Press.

Espositoto, G., & Venuti, P. (2010) Understanding early communication signals in autism: a study of the perception of infants' cry. *Journal of Intellectual Disability Research*, 54, 216–223.

Evanoo, G. (2007) Infant crying: a clinical conundrum. *Journal of Pediatric Health Care*, 21, 333–338.

Fagioli, I., & Salzarulo, P. (1982) Sleep states development in the first year of life assessed through 24 hour recordings. *Early Human Development*, 6, 215–228.

Fagioli, I., Bes, F., & Salzarulo, P. (1988) 24-hour behavioural states distribution in continuously fed infants. *Early Human Development*, 18, 151–156.

Ferber, R. (2006) *Solve Your Child's Sleep Problems*. London: Dorling Kindersley.

Ferrer, M., Morais-Almeida, M., Guizova, M., & Khanferyan, R. (2010) Evaluation of treatment satisfaction in children with allergic disease treated with an antihistamine: an international, non-interventional, retrospective study. *Clinical Drug Investigation*, 30, 15–34.

Field, T., Field, T., Cullen, C., Largie, S., Diego, M., Schanberg, S., & Kuhn, C. (2008) Lavender bath oil reduces stress and crying and enhances sleep in very young infants. *Early Human Development*, 84, 399–401.

Field, T., Grizzle, N., Scafidi, F., Abrams, S., & Richardson, S. (1996) Massage therapy for infants of depressed mothers. *Infant Behavior & Development*, 19, 107–112.

Field, T., Hernandez-Reif, M., Diego, M., Feijo, L., Vera, Y., & Gil, K. (2004) Massage therapy by parents improves early growth and development. *Infant Behavior & Development*, 27, 435–442.

Fifer, W. P., Fingers, S. T., Youngman, M., Gomez-Gribben, E., & Myers, M. M. (2009) Effects of alchohol and smoking during pregnancy on infant autonomic control. *Developmental Psychobiology*, 51, 234–242.

Fisher, J., Feekery, C., & Rowe, H. (2004) Treatment of maternal mood disorder and infant behaviour disturbance in an Australian private mothercraft unit: a follow-up study. *Archives of Women's Mental Health*, 7, 89–93.

Fisichelli, V., & Karelitz, S. (1963) The cry latencies of normal infants and those with brain damage. *Journal of Pediatrics*, 1963, 724–734.

Fisichelli, V., Fisichelli, R., Karelitz, S., & Cooper, J. (1974) The course of induced crying activity in the first year of life. *Pediatric Research*, 8, 921–928.

Fleming, P., & Blair, P. S. (2007) Sudden infant death syndrome. *Sleep Medicine Clinics*, 2, 463–476.

Ford, G. (2002) *The New Contented Little Baby Book*. London: Vermilion.

Forsyth, B. W. C. (1989) Colic and the effect of changing formulas: a double-blind, multiple-crossover study. *Journal of Pediatrics*, 115, 521–527.

Forsyth, B. W., Leventhal, J. M., & McCarthy, P. L. (1985) Mothers' perceptions of problems of feeding and crying behaviors. *American Journal of Diseases in Childhood*, 139, 269–272.

France, K. G. (1992) Behavior characteristics and security in sleep-disturbed infants treated with extinction. *Journal of Pediatric Psychology*, 17, 467–475.

France, K., & Blampied, N. (2004) *Services and Programs Proven to be Effective in Managing Pediatric Sleep Disturbances and Disorders, and their Impact on the Social and Emotional Development of Young Children*. Montreal, Quebec: Centre of Excellence for Early Childhood Development. Retrieved September 21, 2011 from http://www.child-encyclopedia.com/documents/France-Blampied ANGxp.pdf

France, K. G., & Hudson, S. M. (1993) Management of infant sleep disturbance: a review. *Clinical Psychology Review*, 13, 635–647.

Franco, P., Seret, N., Van Hees, J., Scaillet, S., Groswasser, J., & Kahn, A. (2005) Influence of swaddling on sleep and arousal characteristics of healthy infants. *Pediatrics*, 115, 1307–1311.

Freedman, S. B., Al-Harthy, N., & Thull-Freedman, J. (2009) The crying infant: diagnostic testing and frequency of serious underlying disease. *Pediatrics*, 123, 841–848.

Fujiwara, T., Barr, R. G., Brant, R., & Barr, M. (2011) Infant distress at five weeks of age and caregiver frustration. *Journal of Pediatrics*, 159, 425–450

Fukumizu, M., Kaga, M., Kohyama, J., & Hayes, M. J. (2005) Sleep-related crying (Yonaki) in Japan: a community-based study. *Pediatrics*, 115, 217–224.

Galbally, M., Lewis, A. J., Lum, J., & Buist, A. (2009) Serotonin discontinuation syndrome following in utero exposure to antidepressant medication: prospective controlled study. *Australian and New Zealand Journal of Psychiatry*, 43, 846–854.

Gatts, J. D., Fernbach, S. A., Wallace, D. H., & Singra, T. S. (1995) Reducing crying and irritability in neonates using a continuously controlled early environment. *Journal of Perinatology*, 15, 215–221.

Gaylor, E., Burnham, M., Goodlin-Jones, B. L., & Anders, T. F. (2005) A longitudinal follow-up study of young children's sleep patterns using a developmental classification system. *Behavioral Sleep Medicine*, 3, 44–61.

Gekoski, M. J., Rovee-Collier, C. K., & Carulli-Rabinowitz, V. (1983) A longitudinal analysis of inhibition of infant distress: the origins of social expectations? *Infant Behavior & Development*, 6, 339–351.

Gerard, C. M., Harris, K. A., & Thach, B. T. (2002) Spontaneous arousals in supine infants while swaddled and unswaddled during rapid eye movment and quiet sleep. *Pediatrics*, 110, 70–76.

Germo, G. R., Chang, E. S., Keller, M. A., & Goldberg, W. A. (2007) Child sleep arrangements and family life: perspectives from mothers and fathers. *Infant and Child Development*, 16, 433–456.

Ghosh, S., Barr, R., Paterson, J., Huot, S., & Brody, M. (2007) Infants with and without colic demonstrate a similar diurnal pattern of sucrose-induced soothing. *10th International Infant Cry Research Workshop: Puzzles, Progress and Prospects*, 4–7 July 2007 Dragor, Denmark.

Glotzbach, S. F., Edgar, D. M., Boeddiker, M., & Ariagno, R. L. (1994) Biological rhythmicity in normal infants during the first 3 months of life. *Pediatrics*, 94, 482–488.

Goldberg, W. A., & Keller, M. A. (2007) Parent–infant co-sleeping: why the interest and concern? *Infant and Child Development*, 16, 331–339.

Goodlin-Jones, B. L., Burnham, M. M., & Anders, T. F. (2000) Sleep and sleep disturbances: regulatory processes in infancy. In: Sameroff, A., Lewis, M., & Miller, M. (ed.) *Handbook of Developmental Psychopathology*. New York: Kluwer Academic.

Goodlin-Jones, B., Burnham, M., Gaylor, E., & Anders, T. (2001) Night waking, sleep–wake organization, and self-soothing in the first year of life. *Developmental & Behavioral Pediatrics*, 22, 226–232.

Goodman, R. (1997) The Strengths and Difficulties Questionnaire: a research note. *Journal of Child Psychology and Psychiatry*, 38, 581–586.

Gormally, S. (2001) Clinical clues to organic etiologies in infants with colic. In: Barr, R. G., St James-Roberts, I., & Keefe, M. (eds.) *New Evidence on Unexplained Early Infant Crying: Its Origins, Nature and Management*. Skillman, NJ: Johnson & Johnson Pediatric Institute.

Gormally, S., Barr, R. G., Wertheim, L., Alkawaf, R., Calinoiu, N., & Young, S. N. (2001) Contact and nutrient caregiving effects on newborn infant pain responses. *Developmental Medicine & Child Neurology*, 43, 28–38.

Gottlieb, D. J., Vezina, R. M., Chase, C., Lesko, S. M., Heeren, T. C., Mayer, D. E. W., Auerbach, S. H., & Corwin, M. J. (2003) Symptoms of sleep-disordered breathing in 5-year-old children are associated with sleepiness and problem behaviors. *Pediatrics*, 112, 870–877.

Gray, L., Miller, L. W., Philipp, B., & Blass, E. M. (2002) Breastfeeding is analgesic in healthy newborns. *Pediatrics*, 109, 590–593.

Gray, L., Watt, L., & Blass, E. M. (2000) Skin-to-skin contact is analgesic in healthy newborns. *Pediatrics*, 105, e14.

Greenough, W., Black, J., & Wallace, C. (1987) Experience and brain development. *Child Development*, 58, 539–559.

Groh, A. M., & Roisman. G. I. (2009) Adults' autonomic and subjective emotional responses to infant vocalizations: the role of secure base script knowledge. *Developmental Psychology*, 45, 889–893.

Grossmann, K., Grossmann, K. E., Spangler, G., Suess, G., & Unzner, L. (1985) Maternal sensitivity and newborns' orientation responses as related to quality of attachment in Northern Germany. *Monographs of the Society for Research in Child Development*, 50, 233–256.

Grunau, R. V. E., Johnston, C. C., & Craig, K. C. (1990) Neonatal facial and cry responses to invasive and non-invasive procedures. *Pain*, 42, 295–305.

Gunnar, M. R., Herrera, A., & Hostinar, C. E. (2009) Stress and early brain development. In: *Encyclopedia on Early Childhood Development*. Montreal, Quebec: Centre of Excellence for Early Childhood Development. Retrieved September 21, 2011 from http://www.ccl-cca.ca/pdfs/ECLKC/encyclopedia/Enc09_Gunnar-Herrera-Hostinar_brain_en.pdf

Gustafson, G. E., & Green, J. A. (1991) Developmental coordination of cry sounds with visual regard and gestures. *Infant Behavior & Development*, 14, 51–57.

Gustafson, G. E., & Harris, K. L. (1990) Women's response to young infants' cries. *Developmental Psychology*, 26, 144–152.

Gustafson, G., Wood, R., & Green, J. (2000) Can we hear the causes of infants' crying? In: Barr, R. G., Hopkins, B., & Green, J. A. (eds.) *Crying as a Sign, a Symptom, & a Signal.* London: Mac Keith Press.

Hadjistavropoulos, H. D., Craig, K. D., Grunau, R. V. E., & Johnston, C. C. (1994) Judging pain in newborns: facial and cry determinants. *Journal of Pediatric Psychology*, 19, 485–491.

Halász, P., Terzano, M., Parrino, L., & Bódizs, R. (2004) The nature of arousal in sleep. *Journal of Sleep Research*, 13, 1–23.

Harlow, H. E., & Harlow, M. K. (1962) Social deprivation in monkeys. *Scientific American*, 207, 136–146.

Harrington, R. C., Cartwright-Hatton, S., & Stein, A. (2002) Annotation: randomised trials. *Journal of Child Psychology and Psychiatry*, 43, 695–704.

Harrison, D., Stevens, B., Bueno, M., Yamada, J., Adams-Webber, T., Beyene, J., & Ohlsson, A. (2010) Efficacy of sweet solutions for analgesia in infants between 1 and 12 months of age: a systematic review. *Archives of Disease in Childood*, 95, 406–413.

Harrison, Y. (2004) The relationship between daytime exposure to light and night-time sleep in 6–12-week-old infants. *Journal of Sleep Research*, 13, 345–352.

Harrison, Y., & Horne, J. (1995) Should we be taking more sleep? *Sleep*, 10, 901–907.

Hauck, F. R., Omojokun, O. O., & Siadaty, M. S. (2005) Do pacifiers reduce the risk of sudden infant death syndrome? A meta-anaylsis. *Pediatrics*, 116, e716–723.

Hauck, F. R., Signore, C., Fein, S. B., & Raju, T. N. (2008) Infant sleeping arrangements and practices during the first year of life. *Pediatrics*, 22, 113–120.

Hayes, M. J., Parker, K. G., Sallinen, B., & Davare, A. A. (2001) Bedsharing, temperament, and sleep disturbance in early childhood. *Sleep*, 24, 657–662.

Headley, J., & Northstone, K. (2007) Medication administered to children from 0 to 7.5 years in the Avon Longitudinal Study of Parents and Children. *European Journal of Clinical Pharmacology*, 63, 189–195.

Heine, R. (2006) Gastroesophageal reflux disease, colic and constipation in infants with food allergy. *Current Opinion in Allergy and Clinical Immunology*, 6, 220–225.

Heine, R., Jordan, B., Lubitz, L., Meehan, M., & Catto-Smith, A. (2006) Clinical predictors of pathological gasto-oesophageal reflux in infants with persistent distress. *Journal of Paediatrics and Child Health*, 42, 134–139.

Henderson, J. M., France, K. G., Owens, J. L., & Blampied, N. M. (2010) Sleeping through the night: the consolidation of self-regulated sleep across the first year of life. *Pediatrics*, 126.

Heraghty, J. L., Hilliard, T. N., Henderson, A. J., & Fleming, P. J. (2008) The physiology of sleep in infants. *Archives of Disease in Childhood*, 93, 982–985.

Hewitt, C. E., Gilbody, S. M., Brealey, S., Paulden, M., Palmer, S., Mann, R., Green, J., Morrell, J., Barkham, M., Light, K., & Richards, D. (2009) Methods to identify postnatal depression in primary care: an integrated evidence synthesis and value of information analysis. *Health Technology Assessment*, 13, 1–230.

Hewlett, B. S., Lamb, M. E., Shannon, D., Leyendecker, B., & Scholmerich, A. (1998) Culture and early infancy among Central African foragers and farmers. *Developmental Psychology*, 34, 653–661.

Hide, D. W., & Guyer, B. M. (1982) Prevalence of infant colic. *Archives of Disease in Childhood*, 57, 559–560.

Higley, E., & Dozier, M. (2009) Nighttime maternal responsiveness and infant attachment at one year. *Attachment and Human Development*, 11, 347–363.

Hill, D., Roy, N., Heine, R., Hosking, C., Francis, D., Brown, J., Speirs, B., Sadowsky, J., & Carlin, J. (2005) Effect of a low-allergen maternal diet on colic among breastfed infants: a randomized, controlled trial. *Pediatrics*, 116, e709–715.

Hill, J. (2002) Biological, psychological and social processes in the conduct disorders. *Journal of Child Psychology and Psychiatry*, 43, 133–164.

Hirshkowitz, M., Moore, C. A., & Minhoto, G. (1997) The basics of sleep. In: Pressman, M. R., & Orr, W. C. (eds.) *Understanding Sleep: The Evaluation and Treatment of Sleep Disorders, Application and Practice in Health Psychology*, pp. 11–34. Washington, DC: American Psychological Association,

Hiscock, H., Bayer, J., Gold, L., Hampton, A., Ukoumunne, O., & Wake, M. (2007) Improving infant sleep and maternal health: a cluster randomised trial. *Archives of Disease in Childhood*, 92, 952–958.

Hiscock, H., & Wake, M. (2001) Infant sleep problems and postnatal depression: a community based study. *Pediatrics*, 107, 1317–1322.

Hofer, M. A. (2001) Infant crying: an evolutionary perspective. In: Barr, R. G., St James-Roberts, I., & Keefe, M. (eds.) *New Evidence on Unexplained Early Infant Crying: Its Origins, Nature and Management*, pp. 59–70. Skillman, NJ: Johnson & Johnson Pediatric Institute.

Hofer, M. A., & Shair, H. N. (1992) Ultrasonic vocalization by rat pups during recovery from deep hypothermia. *Developmental Psychobiology*, 25, 647.

Hofer, M. A., Shair, H. N., Masmela, J. R., & Brunelli, S. A. (2001) Developmental effects of selective breeding for an infantile trait: The rat pup ultrasonic isolation call. *Developmental Psychobiology*, 39, 231–246.

Hogdall, C., Vestermark, V., Birch, M., Plenov, G., & Toftager-Larsen, K. (1991) The significance of pregnancy, delivery and postpartum factors for the development of infantile colic. *Journal of Perinatal Medicine*, 19, 251–257.

Holditch-Davis, D. (2010) Development of sleep and sleep problems in preterm infants. In: Tremblay, R. E., Barr, R. G., Peters, R. D. V., & Boivin, M. (eds.) *Encyclopdia on Early Childhood Development*. Montreal, Quebec: Centre of Excellence for Early Childhood Development. Retrieved September 21, 2011 from http://www.child-encyclopedia.com/documents/Holditch-DavisANGxp_rev.pdf

Hong, K. M., & Townes, B. D. (1976) Infants' attachment to inanimate objects. *Journal of the American Academy of Child Psychiatry*, 15, 49–61.

Hoppenbrowers, T., Hodgman, J. E., Harper, R. M., & Sterman, M. B. (1982) Temporal distribution of sleep states, somatic activity, and autonomic activity during the first half year of life. *Sleep*, 5, 131–144.

Horne, J. (2006) *Sleepfaring*. Oxford: Oxford University Press.

Horne, J. (2008) Wake up call. *New Scientist*, 200, 36–38.

Horne, R., Franco, P., Adamson, T., Groswasser, J., & Kahn, A. (2002) Effects of body position on sleep and arousal characteristics in infants. *Early Human Development*, 69, 25–33.

Horne, R. S., Franco, P., Adamson, T. M., Groswasser, J., & Kahn, A. (2004)

Influences of maternal cigarette smoking on infant arousability. *Early Human Development*, 79, 49–58.

Hubbard, F. O. A., & van IJzendoorn, M. H. (1987) Maternal unresponsiveness and infant crying: a critical replication of the Bell and Ainsworth study. In: Tavecchio, L. W. C., & van IJzendoorn, M. H. (eds.) *Attachment in Social Networks*. Amsterdam: Elsevier.

Hubbard, F. O. A., & van IJzendoorn, M. H. (1991) Maternal unresponsiveness and infant crying across the first nine months: a naturalistic longitudinal study. *Infant Behavior & Development*, 14, 299–312.

Huhtala, V., Lehtonen, L., Heinonen, R., & Korvenranta, H. (2000) Infant massage compared with crib vibrator in the treatment of colicky infants. *Pediatrics*, 105, e84.

Huizink, A. C., Robles De Medina, P. G., Mulder, E. J. H., Visser, G. H. A., & Buitelaar, J. K. (2003) Stress during pregnancy is associated with developmental outcome in infancy. *Journal of Child Psychology and Psychiatry*, 44, 810–818.

Hunsley, M., & Thoman, E. B. (2002) The sleep of co-sleeping infants when they are not co-sleeping: evidence that co-sleeping is stressful. *Development Psychobiology*, 40, 14–22.

Hunziker, U., & Barr, R. (1986) Increased carrying reduces infant crying: a randomised controlled trial. *Pediatrics*, 77, 641–648.

Iglowstein, I., Jenni, O. G., Molinari, L., & Largo, R. H. (2003) Sleep duration from infancy to adolescence: reference values and generational trends. *Pediatrics*, 111, 302–307.

Iglowstein, I., Latal Hajnal, B., Molinari, L., H, & Jenni, O. G. (2006) Sleep behaviour in preterm children from birth to age 10 years: a longitudinal study. *Acta Paediatrica*, 95, 1691–1693.

Illingworth, R. S. (1954) Three months colic. *Archives of Disease in Childhood*, 29, 165–174.

Illingworth, R. S. (1955) Crying in infants and children. *British Medical Journal*, 1, 75.

Illingworth, R. S. (1985) Infantile colic revisited. *Archives of Disease in Childhood*, 60, 981–985.

Ivanhoe, J. R., Lefebvre, C. A., & Stockstill, J. W. (2007) Sleep disordered breathing in infants and children: a review of the literature. *Pediatric Dentistry*, 29, 193–200.

Jacklin, N. C., Snow, E. M., Gahart, M., & Maccoby, E. E. (1980) Sleep pattern development from 6 through 33 months. *Journal of Pediatric Psychology*, 5, 295–303.

Jenkins, S., Owen, C., Bax, M., & Hart, H. (1984) Continuities of common behaviour problems in preschool children. *Journal of Child Psychology and Psychiatry*, 25, 75–90.

Jenni, O. G., & Carskadon, M. A. (2007) Sleep behaviour and sleep regulation from infancy through adolescence. *Sleep Medicine Clinics*, 2, 321–329.

Jenni, O. G., & O'Connor, B. B. (2005) Children's sleep: an interplay between culture and biology. *Pediatrics*, 115, 204–216.

Jenni, O., Borbély, A., & Achermann, P. (2004) Development of the nocturnal sleep electroencephalogram in human infants. *American Journal of Physiology: Regulatory, Integrative & Comparative Psysiology*, 286, R528–538.

Jenni, O., Fuhrer, H. Z., Iglowstein, I., Molinari, L., & Largo, R. H. (2005) A longitudinal study of bed sharing and sleep problems among Swiss children in the first 10 years of life. *Pediatrics*, 115, 233–240.

Jenni, O. G., Molinari, L., Caflisch, J. A., & Largo, R. H. (2007) Sleep duration from ages 1 to 10 years: variability and stability in comparison with growth. *Pediatrics*, 120, e769–776.

Johnson, N., & McMahon, C. (2008) Preschoolers' sleep behaviour: associations with parental hardiness, sleep-related cognitions and bedtime interactions. *Journal of Child Psychology and Psychiatry*, 49, 765–773.

Jordan, B., Heine, R., Meehan, M., Catto-Smith, A., & Lubitz, L. (2006) Effect of antireflux medication, placebo and infant mental health intervention on persistent crying: a randomized clinical trial. *Journal of Paediatrics and Child Health*, 42, 49–58.

Just, J., Belfar, S., Wanin, S., Pribil, C., Grimfield, A., & Duru, G. (2010) Impact of innate and environmental factors on wheezing persistence during childhood. *Journal of Asthma*, 47, 412–416.

Kagan, J., & Herschkowitz, N. (2005) *A Young Mind in a Growing Brain*. Mahwah, NJ: Lawrence Erlbaum Associates, Inc.

Kalliomäki, M., Laippala, P., Korvenranta, H., Kero, P., & Isolauri, E. (2001) Extent of fussing and colic type crying preceding atopic disease. *Archives of Disease in Childhood*, 84, 349–350.

Karelitz, S., & Fisichelli, V. R. (1962) The cry thresholds of normal infants and those with brain damage. *Journal of Pediatrics*, 61, 679–685.

Kato, I., Scaillet, S., Groswasser, J., Montemitro, E., Togari, H., Lin, J. S., Kahn, A., & Franco, P. (2006) Spontaneous arousability in prone and supine position in healthy infants. *Sleep*, 29, 785–790.

Keefe, M., Karlsen, K., Lobo, M., Kotzer, A., & Dudley, W. (2006a) Reducing parenting stress in families with irritable infants. *Nursing Research*, 55, 198–205.

Keefe, M., Lobo, M., Froese-Fretz, A., Kotzer, A., Barbosa, G., & Dudley, W. (2006b) Effectiveness of an intervention for colic. *Clinical Pediatrics*, 45, 123–133.

Keener, M. A., Zeanah, C. H., & Anders, T. F. (1988) Infant temperament, sleep organisation, and nighttime parental interventions. *Pediatrics*, 81, 762–771.

Keller, P., & El-Sheikh, M. (2010) Children's emotional security and sleep: longitudinal relations and directions of effects. *Journal of Child Psychology and Psychiatry*, 52, 64–71.

Keller, H., Lohaus, A., Völker, S., Cappenberg, M., & Chasiotis, A. (1998) Relationship between infant crying, birth complications, and maternal variables. *Child Care Health and Development*, 24, 377–394.

Kelmanson, I. A. (2010) Sleep disturbances in two-month-old infants sharing the bed with parent(s). *Minerva Pediatrics*, 62, 161–169.

Kerr, M., Jowett, S., & Smith, L. (1996) Preventing sleep problems in infants: a randomised controlled trial. *Journal of Advanced Nursing*, 24, 938–942.

Kirjavainen, J., Kirjavainen, T., Huhtala, V., Lehtonen, L., Korvenranta, H., & Kero, P. (2001) Infants with colic have a normal sleep structure at 2 and 7 months of age. *Journal of Pediatrics*, 138, 218–223.

Kirjavainen, J., Ojala, T., Huhtala, V., Kirjavainen, T., & Kero, P. (2004) Heart rate variability in response to the sleep-related movements in infants with and without colic. *Early Human Development*, 79, 17–30.

Klackenberg, G. (1968) The development of children in a Swedish urban community. A prospective longitudinal study. IV. The sleep behaviour of children up to 3 years of age. *Acta Paediatrica*, 187, 105–121.

Kleitman, N., & Engelmann, T. G. (1953) Sleep characteristics of infants. *Journal of Applied Physiology*, 6, 269–282.

Klinnert, M. D., Nelson, H. S., Price, M. R., Adinoff, A. D., Leung, D. Y., & Mrazek, D. A. (2001) Onset and persistence of childhood asthma: predictors from infancy. *Pediatrics*, 108, 69.

Klougart, N., Nilsson, N., & Jacobsen, J. (1989) Infantile colic treated by chiropractors: a prospective study of 316 cases. *Journal of Manipulative and Physiological Therapeutics*, 12, 281–288.

Kochanska, G., Philibert, R. A., & Barry, R. A. (2009) Interplay of genes and early mother–child relationship in the development of self-regulation from toddler to preschool age. *Journal of Child Psychology and Psychiatry*, 50, 1331–1338.

Kopasz, M., Loessl, B., Hornyak, M., Riemann, D., Nissen, C., Piosczyk, H., & Voderholzer, U. (2010) Sleep and memory in healthy children and adolescents – a critical review. *Sleep Medicine Reviews*, 14, 167–177.

Korner, A. F., & Thoman, E. B. (1972) The relative efficacy of contact and vestibular-proprioceptive stimulation in soothing neonates. *Child Development*, 43, 443–453.

Kotagal, S. (2007) Sleep in children at risk. *Sleep Medicine Clinics*, 2, 477–490.

Kozyrskyj, A. L., Kendall, G. E., Zubrick, S. R., Newnham, J. P., & Sly, P. D. (2009) Frequent nocturnal awakening in early life is associated with nonatopic asthma in children. *European Respiratory Journal*, 34, 1288–1295.

Kramer, M. S., & Kakuma, R. (2009) Optimal duration of exclusive breastfeeding. *Cochrane Database of Systematic Reviews*, 1, CD003517.

Kurth, E., Spichiger, E., Cignacco, E., Kennedy, H. P., Glanzmann, R., Schmid, M., Staehelin, K., Schindler, C., & Stutz, E. Z. (2010) Predictors of crying problems in the early postpartum period. *Journal of Obstetric, Gynecological & Neonatal Nursing*, 39, 250–262.

Lam, P., Hiscock, H., & Wake, M. (2003) Outcomes of infant sleep problems: a longitudinal study of sleep, behavior, and maternal well-being. *Pediatrics*, 111, e203–207.

Latz, S., Wolf, A., & Lozoff, B. (1999) Cosleeping in context: sleep practices and problems in young children in Japan and the United States. *Archives of Pediatrics & Adolescent Medicine*, 153, 339–346.

Lee, K. (1992) Pattern of night waking and crying of Korean infants from 3 months to 2 years old and its relation with various factors. *Developmental and Behavioral Pediatrics*, 13, 326–330.

Lee, K. (1994) The crying pattern of Korean infants and related factors. *Developmental Medicine & Child Neurology*, 36, 601–607.

Lee, K. (2000) Crying patterns of Korean infants in institutions. *Child: Care, Health and Development*, 36, 217–228.

Leerkes, E. M., & Siepak, K. J. (2006) Attachment linked predictors of women's emotional and cognitive responses to infant distress. *Attachment & Human Development*, 8, 11–32.

Lehman, E. B., Denham, S. A., Moser, M. H., & Reeves, S. L. (1992) Soft object and pacifier attachments in young children: the role of security of attachment to the mother. *Journal of Child Psychology and Psychiatry*, 33, 1205–1215.

Lehr, V. T., Zeskind, P. S., Ofenstein, J. P., Cepeda, E., & Warrier, I. (2007) Neonatal facial coding system scores and spectral characteristics of infant crying during newborn circumcision. *Clinical Journal of Pain*, 23, 417–424.

Lehtonen, L. (2001) From colic to toddlerhood. In: Barr, R. G., St James-Roberts, I., & Keefe, M. (eds.) *New Evidence on Unexplained Early Infant Crying: Its Origins, Nature and Management*. Skillman, NJ: Johnson & Johnson Pediatric Institute.

Lehtonen, L., & Korvenranta, H. (1995) Infantile colic – seasonal incidence and crying profiles. *Archives of Pediatrics & Adolescent Medicine*, 149, 533–536.

Lehtonen, L., Gormally, S., & Barr, R. (2000) 'Clinical pies' for etiology and outcome in infants presenting with early increased crying. In: Barr, R. G., Hopkins, B., & Green, J. (eds.) *Crying as a Sign, a Symptom, & a Signal*. London: Mac Keith Press.

Lester, B. M. (1985) *There's More to Crying Than Meets the Ear*. New York: Plenum.

Lester, B. M. (1997) Definition and diagnosis of colic. In: Lester, B. M., & Barr, R. G. (eds.) *Colic and Excessive Crying*. Columbus, OH: Ross Products Division, Abbott Laboratories.

Lester, B. M., & Boukydis, C. F. K. (1985) *Infant Crying: Theoretical and Research Perspectives*. New York: Plenum Press.

Lester, B. M., Boukydis, C. F. Z., Garcia-Coll, C. T., Hole, W., & Peucker, M. (1992) Infantile colic: acoustic cry characteristics, maternal perception of cry, and temperament. *Infant Behavior & Development*, 15, 15–26.

Lester, B. M., Cucca, J., Andreozzi, L., Flanagan, P., & Oh, W. (1993) Possible association between fluoxetine hydrochloride and colic in an infant. *Journal of American Academy of Child and Adolescent Psychiatry*, 32, 1253–1255.

Lewis, M., & Ramsay, D. S. (1995a) Developmental change in infants' responses to stress. *Child Development*, 66, 657–670.

Lewis, M., & Ramsay, D. S. (1995b) Stability and change in cortisol and behavioral response to stress during the first 18 months of life. *Developmental Psychology*, 28, 419–428.

Lewis, M., & Ramsay, D. S. (1999) Effect of maternal soothing on infant stress response. *Child Development*, 70, 11–20.

Liedloff, J. (1975/1986) *The Continuum Concept*. London: Penguin Books.

Lipton, E., Steinschneider, A., & Richmond, J. B. (1965) Swaddling, a child care practice: historical, cultural and experimental observations. *Pediatrics*, 35, 521–567.

Liu, X., Lianqui, L., Owens, J. A., & Kaplan, D. L. (2005) Sleep patterns and sleep problems among schoolchildren in the United States and China. *Pediatrics*, 115, 241–249.

Lothe, L., & Lindberg, T. (1989) Cow's milk whey protein elicits symptoms of infantile colic in colicky formula-fed infants: a double blind crossover study. *Pediatrics*, 83, 262–266.

Louis, J., & Govindama, Y. (2004) Sleep problems and bedtime routines in infants in a cross-cultural perspective. *Archives of Pediatrics*, 11, 93–98.

Lozoff, B., Askew, G., & Wolf, A. (1996) Cosleeping and early childhood sleep problems: effects of ethnicity and socioeconomic status. *Developmental and Behavioral Pediatrics*, 17, 9–15.

Lozoff, B., Wolf, A., & Davis, N. (1984) Co-sleeping in urban families with young children in the United States. *Pediatrics*, 74, 171–182.

Lozoff, B., Wolf, A. W., & Davis, N. S. (1985) Sleep problems seen in pediatric practice. *Pediatrics*, 75, 477–483.

Lozoff, B., & Zuckerman, B. (1988) Sleep problems in children. *Pediatrics Review*, 10, 17–24.

Lucassen, P. L. B. J., Assendelft, W. J. J., Gubbels, J., Van Eijk, J. T., Van Geldrop, W. J., & Knuistingh Neven, A. (1998) Effectiveness of treatments for infantile colic: systematic review. *British Medical Journal*, 316, 1563–1569 (published erratum appears in *BMJ* (1998) 317, 171).

Lucassen, P. L. B. J., Assendelft, W. J. J., Van Eijk, J. T. M., Gubbels, J. W., Douwes, A. C., & Van Geldrop, W. J. (2001) Systematic review of the occurence of infantile colic in the community. *Archives of Disease in Childhood*, 84, 398–403.

Luyster, R., Gotham, K., Guthrie, W., Coffing, M., Petrak, R., & Pierce, R. (2009) The Autism diagnostic observation schedule – toddler module: a new module of a standardized diagnostic measure for autism spectrum disorders. *Journal of Autism and Developmental Disorders*, 39, 1305–1320.

Ly, N. P., Gold, D. R., Weiss, S. T., & Celedón, J. C. (2006) Recurrent wheeze in early childhood and asthma among children at risk for atopy. *Pediatrics*, 117, 1132–1138.

Macknin, M. L., Piedmonte, M., Jacobs, J., & Skibinski, C. (2000) Symptoms associated with infant teething: a prospective study. *Pediatrics*, 105, 747–775.

Mahalski, P. A. (1983) The incidence of attachment objects and oral habits at bedtime in two longitudinal samples of children aged 1.5–7 years. *Journal of Child Psychology and Psychiatry*, 24, 283–295.

Mahle, W. T. (1998) A dangerous case of colic: anomalous left coronary artery presenting with paroxysms of irritability. *Pediatric Emergency Care*, 14, 24–27.

Maldonado-Duran, M., & Sauceda-Garcia, J.-M. (1996) Excessive crying in infants with regulatory disorders. *Bulletin of the Menninger Clinic*, 60, 62–78.

Mao, A., Burnham, M., Goodlin-Jones, B., Gaylor, E., & Anders, T. (2004) A comparison of the sleep–wake patterns of cosleeping and solitary sleeping infants. *Child Psychiatry & Human Development*, 35, 95–105.

Markestad, T. (1997) Use of sucrose as a treatment for infant colic. *Archives of Disease in Childhood*, 76, 356–358.

Marks, I. (1987) The development of normal fear: a review. *Journal of Child Psychology and Psychiatry*, 28, 667–697.

Maughan, B., Taylor, C., Taylor, A., Butler, N., & Bynner, J. (2001) Pregnancy smoking and childhood conduct problems: a causal association? *Journal of Child Psychology and Psychiatry*, 42, 1021–1028.

Maunu, J., Kirjavainen, J., Korja, R., Parkkola, R., Rikalainen, H., Lapinleimu, H., Haataja, L., Lethonen, L., & The Pipari Study Group. (2006) Relations of prematurity and brain injury to crying behavior in infancy. *Pediatrics*, 118, e57–65.

McKenna, J. J. (2005) Sudden infant death syndrome. In: Hopkins, B., Barr, R., Michel, G., & Rochat, P. (eds.) *The Cambridge Encyclopaedia of Child Development*. Cambridge: Cambridge University Press.

McKenna, J. J., & Gettler, L. T. (2010) Co-sleeping, breastfeeding and sudden infant death syndrome. In: Tremblay, R. E., Barr, R. G., Peters, R. D. V., & Boivin, M. (eds.) *Encyclopedia on Early Childhood Development*. Montreal, Quebec: Centre of Excellence for Early Childhood Development.

McKenna, J. J., & Volpe, L. E. (2007) Sleeping with baby: an internet-based sampling of parental experiences, choices, perceptions and interpretations in a western industrialized context. *Infant and Child Development*, 16, 359–385.

McKenzie, S. (1991) Troublesome crying in infants: the effect of advice to reduce stimulation. *Archives of Disease in Childhood*, 66, 1416–1420.

McMahon, C., Barnett, B., Kowalenko, N., Tennant, C., & Don, N. (2001) Post-natal depression, anxiety and unsettled infant behaviour. *Australian and New Zealand Journal of Psychiatry*, 35, 581–588.

McNamara, P., Belsky, J., & Fearon, P. (2003) Infant sleep disorders and attach-ment: sleep problems in infants with insecure-resistant versus insecure-avoidant attachments to mother. *Sleep and Hypnosis* 5, 7–16.

McRury, J. M., & Zolotar, A. J. (2010) A randomized, controlled trial of a behavioral intervention to reduce crying among infants. *Journal of the American Board of Family Medicine*, 23, 315–322.

Meltz, B. F. (2004) Experts speak out against notion of letting babies cry. *Boston Globe*, 16 June.

Meltzer, L., & Mindell, J. (2007) Relationship between child sleep disturbances and maternal sleep, mood, and parenting stress: a pilot study. *Journal of Family Psychology*, 21, 67–73.

Mennella, J. A., & Garcia-Gomez, P. L. (2001) Sleep disturbances after acute exposure to alcohol in mothers' milk. *Alcohol*, 25, 153–158.

Mennella, J. A., Yourshaw, L. M., & Morgan, L. K. (2007) Breastfeeding and smoking: short-term effects on infant feeding and sleeping. *Pediatrics*, 120, 497–502.

Meolie, A. L., Rosen, C. L., Kristo, D., Kohman, M., Gooneratne, N., Aguillard, R. N., Fayle, R., Troell, R., Townsend, D., Claman, D., Hoban, T., & Mahowald, M. (2005) Oral nonprescription treatment for insomnia: an evaluation of products with limited evidence. *Journal of Clinical Sleep Medicine*, 1, 173–187.

Messer, D., & Richards, M. (1993) The development of sleeping difficulties. In: St James-Roberts, I., Harris, G., & Messer, D. (eds.) *Infant Crying, Feeding and Sleeping: Development, Problems and Treatments*. London: Harvester Wheat-sheaf.

Michelsson, K., Rinne, A., & Paajanen, S. (1990) Crying, feeding and sleeping patterns in 1 to 12-month-old infants. *Child: Care, Health & Development*, 16, 99–111.

Milgrom, J., Westley, D. T., & McCloud, P. I. (1995) Do infants of depressed mothers cry more than other infants? *Journal of Paediatrics and Child Health*, 31, 218–221.

Miller-Loncar, C., Bigsby, R., High, P., Wallach, M., & Lester, B. (2004) Infant colic and feeding difficulties. *Archives of Disease in Childhood*, 89, 908–913.

Minde, K., Popiel, K., Leos, N., Falkner, S., Parker, K., & Handley-Derry, M. (1993) The evaluation and treatment of sleep disturbances in young children. *Journal of Child Psychology and Psychiatry*, 34, 521–533.

Mindell, J. A. (2008) Children and sleep. In: Pressman, M. R., & Orr, W. C. (eds.) *Understanding Sleep: The Evaluation and Treatment of Sleep Disorders*. Washington: American Psychological Association.

Mindell, J. A., & Owens, J. (2003) *A Clinical Guide to Pediatric Sleep*. Philadelphia, PA: Lippincott, Williams & Wilkins.

Mindell, J., Kuhn, B., Lewin, D., Meltzer, L., & Sadeh, A. (2006) Behavioral treatment of bedtime problems and night wakings in infants and young children. *Sleep*, 29, 1263–1276.

Mindell, J., Owens, J., & Carskadon, M. (1999) Developmental features of sleep. *Child & Adolescent Psychiatric Clinics of North America*, 8, 695–725.

Mindell, J. A., Sadeh, A., Wiegand, B., Howd, T. H., & Goh, D. Y. T. (2010) Cross-cultural differences in infant and todlder sleep. *Sleep Medicine*, 11, 274–280.

Mindell, J. A., Telofski, L. S., Wiegand, B., & Kurtz, E. S. (2009) A nightly bedtime routine: impact on sleep in young children and maternal mood. *Sleep*, 32, 599–606.

Mitchell, E. A., Blair, P. S., & L'hoir, M. P. (2006) Should pacifiers be recommended to prevent sudden infant death syndrome? *Pediatrics*, 117, 1755–1758.

Moffitt, T. E. (2008) Research review: DSM IV conduct disorder: research needs for an evidence base. *Journal of Child Psychology and Psychiatry*, 49, 3–33.

Montemitro, E., Franco, P., Scaillet, S., Kato, I., Groswasser, J., P, V. M., Kahn, A., Sastre, J. P., Ecochard, R., Thiriez, G., & Lin, J. S. (2008) Maturation of spontaneous arousals in healthy infants. *Sleep*, 31, 47–54.

Montgomery-Downs, H. E., & Gozal, D. (2006) Sleep habits and risk factors for sleep-disordered breathing in infants and young toddlers in Louisville, Kentucky. *Sleep Medicine*, 7, 211–219.

Montgomery-Downs, H. E., Crabtree, V. M., Capdevila, O. S., & Gozal, D. (2007) Infant-feeding methods and childhood sleep-disordered breathing. *Pediatrics*, 120, 1030-1035.

Moore, M., Meltzer, L. M., & Mindell, J. A. (2007) Bedtime problems and night waking in children. *Sleep Medicine Clinics*, 2, 377–385.

Moore, T., & Ucko, L. (1957) Night waking in early infancy: Part 1. *Archives of Disease in Childhood*, 32, 333–342.

Morelli, G. I., Rogoff, B., Oppenheim, D., & Goldsmith, D. (1992) Cultural variation in infants' sleeping arrangements: questions of independence. *Developmental Psychology*, 28, 604–613.

Morley, R., Morley, C., Lucas, P., & Lucas, A. (1989) Comforters and night waking. *Archives of Disease in Childhood*, 64, 1624–1626.

Morrell, C. J., Warner, R., Slade, P., Dixon, S., Walters, S., Paley, G., & Brugha, T. (2009) Psychological interventions for postnatal depression: cluster randomised trial and economic evaluation: The PoNDER trial. *Health Technology Assessment*, 13, 1–153.

Morrell, J. (1999) The role of maternal cognitions in infant sleep problems as assessed by a new instrument, the maternal cognitions about infant sleep questionnaire. *Journal of Child Psychology and Psychiatry*, 40, 247–258.

Morrell, J., & Steele, H. (2003) The role of attachment security, temperament, maternal perception, and care-giving behavior in persistent infant sleeping problems. *Infant Mental Health Journal*, 24, 447–468.

Morris, S., St James-Roberts, I., Sleep, J., & Gillham, P. (2001) Economic evaluation of strategies for managing infant crying and sleeping problems in the first 12 weeks of age: the COSI study. *Archives of Disease in Childhood*, 84, 15–19.

Mosko, S., Richard, C., & McKenna, J., & Drummond, S. (1996) Infant sleep architecture during bedsharing and possible implications for SIDS. *Sleep*, 19, 677–684.

Mosko, S., Richard, C., & McKenna, J. (1997) Maternal sleep and arousals during bedsharing with infants. *Sleep*, 20, 142–150.

Muller, E., Hollien, H., & Murrey, T. (1974) Perceptual response to infant crying: identification of cry types. *Journal of Child Language*, 3, 321–328.

Munck, P., Maunu, J., Kirjavainen, J., Lapinleimu, H., Haataja, L., Lehtonen, L., & Group, P. S. (2008) Crying behaviour in early infancy is associated with developmental outcome at two years of age in very low birth weight infants. *Acta Paediatrica*, 97, 332–336.

Muris, P., Merckelbach, H., Gadet, B., & Moulaert, V. (2000) Fears, worries and scary dreams in 4–12 year-old children: their content, development patterns and origins. *Clinical Child Psychology*, 29, 43–52.

Muris, P., Merckelbach, H., Ollendick, T. H., King, N. J., & Bogie, N. (2001) Children's nighttime fears: parent–child ratings of frequency, content, origins, coping behaviours and severity. *Behaviour Research and Therapy*, 39, 13–28.

Murray, L., & Cooper, P. (2001) The impact of irritable infant behavior on maternal mental state: a longitudinal study and a treatment trial. In: Barr, R. G., St James-Roberts, I., & Keefe, M. R. (eds.) *New Evidence on Unexplained Early Infant Crying: Its Origins, Nature and Management*. Skillman, NJ: Johnson & Johnson Pediatric Institute.

National Health Service (2010) Preventing sudden infant death syndrome. London: NHS. Retrieved September 21, 2011 from http://www.nhs.uk/Conditions/Sudden-infant-death-syndrome/Pages/Prevention.aspx

National Scientific Council on the Developing Child (2010) *Early Experiences can Alter Gene Expression and Affect Long-Term Development. NSCDC Working Paper No. 10*. Cambridge, MA: National Scientific Council on the Developing Child.

Nelson, C. A., Zeanah, C. H., Fox, N. A., Marshall, P. J., Smyke, A. T., & Guthrie, D. (2007) Cognitive recovery in socially deprived young children: the Bucharest Early Intervention Project. *Science*, 318, 1937–1940

Neto, H. J. C., Rosário, N. A., Solè, D., & Mallol, J. (2007) Prevalence of recurrent wheezing in infants. *Journal of Pediatrics (Rio Janeiro)*, 83, 357–362.

Nevarez, M. D., Rifas-Shiman, S. L., Kleinman, K. P., Gillman, M. W., & Taveras, E. M. (2010) Associations of early life risk factors with infant sleep duration. *American Academy of Pediatrics*, 10, 187–193.

Newson, J., Newson, E., & Mahalski, P. A. (1982) Persistent infant comfort habits and their sequelae at 11 and 16 years. *Journal of Child Psychology and Psychiatry*, 23, 421–436.

Nguyen, B. H., Perusse, D., & Paquet, J. (2008) Sleep terrors in children: a prospective study of twins. *Pediatrics*, 122, 1164–1167.

Nikolopoulou, M., & St James-Roberts, I. (2003) Preventing sleeping problems in infants who are at risk of them. *Archives of Disease in Childhood*, 88, 108–111.

O'Connor, T., Caprariello, P., Blackmore, E., Gregory, A., Glover, V., & Fleming, P.

(2007) Prenatal mood disturbance predicts sleep problems in infancy and toddlerhood. *Early Human Development*, 83, 451–458.

Ohgi, S., Arisawa, K., & Shigemori, K. (2004) Randomised controlled trial of swaddling versus massage in the management of excessive crying in infants with cerebral injuries. *Archives of Disease in Childhood*, 89, 212–216.

Olafsdottir, E., Forshei, S., Fluge, G., & Markestad, T. (2001) Randomised controlled trial of infantile colic treated with chiropractic spinal manipulation. *Archives of Disease in Childhood*, 84, 138–141.

Olds, D. L., Sadler, L., & Kitzman, H. (2007) Programs for parents of infants and toddlers: recent evidence from randomized trials. *Journal of Child Psychology and Psychiatry*, 48, 355–391.

Olson, L., Inkelas, M., Halfon, N., Schuster, M., O'Connor, K., & Mistry, R. (2004) Overview of the content of health supervision for young children: reports from parents and pediatricians. *Pediatrics*, 113, 1907–1916.

Osborn, D. A., Jeffrey, H. E., & Cole, M. J. (2010) Opiate treatment for opiate withdrawal in newborn infants. *Cochrane Database of Systematic Reviews*, 10, CD002059.

Osborn, D. A., & Sinn, J. K. H. (2006a) Formulas containing hydrolysed protein for prevention of allergy and food intolerance in infants. *Cochrane Database of Systematic Reviews*, 4, CD003664.

Osborn, D. A., & Sinn, J. K. H. (2006b) Soy formula for prevention of allergy and food intolerance in infants. *Cochrane Database of Systematic Reviews*, 4, CD003741.

Ottaviano, S., Giannotti, F., Cortesi, F., Bruni, O., & Ottaviano, C. (1996) Sleep charateristics in healthy children from birth to 6 years of age in the urban area of Rome. *Sleep*, 19, 1–3.

Owens, J. A. (2004) Sleep in children: cross-cultural perspectives. *Sleep and Biological Rhythms*, 2, 165–173.

Owens, J. (2007) Classification and epidemiology of childhood sleep disorders. *Sleep Medicine Clinics*, 2, 353–362.

Owens, J. A., Babcock, D., Blumer, J., Chervin, R., Ferber, R., Goetting, M., Glaze, D., Ivanenko, A., Mindell, J. A., Rappley, M., Rosen, C., & Sheldon, S. (2005) The use of pharmacotherapy in the treatment of pediatric insomnia in primary care: rational approaches. A consensus meeting summary. *Journal of Clinical Sleep Medicine*, 1, 49–59.

Owens, J. A., Rosen, C., & Mindell, J. A. (2003) Medication use in the treatment of pediatric insomnia: results of a survey of community-based paediatricians. *Pediatrics*, 111, 628–635.

Papoušek, M., & von Hofacker, N. V. (1995) Persistent crying and parenting: search for a butterfly in a dynamic system. *Early Development and Parenting*, 4, 209–224.

Papoušek, M., & von Hofacker, N. V. (1998) Persistent crying in early infancy: a non-trivial condition of risk for the developing mother–infant relationship. *Child: Care, Health and Development*, 24, 395–424.

Papoušek, M., Wurmser, H., & von Hofacker, N. (2001) Clinical perspectives on unexplained early crying: challenges and risks for infant mental health and parent–infant relationships. In: Barr, R. G., St James-Roberts, I., & Keefe, M. (eds.) *New Evidence on Unexplained Early Infant Crying: Its Origins, Nature and Management*. Skillman, NJ: Johnson & Johnson Pediatric Institute.

Parkin, P. C., Schwartz, C. J., & Manuel, B. A. (1993) Randomized controlled trial of three interventions in the management of persistent crying of infancy. *Pediatrics*, 92, 197–201.

Parmelee, A., Schulz, H., & Disbrow, M. (1961) Sleep patterns of the newborn. *Journal of the Newborn*, 58, 241–250.

Parmelee, A., Wenner, W., & Schulz, H. (1964) Infant sleep patterns from birth to 16 weeks of age. *Journal of Pediatrics*, 65, 576–582.

Passman, R. H., & Adams, R. E. (1982) Preferences for mothers for security blankets and their effectiveness as reinforcers for young children's behaviours. *Journal of Child Psychology and Psychiatry*, 23, 223–236.

Passman, R. H., & Halonen, J. S. (1979) A developmental survey of young children's attachments to inanimate objects. *Journal of Genetic Psychology*, 134, 165–178.

Pauli-Pott, U., Becker, K., Mertesacker, T., & Beckman, D. (2000) Infants with "Colic" – mothers' perspectives on the crying problem. *Journal of Psychosomatic Research*, 48, 125–132.

Peirano, P. D., & Algarin, C. R. (2007) Sleep in brain development. *Biological Research*, 40, 471–478.

Peirano, P., Algarin, C., & Uauy, R. (2003) Sleep–wake states and their regulatory mechanisms throughout early human development. *Journal of Pediatrics*, 143, S70–S79.

Pennington, B. F. (2002) *The Development of Psychopathology: Nature and Nuture*. New York: Guilford Press.

Pesonen, A. K., Räikkönen, K., Matthews, K., Heinonen, K., Paavonen, J. E., Lahti, J., Komsi, N., Lemola, S., Järvenpää, A. L., Kajantie, E., & Strandberg, T. (2009) Prenatal origins of poor sleep in children. *Sleep*, 32, 1086–1092.

Petit, D., & Montplaisir, J. (2010) Early childhood parasomnias. In: Tremblay, R. E., Barr, R. G., Peters, R. D. V., & Boivin, M. (eds.) *Encyclopedia on Early Childhood Development*. Montreal, Quebec: Centre of Excellence for Early Childhood Development.

Phaire, T. (1957) *The Boke of Chyldren*. Edinburgh: E & S Livingstone Ltd. (Original work published 1554).

Pinilla, T., & Birch, L. (1993) Help me make it through the night: behavioural entrainment of breast-fed infants' sleep patterns. *Pediatrics*, 91, 436–444.

Plewis, I. (1980) Some simple aproaches to the analysis of dichotomous longitudinal data. *Developmental Medicine & Child Neurology*, 22, 671–674.

Plomin, R., Nitz, K., & Rowe, D. C. (1990) Behavioral genetics and aggressive behavior in childhood. In: Lewis, M., & Miller, S. M. (eds.) *Handbook of Developmental Psychopathology*. New York: Plenum.

Polanczyk, G., Silva De Lima, M., Lessa Horta, B., Biederman, J., & Augusto Rhode, L. (2007) The worldwide prevalence of ADHD: a systematic review and metaregression analysis. *American Journal of Psychiatry*, 164, 942–948.

Pollock, J. I. (1992) Predictors and long-term associations of reported sleeping difficulties in infancy. *Journal of Reproductive and Infant Psychology*, 10, 151–168.

Pollock, J. I. (1994) Night-waking at five years of age: predictors and prognosis. *Journal of Child Psychology and Psychiatry*, 35, 699–708.

Prudhomme White, B., Gunnar, M. R., Larson, M. C., Donzella, B., & Barr, R. G.

(2000) Behavioral and physiological responsivity, sleep, and patterns of daily cortisol production in infants with and without colic. *Child Development*, 71, 862–877.

Quandt, S. (1986) Patterns of variation in breast-feeding behaviours. *Social Science and Medicine*, 23, 445–453.

Ramchandani, P., Wiggs, L., Webb, V., & Stores, G. (2000) A systematic review of treatments for settling problems and night waking in young children. *British Medical Journal*, 320, 209–213.

Ramos, K., & Young Clarke, D. (2006) Parenting advice books about child sleep: co-sleeping and crying it out. *Sleep*, 29, 1616–1623.

Ramos, K. D., Young Clarke, D., & Anderson, J. E. (2007) Parental perceptions of sleep problems among co-sleeping and solitary sleeping children. *Infant and Child Development*, 16, 417–431.

Rao, M., Brenner, R., Schisterman, E., Vik, T., & Mills, J. (2004) Long term cognitive development in children with prolonged crying. *Archives of Disease in Childhood*, 89, 989–992.

Rautava, P., Helenius H., & Lehtonen, L. (1993) Psychosocial predisposing factors for infantile colic. *British Medical Journal*, 307, 600–604.

Rautava, L., Lempinen, A., Ojala, S., Parkkola, R., Rikalainen, H., Lapinleimu, H., Haataja, L., & Lehtonen, L. (2007) Acoustic quality of cry in very-low-birth-weight infants at the age of 1 1/2 years. *Early Human Development*, 83, 5–12.

Reid, M. J., Walter, A. L., & O'Leary, S. G. (1999) Treatment of young children's bedtime refusal and nighttime waking: a comparison of standard and graduated ignoring procedures. *Journal of Abnormal Child Psychology* 27, 5–16.

Reijneveld, S. A., Brugman, E., & Hirasing, R. A. (2001) Parental reports of excessive infant crying: the impact of varying definitions. *Pediatrics*, 108, 893–897.

Reijneveld, S. A., Brugman, E., & Hirasing, R. A. (2002) Excessive infant crying: definitions determine risk groups. *Archives of Disease of Childhood*, 87, 43–44.

Reijneveld, S. A., Van Der Wal, M., Brugman, E., Hira Sing, R. A., & Verloove-Vanhorick, S. P. (2004) Infant crying and abuse. *Lancet*, 364, 1340–1342.

Rhoads, M. J., Fatheree, N. Y., Norori, J., Liu, Y., Lucke, J. F., Tyson, J. E., & Ferris, M. J. (2009) Altered fecal microflora and increased fecal calprotectin in infants with colic. *Journal of Pediatrics*, 155, 823–828.

Ricci, B., Benandi, B., Bellini, F., Patrizi, A., & Masi, M. (2007) Atopic dermatitis: quality of life in young Italian children and their families and correlation with severity score. *Pediatric Allergy & Immunology,* 18, 245–249.

Richardson, H. L., Walker, A. M., & Horne, R. S. (2008) Sleep position alters arousal processes maximally at the high-risk age for sudden infant death syndrome. *Journal of Sleep Research*, 17, 450–457.

Richardson, H. L., Walker, A. M., & Horne, R. S. (2010) Influence of swaddling experience on spontaneous arousal patterns and autonomic control in sleeping infants. *Journal of Paediatrics*, 157, 85–91.

Richman, N. (1981) A community survey of characteristics of 1–2 year olds with sleep disruptions. *Journal of the American Academy of Child Psychiatry*, 20, 281–291.

Richman, N. (1985) A double-blind drug trial of treatment in young children with waking problems. *Journal of Child Psychology and Psychiatry*, 26, 591–598.

Richman N., Douglas J., Hunt H., & Levere R. (1985) Behavioural methods in the treatment of sleep disorders – a pilot study. *Journal of Child Psychology and Psychiatry*, 26, 581–590.

Rickert, V. I., & Johnson, M. (1988) Reducing nocturnal awakening and crying episodes in infants and young children: a comparison between scheduled awakenings and systematic ignoring. *Pediatrics*, 81, 203–213.

Rinne, M., Kalliomäki, M., Salminen, S., & Isolauri, E. (2006) Probiotic intervention in the first months of life: short-term effects on gastrointestinal symptoms and long-term effects on gut microbiota. *Journal of Pediatric Gastroenterology & Nutrition*, 43, 200–205.

Rivkees, S. A. (2007) The development of circadian rhythms: from animals to humans. *Sleep Medicine Clinics*, 2, 331–341.

Roffwarg, H. P., Muzio, J. N., & Dement, W. C. (1966) Ontogenetic development of the human sleep–dream cycle. *Science*, 152, 604–619.

Rogovik, A. L., & Goldman, R. D. (2005) Treating infants' colic. *Canadian Family Physician*, 1209–1211.

Roth, T. C., Rattenborg, N. C., & Pravosudov, V. W. (2010) The ecological relevance of sleep: The trade-off between sleep, memory and energy conservation. *Philosophical Transactions of the Royal Society of London B: Biological Science*, 365, 945–959.

Rubin, S. P., & Prendergast, M. (1984) Infant colic: incidence and treatment in a Norfolk community. *Child: Care, Health & Development*, 10, 219–226.

Ruiz-Contreras, J., Urquia, L., & Bastero, R. (1999) Persistent crying as predominant manifestation of sepsis in infants and newborns. *Pediatric Emergency Care*, 15, 113–5.

Rutter, M. (1972) *Maternal Deprivation Reassessed.* Harmondsworth: Penguin.

Rutter, M. (1977) Classification. In: Rutter, M., & Hersov, L. (eds.) *Child Psychiatry: Modern Approaches*, pp. 359–386. Oxford: Blackwell Publications.

Rutter, M. (2006) *Genes and Behavior. Nature–Nuture Interplay Explained.* Oxford: Blackwell Publishing.

Rutter, M., Kreppner, J., & Sonuga-Barke, E. (2009) Attachment insecurity, disinhibited attachment, and attachment disorders: where do research findings leave the concepts? *Journal of Child Psychology and Psychiatry*, 50, 529–543.

Sadeh, A. (1994) Assessment of intervention for infant night waking: parental reports and activity-based home monitoring. *Journal of Consulting & Clinical Psychology*, 62, 63–68.

Sadeh, A. (1996) Evaluating night waking in sleep disturbed infants: a methodological study of parental reports and actigraphy. *Sleep*, 19, 757–762.

Sadeh, A. (2000) Maturation of normal sleep patterns in childhood through adolescence. In: Loughlin, G. M., Carroll, J. M., & Marcus C. (eds.) *Sleep & Breathing in Children: A Developmental Approach*, pp. 2–25. New York: Marcel Dekker.

Sadeh, A. (2001) *Sleeping Like a Baby: A Sensitive and Sensible Approach to Solving Your Child's Sleep Problems.* New Haven, CT: Yale University Press.

Sadeh, A. (2003) Development of the sleep–wake system and its relationship to children's psychosocial development. In: *Encyclopedia on Early Childhood Development*. Montreal, Quebec: Centre of Excellence for Early Childhood Development. Retrieved Septemerber 21, 2011 from http://www.child-encyclopedia.com/documents/SadehANGxp.pdf

Sadeh, A. (2004) A brief screening questionnaire for infant sleep problems: validation and findings for an internet sample. *Pediatrics*, 113, e570–577.

Sadeh, A. (2005) Cognitive-behavioral treatment for childhood sleep disorders. *Clinical Psychology Review*, 25, 612–628.

Sadeh, A., & Sivan, Y. (2009) Clinical practice: sleep problems during infancy. *European Journal of Pediatrics*, 168, 1159–1164.

Sadeh, A., Dark, I., & Vohr, B. R. (1996) Newborns' sleep–wake patterns: the role of maternal, delivery and infant factors. *Early Human Development*, 44, 113–126.

Sadeh, A., Flint-Ofir, E., Tirosh, T., & Tikotzky, L. (2007) Infant sleep and parental sleep-related cognitions. *Journal of Family Psychology*, 21, 74–87.

Sadeh, A., Horowitz, I., Wolach-Benodis, L., & Wolach, B. (1998) Sleep and pulmonary function in children with well-controlled, stable asthma. *Sleep*, 21, 379–384.

Sadeh, A., Lavie, P., Scher, A., Tirosh, E., & Epstein, R. (1991) Actigraphic home monitoring of sleep disturbed and control infants and young children: a new method for pediatric assessment of sleep–wake patterns. *Pediatrics*, 87, 494–499.

Sadeh, A., Mindell, J. A., Luedtke, K., & Wiegand, B. (2009) Sleep and sleep ecology in the first 3 years: a web-based study. *Journal of Sleep Research*, 18, 60–73.

Sadeh, A., Pergamin, L., & Bar-Haim, Y. (2006) Sleep in children with attention-deficit hyperactivity disorder: a meta-analysis of polysomnographic studies. *Sleep Medicine Review*, 10, 381–398.

Sadeh, A., Tikotzky, L., & Scher, A. (2010) Parenting and infant sleep. *Sleep Medicine Review*, 14, 89–96.

Sagi, A., van, IJzendoorn, M. H., Aviezer, O., Donnell, F., & Mayseless, O. (1994) Sleeping out of home in a Kibbutz communal arrangement: it makes a difference for infant–mother attachment. *Child Development*, 65, 992–1004.

Salzarulo, P., Giganti, F., Fagioli, I., & Ficca, G. (2002) Early steps of awakening process. *Sleep Medicine*, 3, S29–S32.

Sameroff, A. J., & Chandler, M. J. (1975) Reproductive risk and the continuum of caretaker casualty. In: Horowitz, F. D. (ed.) *Review of Child Development*. Chicago, IL: University of Chicago Press.

Santos, I. S., Mota, D. M., & Matijasevich, A. (2008) Epidemiology of co-sleeping and nighttime waking at 12 months in a birth cohort. *Jornal de Pedriatria*, 84, 114–122.

Sarfi, M., Martinsen, H., Bakstad, B., Røislien, J., & Waal, H. (2009) Patterns in sleep-wakefulness in three-month old infants exposed to methadone or buprenorphine. *Early Human Development*, 85, 773–778.

Saskin, P. (2008) Obstructive sleep apnea: treatment options, efficacy and effects. In: Pressman, M. R., & Orr, W. C. (eds.) *Understanding Sleep: The Evaluation and Treatment of Sleep Disorders*, pp. 283–298. Washington, DC: American Psychological Association.

Savino, F., Cordisco, L., Tarasco, V., Palumeri, E., Calabrese, R., Oggero, R., Roos, S., & Matteuzzi, D. (2010) Lactobacillus reuteri DSM 17938 in infantile colic: a randomized, double-blind, placebo-controlled trial. *Pediatrics*, 126, e526–533.

Savino, F., Cresi, F., Vcastagno, E., Silvestro, L., & Oggero, R. (2005) A randomized double-blind placebo-controlled trial of a standardized extract of Matricariae recutita, Foeniculum vulgare and Melissa officinalis (ColiMil) in the treatment of breastfed colicky infants. *Phytotherapeutic Research*, 19, 335–340.

Savino, F., Pelle, E., Palumeri, E., Oggero, R., & Miniero, R. (2007) *Lactobaccillus reuteri* (American type culture collection strain 55730) versus simethicone in the treatment of infantile colic: a prospective randomised study. *Pediatrics*, 119, e124–130.

Schaffer, H. R., & Emerson, P. E. (1964) The development of social attachments during infancy. *Monographs of the Society for Research in Child Development*, 29.

Schechter, M. S. (2002) Technical report: diagnosis and management of childhood obstructive sleep apnea syndrome. *Pediatrics*, 109, 69.

Scher, A. (1991) A longitudinal study of night waking in the first year. *Child: Care, Health and Development*, 17, 295–302.

Scher, A. (2001) Attachment and sleep: a study of night waking in 12-month-old infants. *Developmental Psychobiology*, 38, 274–285.

Scher, A. (2008) Maternal separation anxiety as a regulator of infants' sleep. *Journal of Child Psychology and Psychiatry*, 49, 618–625.

Scher, A., & Asher, R. (2004) Is attachment security related to sleep–wake regulation? Mothers' reports and objective sleep recordngs *Infant Behavior & Development*, 27, 288–302.

Scher, A., & Blumberg, O. (1999) Night waking among 1-year olds: a study of maternal separation anxiety. *Child: Care, Health and Development*, 25, 323–334.

Scher, M. S., Richardson, G. A., & Day, N. L. (2000) Effects of prentatal cocaine/ crack and other drug exposure on electoencephalographic sleep studies at birth and one year. *Pediatrics*, 105, 39–48

Scher, A., Zukerman, S., & Epstein, R. (2005) Persistent night waking and settling difficulties across the first year: early precursors of later behavioural problems? *Journal of Reproductive and Infant Psychology*, 23, 77–88.

Schmid, G., Schreier, A., Meyer, R., & Wolke, D. (2010a) Predictors of crying, feeding and sleeping problems: a prospective study. *Child: Care, Health and Development*.

Schmid, G., Schreier, A., Meyer, R., & Wolke, D. (2010b) Prospective study on the persistence of infant crying, sleeping and feeding problems and preschool behaviour. *Acta Paediatrica*, 99, 286–290.

Schneider, M. (1992) The effect of mild stress during pregnancy on birthweight and neuromotor maturation in rhesus monkey infants. *Infant Behavior & Development*, 15, 389–403.

Schuetze, P., & Eiden, R. (2007) The association between prenatal exposure to cigarettes and infant and maternal negative affect. *Infant Behavior & Development*, 30, 387–398.

Schuetze, P., & Lawton, D. (2006) Prenatal cocaine exposure and infant sleep at 7 months of age: the influence of the caregiving environment. *Infant Mental Health Journal*, 27, 383–404.

Schwebel, D. C., & Brezausek, C. M. (2008) Nocturnal awakenings and pediatric injury risk. *Journal of Pediatric Psychology*, 33, 323–332.

Scott, G., & Richards, M. P. M. (1989) Night waking in infants: effects of providing advice and support for parents. *Journal of Child Psychology and Psychiatry*, 31, 551–567.

Sears, M., & Sears, W. (1999) *The Attachment Parenting Book: A Commonsense Guide to Understanding and Nurturing Your Baby*. New York: Little Brown & Co.

Seifer, R., Dickstein, S., Sameroff, A. J., Hayden, L., Magee, K., & Schiller, M. (1994a) Sleep in toddlers whose parents have psychopathology. *Sleep Research*, 23, 145.

Seifer, R., Sameroff, A. J., Barrett, L. C., & Krafchuk, E. (1994b) Infant temperament measured by multiple observations and by mother report. *Child Development*, 65, 1478–1490.

Seymour, F. W., Brock, P., During, M., & Poole, G. (1989) Reduced sleep disruptions in young children: evaluation of therapist-guided and written information approaches: A brief report. *Journal of Child Psychology and Psychiatry*, 30, 913–918.

Shelton, S. K. (1999) *Sleeping Through the Night . . . and Other Lies*. New York: St Martin's Press.

Shenassa, E. D., & Brown, M. J. (2004) Maternal smoking and infantile gastrointestinal dysregulation: the case of colic. *Pediatrics*, 114, e497–505.

Sherman, M. (1927) The differentiation of emotional response from motion picture views and from observation: (II) The ability of observers. *Journal of Comparative Psychology*, 7, 265–284.

Simonoff, E. A., & Stores, G. (1987) Controlled trial of trimeprazine tartrate for night waking. *Archives of Disease in Childhood*, 62, 253–257.

Skovgaard, A., Houmann, T., Christiansen, E., Landorph, S., Jørgensen, T., Olsen, E., Heering, K., Kaas-Nielsen, S., Samberg, V., Lichtenberg, A., & Copenhagen Child Cohort 2000 Study Team (2007) The prevalence of mental health problems in children 11/2 years of age – The Copenhagen Child Cohort (2000). *Journal of Child Psychology and Psychiatry*, 48, 62–70.

Smart, J., & Hiscock, H. (2007) Early infant crying and sleeping problems: a pilot study of impact on parental wellbeing and parent-endorsed strategies for management. *Journal of Paediatrics & Child Health*, 43, 284–290.

Smyke, A. T., Zeanah, C. H., Fox, N. A., Nelson, C. A., & Guthrie, D. (2010) Placement in foster care enhances quality of attachment among young institutionalized children. *Child Development*, 81, 212–223.

Søndergaard, C., Henriksen, T. B., Obel, C., & Wisborg, K. (2001) Smoking during pregnancy and infantile colic. *Pediatrics*, 108, 342–346.

Søndergaard, C., Olsen, J., Friis-Haschè, E., Dirdal, M., Thrane, N., & Toft Sørensen, H. T. (2003) Psychological distress during pregnancy and the risk of infantile colic: a follow-up study. *Acta Paediatrica*, 92, 811–816.

Sonuga-Barke, E. (1998) Categorical models of childhood disorder: a conceptual and empirical analysis. *Journal of Child Psychology and Psychiatry*, 39, 115–133.

Spock, B. (1979) *Baby & Child Care*. New York: W H Allen & Co Ltd.

St James-Roberts, I. (1989) Persistent crying in the first year of life. *The Psychologist*, 1, 39.

St James-Roberts, I. (1992) Measuring infant crying and its social perception and impact. *Association for Child Psychology and Psychiatry Newsletter*, 14, 128–131.

St James-Roberts, I. (1999) What is distinct about infants' 'colic' cries? *Archives of Disease in Childhood*, 80, 56–62.

St James-Roberts, I. (2001a) Infant crying and its impact on parents. In: Barr, R., St James-Roberts, I., & Keefe, M. (eds.) *New Evidence on Unexplained Early Infant Crying: Its Origins, Nature and Management*. Skillman, NJ: Johnson & Johnson Pediatric Institute.

St James-Roberts, I. (2001b) What do we know; what are the implications of the findings for practitioners; and what do we need to know? In: Barr, R. G., St James-Roberts, I., & Keefe M. (eds.) *New Evidence on Unexplained Early Infant Crying: Its Origins, Nature and Management*. Skillman, NJ: Johnson & Johnson Pediatric Institute.

St James-Roberts, I. (2006a) Helping parents to manage infant colic. *Mims Advances in Infant Nutrition*, 5, 8–10.

St James Roberts, I. (2006b) Infant crying and sleeping problems: recent evidence for best practice. *Workshop for UK Primary Healthcare Service Professionals*, De Montfort University Leicester, May 12.

St James Roberts, I. (2007a) Infant crying and sleeping: helping parents to prevent and manage problems. *Sleep Medicine Clinics*, 2, 363–375.

St James Roberts, I. (2007b) Infant crying and sleeping problems: recent evidence for best practice. *Workshop for UK Primary Healthcare Service Professionals*. United Bristol NHS Trust, Bristol, October 4.

St James-Roberts, I., & Conroy, S. (2005) Do pregnancy and childbirth adversities predict infant crying and colic? Findings and recommendations. *Neuroscience and Biobehavioral Reviews*, 29, 313–320.

St James-Roberts, I., & Halil, T. (1991) Infant crying patterns in the first year: normal community and clinical findings. *Journal of Child Psychology and Psychiatry*, 32, 951–968.

St James Roberts, I., & Peachey, E. (2010) Distinguishing infant prolonged crying from sleep–waking problems. *Archives of Disease in Childhood*, 96, 340–344.

St James-Roberts, I., & Plewis, I. (1996) Individual differences, daily fluctuations, and developmental changes in amounts of infant waking, fussing, crying, feeding and sleeping. *Child Development*, 67, 2527–2540.

St James-Roberts, I., Alvarez, M., Csipke, E., Abramsky, T., Goodwin, J., & Dorgenfrei, E. (2006) Infant crying and sleeping in London, Copenhagen and when parents adopt a "proximal" form of care. *Pediatrics*, 117, e1146–1155.

St James-Roberts, I., Conroy, S., & Wilsher, K. (1995) Clinical, developmental and social aspects of infant crying and colic. *Early Development and Parenting*, 4, 177–189.

St James-Roberts, I., Conroy, S., & Wilsher, K. (1996) Bases for maternal perceptions of infant crying and colic behaviour. *Archives of Disease in Childhood*, 75, 375–384.

St James-Roberts, I., Goodwin, J., Peter, B., Adams, D., & Hunt, S. (2003) Individual differences in reactivity to undressing, handling and a standard neurobehavioural examination predict how much 1-week-old babies cry at home. *Developmental Medicine & Child Neurology*, 45, 400–407.

St James-Roberts, I., Harris, G., & Messer, D. (1993a) *Infant Crying, Feeding and Sleeping: Development, Problems and Treatments*. London: Harvester-Wheatsheaf.

St James-Roberts, I., Hurry, J., & Bowyer, J. (1993b) Objective confirmation of crying durations in infants referred for excessive crying. *Archives of Disease in Childhood*, 68, 82–84.

St James-Roberts, I., Sleep, J., Morris, S., Owen, C., & Gillham, P. (2001) Use of a behavioural programme in the first 3 months to prevent infant crying and sleep problems. *Journal of Paediatric & Child Health*, 37, 289–297.

Steinherz, R. (2004) Dicycloverine for persistent crying in babies: beware recommending dicycloverine treatment in babies. *BMJ*, 328, 956.

Stevens, B., Yamada, J., & Ohlsson, A. (2010) Sucrose for analgesia in newborn infants undergoing painful procedures. *Cochrane Database of Systematic Reviews*, 20, CD001069.

Stifter, C. A., & Bono, M. A. (1998) The effect of infant colic on maternal self-perceptions and mother–infant attachment. *Child: Care, Health and Development*, 24, 339–351.

Stojanovski, S. D., Rasu, R. S., Balkrishnan, R., & Nahata, M. C. (2007) Trends in medication prescribing for pediatric sleep difficulties in US outpatient settings. *Sleep*, 30, 1013–1037.

Stone, K. C., Lagasse, L. L., Lester, B. M., Shankaran, S., Bada, H. S., Bauer, C. R., & Hammond, J. A. (2010) Sleep problems in children with prenatal substance exposure: the Maternal Lifestyle study. *Archives of Adolescent Medicine*, 164, 452–456.

Stone, K. C., Pamela, C., High, P. C., Miller-Loncar, C. L., Lagasse, L. L., & Lester, B. M. (2009) Longitudinal study of maternal report of sleep problems in children with prenatal exposure to cocaine and other drugs. *Behavioral Sleep Medicine*, 7, 196–207.

Stores, G. (2007) Parasomnias of childhood and adolescence. *Sleep Medicine Clinics*, 2, 405–418.

Stores, G., & Wiggs, L. (2001) *Sleep Disturbance in Children and Adolescents with Disorders of Development: Its Significance and Management*. London: Mac Keith Press.

Stremler, R., Hodnett, E., Lee, K., Macmilan, S., Mill, C., Ogcangco, L., & Wilan, A. (2006) A behavioural educational intervention to promote maternal and infant sleep. *Sleep*, 29, 1609–1615.

Super, C. M., Harkness, S., Van Tijen, N., Van Der Vlugt, E., Fintelman, M., & Dijkstra, J. (1996) The three R's of Dutch childrearing and the socialization of infant arousal. In: Harkness, S., & Super, C. M. (eds.) *Parents' Cultural Belief Systems: Their Origins, Expressions, and Consequences*. New York: Guilford Press.

Symon, B. G., Marley, J. E., James Martin, A., & Norman, E. R. (2005) Effect of a consultation teaching behaviour modification on sleep performance in infants: randomised controlled trial. *Medical Journal of Australia*, 182, 215–218.

Tarazona, S., Alfonso, J. D., Madramany, A. A., Escrihuela, L. C., Sáez, E. L., & Monterde, R. B. (2010) Incidence of wheezing and associated risk factors in the first 6 months of life of a cohort in Valencia (Spain). *Anales de Pediatria*, 72, 19–29.

Taubman, B. (1988) Parental counseling compared with elimination of cow's milk or soy milk protein for the treatment of infant colic syndrome: a randomised trial. *Pediatrics*, 81, 756–761.

Taveras, E. M., Rifas-Shiman, S. L., Oken, E., Gunderson, E. P., & Gillman, M. W. (2008) Short sleep duration in infancy and risk of childhood overweight. *Archives of Pediatrics & Adolescent Medicine*, 162, 305–311.

Ter Vrught, D., & Pederson, D. R. (1973) The effects of vertical rocking frequencies on the arousal level in two-month-old infants. *Child Development*, 44, 205–209.

Teti, D. M., Kim, B. R., Mayer, G., & Countermine, M. (2010) Maternal emotional availability at bedtime predicts infant sleep quality. *Journal of Family Psychology*, 24, 307–315.

Thomas, K. A., & Foreman, S. W. (2005) Infant sleep and feeding pattern: effects on maternal sleep. *Journal of Midwifery & Women's Health*, 50, 399–404.

Thorpy, M. J. (2005) *International Classification of Sleep Disorders: Diagnostic and Coding Manual*. Minnesota: American Sleep Disorders Association.

Thygarajan, A., & Burks, A. W. (2008) American Academy of Pediatrics recommendations on the effects of early nutritional interventions on the development of atopic disease. *Current Opinion in Pediatrics*, 20, 698–702.

Tighe, M., & Roe, M. F. E. (2007) Does a teething child need serious illness exclusion? *Archives of Disease in Childhood*, 92, 266–268.

Tikotsky, L., & Sadeh, A. (2001) Sleep patterns and sleep disruptions in kindergarten children. *Journal of Clinical Child Psychology*, 30, 581–591.

Tikotzky, L., & Sadeh, A. (2009) Maternal sleep-related cognitions and infant sleep: a longitudinal study from pregnancy through the first year. *Child Development*, 80, 860–874.

Tikotzky, L., De Marcas, G., Har-Toov, J., Dollberg, S., Bar-Haim, Y., & Sadeh, A. (2010a) Sleep and physical growth in infants during the first 6 months. *Journal of Sleep Research*, 19, 103–110.

Tikotzky, L., Sadeh, A., & Glickman-Gavrieli, T. (2010b) Infant sleep and paternal involvement in infant caregiving during the first 6 months of life. *Journal of Paediatric Psychology*, 36, 36–46.

Tizard, B., & Hodges, J. (1978) The effect of early institutional rearing on the development of eight year old children. *Journal of Child Psychology and Psychiatry*, 19, 99–118.

Tizard, B., & Rees, J. (1975) The effect of early institutional rearing on the behaviour problems and affectional relationships of four-year-old children. *Journal of Child Psychology and Psychiatry*, 16, 61–73.

Tong, S., & McMichael, A. J. (1992) Maternal smoking and neuropsychological development in childhood: a review of the evidence. *Developmental Medicine and Child Neurology*, 34, 191–197.

Treem, W. R. (2001) Assessing crying complaints: the interaction with gastroesophageal reflux and cow's milk protein intolerance. In: Barr, R. G., St James-Roberts, I., & Keefe, M. (eds.) *New Evidence on Unexplained Early Infant Crying: Its Origins, Nature and Management*, pp. 165–176. Skillman, NJ: Johnson & Johnson Pediatric Institute.

Troese, M., Fukumizu, M., & Sallinen, B. J. (2008) Sleep fragmentation and evidence for sleep debt in alcohol-exposed infants. *Early Human Development*, 84, 577–585.

Underdown, A., Barlow, J., Chung, V., & Stewart-Brown, S. (2006) Massage intervention for promoting mental and physical health in infants aged under six months. *Cochrane Database of Systematic Reviews*, 4, CD005038.

Valentin, S. R. (2005) Commentary: sleep in German infants – the "cult" of independence. *Pediatrics*, 115, 269–271.

Valman, H. B. (1981) Sleep problems. *British Medical Journal*, 283, 422–423.

van den Bergh, B. R., & Marcoen, A. (2004) High antenatal maternal anxiety is related to ADHD symtoms, externalizing problems, and anxiety in 8- and 9-year-olds. *Child Development*, 75, 1085–1097.

van den Berg, M. P., van der Ende, J., Crijen, A. A., Jaddoe, V. W., Moll, H. A., Mackenbach, J. P., Hofman, A., Hengeveld, M. W., Tiemeier, H., & Verhulst, F. C. (2009) Paternal depressive symptoms during pregnancy are related to excessive infant crying. *Pediatrics*, 124, e96–103.

van den Boom, D. C. (1995) Do first-year intervention effects endure? Follow-up during toddlerhood of a sample of Dutch irritable infants. *Child Development*, 66, 1798–1816.

van den Boom D. C. (2001) Behavioral management of early infant crying in irritable babies. In: Barr, R. G., St James-Roberts, I., & Keefe, M. (eds.) *New Evidence on Unexplained Early Infant Crying: Its Origins, Nature and Management*. Skillman, NJ: Johnson & Johnson Pediatric Institute.

van der Wal, M. F., Van Den Boom, D. C., Pauw-Plomp, H., & De Jonge, G. A. (1998) Mothers' reports of infant crying and soothing in a multicultural population. *Archives of Disease in Childhood*, 79, 312–317.

van der Wal, M. F., van Eijsden, M., & Bonsel, G. J. (2007) Stress and emotional problems during pregnancy and excessive infant crying. *Journal of Developmental & Behavioral Pediatrics*, 28, 431–437.

van Gelder, R. N. (2004) Recent insights into mammalian circadian rhythms. *Sleep*, 27, 166–170.

van IJzendoorn, M. H., & Juffer, F. (2006) The Emanuel Miller Memorial Lecture 2006: adoption as intervention. Meta-analytic evidence for massive catch-up and plasticity in physical, socio-emotional, and cognitive development. *Journal of Child Psychology and Psychiatry*, 47, 1228–1245.

van Sleuwen, B., L'hoir, M., Engelberts, A., Busschers, W., Westers, P., Bloom, M., Schulpen, T., & Kuis, W. (2006) Comparison of behaviour modification with and without swaddling as interventions for excessive crying. *Journal of Pediatrics*, 149, 512–517.

van Sleuwen, B. E., Engelberts, A. C., Boere-Boonekamp, M. M., Kuis, W., Schulpen, T. W. J., & L'hoir, M. P. (2007) Swaddling: a systematic review. *Pediatrics*, 120, 1097–1106.

van Zeiji, J., Mesman, J., Stolk, M., Alink, L., van IJzendoorn, M., Bakermans-Kronenburg, M. J., Juffer, F., & Koot, H. M. (2006) Terrible ones? Assessment of externalizing behaviors in infancy with the Child Behavior Checklist. *Journal of Child Psychology and Psychiatry*, 47, 801–810.

Vemulapalli, C., Grady, K., & Kemp, J. S. (2004) Use of safe cribs and bedroom size among African infants with a high rate of bed sharing. *Archives of Pediatrics & Adolescent Medicine*, 158, 286–289.

Vik, T., Grote, V., Escribano, J., Socha, J., Verduci, E., Fritsch, M., Carlier, C., von Kries, R., & Koletzko, B. (2009) Infantile colic, prolonged crying and maternal postnatal depression. *Acta Paediatrica*, 98, 1344–1348.

von Kries, R., Kalies, H., & Papoušek, M. (2006) Excessive crying beyond 3 months may herald other features of multiple regulatory problems. *Archives of Pediatrics & Adolescent Medicine*, 160, 508–511.

Vuorenkoski, V., Lind, J., Partanen, T. J., Lejeune, J., Lafourcade, J., & Wasz-

Hockert, O. (1966) Spectrographic analysis of cries from children with maladie du cri du chat. *Annales Paediatriae Fenniae*, 12, 174–180.

Wade, S., & Kilgour, T. (2001) Extracts from "Clinical Evidence". *British Medical Journal*, 323, 437–440.

Wake, M., Hesketh, K., & Lucas, J. (2000) Teething and tooth eruption in infants: a cohort study. *Pediatrics*, 106, 1374–1379.

Wake, M., Morton-Allen, E., Poulakis, Z., Hiscock, H., Gallagher, S., & Oberklaid, F. (2006) Prevalence, stability, and outcomes of cry-fuss and sleep problems in the first 2 years of life: Prospective community-based study. *Pediatrics*, 117, 836–842.

Walker, A. M., & Menaheim, S. (1994) Intervention of supplementary carrying on normal baby crying patterns: a randomized study. *Journal of Developmental & Behavioral Pediatrics*, 15, 174–178.

Walsh, J. K., & Lindblom, S. S. (2008) *Psychophysiology of Sleep Deprivation*. Washington, DC: American Psychological Association.

Wasz-Höckert, O., Lind, J., Vuorenkoski, V., Partanen, T., & Valanné, E. (1968) The infant cry: a spectrographic and auditory analysis. *Clinics in Developmental Medicine, Vol. 29*. Philadelphia, PA: Lippincott.

Wasz-Höckert, O., Michelsson, K., & Lind, J. (1985) Twenty-five years of Scandinavian cry research. In: Lester, B. M., & Boukydis, C. F. Z. (eds.), *Infant Crying: Theoretical and Research Perspectives*, pp. 83–104. New York: Plenum.

Waters, E. (1978). The reliability and stability of individual differences in infant–mother attachment. *Child Development*, 49, 483–494.

Waters, E., Hamilton, C. E., & Weinfield, N. S. (2000) The stability of attachment security from infancy to adolescence and early adulthood: general introduction. *Child Development*, 71, 678–683.

Webster-Stratton, C., & Hammond, M. (1997) Treating children with early-onset conduct problems: a comparison of child and parent training programs. *Journal of Consulting and Clinical Psychology*, 65, 93–109.

Weiss, S. K. (2010) Tips for parents: prevention and management of sleep problems. In: Barr, R. G., Peters, R. D. V., & Boivin, M. (eds.) *Encyclopedia on Early Childhood Development*. Montreal, Quebec: Centre of Excellence for Early Childhood Development.

Weissbluth, M. (1984) Sleep duration, temperament, and Conners' ratings of three year old children. *Journal of Developmental & Behavioral Pediatrics*, 5, 120–123.

Weissbluth, M., Davis, A. T., & Poncher, J. (1984) Night waking in 4–8 month old infants. *Journal of Pediatrics*, 14, 477.

Weizman, Z. & Alsheikh, A. (2006) Safety and tolerance of a probiotic formula in early infancy comparing two probiotic agents: a pilot study. *Journal of the American College of Nutrition*, 25, 415–419.

Weizman, Z., Alkrinawi, S., Goldfarb, D., & Bitran, C. (1993) Efficacy of herbal tea preparation in infantile colic. *Journal of Pediatrics*, 122, 650–652.

Wessel, M. A., Cobb, J. C., Jackson, E. B., Harris, G. S., & Detwiler, A. C. (1954) Paroxysmal fussing in infancy, sometimes called "colic". *Pediatrics*, 14, 421–433.

Willinger, M., Ko, C. W., Hoffman, H. J., Kessler, R. C., & Corwin, M. J. (2003) Trends in infant bed-sharing in the United States, 1993–2000. *Archives of Pediatrics & Adolescent Medicine*, 157, 43–49.

Winnicott, D. W. (1953) Transitional objects and transitional phenomena: a study of the first not-me possession. *International Journal of Psychoanalysis*, 34, 89–97

Wirojanan, J., Jacquemont, S., Diaz, R., Bacalman, S., Anders, T. F., Hagerman, R. J., & Goodlin-Jones, B. L. (2009) The efficacy of melatonin for sleep problems in children with autism, fragile X syndrome, or autism and fragile X syndrome. *Journal of Clinical Sleep Medicine*, 5, 145–150.

Wolf, A. W., & Lozoff, B. (1989) Object attachment, thumb sucking, and the passage to sleep. *Journal of the American Academy of Child & Adolescent Psychiatry*, 28, 287–292.

Wolf, M. J., Koldewijn, K., Beelan, A., Smit, B., Hedlund, R., & De Groot, I. (2002) Neurobehavioral and developmental profile of very low birthweight preterm infants in early infancy. *Acta Paediatrica*, 91, 930–938.

Wolfson, A., Lacks, P., & Futterman, A. (1992) Effects of parent training on infant sleeping patterns, parents' stress and perceived parental competence. *Journal of Consulting and Clinical Psychology*, 60, 41–48.

Wolke, D. (2001) Behavioural treatment of prolonged infant crying: evaluation, methods and a proposal. In: Barr, R. G., St James-Roberts, I., & Keefe, M. (eds.) *New Evidence on Unexplained Early Infant Crying: Its Origins, Nature and Management*. Skillman, NJ: Johnson & Johnson Pediatric Institute.

Wolke, D., Gray, P., & Meyer, R. (1994a) Excessive infant crying: a controlled study of mothers helping mothers. *Pediatrics*, 94, 322–332.

Wolke, D., Gray, P., & Meyer, R. (1994b) Validity of the Crying Patterns Questionnaire: a research note. *Journal of Reproductive and Infant Psychology*, 12, 105–114.

Wolke, D., Meyer, R., Ohrt, B., & Riegel, K. (1995a) Co-morbidity of crying and sleeping problems with feeding problems in infancy: concurrent and predictive associations. *Early Development & Parenting*, 4, 191–208.

Wolke, D., Meyer, R., Ohrt, B., & Riegel, K. (1995b) The incidence of sleeping problems in pre-term and full-term infants discharged from neonatal special care units: an epidemiological longitudinal study. *Journal of Child Psychology and Psychiatry*, 36, 203–225.

Wolke, D., Rizzo, P., & Woods, S. (2002) Persistent infant crying and hyperactivity problems in middle childhood. *Pediatrics*, 109, 1054–1060.

Wolke, D., Schmid, G., Schreier, A., & Meyer, R. (2009) Crying and feeding problems in infancy and cognitive outcome in preschool children born at risk: a prospective population study. *Journal of Developmental & Behavioral Pediatrics*, 30, 226–238.

Wolke, D., Sohne, B., Riegel, K., Ohrt, B., & Osterlund, K. (1998) An epidemiologic longitudinal study of sleeping problems and feeding experience of preterm and term children in southern Finland: comparison with a southern German population sample. *Journal of Pediatrics*, 133, 224–231.

Wood, R. M., & Gustafson, G. E. (2001) Infant crying and adults' anticipated caregiving responses: acoustic and contextual influences. *Child Development*, 72, 1287–1300.

Woodson, R. H., Blurton Jones, N. G., Da Costa Woodson, E., Pollock, S., & Evans, M. (1979) Fetal mediators of the relationship between increased pregnancy and labour blood pressure and newborn irritability. *Early Human Development*, 3, 127–139.

World Health Organization (1992) *The ICD-10 Classification of Mental and Behavioural Disorders: Clinical Descriptions and Diagnostic Guidelines.* Geneva: WHO.

Wright, A. L. (2002) Epidemiology of asthma and recurrent wheeze in childhood. *Clinical Reviews in Allergy and Immunology,* 22, 33–44.

Wright, P. (1993) Mothers' ideas about feeding in early infancy. In: St James-Roberts, I., Harris, G., & Messer, D. (eds.) *Infant Crying, Feeding and Sleeping: Development, Problems and Treatments.* Hemel Hempstead: Harvester Wheatsheaf.

Wurmser, H., Laubereau, B., Hermann, M., Papousek, M., & Von Kries, R. (2001) Excessive infant crying: often not confined to the first 3 months of age. *Early Human Development,* 64, 1–6.

Wurmser, H., Rieger, M., Domogalla, C., Kahnt, A., Janine, B., Kowatsch, M, Kuehnert, N., Buske-Kirschbaum, A., Papoušek, M., Pirke, K. M., & Von Voss, H. (2006) Association between life long stress during pregnancy and infant crying in the first six months postpartum: a prospective longitudinal study. *Early Human Development,* 82, 341–349.

Wyatt, J. K. (2007) Circadian rhythm sleep disorders in children and adolescents. *Sleep Medicine Clinics,* 2, 387–396.

Yalçin, S. S., Orün, E., Mutlu, B., Madendağ, Y., Sinici, I., Dursun, A., Ozkara, H. A., Ustünyurt, Z., Kutluk, S., & Yurdakök, K. (2010) Why are they having infant colic? A nested case-control study. *Paediatric & Perinatal Epidemiology,* 24, 584–596.

Yang, C. K., & Hahn, H. M. (2002) Co-sleeping in young Korean children. *Journal of Developmental & Behavioral Pediatrics,* 23, 151–157.

Zeifman, D. M. (2001) An ethological analysis of human infant crying. Answering Tinbergen's four questions. *Developmental Psychobiology,* 39, 265–285.

Zeifman, D. M. (2004) Acoustic features of infant crying related to intended caregiving intervention. *Infant and Child Development,* 13, 111–122.

Zeskind, P., & Barr, R. (1997) Acoustic characteristics of naturally occurring cries of infants with 'colic'. *Child Development,* 68, 394–403.

Zuckerman, B., Stevenson, J., & Bailey, V. (1987) Sleep problems in early childhood: continuities, predictive factors and behavioural correlates. *Pediatrics,* 80, 664–671.

Zwart, P., Vellema-Goud, M., & Brand, P. (2007) Characteristics of infants admitted to hospital for persistent colic, and comparison with healthy infants. *Acta Paediatrica,* 96, 401–405.

Index